Samuel Rawson Gardiner

The Personal Government of Charles I

A History of England From the Assassination of the Duke of Buckingham...

Samuel Rawson Gardiner

The Personal Government of Charles I
A History of England From the Assassination of the Duke of Buckingham...

ISBN/EAN: 9783744797979

Printed in Europe, USA, Canada, Australia, Japan

Cover: Foto ©Suzi / pixelio.de

More available books at **www.hansebooks.com**

THE
PERSONAL GOVERNMENT
OF
CHARLES I.

A HISTORY OF ENGLAND FROM THE ASSASSINATION OF THE
DUKE OF BUCKINGHAM TO THE DECLARATION
OF THE JUDGES ON SHIP-MONEY

1628—1637

BY

SAMUEL RAWSON GARDINER

LATE STUDENT OF CHRIST CHURCH
PROFESSOR OF MODERN HISTORY AT KING'S COLLEGE, LONDON ; CORRESPONDING
MEMBER OF THE MASSACHUSETTS HISTORICAL SOCIETY, AND OF
THE ROYAL BOHEMIAN SOCIETY OF SCIENCES

IN TWO VOLUMES

VOL. I.

LONDON
LONGMANS, GREEN, AND CO.
1877

PREFACE.

THE two volumes now published will bring the reader to the threshold of the Puritan Revolution, as the demonstration in the streets of London at the execution of the sentence upon Prynne, Burton, and Bastwick, together with the almost simultaneous demonstration at Edinburgh upon the introduction of the new Prayer Book, may fairly be regarded as the starting points of the movement. The period of nine years here treated of is one in which many causes were at work to undermine the Royal authority, and an accurate knowledge of these less exciting times is therefore absolutely indispensable to the formation of a sober judgment on the more stirring events which followed. Hitherto no book has come into existence which has even professed to trace the gradual change which came over English feeling year by year; even Ranke, who has poured a flood of light on the foreign relations of the country, and who has elucidated its domestic affairs so far as he was able to do so by the light thrown on them by the despatches of foreign diplomatists, having left much room for further and more detailed enquiry. Much confusion has been caused by the habit which prevails where it would least be expected, of classifying events rather according to their nature than according to their chronological order, so that the true sequence of the history is lost. It is needless to add that where, as too often happens, no attempt whatever is made to understand the strong points in the case of the King or the weak points in the case of his opponents, the result is a mere caricature.

It is probable that some of my readers may think that I have allotted too large a space to the treatment of foreign affairs. I do not, however, see how it would have been possible to say less about them without injury to the main subject of the narrative. No one can apprehend the truth about Ship-money and the ship-money fleet, unless he understands the relations between England and the Governments of the Continent which first suggested the necessity of a larger fleet than Charles's exchequer could support; and if the bearing upon domestic history of Charles's diplomacy with Spain and Sweden in earlier years is less obvious, it should not be forgotten that the question of the amount of confidence which could be reposed in Charles assumed a pre-eminent importance in 1641 and 1642, in 1646 and 1647; and that the revelation of his earlier diplomatic secrets may not be without considerable weight in helping to the formation of a right judgment on that question. It is impossible, I suppose, for any one to read of the intrigues which Charles carried on alternately with France and Spain, without being forcibly reminded of the very similar intrigues which he subsequently carried on with Presbyterians and Independents, with Parliament and Army. But whatever may be the amount of space which I have assigned to Continental affairs, I have always treated them as subsidiary to those of our own country. It was here and not upon the Continent that religious and political liberty was ultimately adopted as the solution of the difficulties of the time, and my business is to tell the story at least of the earlier stages of the process of the discovery of that solution.

I wish I had been able to penetrate more deeply into the thoughts and feelings of the mass of the nation. Nothing is, however, more difficult than to descend below the surface to the depths of society: nothing more easy than to be led astray into imagining the chance utterance of some poetaster or pamphleteer to be the echo of the popular mind. Nor is it always possible to obtain sufficient information on a subject the knowledge of which would seem to be more easily attainable—the progress of the nation in wealth and prosperity and in the improvement of the social machinery. Such fragments as I have been able to gather will, however, find a more appropriate place in a future volume.

The materials on which I have relied have been brought together from various sources. The *State Papers*, Foreign and Domestic, have been of the greatest value, and *Nicholas's Notes of the Session of* 1629 have been especially helpful as containing an account altogether independent of the original report which formed the basis of all the various journals which have been hitherto accessible. For the despatches of foreign ambassadors I have had to look in various quarters. Copies of those of the Dutch Joachimi, as well as of the newsletters of Salvetti, the Florentine agent, are in the

Museum Library. The letters of the Venetian ambassadors, however, are for this period only to be found at Venice itself, and though much which I found there has been already made use of by Professor Ranke, there is also much which it did not serve his purpose to employ. Though unhappily the French despatches have not been preserved with anything like completeness, still it will be seen that not a little has been gained through the permission accorded to me to examine the volumes in the *Archives des Affaires Étrangères*, the deficiencies of which are, during Seneterre's mission, filled up by the two volumes of that ambassador's letter-book in the *Bibliothèque Nationale*. Much information on the proceedings of the Spanish Government is to be obtained from the *Archives du Royaume* at Brussels, as the Spanish ministers were fortunately in the habit of sending copies of important despatches for the use of the Government of the Netherlands. A visit to Simancas, though not without results, was unfortunately far less productive than former experience had given me reason to expect. The many hundreds of despatches which throw such a flood of light upon the reign of James, find but a scanty counterpart in the reign of Charles. The bundles of *cartas* are entirely missing from 1622 to 1660; and all that we have is the collection of *consultas* of the Council of State, in which are sometimes enclosed copies of those despatches or other official documents which formed the subject of debate.

The recent transmission by the Rev. J. Stevenson of the Panzani letters from the Vatican archives to the Public Record Office occurred at a moment most opportune for my work. They do not indeed shew events in any new light, as there is little general information to be gained from them which is not already known from the Memoirs of Panzani which have been long published. But it would have been impossible to make use of a work of which the origin and authority was uncertain without considerable hesitation, and if I had had nothing else upon which to found my narrative I should have been in considerable doubt at every step as to the propriety on the one hand of omitting all reference to statements so important, or on the other hand of inserting those statements without some stronger assurance of their credibility. Those doubts are now set at rest for ever, and it is thus possible to give the story of Panzani's mission upon indisputable authority.

I ought perhaps to have stated before that I have sometimes allowed myself the liberty of altering into the first person reports of speeches given in the third. It gives a greater interest to the story, and as the speeches and sayings were not taken down in shorthand, and cannot therefore, even when reported in the first person, be more than approximately accurate, the restoration of the first person is merely the removal of one undoubted inaccuracy of the reporter. When, however, this could not be done without effecting some further change, however slight, I have abstained from all alteration, except in one or two special cases to which attention is drawn in the notes.

I should like to draw particular attention to the tables of cases in the Star Chamber and High Commission contained in the Appendix. No doubt every case of actual penalty inflicted in the latter Court implies a great number of cases in which submission was made without appearance in court at all; and, as far as the former court is concerned, the possibility that such transactions as those recorded in the erratum to p. 299 in vol. i., and at p. 152 of vol. ii. must be taken into account, and the discovery of the first of these instances does not leave my argument at p. 182, note [1], of vol. i., as strong as it was. Still, after every allowance has been made on this score, these tables stand in startling contrast to the declamations of popular writers.

I had not intended to say anything here about my view of Wentworth's character. To a great extent, the question between me and my critics has dwindled into a mere difference of opinion on the moral sense attached to the word 'apostate,' and so far as any further objection has been taken, I am quite content to refer my readers to that which they will find in these volumes. At the very last moment, however, I have been allowed to see an unpublished letter of Wentworth's in the collection of the late Mr. John Forster, now in course of arrangement in the South Kensington Museum, of which I have printed a complete copy in the *Academy* for June 2, 1877. There is nothing there which throws any specially new light on Wentworth's character, but it will perhaps not be out of place to notice it here, as this letter, written on September 24, 1632, and probably addressed to the Earl of Carlisle, should be taken in connection with the subsequent letter of October 24, quoted at p. 281 of vol. i.

Wentworth, after a complimentary introduction, gives his opinion of the conduct of Foulis:—

Sir David Foulis, a person raised by the favour and bounty of the Crown to a fair and plentiful fortune, and one I had upon all occasions given the best respects unto I could, as promising myself helps and assistance from him in his Majesty's service, it seemed to me marvellous strange to hear how ill and mutinously affected he was to his Majesty's rights and government, so as taking the report either to be mistaken, or to be grounded upon some personal malice, I gave no great belief or regard thereunto until this late riot of his brake forth with such violence and virulence as might not with my duty be longer silenced.

Foulis, it seems, presented himself before the door of the Council of York, asking to see the President. Wentworth sent to ask whether he wished to see him on private business, or on the King's. He said that he had both, and was in consequence admitted. As soon as he was allowed to speak, however, he explained that his business was only 'touching his own private.' Then, writes Wentworth—

Then I told him I was glad when I heard he had anything to offer for the service of our master, as that which he had never seemed to look after, since I had the honour to serve him in this place, albeit I had expected and promised myself as much from him in that nature as from any other; but seeing that it now all terminated in particulars of our own, the King's Board was no fit place for those discourses; therefore I desired him to excuse me, the matters between him and me being of such a condition as could not be heard betwixt us privately in a chamber, but must pass the file of his Majesty's Courts of Justice, and so rose, went my way and left them.

. . . .

My Lord, you best know how much the regal power is become infirm by the easy way such have found who with rough hands have laid hold upon the flowers of it, and with unequal and swaggering paces have trampled upon the rights of the Crown, and how necessary examples are (as well for the subject as the sovereign) to retain licentious spirits within the sober bounds of humility and fear. And surely if in any other, then in the case of this man, who hath the most wantonly, the most disdainfully demeaned himself towards his Majesty and his ministers that is possible, so as if he do not taste of the rod, it will be impossible to have his Majesty's Council here to be obeyed, and should I say less were to betray the trust my master hath honoured me with. I hear he cries out of oppression; so did my Lord Fauconberg too,—your Lordship heard with what reason or truth,—believe me, this man hath more wit, but his cause is so much the worse as he hath notwithstanding less to say for himself; in this nevertheless they are tied by the tails together, that both of them dared to strike the Crown upon my shoulders without being at all concerned in my own interest, or having any other part to play than such as innocence and patience shall suggest unto me. And truly give me leave to assure your Lordship I have much reason to carry my eyes along with me wherever I go, and to expect my actions, from the highest to the lowest, shall all be cast into the balance and tried whether heavy or light. Content in the name of God! Let them take me up and cast me down. If I do not fall square, and—to use a word of art—paragon, in every point of my duty to my master; nay, if I do not fully comply with that public and common protection which good kings afford their good people, let me perish, and let no man pity me. In the meantime none of these clamours or other apprehensions shall shake me or cause me to decline my master's honour and service, thereby to please or soothe these popular frantic humours; and if I miscarry this way, I shall not even then be found either so indulgent to myself or so narrowly hearted towards my master as to think myself too good to die for him. *El deve bastar.*

.   .   .   .

Only this I will protest to your Lordship in the words of truth, I have been hitherto known to this gentleman only by courtesies. That I bear no malice to his person, or at all consider my own interests in this proceeding, which in truth are none at all, but simply the honour and service of his Majesty and the seasonable correcting an humour and liberty I find reign in these parts, of observing a superior command no farther than they like themselves, and of questioning any profit of the Crown, called upon by his Majesty's ministers, which might enable it to subsist of itself, without being necessitated to accept of such conditions as others might vainly think to impose upon it. 'Tis true this way is displeasing for the present, lays me open to calumny and hatred, causeth me by some ill-disposed people to be, it may be, ill-reported; whereas the contrary would make me pass smooth and still along without noise; but I have not so learnt my master, nor am I so indulgent to my own ease as to see his affairs suffer shipwreck whilst I myself rest secure in harbour. No, let the tempest be never so great, I will much rather put forth to sea, work forth the storm, or at least be found dead with the rudder in my hands; and all that I shall desire is that his Majesty and my other friends should narrowly observe me, and see if ever I question any man in my own interests, but where they are only interlaced as accessories, his Majesty's service and the just aspect towards the public and duty of my place set before them as principals.

No one who has studied Wentworth's letters and speeches can fail to notice his habit of repeating or echoing a phrase which he had used on some other occasions long before, a habit which in some men might be explained as a thoughtless repetition of formulas, but which in a man of Wentworth's character, can only be interpreted as arising from the fixity of his views on the main principles on which he founded his practice. In the extracts given above, two cases of this kind occur. The sentence in the last paragraph about the Crown being enabled 'to subsist of itself without being necessitated to accept of such conditions as others might vainly think to impose upon it,' carries us on to the well-known phrase (vol. ii. p. 328), in which he speaks in 1637 of Ship-money as vindicating 'Royalty at home from under the conditions and restraints of subjects,' and by the way in which the idea is here connected with the proceedings of Foulis, we get a little nearer to Wentworth's conception of the danger which he dreaded as arising from the power of subjects to enforce upon the Crown a policy which suited their own private ends. Another phrase, earlier in the letter, carries us back in quite another direction. When Wentworth speaks of the rights of the Crown as trampled on, and declares 'how necessary examples are—as well for the subject as the sovereign—to retain licentious spirits within the sober bounds of humility and fear,' we are at once reminded of the call made by the writer on the Commons of 1628, to vindicate their 'ancient, sober, and vital liberties, by reinforcing of the ancient laws of our ancestors; by setting such a stamp upon them as no licentious spirit shall dare hereafter to enter upon them.' Then too as here he had declared the interest of sovereign and subject to be the same. "I speak truly," he had said, "both for the interest of the King and people. If we enjoy not these it is impossible to relieve him." Mistaken as Wentworth's idea of government was, there is a unity of conception in both its parts. He waged war against 'licentious spirits' in the country as in the court. Alas! that one so highly endowed by nature and inspired by such rectitude of purpose, should himself have become the 'licentious spirit' to work unwittingly what mischief he could in his day of power.

CONTENTS

OF

THE FIRST VOLUME.

CHAPTER I.

PREPARATIONS FOR A PARLIAMENTARY SESSION.

		PAGE
1628	Charles takes the direction of the government into his own hands	1
	His foreign policy	2
	Character of Lord Treasurer Weston	3
	Demands of the King of Denmark	4
	Negotiations with France	5
	Political ignorance of the Queen	6
	A Spanish alliance suggested by Carlisle	7
	Weston advocates a general peace	8
	Dorchester supports a French alliance	9
	Growing weakness of Spain	10
	Successes of the Dutch	11
	Question of Tonnage and Poundage	12
	Resistance to its payment	15
	Committal of Chambers	16
	He is bailed, but proceeded against in the Star Chamber	17
	Rolle's attempt to obtain back his goods by a replevin	18
	Position taken by the King	19
	Ecclesiastical questions	20
	Cosin and Neile	22
	Cosin's Book of Devotions	23
	Burton and Prynne	25
	Prynne's early life	27
	Ceremonial disputes	28
	Difficulty of enforcing the Elizabethan compromise about the position of the Communion Table	29

VOL. I.   a

		PAGE
	Conflict at Grantham	30
	Decision of Bishop Williams	32
	Heath's letter to Montague	33
	Charles and Laud on dogmatic controversy	34
	The King's Declaration on Religion	36
	Abbot restored to favour	38
	Wentworth's speech at York	39
	Wentworth's political position	41
1629	Fresh disturbances about Tonnage and Poundage	44
	Parliamentary prospects	45

CHAPTER II.

THE SESSION OF 1629.

1629	Opening of the Session	46
	Alleged violation of the Petition of Right	47
	Case of Rolle's privilege	48
	Extension of privileges of Parliament	49
	The King's speech	50
	Postponement of the Tonnage and Poundage Bill	51
	Committee on religion	52
	Pym's views	53
	Eliot's speech on religion	54
	Resolution of the Commons	58
	Difficulty of interpreting it	59
	Eliot proposes to take the aggressive	60
	Montague's bishopric questioned	62
	The Durham ceremonialists	63
	Smart's sermon	64
	Cosin on the Royal supremacy	65
	The pardons questioned	66
	Attack on the Article relating to the authority of the Church	67
	Charges against Heath and Neile	68
	Selden on the liberty of the press	70
	Oliver Cromwell's early life	71
	His first speech in Parliament	75
	Curious charges against the ceremonialists	76
	The Jesuits' College at Clerkenwell	77
	Tonnage and Poundage again discussed	78
	Eliot proposes to call in question the farmers of the customs	80
	Proposals of Noy and Selden	81
	The Court of Exchequer rejects the dictation of the Commons	82

THE FIRST VOLUME. xix

	PAGE
Pym's warning	83
Eliot refuses to accept it	84
The House insists that the farmers have broken the privileges of the House	85
The King protects them	86
The Resolutions on Religion	87
Attempts to avert a rupture	89
The King's order to adjourn the House resisted	90
The Speaker held down in his chair	91
The door of the House locked	93
Eliot's charge against Weston	94
The Speaker refuses to put the resolutions proposed	95
Jerome Weston defends his father	96
Confusion in the House	97
The Speaker threatened	98
Adjournment of the House after the adoption of the resolutions by acclamation	99

CHAPTER III.

PRIVILEGE OF PARLIAMENT BEFORE THE JUDGES.

1629	Dissolution of Parliament, and imprisonment of the members concerned in the last scene	100
	The King's intentions announced	101
	Examination of the prisoners	103
	Firm stand taken by Eliot	104
	Proclamation against rumours of another Parliament	105
	Tonnage and Poundage exacted	106
	Sentence upon Chambers in the Star Chamber	108
	He refuses to submit, and brings an action against the Custom House officers	110
	He questions the jurisdiction of the Star Chamber	111
	The Judges consulted on the proper mode of dealing with the imprisoned members	112
	The prisoners apply for a *Habeas Corpus*	115
	The Attorney General's information in the Star Chamber	116
	Demurrer of the defendants	117
	Arguments in the King's Bench on the prisoners' demand to be bailed	118
	The Judges consult the King	119
	Charles does not produce the prisoners	120
	The King's foreign policy	123
	The Edict of Restitution in Germany	124
	Roe advocates a warlike policy	125

		PAGE
	The Treaty of Susa	126
	Vane's mission to Holland	127
	The peace of Lübeck	128
	Rohan's rebellion	128
	Rubens in England	129
	Roe's mission to the Baltic	130
	Charles listens to the overtures of Spain	131
	Resolves on sending Cottington to Madrid	132
	Charles and the Queen	133
	Further negotiations with Spain	135
	The Star Chamber prosecutions dropped	136
	Charles's letters to the Judges	137
	The prisoners refuse to be bound to good behaviour	138
	Suspension of Chief Baron Walter	140
	Chambers's case in the Exchequer	142
	Eliot in the Marshalsea	143
1630	The Attorney General's information in the King's Bench	144
	The prisoners deny the jurisdiction of the Court	145
	The Judges claim jurisdiction	146
	Judgment pronounced	148
	Eliot's imprisonment	150

CHAPTER IV.

LAUD, WENTWORTH, AND WESTON.

1629	The Judges and the Petition of Right	153
	Laud's view of toleration	154
	His eagerness to enforce uniformity	157
	His view of the Royal authority	158
	He becomes the centre of the opposition to Puritanism	159
	Sentence on Peter Smart	160
	Prohibition of nonconformity	161
	The lecturers	162
	The King's instructions	163
1630	Death of Pembroke	164
	Laud Chancellor of the University of Oxford	165
1629	Wentworth at York	166
	Character of his policy	167
	He brings Dudley's paper of advice to the King, and becomes a Privy Councillor	170
	History of Dudley's paper	171
1630	Prosecution of those who circulated it put an end to in consequence of the birth of a Prince	173
	Death of Sir R. Cotton	174
	The Puritans regret the birth of a Prince	175

	PAGE
Alexander Leighton	176
Sion's Plea against Prelacy	177
Leighton's sentence in the Star Chamber	181
Execution of the sentence	185
John Winthrop	187
Resolves to emigrate to New England	189
Early settlements in Massachusetts	190
Transference of the Massachusetts charter to America	191
Winthrop sails for America	192
Ecclesiastical and political system of Massachusetts	193
Toleration rejected in England and America	194
Wentworth in the Privy Council	196
Attempt of the Council to restrict the ravages of the plague	197
Measures taken to avert famine	198
Commissions for the relief of debtors and for the relief of the poor	200
Cromwell's objections to the charter of Huntingdon	202
Weston's financial difficulties	203
The knighthood fines	204
Enforcement of Tonnage and Poundage	205

CHAPTER V.

ENGLISH DIPLOMACY AND SWEDISH VICTORIES.

1630	Domestic and foreign policy of Charles	207
	Result of Vane's mission to the Hague	208
	Opening of Cottington's negotiations at Madrid	209
	Proposed league with Spain against the Dutch	211
	Mission of Anstruther to Vienna	212
	Dismissal of Wallenstein, and landing of Gustavus in Germany	213
	The treaty of Madrid	214
1631	Result of Vane's second mission to the Hague	215
	Secret treaty with Spain for the partition of the Dutch territory	216
	Money convoyed to the Spanish Netherlands	217
	Richardson's diplomacy	218
	Progress of the war in Germany	219
	Hamilton levies volunteers for Gustavus	221
	Lord Reay's charge against Hamilton	222
	Hamilton allowed to start	223
	Richelieu's overtures to Weston	224
	Mary de Medicis in the Netherlands	225
	Quarrel between Henrietta Maria and the French ambassador	226

		PAGE
	Failure of Anstruther's mission	228
	Vane's mission to Gustavus	229
	Charles offers aid to the Emperor	231
	Hamilton's misfortunes	232
	Eliot in prison	233
	Charles receives the demands of Gustavus	235
1632	Further negotiation with Gustavus	236
	Failure of Richelieu's expectations	237
	Charles's propositions to Gustavus	239
	Advance of the French	240
	Roe's political advice	241
	Windebank Secretary of State	243
	Massinger's political Plays	244
	Jerome Weston's mission	247
	Gustavus rejects Charles's propositions	248
	Failure of Charles's diplomacy	249
	Deaths of Gustavus and Frederick	250
	Boast of material prosperity in England	251
	Elizabeth refuses to come to England	252
	Discontent in the Spanish Netherlands	253
	Meeting of the States General at Brussels	254
	Charles offers to protect them	255
	Strong position of Richelieu	257
	Charles hesitates between France and Spain	258
1633	Richelieu's offers to the Dutch	259
	Charles's offer to the Swedes	260
	Weston created Earl of Portland	261
	The Queen's letter intercepted	262
	Quarrel between the Queen's Court and the Westons	263
	Understanding between Richelieu and Portland	265

CHAPTER VI.

DIVERGENT TENDENCIES IN POLITICS AND RELIGION.

1631	The lawyers rally round the Government	265
	Views of the antiquaries	268
	Eliot's *Monarchy of Man*	269
1632	His last days and death	272
1631	Wentworth in the North	275
	Is insulted by Bellasys	276
	Death of Lady Wentworth	277
1632	Case of Sir D. Foulis	278
	Lord Eure's resistance	279
	Foulis offers to use his influence on the King's behalf	280
	Wentworth's protest	281

		PAGE
	Sentence on Foulis	282
	Wentworth defends the jurisdiction of the Council of the North	283
1633	He leaves for Ireland	284
	The Government and the country gentlemen	285
1631	Laud's influence in the Church	286
	Bowing in church	287
	The consecration of St. Catherine Cree	288
	Laud's buildings at St. John's	290
	The repair of St. Paul's	291
	Controversy between Prynne and Widdowes	293
	Party feeling at Oxford	294
	Laud's view of conformity	295
	Laud's treatment of the Puritan clergy	296
1632	Matrimonial cases in the Court of High Commission	298
	Cases of Antinomianism and Separatism	299
	Case of John Vicars	301
	Sherfield breaks a painted window at Salisbury	302
1633	His trial and sentence in the Star Chamber	304
	The feoffees for impropriations dissolved by the Court of Exchequer	305
	William Gouge	307
	Richard Sibbes	308
	Nicholas Ferrar	311
	George Herbert	314
	Comparison between Herbert and Milton	319
	Tone of Milton's early poems	321
	The disruption of the nation yet incomplete	322

CHAPTER VII.

THE KING'S VISIT TO SCOTLAND.

1612	Effects of the establishment of episcopacy	324
1616	The Assembly at Aberdeen authorises the preparation of a liturgy	325
	The five Articles proposed by the King	326
	Preparation for James's visit to Scotland	327
1617	Adornment of the chapel at Holyrood	328
	James in Scotland	329
	He urges on the nobles the duty of abandoning their heritable jurisdictions	330
	Proposes an act on ecclesiastical ceremonies	331
	Hewat's Prayer Book	332
	The King's speech at St. Andrew's in recommendation of the five Articles	333

CONTENTS OF THE FIRST VOLUME.

		PAGE
	Feeling about them in Scotland	334
	Patrick Forbes	335
	Archbishop Spottiswoode	338
1618	Preparations for an Assembly at Perth	339
	Proceedings of the Assembly	340
	The five Articles accepted	343
	Difficulties of the Bishops in enforcing them	344
	The Articles confirmed by Parliament	346
	First measures of Charles I.	347
1625	The act of revocation	348
1629	The commutation of tithes	350
	The Crown and the aristocracy	351
1633	Charles's coronation at Edinburgh	353
1629	Question of a new Prayer Book discussed	354
	Position of the Scottish Bishops	356
1633	Ceremonies observed at the Coronation	358
	Difficulty of opposition in the Scottish Parliament	359
	The bills proposed by the Government accepted	362
	The introduction of the Prayer Book postponed	363
1634	William Forbes, the first Bishop of Edinburgh	364
	The King and the Lords of the Opposition	366
	The supplication	367
1635	Lord Balmerino's trial	369
	Composition of the Privy Council	371
	Archbishop Spottiswoode made Chancellor of Scotland	373

Errata.

Page 48, line 5, *for* "Henry" *read* "John."

" 71 " 8 from bottom, and p. 72, lines 8 and 12, *for* "Hinchinbroke" *read* "Hinchinbrook."

" 74 " 11 " *for* "judgment" *read* "judgments."

" 172 " 7 " *dele* "but who was commonly reported to be his own natural son," *and add as a footnote*, "The statement that he was really Cotton's natural son is suspicious, as resting on the authority of D'Ewes, who is not to be trusted when he brings charges of this kind."

" 299 note 2. After all it appears from a release to Sir T. Hatton (*Patent Rolls*, 13 Charles I., Part 33, No. 5) that in reality Alington's fine, reduced to 10,000*l.*, was paid over to the Queen, a pardon being granted to conceal the transaction.

" 301 line 2 from bottom, *after* "reinstated" *read* "in the ministry but not in his cure." To the footnote in the same page *add the reference* "295, b."

THE PERSONAL GOVERNMENT OF CHARLES I.

CHAPTER I.

PREPARATIONS FOR A PARLIAMENTARY SESSION.

THE murdered Buckingham had no successor in Charles's affections. No other man could bring with him the long habitude of personal friendship, or the promptness of decision made palatable by winning gracefulness of manner, which had enabled the late Lord Admiral, under the show of deference, to guide his sovereign at his pleasure.

1628. Sept. Buckingham not replaced in Charles's favour

It was easy to dispose of Buckingham's offices, to give the Mastership of the Horse to Holland, and to place the Admiralty in commission in order that the profits of the place might be applied to the payment of debts which Buckingham had contracted, for the most part, in his master's service. But Charles marked his sense of personal loss by refusing to give away the vacant Garter which his friend had worn.[1]

His offices given away.

Buckingham had been more than a Master of the Horse or a Lord Admiral. He had been even more than a Prime Minister is in a modern Cabinet. His word had given the impulse to the whole machine of government. Every act had been submitted to his

The government undertaken by the King.

---

[1] Contarini's Despatch, $\frac{\text{Sept. 29}}{\text{Oct. 6}}$. *Ven. MSS.*

approval. Every office had been filled by personal followers, who had learned that their fortunes could be made or marred by his nod. Into this supreme direction of affairs Charles stepped at once. He announced his intention of presiding continually at the Council, and ordered each minister to report directly to himself on the business entrusted to his charge.

Of industrious attention to business Charles was eminently capable. Countless corrections upon the drafts of despatches and state papers show how diligent he was in moulding the minutest turns of expression to his taste, and how little latitude he allowed to those who served under him. For government in the higher sense he had no capacity. He was as obstinate in refusing to abandon any plan which he had once formed, as he was irresolute in the face of any obstacles which might arise in the way of their execution. Hence the contrast between his treatment of difficulties at home and abroad. Within the kingdom, where his authority was undisputed, he required prompt obedience without troubling himself with the growing ill-will which was storing itself up to become the source of future trouble. But with the Kings and States of the Continent who had no thought of taking his word for law, he never succeeded in gaining his ends. Constant repetition of the same demand without any intention to offer advantages in return, or any power to extort by prompt action the object which he sought, made Charles's diplomacy a byword on the Continent, as his father's had been before.

From the beginning of the reign it had been the fault of Charles's foreign policy that it rested rather on the supposed necessity of giving satisfaction to the personal honour of the king than on the well-understood interests, either of England or of the nations of the Continent. Because the Elector Palatine was Charles's brother-in-law, and because he had himself failed to secure a wife at Madrid, he had engaged in war against Spain. Because his guarantee to the treaty between Lewis XIII. and his Huguenot subjects had been disregarded, he had engaged in a war with France. As long as Buckingham lived, Charles had struck blow after blow in the vain hope of recovering the Palatinate, and saving Rochelle. With Buckingham no longer at his side, it was likely that words would take the place of deeds, and that he would write despatches and instruct ambassadors, instead of arming fleets and appointing generals. But it was not likely that he would frankly acknowledge that events were stronger than himself, or that he would give up the hope of obtaining objects which he still believed to be desirable, because they were beyond his reach.

Everything thus combined to increase the influence of the minister whose voice was persistently raised in favour of peace. Weston, the Lord Treasurer, was neither a highminded nor a farsighted politician. His wife and some of his children were acknowledged Recusants; and though he himself conformed to the English Church, it was generally believed that but for the allurements of temporal interest he would have followed in their steps. He was outrageously rude to those whom he could afford to despise, and obsequiously subservient to those upon whom he was obliged to depend. He alone of all those who had advocated the maintenance of peace in 1624 had contrived to keep his place in Buckingham's favour by promptly accommodating his actions to the wishes of the favourite, and men were already beginning to laugh at the timidity with which he shifted his ground whenever a persistence in the course which he had adopted would be likely to be accompanied by consequences unpleasant to himself.

Like Middlesex, Weston was a careful and economical administrator of the treasury, though he took good care to fill his own pockets as well by means even more unscrupulous than those to which Middlesex had resorted. Like Middlesex, too, he was now endeavouring to impress upon the Government the policy of complete abstention from foreign complications, except when intervention was absolutely required by the material interests of England. The men of the sixteenth century had handed down traditions of heroism displayed on behalf of the Continental Protestants. Weston wished to hear of nothing of the kind. He cared for England alone. But he cared for England with no exalted patriotism. It was not to him the land of ordered liberty and ancient pre-eminence in arts and arms. It was a land the people of whom it was his business to make rich, in order that they might be more easily made obedient.

The influence of Weston would thus bring itself to bear on that side of Charles's character which had been neglected by Buckingham. Buckingham had encouraged his unyielding persistency, and had relieved his helplessness by his own promptness in action. Weston taught him that inactivity was in itself a virtue, that the best policy was to do nothing. But he did not weary him by contradiction. He offered himself as the instrument of his will, whatever it might be, certain that something would occur in the end to throw insuperable difficulties in his way. No minister, in fact, could hope to keep his place for an hour who should venture to inform Charles that the recovery of the Palatinate was beyond his power to effect.

In the beginning of September, the Danish ambassador, Rosencrantz, arrived to represent King Christian's desperate need of men and money. In reply, Morgan was ordered to carry to Glückstadt the 1,200 men who formed the shattered remains of the garrison of Stade, and to do his utmost to relieve Krempe. Before the end of the month, commissioners were appointed to treat with Rosencrantz on the best means of rendering more considerable assistance.[1]

It was more easy to induce Charles to consent to make peace with France than to bring him to make peace with Spain and its allies, as long as they were in possession of the Palatinate. Contarini, the Venetian ambassador, continued to offer the mediation which had been interrupted by Buckingham's assassination. He had the unusual satisfaction of finding his advances accepted by men of every shade of opinion. Weston was delighted to help on peace in any shape; whilst Pembroke and Dorchester looked upon a treaty with France as a necessary preliminary to an active co-operation with the German Protestants.

In this last view Charles apparently concurred. He averred that he could not make terms with Lewis as long as Rochelle was besieged and the Huguenots unsatisfied. But he gave it to be plainly understood that, if once these obstacles were removed, he was quite prepared for a military alliance. He even went so far as to express a preference for the plan which he had rejected when proposed by Gustavus in 1624, that France should carry on war with Spain in Italy, whilst England and the Protestant Powers combated the Emperor in Northern Germany.[2]

[1] Proposition by Rosencrantz, Sept. 4. Commission to Weston and others, Sept. 28; *S. P. Denmark*. Carleton to the Privy Council, Oct. 20; *S. P. Holland*.

[2] Contarini's Despatches give full particulars on his conversations with the King and others.

1628.
Sept.
The Queen supports the French alliance.

Contarini found a warm ally in the Queen. Henrietta Maria had been gradually accustoming herself to the loss of her French attendants. Buckingham's death was the removal of a wall of separation between herself and her husband. When the confidential friend was gone, Charles turned for consolation to his wife. At last he tasted the pleasures of a honeymoon. She was now in her nineteenth year, ignorant and undisciplined, but bright and graceful, with flashing eyes and all the impulsive vehemence of her race. Her pouting sulkiness had been the response to her husband's cold assertion of superiority, and when he threw aside his reserve and sought but to bask in the sunshine of her smiles, she repaid him with all the tenderness of a loving woman. Courtiers had many stories to tell of the affection of this pair so long estranged, and it was soon announced that a direct heir to the English throne was to be expected.

Oct.

Of politics the Queen was completely ignorant, and it was always difficult to interest her in them, unless some personal question was involved. But she could not be indifferent to the continuance of strife between her brother and her husband.

Nov. Effect of the news of the capture of Rochelle.

Charles listened, but he did not listen too eagerly. Even the news of the fall of Rochelle did not at once produce a better understanding between the Governments. Charles took it ill that Richelieu did not immediately despatch messengers to England to sue for peace.[1] He began to cast about for other means of regaining the Palatinate. In Buckingham's lifetime Porter had been sent to Madrid, and Carlisle after passing through Brussels and Lorraine, had arrived at Turin, to knit together, if possible, a general league of the enemies of France. Ever since the failure of the

Carlisle's mission to Turin.

---

[1] Contarini to Zorzi, Nov. $\frac{11}{21}$. Contarini's Despatch, $\frac{\text{Nov. 22}}{\text{Dec. 2}}$. *Ven. MSS.*

French alliance, which he had negotiated in 1624, Carlisle had thrown himself warmly into opposition to Richelieu, by whose arts, as he held, the honest intentions of the English Government had been thwarted. There was, indeed, much to complain of on both sides. If Charles had broken his word in the matter of the marriage treaty, Lewis had broken his word in the matter of Mansfeld's expedition; and whilst the expulsion of the Queen's attendants and the renewed persecution of the English Catholics were bitterly remembered at the Louvre, the utter failure of the first military expedition of the war was by no means forgotten at Whitehall. Carlisle now urged the continuance of the war with France. "If the present government of France," he wrote, "were such as good and honest patriots do wish and desire, many questions would fall to the ground." The King of France, however, he continued, had neither the power nor the will to recover the Palatinate, and he certainly designed the ruin of Protestantism in his own country. If Charles listened to the overtures of Spain, without accepting them too impatiently, he might have full satisfaction in all that he desired. Charles caught at the suggestion. He hoped that no one would suspect him of 'so great a villainy' as a peace with France which failed to secure terms for the Huguenots. He at once invited the Savoyard diplomatist, the Abbot of Scaglia, to England, to act as an intermediate agent between Spain and himself, and he assured the Duke of Rohan that he would continue to support him in spite of 'the late mis-accident of Rochelle.'[1]

It was the fundamental weakness of Charles's

---

[1] Carlisle and Wake to Conway, Nov. 1; Conway to Carlisle and Wake, Nov. 23. The King to Carlisle, Nov. 24; *S. P. Savoy*. Conway to Rohan, Nov. 23; *S. P. France*.

foreign policy that he had no moral sympathy with any single party on the Continent. The States which he courted were nothing more in his eyes than instruments which might help him to gain his own objects. If one King would not help him, another might. He forgot that it was unlikely that anyone would care to help him at all, unless he had something to offer in return.

Oct. Arundel in the Council.

In the meanwhile, Weston's influence was daily growing. He effected a complete reconciliation between the King and Arundel. That stately nobleman once more took his place at the Council Board, ready when the moment came to give his vote in favour of peace.

Nov. 12. Cottington a Councillor.

He was soon joined there by Cottington, a man of the world without enthusiasm, believing that the Roman Catholic belief was the safest to die in, and that Weston's policy ran less risk than any other in the immediate present. Weston was thankful for his support, and marked him out for the Chancellorship of the Exchequer as soon as a vacancy could be made.

Weston's economy.

Weston's voice was always raised in favour of economy. Charles proposed to raise a sumptuous monument to Buckingham's memory. "I would be loath," said Weston, "to tell your Majesty what the world would say, not only here but all Christendom over, if you should erect a monument for the Duke before you set up one for King James, your father." [1]

He holds back from interference in Germany.

With still greater persistency he opposed any opening for fresh warlike expenditure. Rosencrantz was urgent that some of the ships and troops returning from Rochelle might be sent to the King of Denmark's assistance. Weston hastened to pay off the landsmen, and gave an unfavourable answer about the ships.[2]

---

[1] Meade to Stuteville, Nov. 1. *Court and Times,* i. 419.
[2] *Council Register,* Oct. 26, Nov. 12. Contarini's Despatches, Oct. 24 Nov. 3 Nov. 22 Dec. *Ven. MSS.*

When news arrived that Krempe had surrendered to the Imperialists, Charles resolved to send no present aid to Denmark, and Morgan was ordered to keep quiet at Glückstadt till the winter was over. Yet though Charles allowed himself to be persuaded into inaction for the present, he could not be induced to forego the luxury of promising large aid in the future. His ambassador, Anstruther, was directed to inform the King of Denmark that though the aid which he sorely needed was postponed, it was not refused. Parliament would, doubtless, grant the necessary supplies, and help would be sent in the spring. Morgan's regiment should be reinforced, and a fleet of forty ships should be despatched to the Elbe.[1]

In the course of December a nomination was made which showed that Charles did not place himself unreservedly in Weston's hands. Conway was old and sickly, and was removed from the Secretaryship to the less troublesome office of President of the Council, which the still older Marlborough was induced to vacate. He was succeeded by Dorchester, a warm advocate of the French alliance. It was not long before Dorchester had the satisfaction of seeing the difficulties in the way of peace with France gradually removed; and in January a treaty sent over by Richelieu was, with the exception of one not very important particular, agreed to by the English Council.[2]

Almost at the same time Carlisle and Porter returned from their respective missions. The most dazzling offers were dangled before Charles's eyes as the price of an alliance with Spain. With the help of Olivares, Frederick and Elizabeth would soon be re-

---

[1] Coke to Morgan, Nov. 24; Anstruther to Conway, Dec. 29. Answer of the Commissioners, Jan. *S. P. Denmark.*

[2] Contarini's Despatches, $\frac{\text{Dec. 20}}{\text{Jan. 9}}$, Jan. $\frac{10}{20}$. *Ven. MSS.*

installed at Heidelberg, whilst Denmark and the Dutch Republic should be relieved from the attack of the Catholic Powers. Already the two great rivals, Richelieu and Olivares were measuring one another's strength with hostile glances, and were anxious to secure the neutrality, if not the alliance, of England in the inevitable conflict.

Progress of the negotiation with France.

A negotiation almost completed and publicly avowed for a treaty with France, which might possibly lead to an alliance against Spain and the Emperor—an inchoate and unavowed negotiation for a treaty with Spain, which might possibly lead to an alliance against France—and a promise to send active aid to Denmark in its war against the Emperor; such were the bewildering results of three months of Charles's diplomacy since he had lost Buckingham's assistance. What likelihood was there that he would succeed in making his policy intelligible to the House of Commons, or that he would gain the support of the nation for his plans?

Results of Charles's diplomacy.

Feeling of the nation.

As far as it is possible to gauge the feeling of the nation, it may be asserted that, though any favour shown to Spain would be unpopular, there was no longer that burning zeal for war which had animated the political classes when the news of the loss of the Palatinate first reached England. Not only had the thoughts of the nation been diverted to domestic affairs, but Spain itself was far less formidable in 1629 than she had been in 1621. The reduction of Breda in 1625 had been followed by a long period of quiescence, during which the Spanish generals had not even attempted to push home the advantage which they had gained. In Germany, though Spanish troops continued to occupy Frankenthal and the Western Palatinate, they stood aloof from all active participation in the

Growing weakness of Spain.

war, and left Tilly and Wallenstein to stamp out if they could the last embers of resistance on the coasts of the Baltic. Nor, if Spain failed to make any show of strength in Germany or the Netherlands, was it able to explain its inertness by any increased activity in opposing England. Even at the height of Buckingham's mismanagement, when Wimbledon returned discomfited from Cadiz, when Buckingham himself brought back the beaten remnants of his army from Rochelle, she had not ventured on a single aggressive movement. And now at last it was seen that she could no longer hold her own. In the summer of 1628, the stadtholder, Frederick Henry, for the first time, quitted the defensive tactics which necessity had for so many years imposed on the guardians of the Dutch Republic, and had attacked and taken Grol under the eyes of Spinola. Before the year was out, still more glorious tidings were wafted across the Atlantic. The prize which Drake and Raleigh had failed to secure, and for which Wimbledon had waited in vain, had been secured by the conduct and courage of a Dutch mariner. Peter Hein had captured the Plate fleet, and the treasure which had been destined for the payment of Spanish soldiers was on its way to support the arms of the Republic in a more daring campaign that any Dutchman had dared to contemplate since the day when Ostend had surrendered to the skill and resources of Spinola.

It had thus become plain in England that the danger of the erection of a universal monarchy having its seat at Madrid had passed away. Nor were the imaginations of Englishmen much moved by the risk of the establishment of a strong military and Catholic empire having its seat at Vienna. No doubt there was sympathy with the German Protestants, and much angry talk about the devastations of Wallenstein and Tilly. But after all, the coast of the Baltic was far away, and the fall of Krempe did not touch Englishmen as the fall of Ostend had touched them in earlier days. It did not bring home to them any sense of immediate danger to themselves, nor were the conquerors men of that race whose very existence had been a standing menace to England ever since the early days of Elizabeth's reign. Tilly's veterans were not the military representatives of the troops who had contended with Sidney under the walls of Zutphen, or who had waited on the Flemish sandhills under Parma till the Armada should appear to convey them to the invasion of the island realm.

The fear of Spanish interference at home removed.

Above all, neither the King of Spain nor the Emperor threatened now to undermine the institutions of England by secret sap. There was no longer any fear of the arrival of an Infanta to be the bride of a King of England ; and it is difficult to say how much of the warlike ardour of 1621 was to be attributed rather to the fear of the intrigues of Spain in the English Court, than to the fear of its warlike predominance in Germany and the Netherlands. Those who in 1621 were eager to avert a domestic danger by engaging in a foreign war, were ready in 1628 to allow the Continental nations to shift for themselves.

Weston hopes to conciliate Parliament.

Thus it came about that Weston's foreign policy was in greater danger from his master's reluctance to abandon the hope of regaining the Palatinate, than from the warlike zeal of the House of Commons. He would have a harder task in assuaging the asperities which had sprung up at home during the last session than in putting an end to the war.

July. Tonnage and Poundage.

Weston's first difficulty was the question of Tonnage and Poundage. The Commons had not only declared the levy of these dues to be illegal in itself, but had encouraged individual merchants to refuse payment to the King's officers.[1] To the merchants, whose trade had suffered severely from the ravages of the Dunkirk privateers, the suggestion that they might free themselves from such a burthen fell upon willing ears. The spirit of the old English constitution was on their side, and they were assured by no less a body than the House of Commons, that they had the letter on their side as well. The King was certain to take a different view of the case. He held it to be the duty of subjects to give him a revenue sufficient to enable him to conduct the regular administration of government without interruption; and it was certain that, unless Tonnage and Poundage and the still more questionable impositions continued to be paid, little short of half of his income would be lost at a stroke.

CHAP. I.
1628.
July.

At the close of the last session the King had taken strong ground, in asserting that the interpretation of the law belonged to the Judges, not to the House of Commons. Such then, as now, was the accepted rule of the constitution. Yet it was impossible to allow any mere interpretation of the law to decide the question at issue.[2] As well might two men engaged in deadly

The King's appeal to the Judges.

---

[1] *England under Buckingham and Charles I.*, ii. 307.

[2] A possible instance may be taken to illustrate the position. The present constitution rests upon the maintenance of tolerable harmony between the two Houses. Suppose it should happen that the House of Lords placed itself in deliberate opposition to the House of Commons, even after a general election had shown that the House of Commons was in accordance with the feelings of the constituencies. Suppose that the House of Lords rejected every Bill sent up to it by the Commons. What would be the use of applying to the Judges as arbitrators? They could but decide that the Lords were legally in the right. They could not decide whether they were politically in the right. That would depend partly upon their chance of converting the nation to their views, partly upon the extent to which the existing constituencies were a fair representation of the nation. It would be quite possible for a national feeling to spring up which had no representation in the House of Commons, though that is far less likely to happen now than it was with the unreformed House.

strife ask an impartial arbiter to decide the question of property in the dagger to which both were clinging with convulsive grasp. Nothing less than the supreme authority in England was at stake.

Question at issue.

If the King could collect money without opposition, he might govern as he pleased till he provoked a revolution. If he could not collect it without the consent of the Commons, they might dictate their own terms. The impositions had been adjudged to James simply because certain words had been used instead of others in Acts of Parliament three centuries old. If Tonnage and Poundage were now to be declared leviable as impositions had been levied, at the sole will of the King, it would be because certain technical words had been omitted in the Petition of Right. Such considerations would never be suffered to weigh very heavily in the balance. However accurate men might try to be in their reading of the law, they could not avoid being influenced by the enormous consequences of the interpretation which they gave to it. They would not scan statutes and year-books with the serene impartiality with which a botanist scans the claims of a newly-discovered plant to be classed in one natural order or another. Those who thought that it was better that authority should remain in the King's hands, than pass into the hands of the House of Commons, would naturally be of one opinion. Those who thought that it was better that England should be ruled in accordance with the wishes of the House of Commons, than that her destinies should be left to the good pleasure of the King, would naturally be of another opinion.[1]

---

[1] An able writer who reviewed my former volumes in the *Edinburgh Review* for January 1876, has undoubtedly made out that the word 'tax' was sometimes used even officially to cover customs duties. But the Crown lawyers would, I believe, hold that when a doubt existed the judgment should be for the King, and, therefore, the absence of a more

Whatever the views of the Judges might be, a grave political question would never be settled by other than political arguments or political forces.

The immediate danger arose from the appeal of the House of Commons to the private action of individuals. The first result of that appeal was that some merchants refused to pay the imposition on wines. Those who resisted were committed to the Fleet, but were speedily liberated on entering into bonds to pay the required sum. The imposition on currants, the very article which had been the subject of the Judges' decision in James's reign, was next challenged. Importers began to land goods without paying duty. Charles took a firm stand against this attempt of individual merchants to take the law into their own hands. In full council he declared that these impositions were his 'by a solemn and legal judgment.' Finding the warning ineffectual, the Council issued orders to seize all goods landed without payment.[1]

The example of the recalcitrant merchants spread. Goods liable to Tonnage and Poundage were seized for non-payment of dues. The owners had recourse to the Sheriff's Court of the City of London, and sued out a replevin, as if to regain property of their own which had been illegally distrained. Popular feeling was on the side of the merchants; and it was feared that an

definite word shows, I still think, that the framers of the Petition did not mean to cover the case of impositions, probably, as the Reviewer thinks, because they expected to pass their Bill of Tonnage and Poundage, and also because they were unwilling to encumber the Petition with more matter disagreeable to the King than was absolutely needful. If the King on his part did not directly say that he levied all these duties as impositions, it was because he thought it inexpedient to do so. Logically there was nothing to prevent him, and his expressions show that he kept this argument in reserve. He was, however, in a stronger position by leaving his case generally to the Judges, than he would have been if he had settled upon a special plea for himself.

[1] *Rushworth,* i. 639; *Council Register,* July 20, Aug. 13.

attempt would be made to carry off the goods by force. The Council directed that assistance should be given to the Custom-house officers in the execution of their duty, and that those who resisted them should be imprisoned 'until this Board give other order, or that they be delivered by order of law.'[1] Evidently the Government wished to conform to the Petition of Right, and to make the Judges the arbitrators of the dispute.

Resistance did not cease. To the merchants it was a question of refusing to submit to an unblushing attempt to extract illegal duties by force; and this question was mixed up in the minds of some of them with the injury done to trade by compelling them to pay duties at all. On September 28, the refusers were summoned before the Council. One of them, Richard Chambers, flung out defiant words. "Merchants," he said, "are in no part of the world so screwed and wrung as in England. In Turkey they have more encouragement."[2] The words themselves, perhaps still more the tone in which they were spoken, were treated as a contempt of the Board, and Chambers was committed to the Marshalsea.

In the midst of such agitation it would hardly be wise to allow Parliament to meet in October, as had been originally proposed. Two days after the committal of Chambers, it was resolved to prorogue it to January 20. It was fervently hoped by the Councillors that time would thus be gained for establishing a better understanding with the Commons; 'the medicine of a constant and settled form of government' being 'the only remedy for the distemper' of the times.[3]

[1] *Council Register*, Aug. 31.
[2] Form of Submission; *Rushworth*, i. 672.
[3] Dorchester to Carlisle, Sept. 30; *Court and Times*, i. 403.

Chambers was not the man to give any assistance to the establishment of a constant and settled government. He applied to the Court of King's Bench for a writ of *habeas corpus*. For the first time the Judges were called upon to exercise the authority secured to them by the Petition of Right. The warrant of committal was produced in Court, stating that the cause of imprisonment was 'insolent behaviour and words spoken at the Council Table.' The Judges did not dispute that the Council, like any other superior Court, might commit for contempt. But they held that the words spoken ought to be set down for their information, in order that they might convince themselves that they really amounted to a contempt. As no account of the words had been given, they admitted Chambers to bail, though they advised him to make his submission to the Board, and warned him that they might, if they pleased, order an indictment or information to be drawn against him in their own Court for his contemptuous words. The Lord Keeper and other members of the Council complained that the Judges had failed to give them due notice of what they intended to do; but they did not deny the principle on which the Court had acted, that the Judges had the right of examining whether the cause named on the warrant was truly given.[1]

The Crown lawyers took another course than that suggested by the Judges. The Petition of Right had not in any way lessened the powers of the Star Chamber, and the Attorney General preferred an information against Chambers in that Court. It is likely enough that the Government was by no means sorry that some months would pass away before the case came on for trial.[2]

---

[1] *Rushworth*, i. 639.
[2] Meade to Stuteville, Nov. 15. *Court and Times*, i. 429. Meade

CHAP. I.
1628.
Renewed resistance to the duties.

Nov. 12.

Nov. 13. Interference of the Court of Exchequer.

Nov. 27. Final decision of the Court.

The question referred to Parliament.

Whatever fate might be reserved for Chambers, it was necessary to take an instant decision on the collection of the duties. Some thirty of the principal merchants, amongst them John Rolle, a member of the House of Commons, refused to pay, though they offered to give security for any sum which might ultimately be adjudged to the King by law. On November 12, Rolle and three others made a fresh attempt to regain their goods by a replevin. The Attorney General applied to the Court of Exchequer, and the Barons at once ordered that the goods should remain in the officers' hands. The question at issue, they held, was too important to be determined in an off-hand fashion by a City Court. It was 'only fit for the Parliament now shortly to be reassembled, there to be finally settled, as the desire of His Majesty and the discreeter sort of merchants is it should be.' A fortnight later the Court of Exchequer finally decided that a replevin was not the proper method of taking 'goods out of His Majesty's own possession,' and that in this case the property must be held to be in the King's possession.[1]

The question between the Crown and the merchants was thus narrowed to a difference of opinion as to which party was so far entitled to be considered *primâ facie* in the right, as to be allowed to retain the custody of the goods whilst the legality of the demand for duty was submitted to a superior Court. Weston, however, says that he was 'committed a second time to one of the tipstaves of that Court.' Does that mean that he was actually imprisoned till the case came on?

[1] *Orders and Decrees in the Exchequer*, Nov. 13, 27, 4 Charles I., fol. 254, 262; Att. Gen. *v.* Rolle. In *S. P. Dom.* clv. 1, is an undated collection of orders, 'apparently granted by the Court of Exchequer to stay proceedings in suits at the Common-law brought against the King's officers for levying his duties.' It must have been made either now, or during the subsequent session of Parliament, and must have formed a valuable support to the decision of the Court.

who, as Lord Treasurer, had a seat on the Bench of the Exchequer, announced that he looked to another quarter for a solution of the difficulty. The Court, he said, would now 'by no means meddle with the question of right, but did refer it wholly to the Parliament, where he made no doubt there would be perfect agreement between the King and subject.'[1]

Thus far, under Weston's guidance, Charles had proceeded with no inconsiderable tact. He had retreated from the defiant position which he had taken up at the close of the last session, and without openly abandoning his claim to levy the whole of the customs duties of the realm under the name of Impositions, had refrained from irritating his subjects by bringing it prominently forward. He would not suffer the rights which he believed to be his own to be trampled under foot by mob violence. But he was ready to submit them to the decision of the Judges. At the same time he acknowledged that the question went too deep to be settled by legal arguments. It was pre-eminently a political question, and he hoped to be able to come to an amicable arrangement on it with his Parliament.

It was not unlikely that Parliament, and especially the House of Commons, would regard the question from a very different point of view. They might resent the levy of the duties as an infraction of the law, according to the interpretation which they had persistently put upon it since 1610. They might even pronounce it, as they had pronounced it in the last session, to be contrary to the Petition of Right. Further, if there was any object upon which they had set their hearts, and which the King declined to grant, they might use their power of refusing to pass a bill of Tonnage and

[1] Pory to Meade, Nov. 28. *Court and Times,* i. 437.

CHAP. I.
1628.
Nov.
Difficulties of the Church.

Poundage in order to extort that object from their unwilling Sovereign.

It was only too probable that contention would arise on some question of ecclesiastical politics. At the close of the last session the Remonstrance of the Commons had spoken bitterly of Laud and Neile, and had demanded the suppression of Arminianism in the Church. The Church of England, in fact, was called upon to face the difficulty which meets every society which renounces old authority and relaxes the bonds of ancient discipline. The victory over external enemies was won. But there was danger of divisions and distractions within. Those who questioned the received Calvinistic doctrines were regarded as renegades from the faith, as traitors ready to replace a Protestant Church under the Papal yoke. But though the repulsion to Arminianism, or to what passed as Arminianism, was real and strong, a political element was mingled with the religious element in the popular feeling. Montague had closed his obnoxious book with alarming words: "Do thou defend me with the sword, and I will defend thee with the pen." It was probably unavoidable that a body of clergy whose views were proscribed by popular religious opinion should lean upon the Royal authority which they regarded as raised above popular opinion. Elizabeth had kept Puritans at bay, and why should not Charles follow in her steps? Was not the Church the King's peculiar province, to be ruled without reference to Parliament? Montague had been followed by others who carried the attack into the enemies' quarters. Sibthorpe and Manwaring had publicly maintained doctrines concerning the State which stripped Parliament even of those powers which had hitherto been universally allowed to belong to it. It seemed as if a league had been struck by which the

King was to maintain the anti-Calvinist clergy in their places, whilst they in return were to inculcate the duty of obeying the absolute authority of the King.

<small>CHAP. I.
1628.
July.
Promotions of Montague and Manwaring.</small>

The King had done everything that lay in his power to give strength to this impression; for he had raised Montague to the bishopric of Chichester, and had granted a rich living to Manwaring. How could men doubt that Charles was bent not merely on providing for liberty of opinion,—which would have been unpopular enough,—but on closing the mouths of Calvinistic preachers, and on breeding up a race of clergy ready to inculcate doctrines of a different cast?

Abstruse as the prevailing doctrine of grace and predestination was, it struck its roots deeply into the moral nature of those who valued it as a pearl of great price. It made them braver and more self-reliant. It imparted to them a contempt for merely human authority, by impressing on them the duty of an absolute surrender of the will to a Perfect and Divine Being. Yet strong as the sentiments were which gathered round it, a nation would hardly have been roused in the defence of a merely theological dogma, if the question at issue had not been presented in some more palpable form. The human mind requires considerable cultivation before it is seriously impressed by that which appeals to it through the ear: it is easily moved by sights which reach the eye. Already there were signs, though few as yet, that the quarrel would soon take a new form. The men who looked back for their doctrine to the early Reformers and to the earlier Fathers were likely to look in the same direction for their ceremonies. In proportion as they broke loose from the logical bonds of Calvinism, necessity led them to seek to order their lives by the requirements of a ceremonial devotion which might constantly

<small>Moral side of the theological dispute.</small>

<small>Ceremonial dispute.</small>

remind them that they were the servants of a Heavenly Master.

1628. John Cosin.

Amongst those who were repelled by the baldness of the ordinary Church worship of the day was John Cosin. Early in life he had attracted the notice of men as distinguished as Overall and Andrewes. After Overall's death he attached himself to Bishop Neile of Durham, and joined the circle which comprised Laud and Montague, and which met constantly at Durham House, once the splendid habitation of Raleigh, to discuss the prospects of the Church and the possibility of resisting the tide of Puritanism. Neile was as strict a disciplinarian as Laud himself. He is described as a good preacher, but a poor scholar; and he left no mark upon the theological literature of the time. He had the good sense to make no attempt to conceal his deficiencies. One day he reproved a Durham schoolmaster for flogging his pupils unmercifully. He himself, he said, was an example of the uselessness of so ferocious a discipline. He had been flogged so constantly at Westminster that he had never mastered the difficulties of the Latin language.[1] Yet he had that undefinable quality which enables some men in no way distinguished by their intellectual achievements to gather disciples round them, and to utilise the efforts of men whose powers are more productive than their own. He was a man of sumptuous habits, and displayed a marked preference for architectural and ceremonial splendour.

Bishop Neile.

1625. Cosin assists Montague.

Cosin had mingled early in controversial strife. In 1625 the sheets of the *Appello Cæsarem* were placed in his hands as they came from the press, and he was invited by the confiding author to alter or to omit

---

[1] The story is told by Leighton (*Epitome*, 75) as being to the Bishop's disadvantage.

passages at his pleasure.¹ In 1626 he took part in the conference at York House between Montague and his opponents. The next year he was brought more prominently before the eyes of the world. The King was alarmed at the discovery that his wife and her priests were practising upon the religion of the English ladies of the Royal household. Religious books were thrown in their way, and conversation was led to the contrast between the English forms of worship and the imposing ceremonial of the Catholic Church. Either Lady Denbigh or Charles himself asked Cosin to provide a manual of private prayer which might fitly be used by members of the English Church.²

The result was a Book of Devotions, which was ready for publication early in 1627. It was founded upon the Primer which had been issued in 1560, as that had been founded upon an earlier Primer issued in 1546. But much was added which had no authority from the book published by the direction of Elizabeth.

The devotion of Cosin was as precise and methodical as the logic of a Puritan's creed. In it every external form was to be taken advantage of to quicken the aspirations of the soul. Classification and arrangement have here a supreme importance. Certain days are to be kept for special abstinence or for special rejoicing. The Apostles' Creed is to be divided into twelve articles, the Lord's Prayer into seven petitions, each of which is to be separately regarded. Every one of the Commandments has its appended list of duties to be

---

[1] This we learn from Montague's letters in Cosin's *Correspondence*. Surtees Society.

[2] Cosin's *Works*, i. xxi.

[3] *Ibid.* ii. 82.

performed and of offences to be avoided. Prayers are to be said at certain specified hours. The distinction between good and evil threatened to become involved in considerations of time and number. There were three theological virtues, three kinds of good works, seven spiritual and six corporal works of mercy, seven deadly sins, and seven virtues opposed to them, whilst Death, Judgment, Hell, and Heaven are duly catalogued as the four last things which may befal a man.[1]

Contrast between Cosin and the Puritans.

The gulf between this religion and the religion of the ordinary English Protestant was wide and deep. As the central point of the Puritan system lay in preaching and conversion, the central point of the system of their opponents lay in the Sacrament of the Lord's Supper. In preparing for it Cosin laid stress upon the words in the Prayer-book in which those who required counsel and comfort were admonished to seek out some discreet minister of God's Word, in order that they might receive absolution from him, though he never thought of proposing that such applications should be general or compulsory. For the Communion Service itself he provided a form of words to be repeated by the worshipper 'prostrate before the altar,' and he spoke of a real though spiritual presence of Christ in the Sacrament itself, and reminded Christians that they were here enabled to offer a 'sacrifice of praise and thanksgiving' as a memorial of the sacrifice of the Cross.

His views not to be suppressed.

Such a doctrine would offer a refuge to many who but for it would have fled from the uncongenial teaching of Puritanism into the arms of the Church of Rome. It would gather round it all the growing love of æsthetic decoration, of colour, and of music. Beyond

---

[1] Except the special hours of prayer, there is nothing of all this in Elizabeth's book.

that, it appealed to one whole side of human nature, its weakness, its dependence upon outward surroundings, its need of a curb upon irreverence and thoughtlessness. But to men of a strong and highsouled temperament it was nothing but Popery in disguise, bringing the spirit under outward and material bondage.

Puritanism had a noble and vigorous protest to urge against the attempt to confine religion within the bonds of ceremonial forms. It had too its own narrowness, its prostration before a logical system of theology. The first assault upon Cosin came from men who had no broad intelligence or spiritual insight, no quality to inspire respect, except that dogged persistency in support of that which they believed to be true, which is in itself a virtue. One of these men, Henry Burton, had been attached to the service of Henry Prince of Wales, and had afterwards been taken into his brother's household. Before Charles's accession he had taken orders. As soon as the new reign commenced he gave offence by an untimely recommendation to the King to dismiss Neile and Laud from Court.[1] After this, Whitehall was no place for him. As Rector of St. Matthew's in Friday Street he found a more sympathetic audience, and declaimed against Popery and Arminianism to his heart's content. He had criticised Montague's book with unsparing bitterness, and he now followed up his blow by an equally violent criticism of Cosin's Devotions.

William Prynne deserves fuller recognition. Born at Swainswick in the neighbourhood of Bath in 1600, he grew up under the influence of his father, a Puritan farmer, and of his maternal grandfather, a Puritan clothier, who had been Mayor of Bath, and had repre-

[1] *A Narrative of the Life of Henry Burton.*

sented his native city in Parliament. His was not the genial nature to seek out new paths for himself, or to learn from contact with the world a softer, gentler view of life than that which he had brought with him from home. He came to Oxford in 1616 to listen, at the most impressionable age, to tales of James's defection from the Protestant cause, and to be stirred to indignation by the diplomacy which aimed at placing a Catholic Queen upon the English throne. Then came the war in Bohemia, and after the war in Bohemia came the war in the Palatinate. Protestantism, it seemed, was betrayed abroad, and from his Calvinistic teachers, still, at that time, dominant in the University, he learned to look upon Neile and Laud as the traitors who were undermining it at home.

In 1621, after his father's death, Prynne established himself as a student of law at Lincoln's Inn. His untiring industry, and his stupendous memory soon enabled him to make himself master of the whole store of legal knowledge, and to combine with his legal knowledge an acquaintance with ecclesiastical writers which Selden could hardly equal. The preachers at Lincoln's Inn had always been selected as men of large and liberal culture, but they had always been prominent exponents of that Calvinistic theology, the formal completeness of which had special attractions for the legal mind. There it was that Reynolds and Field had preached. There, soon after Prynne's arrival, Donne gave place to Preston, the noted Master of Emanuel College, whose influence over Buckingham only paled before the rising star of Laud. When the Society opened its new chapel in 1623, the young Prynne found himself in the presence of many of the occupants of the judicial Bench, of Hobart and Ley, of Denham and Crewe, as well as of others whose names were in various ways to become noted in the stirring times to come. There was Noy who had not yet invented ship-money, and Sherfield who had not yet broken the painted window at Salisbury. There, too, were Lenthall the future Speaker of the Long Parliament, and St. John the future advocate of Hampden. With such companions around him Prynne kept on his steady course. He watched the dangers to English Protestantism from the entanglement in the Spanish alliance and the marriage treaty with France; watched, too, the growing strength of that party which appealed to the early Fathers rather than to the Protestant divines of the Continent and the Puritan divines of Elizabethan England; and he saw in Montague's attack upon predestination a blow struck at the root of Protestant theology.[1]

In 1627 Prynne's first book appeared, *The Perpetuity of a Regenerate Man's Estate*. Under the forms of theological argument, Prynne's contention is, in the main, a contention for the central idea of Protestantism, the immediate dependence of the individual soul upon God without the intervention of human or material agencies. But in Prynne's hands the theme was stripped of all the imaginative grandeur with which it has been so often clothed. His pages, with their margins crowded with references, afforded a palpable evidence how much he owed to his reading and his memory. He had no formative genius, no broad culture, no sense of humour. He had no perception of the relative importance of things distasteful to him. *Health's Sickness*, a violent diatribe on the supreme wickedness of drinking healths, was followed by *The Unloveliness of Lovelocks*, an equally violent diatribe on the supreme wickedness of the long lock of hair floating

---

[1] Up to this point I have made use of Mr. Bruce's fragment of Prynne's biography published by the Camden Society.

over the shoulder, which was the latest fashion amongst courtiers. The folly of the day was chastised with a torrent of learned objurgation which would not have been out of place in a harangue directed against the seven deadly sins. He had nothing worse to say when he sat down to prepare *A brief Survey and Censure of Mr. Cosin's cozening Devotions.*

<small>His resistance to Cosin.</small>

It is easy to turn scornfully upon the aridity of Prynne's mind, far easier than it is to read his books. Yet hard and unintelligent as his assault upon Cosin was, he was but giving voice in his own peculiar way to the repugnance felt by strong men to the feminine neatness of Cosin's devotional exercises. They threatened to 'take the imprisoned soul and lap it in Elysium,' to teach the ardent spirit to forego the stern wrestling for truth and to content itself with the passive acknowledgment of an order in the formation of which it was to take no part. Cosin would teach men to regard the State as dependent on the authority of the King, and the Church as dependent on the authority of the clergy.

<small>He demands the silencing of the Arminians.</small>

The problem presented by these disputes was a hard one for a statesman to solve. To Prynne it presented no difficulty at all. No man was to be allowed to speak or write against the Calvinistic doctrines. The conclusions of the Synod of Dort were to be offered as a test to every clergyman in England. Those who refused to subscribe were to be at once excluded from holding any ecclesiastical office.[1]

<small>Ceremonial differences.</small>

If it was difficult for a ruler to mediate between forms of thought so hostile, it was still more difficult to mediate when adverse thoughts clothed themselves in ceremonial. To the Calvinist the pulpit was clearly the first thing in the Church, the place

---

[1] See the Address to Parliament prefixed to the *Survey of Cosin's Devotions.*

where the Divine Word, through the intervention of the understanding, was dispensed to hungry souls. To those who recurred to older Church traditions the Communion-table, or—as they loved to call it—the Altar, was worthy of the highest reverence, the place where holy mysteries were dispensed which raised man into communion with God without the intervention of the understanding. The one party would have had the Table either standing permanently under the pulpit or brought out occasionally for its special purpose, to be placed 'table wise,' or East and West. The other party would have had it placed permanently 'altar wise,' or North and South, in the place of honour at the East end.

Elizabeth, as usual, had done her best to effect a compromise. In the Injunctions issued soon after her accession, she had followed the second Prayer-book in directing 'that the holy table in every church be decently made and set in the place where the altar stood, and there commonly covered as thereto belongeth, and as shall be appointed by the visitors; and so to stand, saving when the Communion of the Sacrament is to be distributed; at which time the same shall be so placed in good sort within the chancel as whereby the minister may be more conveniently heard of the communicants in his prayer and ministration, and the communicants also more conveniently and in more number communicate with the said minister; and after the Communion done, from time to time, the same holy table to be placed where it stood before.'

Elizabeth's compromise.

This compromise, which was substantially adopted in the Canons of 1604,[1] was decidedly in favour of the Puritan view, the balance being weighted on the other

Difficulty of enforcing conformity.

---

[1] The Injunctions only contemplate a removal within the chancel; the 82nd Canon goes further, and allows the Table to be placed *in ecclesiâ vel ejusdem cancello.*

side by a strict order that the Communion should be received in a kneeling posture. It was one thing to direct conformity, another to enforce it. It was above all difficult to obtain compliance with a rule which demanded that a heavy piece of furniture should be moved backwards and forwards from one part of the church to the other. Before the end of James's reign the Table was permanently established at the East end in the Royal Chapel and in all Cathedrals, whilst in most parish churches it was permanently established in the middle of the church or chancel. Any attempt to remove it to the East end was sure to be regarded as an unwarranted innovation by those who had grown accustomed to the existing practice.

Such an attempt was made at Grantham. The acting vicar,[1] a young man named Tytler, had engaged in various disputes with his parishioners. There had been quarrels about the rights and income of the vicarage, quarrels about a lectureship which the townspeople had set up in opposition to his teachings. In 1627 he had preached vigorously in defence of the forced loan, threatening, unless report spoke falsely, everlasting punishment to those who refused to pay it.[2] In the heat of this contention he resolved to restore the Communion-table, or the Altar as he termed it,[3] to that

---

[1] There were two vicars of Grantham.

[2] Valentine's Speech in the House of Commons, Feb. 7, 1629. *Nicholas's Notes.*

[3] Bishop Andrewes, preaching in 1612, puts it thus: "This is it in the Eucharist that answereth to the sacrifice in the Passover, the memorial to the figure. To them it was *hoc facite in Mei præfigurationem*; do this in prefiguration of Me; to us it is 'Do this in commemoration of Me' .... By the same rules that theirs was, by the same may ours be termed a sacrifice. In rigour of speech, neither of them; for to speak after the exact manner of divinity, there is but one only sacrifice, *veri nominis* 'properly so called;' that is Christ's death. While yet this offering was not, the hope of it was kept alive by the prefiguration of it in theirs. And after it is past, the memory of it is still kept fresh in the

which he held to be its appropriate site. Hitherto it had stood in the 'upper part of the choir,' probably in front of the ancient rood-screen which then divided the chancel from the body of the church.[1] Bringing workmen with him, he carried it inside the screen and placed it against the wall at the East end. Alderman Wheatley, the chief magistrate of the town, asked him by what authority he acted, "My authority," answered Tytler sharply, "is this,—I have done it, and I will justify it." Wheatley and his friends carried the table back to its old position. There was a scuffle in the church. Rough words were spoken and blows were struck. "I care not," said the angry Vicar, "what you do with your old trestle. I will build me an altar of stone at my own charge, and fix it in the old altar place. I will never officiate at any other." "You shall set up no dressers of stone within our church," was the equally angry reply. "We will find more hands to throw

mind by the commemoration of it in ours. So it was the will of God that so there might be with them a continual foreshowing, and with us a continual showing forth the Lord's death till He come again. Hence it is that what names theirs carried, ours do the like, and the Fathers make no scruple at it; no more need we. The Apostle in the tenth chapter compareth this of ours to the *immolata* of the heathen, and to the Hebrews *habemus aram* matcheth it with the sacrifice of the Jews. And we know the rule of comparisons, they must be *ejusdem generis*." The ecclesiastical teaching of Charles's reign was so deeply leavened by the teaching of Andrewes; and Laud, in particular, reverenced him so highly, that these words are worth particular consideration.

[1] Much information about Grantham is collected in a work by the Rev. B. Sweet, a sight of which I owe to the kindness of the author, as there is no copy in the Museum Library; and this special quarrel has recently been illustrated by the Rev. E. Venables in a paper published in the Transactions of the *Lincoln Diocesan Architectural Society*. I am unable to concur in his view that the Vicar did not mean the Table to stand permanently at the East end. Williams at least understood that he did. In his unsigned letter to the Vicar, he quotes him as saying of the Table, 'that the fixing thereof in the choir is so canonical that it ought not to be removed upon any occasion to the body of the church.' *The Holy Table, Name and Thing,* 13.

your stones out, than you will do to bring them in. We will all in a body make our journey to the Bishop before we will endure it."

Grantham was in the diocese of Lincoln, and the Bishop of Lincoln was Williams. Williams had no strong prejudices on either side. He was fond of pomp and ceremony, and in the chapel of his episcopal residence at Buckden, the Table stood against the Eastern wall. But he had no sympathy with the doctrinal teaching which was held to be involved in this position, and he had a strong conviction of the impolicy of estranging a whole population by imposing upon it ceremonial forms which they regarded with detestation. He decided, as every unprejudiced person would decide now, that the meaning of the Injunctions and Canons was that the Table should ordinarily stand at the East end, and should be moved down when required for use. More questionable was his ruling, that the Table when placed at the East end should stand East and West as a table, and not along the wall as an altar.

"Lastly," wrote Williams to the Vicar, "whether side soever, you or your parish, shall first yield unto the other in these needless controversies shall remain, in my poor judgment, the more discreet, grave, and learned man of the two; and by that time you have gained some more experience in the cure of souls, you shall find no such ceremony equal to Christian charity."[1]

Williams has many faults to answer for. He was hot tempered and worldly minded, and when driven to bay he had resort to the most discreditable means in order to overpower his pursuers. But he had the

---

[1] Printed in *The Holy Table, Name and Thing*. Williams appeals to general practice, "If you mean by altar wise," he writes, "that the Table should stand along close to the wall, I do not believe that ever the Communion-tables were, otherwise than by casualty, so placed in country churches."

strong conviction that men were greater than either intellectual or ceremonial forms. On the one hand, he repelled Prynne's assumption that the human mind could only be purified by submission to the strictest Calvinistic dogmatism. On the other hand, he repelled Laud's assumption that the human mind could only be purified by submission to a certain external order. It is impossible not to think the better of Charles for refusing to look up to a man so shifty as Williams. But it is impossible not to regret that Charles was not great enough to utilise the counsel of one who, if he could have kept himself aloof from trickery and intrigue, might have been the Burke of the ecclesiastical politics of the seventeenth century.

It soon became evident how much need Charles had of a councillor who could have taught him that a ruler can no more afford to despise the currents of opinion than a navigator can afford to despise the set of the tides. It was only natural that Charles should do his best to shield from future attack the Churchmen who had been assailed in the last session, and he accordingly ordered the preparation of a pardon for Montague, which, as he hoped, would place out of the question the continuance of his impeachment. A letter addressed to the new Bishop by Heath, the Attorney General, shows the disquietude felt, by men most devoted to the prerogative, at the danger lest the King should involve himself in the quarrels of ecclesiastical controversialists. "I know," he wrote, "you are wise, and I presume you are charitable, and will make no misconstruction of my honest intentions. Haply this pardon may set your lordship free *in foro civili*; and yet I must put your lordship in mind that the Court of Parliament may peradventure call things past into question, notwithstanding your pardon; nay, perhaps, by your pardon they will rather be stirred to question you: not but that the King by his supreme power may pardon whatsoever may be questioned by any Court; yet that is not all, a scar to one is worse than a wound to another. You are now a father of our Church; and, as a father, you will, I know, tender the peace and quiet of the Church. Alas, a little spot is seen on that white garment, and a little fire, nay a spark, may influence a great mass; and how glad would the common adversary be to see us at odds amongst ourselves. We are not bound to flatter any in their humours; but we are bound in conscience to prevent, nay to avoid, all occasions of strife and contentions in those things specially which are so tender as the peace of the Church and the unity of religion. My lord, I take not upon me to advise your lordship,—but I pray, give me leave to put your lordship in mind of thus much,—that if your lordship will be pleased to review your book, to consult first with Almighty God the God of peace, the bond of peace, the spirit of peace; next, with our most gracious and good King, and by his approbation take away the acrimony of the style, and explain those things which are therein left doubtful and undefined, that the orthodoxal tenets of the Church of England might be justified and cleared by your own pen,—I am persuaded all scandal would be taken away, and your lordship may be a happy instrument of reconciling and giving a stop to these unhappy differences and jealousy which else may trouble the quiet of our Church, and may occasion the disquiet of our commonwealth."[1]

Heath's recommendation met with ready acceptance from those in whose hands the decision lay. Neither Charles nor Laud, by whose advice in ecclesiastical matters Charles was more than ever guided, had any taste for dogmatic controversy. Laud believed

[1] Heath to Montague, Oct. 7. *S. P. Dom.* cxviii. 33

that it only served to distract the clergy from their real work, and he looked with the contempt of a practical man upon the endless discussions upon problems which it was impossible for the human intellect to solve. It was only, he thought, to lose themselves in wandering mazes, that reasonable beings, with the world's sin and shame before them, could rack their brains to divine the secret

> Of Providence, Foreknowledge, Will, and Fate,
> Fixed fate, free will, foreknowledge absolute.

Nor had he less contempt for public opinion than he had for abstract thought. There was something in his eyes inexpressibly mean in the notion that a teacher was to be bound to deliver the sentiments and inculcate the doctrines of which his disciples happened to approve. In the combat which he waged against this double danger lay the strength of his position. Prynne's demand for the imposition of the test of agreement with certain abstruse doctrines contained in it a tyranny which deserved to be resisted as sternly as the demand that what was believed by the mass of ordinary Englishmen must be stereotyped for ever on the minds of the rising generation. Unhappily Laud did not catch a glimpse—no man at that time could be expected to do more—of the truth that in full liberty of utterance lies the true corrective of the tyranny of public opinion.

Laud had no hesitation in recommending that the substance of the Royal Proclamation for the peace of the Church which had been drawn up in 1626 should be issued in a form calculated to reach the ears of every one. Orders were accordingly given for the preparation of a new edition of the Articles of Religion, to be prefaced by a Declaration which every minister entering upon a new cure would be bound to read.[1]

[1] Heylyn's *Life of Laud*, 187.

CHAP. I.
1628.
Nov.
The King's Declaration.

"Being by God's ordinance," thus ran Charles's last word in the controversy, "according to our just title, Defender of the Faith, and supreme governor of the Church, within these our dominions, we hold it most agreeably to this our kingly office, and our own religious zeal, to conserve and maintain the Church committed to our charge in unity of true religion and in the bond of peace; and not to suffer unnecessary disputations, altercations, or questions to be raised which may nourish faction both in the Church and Commonwealth.

"We have therefore, upon mature deliberation, and upon the advice of so many of our Bishops as might conveniently be called together, thought fit to make this Declaration following:—That the Articles of the Church of England, which have been allowed and authorised heretofore, and which our Clergy generally have subscribed unto, do contain the true doctrine of the Church of England agreeable to God's Word: which we do therefore ratify and confirm; requiring all our loving subjects to continue in the uniform profession thereof, and prohibiting the least difference from the said Articles; which to that end we command to be new printed, and this our Declaration to be published therewith:

"That we are supreme governor of the Church of England; and that if any difference arise about the external policy concerning Injunctions, Canons, and other Constitutions whatsover thereto belonging, the Clergy in their Convocation is to order and settle them, having first obtained leave under our broad seal so to do, and we approving their said ordinances and constitutions, providing that none be made contrary to the laws and customs of the land:

"That out of our princely care that the Churchmen may do the work which is proper unto them, the Bishops and Clergy, from time to time in Convocation, upon their humble desire, shall have license under our broad seal to deliberate of, and to do all such things, as being made plain by them, and assented to by us, shall concern the settled continuance of the doctrine and discipline of the Church of England now established; from which we will not endure any varying or departing in the least degree:

"That for the present, though some differences have been ill raised, yet we take comfort in this, that all clergymen within our realm have always most willingly subscribed to the Articles established; which is an argument to us that they all agree in the true, usual, literal meaning of the said Articles; and that even in those curious points in which the present differences lie, men of all sorts take the Articles of the Church of England to be for them; which is an argument again that none of them intend any desertion of the Articles established:

"That therefore in these both curious and unhappy differences, which have for so many hundred years, in different times and places, exercised the Church of Christ, we will that all further curious search be laid aside, and these disputes shut up in God's promises as they be generally set forth to us in the holy Scriptures, and the general meaning of the Articles of the Church of England according to them; and that no man hereafter shall either print or preach to draw the Article aside any way, but shall submit to it in the plain and full meaning thereof, and shall not put his own sense or comment to be the meaning of the Article, but shall take it in the literal and grammatical sense:

"That if any public reader in either of our Universities, or any head or master of a college, or any other person respectively in either of them, shall affix any new sense to any Article, or shall publicly read, determine, or hold any public disputation, or suffer any such to be held either way, in either the Universities or colleges respectively, or if any divine in the Universities shall preach or print anything either way, other than is already established in Convocation with our Royal assent; he or they the offenders shall be liable to our displeasure, and the Church's censure in our Commission ecclesiastical, as well as any other; and we will see there shall be due execution upon them."[1]

The Declaration approved by the Council.

The draft of the document thus prepared was approved by the Privy Council in the end of November or the beginning of the following month.[2] The next step was to obtain the assent of both parties amongst the Bishops. Montague was induced to write a letter to Abbot in which he disclaimed any wish to uphold Arminianism.[3] Abbot accepted the hand thus held out to him, and was restored by Charles to such favour as Charles had to bestow upon one with whom he had so little sympathy. On December 11 the Archbishop appeared once more at Whitehall, kissed the King's hands, and was graciously bidden to attend the meetings of the Council.

Dec. 11. Abbot restored to favour.

Dec. 12. Meeting of Bishops at Lambeth.

The next day such Bishops as could be brought together on so short an invitation met in Council at Lambeth.[4] As soon as they had declared their acceptance of the proposed Declaration, it was sent to the press.

1629. Jan. 17. Appello Cæsarem called in.

The first step taken to emphasise the Declaration was the issue of a Proclamation calling in Montague's *Appello Cæsarem*, in order that men might ' no more

[1] The Declaration is prefixed to the edition of the Articles of 1628, and is to be found in the present Book of Common Prayer. How many people who see it there are aware of its historical importance?

[2] It is mentioned in Contarini's Despatch of Dec. $\frac{2}{12}$. *Ven. MSS.*

[3] I do not believe that he went beyond this, which he might honestly do, on the same grounds as Laud. Pory in his letters makes him really to subscribe to the Synod of Dort, which is incredible.

[4] Pory to Meade, Dec. 12, 19, *Court and Times*, i. 448, 451.

trouble themselves with these unnecessary questions, the first occasion being taken away.' If writers continued to carry on the dispute, such order should be taken with them, that they 'should wish that they had never thought upon these needless controversies.'[1] The Proclamation had been preceded by the grant of special pardons to Montague, Sibthorpe, Manwaring and Cosin, in order that the Commons might be warned not to rake up the embers of the old quarrel.

CHAP. I.
1629. Jan. 17.
Pardons issued.

Oblivion for the past and silence for the future were the terms offered by Charles. It remained to be seen how acceptable they would be to the Commons, whose competency to deal with religious questions at all was implicitly denied by the reference in the Declaration to the King and the Convocation as the sole constitutional authority in such matters.

Charles's terms.

It was hardly likely that the Commons would be content with this. But there was one man who had played a leading part in the preceding session who asked nothing better. Immediately after the close of that session, Wentworth had been raised to the peerage, and had been promised the Presidency of the North. On December 10, he became Viscount Wentworth, and five days later he received the patent of his Presidency.

1628. Dec. Wentworth President of the North.

On the 30th he entered upon the duties of his office at York. In the speech[2] which he there delivered amongst his old friends and neighbours, he showed no signs of regret for the part which he had played in the preceding session. He thanked them for the kindness with which they had received him after his exile for resisting the forced loan. What confidence or affection could be greater? Yet he had not thanks for them alone. "Cast," he said, "the free bounties of my gracious

Dec. 30. His speech at York.

He does not repudiate the past.

---

[1] Proclamation, Jan. 17. *Rymer*, xix. 26.
[2] Printed from *Tanner MSS.* lxxii. 300; in the *Academy*, June 5, 1875.

master into the other scale: there weigh me, within the space of one year, a bird, a wandering bird cast out of the nest, a prisoner, planted here again in my own soil, amongst the companions of my youth; my house honoured, myself entrusted with the rich dispensation of a sovereign goodness, nay assured of all these before I asked, before I thought of any."

If Wentworth did not repudiate the Petition of Right, he repudiated the challenge of sovereignty put forward on behalf of the Commons at the close of the session. "To the joint individual wellbeing of sovereignty and subjection," he said, "do I here vow all my cares and diligences through the whole course of my ministry. I confess I am not ignorant how some distempered minds have of late very far endeavoured to divide the considerations of the two; as if their ends were distinct, not the same, nay, in opposition; a monstrous, a prodigious birth of a licentious conception, for so we would become all head or all members. But God be praised, human wisdom, common experience, Christian religion, teach us far otherwise."

Wentworth's conception of the Constitution was in the main the same as Bacon's. "Princes," he continued, "are to be indulgent, nursing fathers to their people; their modest liberties, their sober rights ought to be precious in their eyes, the branches of their government be for shadow for habitation, the comfort of life. They[1] repose safe and still under the protection of their sceptres. Subjects, on the other side, ought with solicitous eyes of jealousy to watch over the prerogatives of a Crown. The authority of a King is the keystone which closeth up the arch of order and government, which contains each part in due relation to the whole,

---

[1] "They" is added by conjecture and inserted here and elsewhere when it is needed.

and which once shaken, and infirmed, all the frame falls together into a confused heap of foundation and battlement, of strength and beauty.[1] Furthermore, subjects must lay down their lives for the defence of kings freely till those offer out of their store freely, like our best grounds, *qui majore ubertate gratiam quietis referre solent.*

"Verily there are those mutual intelligence of love and protection descending and loyalty ascending which should pass and be the entertainments between a King and his people. Their faithful servants must look equally on both, weave, twist these two together in all their counsels; study, labour, to preserve each without diminishing or enlarging either; and by running in the worn wonted channels, treading the ancient bounds, cut off early all disputes from betwixt them. For whatever he be which ravels forth into questions the right of a King and of a people shall never be able to wrap them up again into the comeliness and order he found them."

The obligation mutual.

Had he not himself ravelled forth these rights into questions? In his heart doubtless he believed that it was not so. He had always in his fiercest denunciation of the King's ministers preserved his respect for the King, and had spoken of the King's prerogative in terms far more reverential than any other member of the House of Commons not in the actual service of the

Had Wentworth changed?

---

[1] Shakspere's Coriolanus says much the same thing (act iii. scene 1):

"My soul aches
To know, when two authorities are up,
Neither supreme, how soon confusion
May enter 'twixt the gap of both and take
The one by the other . . . . . .
That is the way to lay the city flat;
To bring the roof to the foundation,
And bury all, which yet distinctly ranges,
In heaps and piles of ruin."

Crown. The utmost which he had claimed for the assembly of which he was a member had been the right of lifting up its voice against oppression and wrong; and, if its voice were disregarded, of refusing to grant those supplies for carrying on a useless and extravagant war which it was in its power to grant or to refuse. And yet they were not in the wrong who held that he had ranged himself on the side of the nation against the Crown. Facts had been too strong for even Wentworth's theories; and when, in his lofty impassioned eloquence he denounced attacks upon property and law, it was impossible that the blow which was aimed at Buckingham should not light upon Charles, who had in reality been the author of the mischief as much as Buckingham. Yet there is no rashness in affirming that Wentworth was himself unconscious of any change in himself. It was the House of Commons which had changed. In March he had argued that the danger of anarchy and disorder came from the Government. In June he might have argued that it came from the Commons. The invitation addressed to him to take part in the work of government would do the rest. The condescension of the King, the affable unbending of a Sovereign usually so reserved, would strengthen him in the conviction that all danger from the Crown was past. As a defender of order against disorder he had raised his voice in Parliament; as a defender of order against disorder he would exercise at York the authority entrusted to him by his Sovereign.

His view of the ecclesiastical question.

As he continued his speech he let fall not a few words which showed how little sympathy he had with Eliot in those ecclesiastical questions which had risen to such sudden prominence during the last days of the session. " I not only," said he, " profess my entire filial obedience to the Church, but also covet a sound, a close conjunction with the grave, the reverend clergy, that they to us, we to them, may as twins administer help to each other; that ecclesiastical and civil institutions, the two sides of every State, may not stand alone by themselves upon their own single walls, subject to cleave and fall in sunder; but joined strongly together in the angle, where his Majesty under God, is the Mistress of the corner, the whole frame may rise up *unitate ordinatâ* both in the spirituals and the temporals."

CHAP. I.
1628.
Dec. 30.

Wentworth, it is plain, had accepted without hesitation, the King's Declaration. He was ready too to accept his general supervision in confidence that it would be used for the benefit of the State. It was for him, not for the Judges at Westminster, who might be actuated by professional jealousy, to settle the limits of the jurisdiction of the Council of the North. Wentworth's idea of government, indeed, was not one in which the people had no part. They were not to control the King, they were to counsel and co-operate. The objection which had been raised that there was no statute compelling attendance upon musters stirred him to indignation. There was such a statute, he replied in the first place, declaring service in the militia to be obligatory. What, however, if no such statute had been in existence! "Admit," he said, "the law were defective, yet then it will be confessed a necessary service for the State, for the defence of yourselves, wives, and children, so as we might manifest more discretion to wink at it than thus narrowly to pry into it."

Accepts the general supervision of the Crown.

The people to co-operate.

A King thoroughly well meaning and prudent, counsellors intelligent and patriotic, a people even outstripping the government in its zeal to carry out the royal commands, such was Wentworth's vision of the

Commonwealth which he hoped to see flourishing upon English soil. Arthur, it would seem had come again in Charles, now that Buckingham was gone. England had but to sing the song of Arthur's knights:—

> 'Blow trumpet, for the world is white with May;
> Blow trumpet, the long night hath roll'd away,
> Blow through the living world, "Let the King reign."'
>
> . . . .
>
> 'The King will follow Christ, and we the King,
> In whom high God hath breathed a secret thing.
> Fall battleaxe, and flash brand! Let the King reign.'

The powers of evil, as Wentworth would have reckoned them, were, however, still stirring. Before the opening of the session arrived, fresh tumults at the Custom-house came to trouble the hopefulness of the Government. In defiance of the order of the Court of Exchequer, another attempt was made to carry off goods by force under cover of a replevin. The attack was repulsed, and the leaders committed to prison to await proceedings in the Star Chamber.[1] A few days later the King consulted his principal Councillors on the best mode of dealing with so agitating a question. It was resolved that if the Houses would 'pass the Bill as his ancestors had it, his Majesty' would 'do any reasonable thing to declare that he claims not Tonnage and Poundage otherwise than by grant of Parliament, but if this do not satisfy, then to avoid a breach upon just cause given, not sought by the King.'[2]

Those who watched the position of affairs with an impartial eye were of opinion that Charles was really anxious to avert all chance of a quarrel with the House of Commons.[3] The dark side of the picture may be

---

[1] *Council Register*, Jan. 5, 7. *Rushworth*, i. App. 7.
[2] *Rushworth*, i. 642.
[3] "Fra dieci giorni si radunerà il Parlamento con opinione di buon successo, già S. M. invigila con ogni sollecitudine di ben preparar tutte

shown in words which had not long before been addressed to Carlisle by a correspondent in England. "At home," he wrote, "the little thing that is done is done by my Lord Treasurer. They are about to satisfy some things both in religion and government to sweeten things to the Parliament, but most men doubt that they are not sincerely intended, and so will give little satisfaction. The Parliamentary men have an eye on your Lordship, and are afraid that you will join with my Lord Treasurer, who, though as I think an honest man and good patriot, has much ado to overcome and dissipate those clouds of suspicion concerning religion that are hung over him all this while."[1]

It was a fair account of the situation. It was not enough for Charles to be well intentioned. He could not in a moment do away with the impression produced upon his subjects by the errors of the past four years, or by his own moral and mental isolation amongst the people whom he ruled. No electric cord of sympathy stretched from his heart to the heart of the nation. From their aims, their hopes, their prejudices he stood apart. His Court was no place where the independent gentlemen of England could find a chance of reaching his ear. His progresses were made to some hunting seat of his own, not to the houses of his subjects, where Elizabeth had been wont to win all hearts by her queenly condescension. Above all, he did not understand the meaning of 'those clouds of suspicion concerning religion,' which were so exaggerated, but so natural, and which needed to be treated with judicious but sympathetic firmness if they were not to burst up in the fiercest intolerance, or to give rise to the most deep-seated discord.

le cose e di proceder più consultatamente di quello si fece per l' adietro." *Contarini's Despatch*, Jan. 12/20. *Ven. MSS.*

[1] Aston to Carlisle, Dec. 19. *S. P. Dom.* clii. 58.

CHAPTER II.

THE SESSION OF 1629.

CHAP. II.
___
1629.
Jan. 20.
Opening of the Session.
Jan. 22.

So confident was Charles of the issue that, when the Houses met on January 20,[1] he did not even think it necessary to explain what he has done. The Commons, as soon as they proceeded to business on the 22nd, showed that they looked upon the events of the past months from a point of view of their own. Complaints were at once heard that the speech in which the King at the close of the last session had claimed Tonnage and Poundage as his due, had been enrolled with the Petition of Right, and that a printed copy of the great statute had been circulated in the country 'with an answer which never gave any satisfaction,' that is to say, with the answer which had been rejected as insufficient, in addition to the final answer and the speech by which it was finally expounded by the King.[2]

[1] The ordinary account of the debates of this session appears in its best form in a volume in the possession of Lord Verulam, which was described by Mr. Bruce in the 38th volume of the *Archæologia*. Mr. Bruce's copy has, through Lord Verulam's kindness, been placed in my hands. The Parliamentary history has additional matter from other sources, and Nicholas's Notes (*S. P. Dom.* cxxxv.) give a report entirely independent commencing with Jan. 26. Mr. Forster (*Sir J. Eliot*, ii. 197) gives from the MSS. at Port Eliot a speech said to have been spoken by Eliot on Jan. 20. I am afraid this must be relegated to the domain of speeches never uttered. Lord Verulam's MS. distinctly says of that day that on it 'nothing was done but only the settling of the Committees,' and Nethersole, in the letters in which he details the main occurrences of the session, has no mention of any such speech.

[2] The copy of the Statutes of the last session in the Museum Library

Selden then stepped forward with a weightier charge. The Petition of Right, he said, had been actually broken. For liberties of state, he said, "we know of an order made in the Exchequer that a sheriff was commanded not to execute a replevin, and men's goods are taken away and must not be restored." Further, "one had lately lost his ears by a decree of the Star Chamber, by an arbitrary judgment. Next," he said, "they will take away our arms, and then our legs, and so our lives; let all see we are sensible of this. Customs creep on us, let us make a just representation hereof unto his Majesty."

1629. Jan. 22. Has the Petition of Right been violated?

The case of Savage, of which Selden spoke so bitterly, had been one of extreme harshness. Either from a foolish love of notoriety or from actual insanity he had announced that Felton had asked him to join in killing Buckingham.[1] He was sentenced in the Star Chamber to lose his ears.[2] It was well that Selden should raise his voice against the scandal. It was well that a limit should be placed to the swelling jurisdiction of the Star Chamber.[3] But it was absurd to argue

Savage's case.

shews that this was what was really done, and it is so put in Nethersole's letters to Elizabeth. *S. P. Dom.* cxxxiii. 4.

[1] Meade to Stuteville, Sept. 27, Nov. 8. *Court and Times,* i. 402, 422.

[2] Hudson, in his treatise in the Star Chamber, written before any controversy arose, holds that the Court had the power of cutting off ears in certain cases.

[3] According to Nethersole, Chambers's case was expressly mentioned, "They began to complain that the Petition of Right granted the last session had been already invaded in all the parts thereof: that of the liberty of men's persons, by the imprisonment of a merchant without showing a lawful cause, the difficulty in showing a *corpus habeas*: that against the use of martial law, by the taking a man's ears off by a sentence in the Star Chamber, being an arbitrary Court, and having no power of life or limb: that of the property of men's goods, by the seizure of the wares of divers merchants, for refusing to pay the customs and impositions, there being no law to demand this, and the refusing of the grant of a writ of replevin when it was demanded." Nethersole to Elizabeth, Jan. 24. *S. P. Dom.* cxxxiv. 4. Not one of these charges

that the jurisdiction of that Court was in any way affected by the Petition of Right.

Unluckily the question of Tonnage and Poundage, embarrassing enough in itself, was complicated by the fact that Henry Rolle, one of the merchants whose goods had been seized, was a member of the House, "Cast your eyes," said the impetuous Phelips, "which way you please, and you shall see violations on all sides. Look on the privileges of this House! Let any say if ever he recall or saw the like violations by inferior ministers that ever do their commands. They knew the party was a Parliament man. Nay, they said, 'if all the Parliament were in you, this we would do and justify.'" Phelips concluded by moving for a Committee on the whole question of the levy of Tonnage and Poundage.[2]

It was hardly possible to dwarf a great question more completely than to convert the mighty struggle against unparliamentary taxation into a mere dispute about privilege. Yet this was what the House seemed disposed to do. "Let the parties," said Littleton, "be sent for that violated the liberties." The Commons did not notice that in so doing they were leaving a strong position for a weak one. In resisting the King's claim to levy duties without consent of Parlia-

---

necessarily involved a direct breach of the Petition, the question of property being the very one which the Judges had to decide. The line taken here involved the assertion that the interpretation of the Petition belonged to the House of Commons, not to the Judges.

The case of billeting at Chichester, *Rushworth*, ii. 32, is sometimes alleged as a breach of the Petition. But the Petition forbade billeting against the householder's will. The authorities of Chichester barred the gates of the city against the soldiers so as to prevent the householders from exercising an option.

[2] Mr. Forster (*Sir J. Eliot*, ii. 205) says that Phelips alleged that 5,000*l.* worth of goods had been sold for dues not exceeding 200*l.* He gives no authority for the selling, and it is altogether improbable.

ment, they were guarding the purse of the subject from encroachments to which no limit could be placed. In resisting his claim to seize the goods of a member of Parliament, they gave a direct advantage to a merchant who happened to be a member of the House over one who was less fortunate. In point of fact, the claim of privilege for goods in the case of legal proceedings was one which has long ago been abandoned by a triumphant Parliament.

The privilege of Parliament had, of late years, been on the increase. Up to the accession of James, only three cases could be shown in which a member had made good his claim to freedom for his goods, and in two of these the claim had been expressly limited to such goods as it was necessary for him to have with him during his attendance at Westminster or on his return home.[1] In James's reign the interference of the House to protect members' goods in general had become frequent, and was justified on the principle that those who were engaged on the public service ought not to be distracted from their duties by the care of defending their own property. But nothing was settled as to the exact time before and after each session during which the privilege was to last.[2] It was only indeed by a technicality that Rolle's case could be brought within the largest limits which had ever been suggested. The seizure of his goods had been effected on October 30, more than four months after the close of one session, and more than two months before the commencement of another. But it so happened that Parliament had been originally prorogued to October 20, and Rolle was therefore supposed, by a legal fiction, to have been hindered in the fulfilment of duties which, as

[1] *Hatsell*, i. 67.   [2] *Ibid.* i. 99.

he was perfectly aware at the time, were not to be imposed upon him for many weeks to come.

At last Charles discovered that it was unwise to allow the debates to proceed without a word from himself. Summoning the Houses to Whitehall, he assured them that he had had no intention to levy the duties by his 'hereditary prerogative.' "It ever was," he declared distinctly, "and still is my meaning, by the gift of my people to enjoy it; and my intention in my speech at the end of the last session was not to challenge Tonnage and Poundage of right, but for expedience *de bene esse*, shewing you the necessity, not the right, by which I was to take it until you had granted it unto me; assuring myself, according to your general profession, that you wanted time and not good will to give it me." He had been startled, he added, by some things which had been said amongst them. But he would not complain. "The House's resolution," he ended by saying, "not particular men's speeches, shall make me judge well or ill, not doubting but, according to mine example, you will be deaf to all reports concerning me, until my words and actions speak for themselves, that this session beginning with confidence one towards the other, it may end with a perfect good understanding between us; which God grant."[1]

It would be easy to find fault with the account given by Charles of the language which he had employed at the close of the last session. But it was not of the slightest importance whether he had contradicted himself or not. It was enough that he had renounced plainly all claim to levy Tonnage and Poundage as his right. Accordingly, the first impression made by

---

[1] Contarini, who tells this, adds, however, significantly, "Parmi nondimeno che primo d'avantarsi in questa materia vogliono aggiustar i punti della religione." Contarini's Despatch, Jan. 30/Feb. 9. *Ven. MSS.*

the speech was extremely favourable. It was not then the decent custom to listen to announcements from the throne in respectful silence, and the King was many times interrupted by sounds of applause. As the Commons left his presence, one of them observed that it was easy to see that Buckingham was no longer alive. "This speech," wrote Nethersole, "hath given great satisfaction for the present." But Nethersole was too old a member to be ignorant where the real danger lay. "In matter of religion," he proceeded to say, "they are quiet as yet. For it is early days. But the greatest business is like to be about that, notwithstanding that his Majesty hath called in Montague's book by a special proclamation... His Majesty hath also granted his pardon to Montague, Cosin, Manwaring, and Sibthorpe. But that will hardly save some of them. God keep us in good temper."[1]

On the 26th Sir John Coke offered to bring in a Bill of Tonnage and Poundage. But he was told that it was not the custom of the House to vote on a Bill of supply, except upon resolutions debated in Committee. Besides, the question of Impositions must be cleared up before anything could be done.[2]

The question of Impositions had not been taken into account by Charles. Still, it was one on which compromise was possible, and it is unlikely that, if the House had proposed to include existing impositions in the new Tonnage and Poundage Bill, in return for an abandonment of the King's claim to levy further impositions by prerogative, Charles would have offered any decided resistance to an amicable settlement of the long dispute. But the hearts of the members were elsewhere than in the question of impositions. Scarcely

[1] Nethersole to Elizabeth, Jan. 24. *S. P. Dom.*, cxxxiii. 4.
[2] This debate is only to be found in *Nicholas's Notes*.

1629.
Jan. 26.
Rouse's speech on religion.

was the mode of procedure on the Tonnage and Poundage Bill settled, when Francis Rouse rose. He lived to be the author of that metrical version of the Psalms which was one day to be the cherished treasure in joy or in affliction of every Scottish household. He lived, too, to be the speaker of that strangest of all English political assemblies which strove in vain to hurry conservative England into the path of social revolution. He now called upon no inattentive hearers to stand firm against the encroachments of Popery, that confused mass of errors which cast down 'Kings before Popes, the precepts of God before the traditions of men, living and reasonable men before dead and senseless stocks and stones,' and against the encroachments of Arminianism, ' an error that makes the grace of God lackey it after the will of man, that makes the sheep to keep the shepherd, and makes a mortal seed of an immortal God.'

Kirton's explanation.

Kirton rose to explain the source of the mischief. The new doctrines, he argued, had been introduced in order to pave the way for the betrayal of Protestantism to Rome. The personal ambition of the clergy was the cause of it all. "The highest dignity," he said, " they can attain to here in England is an Archbishopric, but a Cardinal's cap is not here to be had. Our endeavour must be to take away the root, and then the branches will decay of themselves. It is not the calling in of the Appeal to Cæsar that will do it; for if they can get Bishoprics for writing of such books, we shall have many more that will write books in the same kind."

Committee on Religion.

So flowed on confusedly and without restraint the pent-up waters of indignation. In the end the whole subject of religion was referred to a Committee; and in spite of a message from the King urging the House to proceed at once with the Tonnage and Poundage Bill, it was resolved that the report of the Committee should first be heard.

The reporter, or as we should now say, the chairman of the Committee, was Pym, as he had been the reporter of every Committee on religion in the reign. He combined a firm persuasion of the truth and importance of the Calvinistic creed with a knowledge of the world, and with a tact in the management of men, which was hereafter to raise him to the supreme leadership of the Long Parliament.[1] He clearly saw the intimate connexion between all the various questions by which the reign had been agitated. He held that the path of safety lay in the combined supremacy of King and Parliament. The time had not yet come when men could venture, even in thought, to separate between the two. All other institutions, ecclesiastical, judicial, military, must work in accordance with rules laid down by King and Parliament together. They must not claim to be independent of the nation itself, revolving in orbs of their own, and careless of the national conscience and the national will.

Such a view of government was alien to the mind of Charles. He was himself, he held, the sun of the constitutional system. Parliament was but one of the many planets revolving round his throne. Against this view of the case Pym's report was a decided protest. Parliaments, he ominously said, 'have enacted laws for the trial of heretics.' The two Convocations were but Provincial Synods. 'The High Commission derived its authority from Parliament, and the deriva-

---

[1] Pym is frequently spoken of as a statesman for whom religious questions had only a secondary interest. I believe this view of his character to be incompatible with his course in these early Parliaments. See especially his speech in the Parliament of 1621.

tive could not prejudice the original.' What Pym had said on the religious question was said by Eliot on the temporal question. "I find," he declared upon the reading of a petition from Chambers, "the Judges, the Council, Sheriffs, Customers, the Attorney and all conspire to trample on the liberty of the subjects." Chambers, however, ought to take a legal course that it might be known who were the ministers who had declined to do their duty. Eliot, in short, refused to acknowledge that even the Judges could be the final arbitrators of the constitution. King and Parliament together were the highest authority; and there can be no doubt that in his own mind he believed that the authority of King and Parliament ought to be exercised in accordance with the decision of the House of Commons.

In spite of renewed protests from Secretary Coke, the House went into Committee on Pym's report. The tone of the whole debate was given by a great speech from Eliot.[1] He began by warning the House of the danger of turning its debates into a theological conference. "I presume, Sir," he said, "it is not the intention we now have to dispute the religion we profess. After so long a radiance and sunshine of the Gospel, it is not for us to draw it into question. The Gospel is that truth which from all antiquity is derived, that pure truth which admits no mixture or corruption, that truth in which this kingdom has been happy through a long and rare prosperity. This ground, therefore, let us lay for the foundation of our building,

---

[1] Mr. Forster (*Sir J. Eliot*, ii. 210) gives the speech from Eliot's own MS. and follows the Parliamentary History in assigning it to an earlier day. Lord Verulam's MS. gives it to the 26th, and explains the allusion to Eliot's countryman, as referring to Rouse, not to Coryton, as Mr. Forster supposed. Nicholas, however, gives the 29th, and his shorthand notes must be accepted as conclusive on a question of this kind.

that that truth, not with words but with actions, we will maintain. Sir, the sense in which our Church still receives that truth is contained in the Articles. There shall we find that which the acts of Parliament have established against all the practice of our adversaries. Not that it is the truth because confirmed by Parliament, but confirmed by Parliament because it is the truth."

Then, aiming not, like Kirton, at imaginary ambitions, he pointed fearlessly to the root of the mischief: "Among the many causes of the envy we have contracted," he said, "there is none comes with a fuller face of danger to my thoughts than the late Declaration that was published in the name and title of his Majesty." It could not, he continued, have really proceeded from the King, or it must have been won from him by misinformation. "I will so believe it," he cried, "of this Declaration—by which more danger is portended than in all that has been before. For by the rest, in all other particulars of our fears concerning Popery or Arminianism, we are endangered by degrees; the evils approaching by gradation, one seeming as a preparation to another; but in this, like an inundation, they break on us with such impetuous violence that, leaving art and circumstance, they threaten at once to overwhelm us by plain force. For, I beseech you, mark it. The Articles contain the grounds of our religion; but the letter of those Articles, as the Declaration doth confess, implies a doubtful sense, of which the application makes the difference between us and our adversaries; and now the interpretation is referred to the judgment of the prelates who have, by this Declaration, the concession of a power to do anything for the maintenance or overthrow of the truth. The truth, as I said, being contained in the Articles, and they having a double sense, upon which the differences arise, it is in the prelates now to order it which way they please, and so, for aught I know, to bring in Popery or Arminianism, to, which we are told, we must submit. Is it a light thing to have canons of religion rest in the discretion of these men? Should the rules and principles of our faith be squared by their affections?" Some of the Bishops, it was true, might 'be fathers to all ages.' "But," continued the orator, "they are not all such, I fear. Witness those two, complained of in the last Remonstrance we exhibited, Doctors Laud and Neile; and you know what place they have! Witness, likewise Montague, so newly now preferred. I reverence the order, though I honour not the man. Others may be named, too, of the same bark and leaven, to whose judgments if our religion were committed, it might easily be discerned what resolutions they would give; whereof even the procuring of this reference, this manifesto, to be made, is a perfect demonstration."

Meaning of the difference between Eliot and his opponents.

Eliot had singled out the true rock of offence. Between the controversialists, whom Charles had hoped to silence, there was a difference not to be measured by words or terms. It was a difference reaching deep down into the moral and spiritual basis upon which all conceptions of theology rest, a difference of habit of mind and religious instinct. To Eliot and to such as Eliot, the helps and assistances to faith upon which Cosin dwelt so lovingly only served to distract the mind from the contemplation of the great Taskmaster in whose eye they lived, even if they did not threaten to occupy His place. To them even the hard Calvinistic dogmatism, so repulsive in the pages of Prynne, was full of a precious and tender reality. Through it they entered into the sweet contemplation of a ruling Personality, who had raised them from the dust, and who guarded them from the sin which so easily beset them. To the harder, sterner features of that creed they closed their eyes.

Where then was the remedy? It is easy for us to say that it was to be found in liberty, in the permission to each new thought to develope itself as best it might. But the very notion of religious liberty was as yet unheard of, and even if it had been as familiar as it is now, its bare proclamation would have been of little avail. Bishops, it seemed, of the stamp of Laud and Montague were to rule the Church, to exercise the enormous powers of the Episcopate and of the High Commission to depress one mode of thought and to elevate another. All the patronage of the Court, all the patronage of the Bishops, would flow in one direction. The ideas of a minority of religious men would prevail by other means than their own persuasiveness. The religion dear to the gentlemen of England was thrown on the defensive, and the House of Commons was not inclined to abandon it without a struggle.

Eliot refused to allow that his faith was a matter for argument. "Some of our adversaries, you know," he said, "are masters of forms and ceremonies. Well, I would grant to their honour even the admission at our worship of some of those great idols which they worship. There is a ceremony used in the Eastern Churches of standing at the repetition of the Creed to testify their purpose to maintain it, and as some had it, not only with their bodies upright, but with their swords drawn. Give me leave to call that a custom very commendable. It signified the constancy and readiness of their resolution to live and die in that profession; and that resolution I hope we have with as much constancy assumed, and on all occasions shall as faithfully discharge, not valuing our lives where the adventure may be necessary, for the defence of our Sovereign, for the defence of our country, for the defence of our religion."

Eliot's conclusion.

"I desire," said Eliot, in conclusion, "that we may avoid confusion and distraction; that we may go presently to the grounds of our religion, and lay that down as a rule. Then, when that is done, it will be time to take into consideration the breakers and offenders against this rule, and before we have done that, our work will be in vain. Therefore, first lay down the profession wherein we differ from the Arminians, and in that I shall be ready to deliver my opinion."

Position taken by the House.

It was the inevitable consequence of the failure of Charles to stand forth as the representative of the nation, that the House of Commons should thrust itself into a position which it could not with credit occupy. Because Charles treated the religion of the nation as a matter with which the nation had no concern whatever, therefore the Commons attempted to define the doctrine of the nation and to inflict penalties upon those who refused to accept it. Eliot and Pym said in effect, "We will not allow the religion of England to be changed." To carry out their purpose they were forced much against their will to convert the House of Commons into a school of theology one day, as they would have to convert it into a school of law on the next. At one time the Bishops, at another time the Judges, would be called to account before a body which had never studied profoundly the subjects with which Bishops and Judges were respectively conversant.

Resolution of the Commons.

The House shrunk from the uncongenial path which it was called on to enter. It was not till after many suggestions had been made, that the following Resolution was finally adopted:—

"We the Commons now in Parliament assembled do claim, profess, and avow for truth the sense of the Articles of Religion which were established in Parliament in the reign of our late Queen Elizabeth, which by public act of the Church of England, and by the general and concurrent exposition of the writers of our Church, have been delivered to us, and we do reject the sense of the Jesuits and Arminians."

1629. Jan. 27.

Like many other celebrated Parliamentary documents, this famous Resolution was by no means a model of precision. The clause about the Parliamentary title of the Articles, which had been suggested by Selden, was evidently intended to deny the claim of Convocation to legislate even in religious matters. But nothing of the kind was said, and the rest of the document was still more indefinite. When the Committee met two days afterwards, even friendly criticism professed that it was impossible to understand what was really meant by the Resolution.[1] What, for instance, were the public acts of the Church to what it appealed? According to Sir Nathaniel Rich, they were the Catechisms, the Lambeth Articles, the Irish Articles, the Acts of the Synod of Dort which had been approved by King James, the readings of professors in the Universities, the Homilies, and all other books of divines printed by authority. To this portentous list the lawyers demurred. Nothing, said Selden, could be called a public act of the Church which had not received the assent of Convocation. Serjeant Hoskins refused to give the title even to acts of Convocation. "That only," he argued, "is said to be a public act which is considered of, debated, disputed, and resolved on by the King and all the State."

Jan. 31. Its meaning doubtful.

Was Convocation or Parliament to lay down the

---

[1] This debate is only to be found in *Nicholas's Notes*.

rule of faith for England? Practically the Bishops were supreme in Convocation, and, as every one knew, the Bishops owed their appointment to the King. However much the Commons might shrink from avowing it, they had to ask themselves whether their religion was safe in Charles's hands. The House at least felt it necessary to explain their conduct in interrupting the progress of the Bill of Tonnage and Poundage. Charles restrained his vexation, but not without showing signs of irritation beneath his friendly words. He was thankful to the House, he said, for their confidence in his good intentions, but they must think that he either wanted power, which could not be, or that he was very ill counselled, if religion was in such danger as they affirmed. Eliot, at least, was not afraid of drawing the inference. "If these things be thus as we see," he said, "then he is not rightly counselled."

As soon as Pym had once more taken the chair in the Committee on Religion, Eliot rose again. The result of the last meeting had not been satisfactory. The Committee had been unable to discover with certainty what were those public acts to which so solemn an appeal had been made. Eliot now proposed to drop the investigation. Whether the Lambeth Articles had been formally accepted by the Church or not, they all believed them to be true. Let them, therefore, boldly rely upon that. "Are there Arminians?—for so are they properly called—Look to those: see to what a degree they creep; let us observe their books and sermons; let us strike at them, and make our charge at them, and vindicate our truth that yet seems obscure, and if any justify themselves in their new opinions, let us deal with them, and these testimonies will be needful. Our truth is clear, our proofs will be manifest, and if these parties will dare to defend themselves, then seek for proofs."[1]

It is impossible to deny that Eliot's proposal could only be justified by the arguments which may be used to justify a revolution. The mere assent of the House of Commons to certain doctrinal propositions which had never been legally binding upon any one was to be made the touchstone of orthodoxy. Unpopular theologians were to be summoned to give account of their actions and opinions before a tribunal which recognised no fixed legal procedure, and which would decide according to the popular instinct rather than according to any certain rule of law. It was perhaps inevitable that it should be so. The King's claim to rule as seemed right in his own eyes without taking the national conscience into account was met by the claim of the House of Commons to rule as seemed right in its own eyes without taking the rights of individual conscience into account. The time would come when it would be understood that liberty of speech and action is all that either a majority or a minority can fairly claim. But that time had not yet arrived. The Declaration on Religion nominally imposed silence on both parties alike. Practically it imposed silence on those to whom the Calvinistic doctrines were precious, not upon those who cared far more about other doctrines on which they were at liberty to talk as much as they pleased. The restraint upon freedom which the Declaration undoubtedly was, was therefore answered by an attack upon the men from whom the restraint proceeded.

As usual, Charles had studied the letter rather than the spirit of history. It was undoubtedly true that

---

[1] This debate I take from Lord Verulam's MS. and Nicholas. The *Parl. Hist.* (ii. 457) is confused, giving speeches really delivered on the following day.

religious changes had been effected by the authority of Kings. It was undoubtedly true that Henry and Elizabeth had made use of the Bishops in Convocation and out of Convocation with scant respect for any objections which might reach them from the House of Commons. But they had allowed it to be plainly seen that they were not wedded to any particular Church party. They took their stand as moderators above all. Charles could not do this. What he believed he believed thoroughly. He had no notion of watching the tides to gain the port which he had in sight. He had honestly believed his Declaration to be a healing measure, and it was perfectly incomprehensible to him how men, except from factious motives, could lash themselves into a fury against it.

The adoption of Eliot's proposal by the House therefore meant nothing less than a declaration of war against the King. The House was ready to follow him. It resolved to make enquiry into the pardons lately granted, and more especially to take up once more the charges against Montague. Addresses and remonstrances to the King had come to an end. They were to give place to sharp action against the men who owed to the King's favour their power to do good or evil.

The appointment of Montague to a Bishopric had been one of Charles's most indiscreet actions. In the House of Commons it was felt most bitterly. What, Seymour had argued in the late debates, was the use of suppressing a book, if its author was made a Bishop? The House caught eagerly at a suggestion that, after all, he was not legally a Bishop. One Jones, a bookbinder, had declared in a petition that at Montague's confirmation he had presented objections which had been passed over as irregular in form, and though the Solicitor General explained that the confirmation nevertheless was perfectly legal, it was resolved that the question should be argued at the bar.

The quarrel of the Commons with Montague was a quarrel about doctrine. Their quarrel with Cosin was a quarrel about ceremonies. Since the publication of his Book of Devotions, Cosin had been involved in charges on which he would hardly receive a fair hearing from the House of Commons. During the last summer the old Norman pile which looked down from its green height upon the then limpid waters of the Wear had been the scene of religious strife. Durham Cathedral had remained longer than most other Cathedrals in the state in which a Puritan would have wished to see it. It was not so very long ago that the Communion-table and the Font had stood one on each side of the North door which leads into the choir. Before James I. died the hand of the reformer had come. The font was moved first into the nave, then into the galilee, the Lady Chapel as it had been of old days, the only Lady Chapel in England which stood at the West end of a church, whither it had been driven, as local legends told, by the persistent refusal of St. Cuthbert to surrender a site which he had already occupied. The Communion-table was altogether removed, and a new table of stone, supported on marble pillars and adorned with figures of cherubim, was erected in the place were the altar had originally stood, and where the very same table stands somewhat mutilated at the present day. The services assumed a statelier form. The congregation were bidden to stand up at the recital of the Nicene Creed, which was now sung to the music of an organ and of other instruments. Old copes, according to the directions of the Canons of 1604, were sought out and refurbished for the use of the officiating ministers. The custom of bowing towards the East on entering

CHAP. II.
1628.

The ceremonies at Durham.

the Church, which had been prescribed by ancient statutes, was revived, and two large candlesticks appeared upon the Communion-table, though they do not seem to have been lighted except when it was dark.

Such things could not be done without awakening opposition, and that opposition found a mouthpiece in one of the prebendaries of the Cathedral, Peter Smart. For seven years he abstained from preaching in a Church which he held to be contaminated by these innovations. His subsequent history shews him to have been an inaccurate, if not a consciously mendacious, reporter of things which had passed before his eyes. On July 27, 1628,[1] he resolved to ascend the Cathedral pulpit to bear testimony against the changes which he disliked. It may be that the Remonstrance of the Commons filled his mind with zeal, as it had filled the disordered mind of Felton. His sermon was a bitter invective against his colleagues. He charged them with attempting to revive and raise up again Jewish types and figures long since dead and buried, in bringing in altars instead of tables, priests instead of ministers, propitiatory sacrifices instead of sacraments. In all this, he added, they had but copied ' that painted harlot, the Church of Rome.' In short, they were bent on introducing the Mass into the midst of an English congregation.

Smart was at once convented before the Ecclesiastical Commissioners for the Province of York. He appealed to the secular Courts. At the summer assizes he preferred an indictment against the principal prebendaries for their conduct relating to the Communion-table, standing at the Nicene Creed, and other

---

[1] The edition of his sermon printed in 1640, gives July 7, instead of the true date, as appears from the Act of the Ecclesiastical Commissioners. See *An Illustration of Neal's Hist. of the Puritans*, Durham, 1736.

ceremonies of the Church. Whitelocke, the Judge on Circuit, had taken care in the new chapel at his own house at Fawley, to place the Communion-table by the side of the pulpit.[1] But he seems to have thought, as many others thought, that a Cathedral was not to be bound by the regulations which were fitted for a parish Church. He allowed himself to be conducted over the Cathedral, expressed his approval of all that he saw, and refused Smart's application. Upon this the Dean and Chapter sequestered Smart's prebend for an offence 'against good manners, Christian charity, and the statutes of the Church of Durham.' In the following January he was transmitted to the High Commission Court of the Province of Canterbury, where his judges would at least be so far impartial that they would not feel personally aggrieved by his sermon.[2]

Sept. 20.

1629. Jan. 29.

Amongst the Durham prebendaries Cosin was the most active and influential. In the preceding spring he had been present at a conversation which turned upon the right of excommunication. Cosin maintained that the clergy held it directly from Christ. A certain Mr. Pleasance, who was present, was of a different opinion. "You have it," he said, "from the King. He can excommunicate as well as you." "The exercise of it indeed," replied Cosin, "is under the King. But the power is derived from Christ and by virtue of Holy Orders." The discourse then took a wider turn. "How," said Pleasance, "can the King be said to be Head of the Church?" "Who says it now?" was Cosin's reply. The title, he explained, though capable of innocent interpretation, was liable to be misunderstood. It had been dropped by Queen Elizabeth,[3]

1628. April. Cosin's conversation about the Royal Supremacy.

---

[1] This appears from Lord Bute's MS. of Whitelocke's Memorials.
[2] *Illustration of Neal*, 47–58. The Dean and Chapter to Neile, Aug. 23. *S. P. Dom.*, cxiii. 65.
[3] See, however, Coke's argument on the other side, 4 *Inst.* cap. 74.

and had ceased to be binding upon any one. It was enough to say that the King was 'supreme governor of Church and State,' and that he might by his 'power of supreme dominion command churchmen at any time to do their office, or punish them for neglect of it . . . External co-action. . . . whereby men were forced to obey the jurisdiction of the Church was only from the King; but the power of spiritual jurisdiction itself was from Christ, who had given it to his Apostles, and they to their successors by ordination.'

Such a conversation, after passing over the tongues of a few gossiping reporters, was easily converted into an attack upon the Royal Supremacy. The attention of the Attorney General was called to it by one of Smart's friends.[1] Charles was not likely to pay attention to such a charge against such a man; and another of Smart's friends, thinking that he would find a more favourable hearing in the House of Commons, drew up a petition full of charges against Cosin, some of them perhaps true, some of them afterwards proved to be entirely false.

Before any enquiry could be made into the truth of the petition, Phelips, who had been sent to ask the Attorney General by whose authority he had drawn the obnoxious pardons, returned with the answer. Heath explained that he had drawn Montague's pardon by his Majesty's express command. The order for preparing the pardons for Sibthorpe, Manwaring and Cosin, had been conveyed to him by Bishop Neile.[2] The House ordered that a sifting enquiry should be instituted into the history of these pardons, and into the reasons why the charges brought against Cosin had

---

[1] Cosin to Laud, Nov. 22. *S. P. Dom.*, cxxi. 33.

[2] The Bishop of Chichester is the name given in Lord Verulam's MS. Nicholas is surely right in giving that of the Bishop of Winchester, whose connection with the affair is referred to in a subsequent speech of Eliot's.

been allowed to sleep. Cosin himself was ordered to appear on the 23rd. The House, it seemed, was more jealous of the King's honour than he was himself.

In one form or another, the vital question, whether Parliament or Convocation were the supreme legislators in religious matters was constantly recurring. It was suggested that the Articles as usually printed differed in one important clause from the Articles as mentioned in the Act of Parliament of 1571, from which, according to the contention of the House of Commons, the Articles derived their binding force. The twentieth Article now contained a clause asserting that "The Church hath power to decree rites and ceremonies, and authority in controversies of faith." Such a clause might easily be quoted in support of the pretensions of Convocation. It had been absent from the printed book acknowledged by Parliament in 1571. "By adding these two lines," it was said of the existing addition, "it gives power to alter religion."[1]

In all probability the clause in question had been added by Elizabeth after the Articles passed through Convocation in 1562, though the alteration had been tacitly accepted by the clergy. For some time editions of the Articles accepted or omitted the clause at pleasure. In the edition acknowledged by Parliament in 1571 it was not to be found. In the same year it was adopted by Convocation; and though for a few years longer the practice of the printers continued to vary, it had found a place in every edition subsequent to 1581. Till the question arose between Parliament and Convocation in 1629, no practical importance had attached itself either to its adoption or its omission.[2]

CHAP. II.
1629.
Feb. 5.
Question about the authority of the Church.

Clause alledged to have been foisted upon the Articles.

History of the Clause in dispute.

---

[1] *Nicholas's Notes.*
[2] Hardwick, *Hist. of the Articles*, 143. Cardwell, *Synodalia*, i. 34, 53.

1629.
Feb. 6.
Attack upon Heath.

The question of authority reached too far to be settled without a struggle. Unhappily, its existence jaundiced the minds of those who felt strongly on one side of the conflict. The simple question of Cosin's very innocent conversation about the Royal Supremacy assumed portentous dimensions in Eliot's eyes. It was always a satisfaction to the men who were opposing the King's claims to persuade themselves that they were in reality on his side, and Eliot charged Heath with stifling a charge which amounted to little less than high treason. Yet Heath's account given to the House must have been accepted as satisfactory, as no further proceedings were taken in the matter. In the course of the defence, however, he mentioned the name of the person who had communicated to him the King's directions that he should drop the prosecution, and Charles took offence at this revelation of his secrets. It was only after making very humble apologies indeed, that he was restored to favour.[1]

Feb. 9.

The question of Montague's confirmation.

The attempt to prove that Montague was not a Bishop failed as completely as the attempt to prove that Cosin was a traitor. Counsel was heard in support of the objection which had been taken; but an argument of Sir Henry Marten satisfied the House that it could not be sustained.

Feb. 7.
Charges against Neile.

Great as was the eagerness of the Commons to listen to charges against the men whom they disliked, they had not ceased to be amenable to reason. At last it was hoped that an unanswerable case had been found. Sherfield, the member for Salisbury, whose name was a few years later to blaze forth into notoriety in a Star Chamber prosecution, reported to the Committee on Religion that Neile had caused the insertion in the

[1] Contarini's Despatch, Feb. $\frac{13}{23}$. *Ven. MSS.*

pardons to Montague and the others of words, freeing them from the penalties for erroneous, unorthodox, and false opinions;[1] words which were doubtless simply intended to guard against accusations founded upon the utterance of opinions which might be alleged by Parliament to be erroneous, unorthodox, or false, but which looked like a premeditated attempt to encourage the promulgation of heretical doctrine. Sir Daniel Norton followed by a still more telling accusation. Neile, he said, had sent for Dr. Moore, one of the Prebendaries of his Cathedral at Winchester, and told him 'that he had oftentimes heard him preach before King James, and that he had used to preach against Popery.' "This," the Bishop was alleged to have said, "was well liked of then, but now you must not do so." "If occasion serves," Moore had replied, "I will not spare to do the like again." "The times," rejoined Neile, "are not the same, and therefore you must not do so."

What Neile in all probability had intended to say was, that the King disapproval of the violent polemical objurgations which too often took the place of moral or religious instruction which ought to form the staple of a preacher's work. But no such explanation in favour of the Bishop who had been so busy in obtaining the pardons was likely to gain a hearing. "In this Lord,"[2] said Eliot, "is contracted all the danger we fear; for he that procured those pardons, may be the author of these new opinions; and I doubt not but his Majesty, being informed thereof, will leave him to the justice of the House, and I hope their exhalations will not raise jealousies between his

---

[1] Erroneas opiniones vel minus orthodoxas, doctrinas falsas, earumque publicationes, scandalize dicta, male gesta. *Nicholas's Notes*.

[2] Not "Laud," as in the *Parl. Hist.*

Majesty and us. Let the Doctor be sent for, to justify it."

The power to silence opponents was the real object in dispute. Hitherto the Commons had shown themselves far more inquisitorial than the Bishops. Yet there was one voice amongst them which was raised in favour of liberty. Selden's unenthusiastic nature and wide learning had made him utterly indifferent to the theological disputes with which the air resounded, and he thought it very hard that any one should suffer because he held one view or another on a speculative question. He was no more born to be a martyr of liberty than a martyr of orthodoxy. In his chambers in the Temple he loved to pose his friends with sudden questions, revealing his indifference to the issues which seemed so momentous. On the whole, he attached himself to the popular party. But his object was not to seize upon power in order that it might be turned against those who held it. Power itself, he held, needed to be diminished. His friends had, therefore, to resign themselves to listen to arguments which must have appeared to them to be the merest quixotry, and which made it certain that if ever, by some unexpected turn of the wheel of fortune, they found themselves in the possession of authority, they might count on Selden's opposition. In the last session, he had startled the House by an opinion, that no Englishman could legally be pressed into military service. At the opening of this session he had declared, with more applause, that the Star Chamber had no legal right to cut off ears. He now threw out a far more startling suggestion. Certain printers presented a petition, complaining that Laud's chaplain had refused to license books which they described as orthodox, whilst he had licensed books which they described as 'holding opinions of Arminianism and Popery,' and that the printers who had acted in defiance of this decision had been punished by the High Commission. To this Selden rose. "There is no law," he said, "to prevent the printing of any book in England, but only a decree in the Star Chamber. Therefore that a man should be fined, imprisoned, and his goods taken from him, is a great invasion of the liberty of the subject; and therefore, I desire that a law may be made on this." Selden was before his time. The question was referred to a select committee, and no more was heard of it. If the Commons had taken any step at all in the matter it would only have been to wrest from their adversaries a power which they would gladly have exercised themselves.

The debate which followed upon Neile's share in procuring the pardons is memorable for the first public appearance of a man who was one day to have something to say upon liberty of conscience far more determinately than Selden.

Oliver Cromwell was born at Huntington in 1599. His father, Robert, was a younger son of Sir Henry Cromwell, the Golden Knight, whose splendour at Hinchinbroke had been the subject of wonder to a past generation. The family, like so many others which rose to historical fame in the sixteenth and seventeenth centuries, had thriven by the dissolution of the monasteries. The old nunnery at Hinchinbroke had been given by Thomas Cromwell to a young kinsman who took the name of Cromwell in addition to, or in exchange for, that of Williams which he inherited from his father. Sir Richard Cromwell was fortunate enough to preserve the King's favour after his patron's fall. His descendants were not as prudent as himself, and the prodigality of his son and grandson wasted estates

CHAP. II.

1629.
Feb. 11.
The Golden Knight.
Sir Oliver Cromwell.

which had been suddenly acquired. When James arrived in England, the Golden Knight was dead. His son, Sir Oliver, the uncle of the future Lord Protector, welcomed his new Sovereign with that magnificence and prodigality which was the failing of the family. Such vast expenditure could not be supported for ever, and in 1627, Sir Oliver Cromwell was compelled to sell Hinchinbroke to Sidney Montague, a brother of the Earl of Manchester, and to retire to Ramsey, where he ended his days in such circumstances as his reduced income would allow.

Robert Cromwell.

Oliver's childhood.

Robert Cromwell settled close by Hinchinbroke, at the little town of Huntington. He had a younger brother's portion, and a younger brother's encouragement to thrift. His son Oliver grew up connected, through his uncle, with the chief families of the county, and connected, through his place of residence, with the townsmen, amongst whom his father occupied a leading position. Educated at the free grammar-school of the place, under Dr. Beard, and then passing to Cambridge in 1616, he was probably recalled to Huntington by his father's death in the following year, to take charge of the land which Robert Cromwell had owned, and to care with all the strength and tenderness of his nature for his mother and his sisters. Early responsibility developed his sterling qualities. A visit made to London for the purpose of studying law, a study without which, in that age, no gentleman's education was complete, led, when he was only in his twenty-second year, to a marriage with Elizabeth Bourchier, the gentle sharer of his anxieties and greatness, who preserved the whiteness of her simplicity alike in the modest house at Huntington and in the stately galleries of Whitehall. It is generally believed that the marriage was arranged by Oliver's aunt, the mother of

His marriage.

John Hampden. In the beginning of 1628, his fellow townsmen chose him to represent them in the great Parliament which was to claim the Petition of Right. To be so chosen whilst still in his twenty-ninth year, by those who had the most intimate acquaintance with his daily life, is the best possible testimony to his high character.

<small>CHAP. II.
1629.
Feb. 11.
Is chosen Member for Huntington.</small>

Of the wild calumnies repeated of him in after years it is unnecessary to say a word.[1] So far as it is possible to catch a glimpse of the human figure which they surround, we see a youth endowed with a vigorous frame and strong animal spirits, not unmindful of his studies, mastering the difficulties of the Latin language, so far at least as to be able to converse in it in later years, though he did not satisfy the requirements of professed scholars. It was the same with his other studies. From mathematics, history, and law, he extracted just as much as would be serviceable to him in his battle with the world; and it may perhaps be taken as the residuum of a vast mass of scandal, that he loved his jest, and was fond of outdoor exercise, sometimes allowing his pursuit of amusement to interrupt his severer studies. On the whole, there was in him a balance of the mental, the moral, and the physical powers which must have rendered him a notable example of the sound mind in the sound body, without which but little can be accomplished in the world.

<small>His moral character.</small>

Not one man in a thousand who is possessed of a sound mind and a sound body raises himself from obscurity. Great achievements come but to those who have learned to sacrifice themselves to the ideal which flashes before the inner eye of conscience. To some the wakening to higher aims and a nobler life

<small>Crisis in his life.</small>

---

[1] They are collected, accompanied by judicious reflections, in Sanford's *Studies of the Great Rebellion*, 174.

comes gradually and insensibly; to some it comes with a painful struggle: but to none was the sense of change so complete, and the struggle so intensified as to the Puritan of the seventeenth century. It may be that Cromwell's marriage and return to Huntington may have awakened new thoughts in his mind. The pleadings of his young wife may have wound themselves round his heart, and the return to the teaching of his schoolmaster, Dr. Beard, may have influenced him deeply. The struggle was great in proportion to the energy of his character. No mere resolution to improve would satisfy him. He learned to look upon his old life as utterly vile in the sight of God and man. "You know," he wrote, not many years afterwards, "what my manner of life hath been. Oh! I lived in and loved darkness, and hated light. I was chief, the chief of sinners. This is true, I hated godliness, yet God had mercy on me."[1] It is not necessary to take these words literally. It is enough to believe that his soul was crushed with a sense of sinfulness. Dr. Beard, it may be suspected, had much to do with strengthening him in this frame of mind. The book of which he was the author, *The Theatre of God's Judgment displayed*, is full of instances of immediate temporal penalties inflicted on the breach of God's laws. The higher spiritual penalty would be that upon which Cromwell's mind would fix itself. But the feeling of his own inability to meet the requirements of the Judge would be all the more intense for that. His strong nature could find no nurture in dogmatic assertions or in ceremonial devotion. He longed for purity of heart, for reality of life. What was he that he should silence the voice of judgment,—of a judgment which searched to the very depth of his being, pronouncing

[1] *Carlyle* (ed. 1857), i. 80.

him unclean. We may well believe that long months of inward conflict harrowed his soul, a time of impaired health, of strange visionary imaginations and of drear melancholy despondency. Then at last came light, as it has come to so many others, in the beaming forth from that Bible which he cherished, of the bright image of the Redeemer, of the Helper whose loving kindness would purify his life and ennoble his aims. Cromwell's misery lasted as long as he gazed with painful introspection into himself; it was lightened as soon as he forgot himself. Yet he ever held that the misery was a necessary preliminary to the joy, "Who ever," he assured his daughters, " tasted that the Lord is gracious, without some sense of self, vanity, and badness?"

CHAP. II.
1629. Feb. 11.

There was no vanity in the course which Cromwell took in Parliament. During the long session of 1628 he had remained silent. He was quite conscious that he was not master of the burning oratory of Eliot, or of the clear precision of Selden. The great lawyers who bore the weight of the struggle for the Petition needed no help from him. But as the battle changed its ground, it must have gained in interest in his eyes. The growing fondness for ceremonial observances was to him a return to the dark ways of carnal ordinances. But he watched it all in silence. At last a moment came when he became aware that he was in possession of the knowledge of a fact which might be of interest to the House. When Sherfield had charged Neile with originating the pardons, Cromwell remembered that he had heard a story in Neile's disfavour from Dr. Beard. It was an old story enough now. It was the custom that on the Sunday after Easter, a preacher should be selected to sum up and repeat the main points of three other sermons which had been preached before the Lord Mayor and Aldermen from a pulpit in the open air in Spital Square. In some year

His conduct in Parliament.

His first speech.

not later than 1617, the first sermons had been assigned to Dr. Alablaster. It became known that Beard, who was appointed to recapitulate what he had said, intended to contravert him as having preached 'tenets of Popery.' Cromwell now told in a few plain words how Neile, who as Bishop of Lincoln was at that time Beard's diocesan, had sent for him, charging him 'not to preach any doctrine contrary to that which Alablaster had delivered.' Beard, however, had persisted in his intention, had attacked Alablaster's opinions, and had been reprimanded by Neile for his conduct.[1]

We have no means of knowing what Alablaster's arguments were; and it is easy to understand that the sight of one preacher ascending the pulpit to criticise the opinions of another which he was expected to condense would be regarded as unseemly by a Bishop like Neile. The House was in no mood to examine into details. Phelips quoted a Dr. Marshall, who had been treated by Neile as Moore and Beard had been treated. Stronger charges followed. Sir Robert Crane had heard from 'a very honest man, and a good divine' that Cosin had been seen reading a book called *The Preparation for the Mass*, during the administration of the Communion. Mr. Waller, too, had heard that Cosin had ordered a printer who was setting up the type for an edition of the Prayer-book, to substitute

[1] Nicholas, who took down the speeches in short-hand, gives the speech thus: "Mr. Cromwell saith that Dr. Beard told him that one Dr. Alablaster did at the Spital preach in a sermon tenets of Popery, and Beard being to repeat the same, the now Bishop of Winton, then Bishop of Lincoln, did send for Dr. Beard, and charge him, as his diocesan, not to preach any doctrine contrary to that which Alablaster had delivered, and when Dr. Beard did, by the advice of Bishop Felton, preach against Dr. Alablaster's sermon and person, Dr. Neile, now Bishop of Winton, did reprehend him, the said Beard, for it." The remainder of the speech, as printed from the *Parl. Hist.* by Carlyle, referring to Manwaring, and concluding, "If these are the steps to Church-preferment, what are we to expect," is taken from another speech by another speaker on a different occasion.

the word 'priest' for 'minister.' Marshall and Beard were sent for to give their evidence; and a select committee was appointed 'to consider of those things that have been already agitated concerning the innovation of our religion, together with the cause of the innovation and the remedy.'

Some time must elapse before all the witnesses could appear. Dr. Moore arrived on the 13th. It was quite true, he said, that Neile had forbidden him to preach against Popery. At Winchester Cathedral, since Neile's arrival, the Communion-table had been removed to the place of the Altar. On it had been placed 'two high candlesticks, which, they say, were the same that were used at the marriage of Queen Mary.' Then came a story which looks as if it was but the repetition of the wildest gossip. 'Dr. Price .... hath used at his house to have two napkins laid across, which done, he himself maketh a low obeisance to that cross, and causes his man to put at one end of that cross a glass of sack, at another end a glass of claret, at another a cup of beer, and in the midst a cup of March beer.'[1]

As this was all the evidence to be had for the present, the House had time to turn its attention to the Roman Catholics. Selden, who had no thought of including them in his anticipations of liberty, complained that of the ten priests seized in that College at Clerkenwell, which had played such a curious part at the opening of the last session, only one had been condemned. Sir Francis Davey said that only three had even been tried, and that though two of these who were acquitted, together with the seven who had not been brought to trial, had refused to take the oath of allegiance, they had not been retained in prison on that

[1] *Nicholas's Notes.*

1629.
Feb. 14.

score. The next day it came out that the condemned priest had been reprieved by a warrant from Chief Justice Hyde. The other nine persons had been released on bail by an order conveyed from the King by the Earl of Dorset. In the eyes of the House this carefulness not to shed blood for religion's sake was treason to Protestantism. Yet what could they do? They repeated in chorus that the King was innocent: his ministers had done it all. It was very natural. All the old hereditary respect for the monarchy, all the consciousness of services rendered in the days of their fathers, stood in the way of a rupture with the King, if it could by any means be avoided. It would be difficult to avoid it much longer.

The Commons accusers, not judges.

After all, ready as the Commons had been to welcome every suspicion against Neile and Cosin, it must not be forgotten that they were not judges, but accusers. When the evidence was brought into shape, it would have to be carried before the Lords, and the Lords would have to listen to the defence and to pronounce judgment.

Tonnage and Poundage again.

No House of Lords could intervene in the other great question of the session. The enforced cessation of the debates on religion till the witnesses appeared gave time for the resumption of the debates on Tonnage and Poundage. A compromise was far less probable than it had been a fortnight before. Angry feelings had arisen, and they were not likely to be soothed by the knowledge that the possession of these duties would enable the King to set the ecclesiastical feeling of the House at defiance. Charles, on the other hand, could not forget that for more than a century the duties had been granted formally at the commencement of every reign, and the attempt of the House of Commons to convert this formal consent into a right of refusal must have seemed to him an unwarrantable shifting of the balance of the Constitution; much in the same way as we should regard an attempt of the Sovereign to exercise the right of veto upon Bills presented by Parliament.

1629. Feb. 14.

There was one circumstance, however, which Charles had forgotten. Beyond the legal question, lay the question of the safety of property. If the Commons gave way, they not merely conceded the right of levying an ascertained revenue, but of extracting from commerce an undefined amount, which might entirely ruin the trade of the kingdom.

It cannot be settled without settling the questions of Impositions.

The 12th had been fixed as the day on which the discussion was to be resumed in a Committee of the whole House. Before the day had arrived the feeling on both sides was embittered by mutual provocation. On the one hand, a sheriff of London had been sent by the Commons to the Tower for giving unsatisfactory answers about the seizure of the merchants' goods. On the other hand, proceedings had been commenced in the Star Chamber against some of the merchants, apparently to punish them for the riotous manner in which they had carried off these very goods.[1] In the course of these proceedings a subpœna was directed to Rolle, commanding his attendance.

Feb 10. Mutual provocation.

It was impossible to deny that a breach of privilege had been committed in summoning a member during the actual session. The Attorney General frankly acknowledged the mistake. But the House was not satisfied. "We heard the King say," observed Kirton, "he took not nor did claim the subsidy of Tonnage and Poundage as his right; and yet, by the

Feb. 11. Further enquiry demanded.

---

[1] In *Nicholas's Notes* the information is said to have been for not paying the duties; but the account given above seems the only way of explaining how the matter got into the Star Chamber. The non-payment would be for the Exchequer Court to punish if it chose to do so.

CHAP. II.
1629.
Feb. 12.

information exhibited in the Star Chamber, we see his Majesty's ministers do proceed otherwise." It was resolved to take these proceedings into consideration, together with the grievances of the merchants.

Eliot's leadership makes an arrangement impossible.

It is most unlikely that, until the ecclesiastical difficulties had been settled, any arrangement satisfactory to both parties could have been made on this question of Tonnage and Poundage. Under Eliot's leadership no such arrangement was possible. Full of enthusiasm for the supremacy of the House of Commons, he reverted to his old tactics of calling the King's ministers to account, whilst he treated the King himself with the highest respect, a respect which was doubtless altogether unfeigned. He could not see that he was striking away all the supports of the Royal authority, as it had established itself under the Tudor Sovereigns, and that whether his course was to be justified by precedents and reason or not, it was one to which no Sovereign with the slightest feeling of self-respect was likely to submit. He now proposed to

He advises an attack upon the farmers of the customs.

dissociate the farmers of the customs from the King. He argued that as these men had paid a certain sum into the Exchequer for the right of levying the duties, the Crown was not involved in the matter at all. If the farmers failed to recoup themselves by levying duties, it was upon them, and not upon the King, that the loss would fall. Let the Barons of the Exchequer be told that they had been misinformed. If they once knew that the goods had been seized for the farmers, and not for the King, the ground of their decision would be taken away, and they would allow the replevins to take their course.

Noy's suggestion.

Eliot's proposal to go round the difficulty was met by an argument from Noy, that it would be better to

---

[1] The fullest report is in *Nicholas's Notes*. The *Parl. Hist.* transfers the speech to the 11th.

meet it in the face. As he had attempted to mediate in the last session, he attempted to mediate now. He began by stating his opinion that Tonnage and Poundage was 'an aid and subsidy,' which ultimately fell upon the whole body of the nation. They were the greatest hinderers who sought to take it by force. It would be necessary to rid themselves of the proceedings in the Exchequer and in the Star Chamber, or the King's claim would be confirmed by their silence. The best way to do this would be to go on with the grant, inserting in the Bill a clause declaring that all judgments based on the King's claim to levy the duties were void and of no effect. As soon as such a Bill was drawn up, the King would doubtless restore the goods which had been seized.[1]

Whatever chance there was of maintaining the right claimed by the House without a breach with the King lay in the prompt adoption of Noy's proposal. Unhappily Selden threw the weight of his authority on the other side. It is possible that his constitutional timidity led him to approve of the less direct mode of facing the difficulty. Whatever his motive may have been, he argued that what had been done had been the act of the King's ministers, not of the King himself. Let a message be sent to the Barons of the Exchequer to

Selden proposes a message to the Court of Exchequer.

The message.

[1] *Nicholas's Notes.* The feeling of the House was probably well expressed by Nethersole. "On Thursday last," he writes, "the matter of Tonnage and Poundage was taken into consideration, and by what was then said, it is easy to see that the House will give it to the King your brother, without any diminution in point of profit, but not without a very full acknowledgment and declaration of the right of the subject and cessation of all that hath been done to the prejudice thereof either by the King your father or your brother." The question of impositions, in short, was to be settled as well as that of Tonnage and Poundage. But there was more behind. The writer adds that nothing had been done since 'nor will be much till religion be settled, whereon the hearts of all the House are earnestly set.'—Nethersole to Elizabeth, Feb. 14. *S. P. Dom.* cxxxv. 40.

inform them that the goods in question had been seized for Tonnage and Poundage. When they knew that, they would doubtless alter their decree. Noy and other members who agreed with him urged that it would be better for the merchants to plead their own cause in the Exchequer; but the House refused to accept the suggestion, and ordered that a message should be sent drawing the attention of the Barons to the fact that the goods seized had been seized for Tonnage and Poundage.[1]

As yet the House had not openly engaged in a conflict with the Courts of Law. But such a conflict was perilously near. The Barons of the Exchequer were not likely to submit to dictation from the Commons in whatever words it might be veiled. They replied that the attempt to recover the goods by replevin 'was no lawful action.' If the owners considered themselves to be wronged, they might 'take such order as the law requireth.'

What answer could the Commons make? They appointed a Committee to search the records of the Exchequer in the hope of convicting the Barons of acting in defiance of their own precedents. In the meanwhile Eliot's proposal of the 12th was adopted, and the Custom House officers were summoned to the Bar.

When the officers appeared, the questions put to them shewed that those who guided the deliberations of the House had resolved to restrict the ground of dispute to a question of privilege. They were asked whether they had known Rolle to be a member of Parliament when they seized his goods. The officer to whom the question was put replied that he was not aware that a member's goods as well as his person were covered by the privilege, and May, who alone, with the

[1] *Nicholas's Notes.*

feeble Coke, sustained the weight of the defence of the Government, declared that it had never been heard 'till this Parliament' that a member 'should have his goods privileged against the King, and he is not yet satisfied that he ought.' Eliot urged the House simply to discuss the question whether the officers were delinquents or not. The Commons were indeed in a great strait. But voices were not wanting to urge them to take some broader course. Those who objected to see a great constitutional question narrowed to a mere dispute over privilege had the weighty support of Pym. "The liberties of this House," he said, "are inferior to the liberties of this kingdom. To determine the privilege of this House is but a mean matter, and the main end is to establish possession of the subjects, and to take off the commission and records and orders that are against us. This is the main business; and the way to sweeten the business with the King, and to certify ourselves, is first to settle these things, and then we may in good time proceed to vindicate our own privileges."

<small>CHAP. II.
1629.
Feb. 19.</small>

<small>Pym's objection to narrow the dispute.</small>

In Pym's words was to be heard the prudence of the great tactician of the Long Parliament. His skill was formed upon the truest perception of the conditions of action. He felt instinctively that the great cause of the subject's rights ought to be brought into the foreground, and that the petty question of Rolle's privilege, resting as it did on precedents not absolutely certain, and involving an unfair advantage to members of the House over other merchants, ought to be kept in the background.

<small>Pym's procedure.</small>

Once more Selden failed to rise to the height of the argument. If a point of privilege was raised, he said, all other matters must give place. Sir Nathaniel Rich pointed out the risk into which Selden was bringing the

<small>Selden's course.</small>

<small>Rich's suggestion.</small>

House. He asked whether it was true that a member of Parliament had privilege for his goods against the King. "We have not used," he added, "when anything has been done by the King's command, to the breach of a privilege of this House, to fly on the officer that hath put such commands in question; but have by petition gone to the King, and it hath ever succeeded well." He suggested that the mode of proceeding should be referred to a Committee.

Eliot would not hear of such a suggestion. "Place your liberty," he cried, "in what sphere you will, if it be not to preserve the privileges of this House; for if we were not here to debate and right ourselves and the kingdom in their liberties, where had all our liberty been at this day?" The course proposed by Pym, however, was not left unsupported. Digges and Seymour spoke warmly for it. May thought that the time was come to strike in for the King. "God forbid," he said, "that the King's commands should be put for delinquency. When that is done his crown is at stake."[1] Eliot turned aside from the main issue to wrap himself once more in the robes of privilege. "Mr. Chancellor of the Duchy," he replied to May, "said we were making a question of bringing the King's command for a delinquency. But the question is whether an act done on pretence of the King's command, to the breach of the privileges, be a delinquency or no. I have heard the King cannot command a thing which tends to the breach of Parliament privilege, and the Chancellor of the Duchy said that if we did go about to bring the King's commands for a delinquency, the King's crown was at stake, which if we should go about were an act of the highest treason." May rose

[1] "Actum est de imperio" in May's words, as in Eliot's and his own second speech.

to explain. He had accused no one, but if the officers were punished after justifying themselves on the King's command, the King might think that his crown was at stake, 'seeing he should be no more obeyed.'[1]

<small>CHAP. II.
1629.
Feb. 19.</small>

May had touched the heart of the question. The question of responsibility was the question of sovereignty. If that was decided against Charles a complete revolution would have been effected in the relations between the King and his subjects, as those relations had been understood by four generations of Englishmen.

<small>Importance of the question raised.</small>

The Commons shrank, as well they might, from facing so tremendous an issue. After two days of further discussion the Committee came to a vote on the restricted question of privilege. Their resolution declared that a member of the House ought to have privilege for his goods as well as for his person. Did this mean, asked May, that he ought to have privilege against the King. The Committee did its best to avoid a reply. Many of the members expressed a conviction that the goods had been seized without orders, till the production of the King's warrants made the subterfuge no longer possible. In the vote which was taken, the King's name indeed was not mentioned, but it was resolved that Rolle was to have privilege for his goods.[2]

<small>Feb. 21.
Decision of the Commons.</small>

It was impossible for Charles to keep silence any longer. The next day was Sunday, and, as usual, a full Council was held in the afternoon. The King attended its meeting, and declared 'that what was formerly done by his farmers and the officers of the Customs was done by his own direction and commandment of his Privy Council, himself for the most part

<small>Feb. 22.
The King intervenes.</small>

---

[1] Only from *Nicholas's Notes* do we learn the full importance of this debate. Hitherto we have only had a fragment of it.

[2] *Nicholas's Notes.*

being present in Council,' and if he had been at any time from the Council Board, yet he was acquainted with their doings, and gave full direction in it; and therefore could not in this sever the act of the officers from his own act, neither could his officers suffer from it without high dishonour to his Majesty.' To this declaration the Council assented unanimously, and Sir John Coke was ordered to inform the House of the King's words.[1]

When the morning came, however, Coke did not at first deliver the message, waiting perhaps to see if the House might be inclined to extricate itself without the intervention of the King. May pleaded hard for an amicable solution. "We all agree," he said, "that a wound is given, and there is oil and vinegar to put into it. If we put in oil, we may cure it; if vinegar, I know not what may be the success. Think upon some course to have restitution made."[2]

Eliot waved the suggestion haughtily away. He had confidence, he said, in the justice of the King. Let them go to the delinquency of these men. It may be that a murmur of applause shewed that Eliot had carried the Committee with him. At all events Coke thought that the time was come for the fulfilment of his mission. "I must now," he said, "speak plain English." The officers had acted by the King's command, and the step proposed to be taken against them concerned him highly 'in point of government.' He could not sacrifice his honour by giving way to the distinctions which appeared to satisfy others.

It was now plain to the dullest understanding that the House would have to deal with the King and not with his officers. Charles would not follow the Tudor

---

[1] *Rushw.* i. 659.
[2] So far from Nicholas; what follows is from Lord Verulam's MS.

habit of throwing over his ministers to escape responsibility. The House adjourned to the 25th to afford time for consideration.

If anything was needed to confirm Charles in his resolution, it must have been the knowledge that if he surrendered the Custom House officers he would next be called upon to surrender the Bishops. On the 26th a Sub-committee completed the Resolutions which were to be submitted to the House on the religious difficulty.[1]

The Resolutions repeated the grievances of which complaints had been made in the debates. Popery and Arminianism were spreading, Communion-tables had been removed, to be set as altars at the Eastern end of churches. Candlesticks had been placed on them, and obeisance made towards them. Congregations had been ordered to stand up at the singing of the *Gloria Patri*, and women coming to be churched had been compelled to wear veils. Then there was the 'setting up of pictures and lights and images in churches, praying towards the East, crossing' and other objectionable gestures. The orthodox doctrine had been suppressed, the doctrine which was supported by the Prayer book, the Homilies and Catechism, by Jewel's writings, the public determination of divines, the Lambeth articles, the Irish articles, and the resolutions of the Synod of Dort, by the uniform consent of writers whose works had been published by authority, and by the submission enjoined by the two Universities upon the opponents of the Lambeth articles. Those who now opposed this orthodox doctrine had

---

[1] *Parl. Hist.* iii. 483. There is some difficulty about the date of this. Lord Verulam's MS. here becomes utterly confused, and other MSS. give varying dates. I have followed *Harl.* 4296. We know that this Sub-committee was at work, and there is no reason to think that the resolutions were ever accepted by the House.

been preferred to Bishoprics and Deaneries, and some prelates, Neile and Laud in particular, had been taken into special favour, and having gotten the chief administration of ecclesiastical affairs under his Majesty, had discountenanced and hindered the preferment of those that are orthodox, and favoured and preferred such as are contrary.

Remedies proposed.

In the last clause lay, to modern ears, the real weight of the Commons' case. The King's authority was being used in a one-sided way to secure the undue preponderance of unpopular opinions. The remedy proposed was the old remedy of compulsory uniformity. The laws were to be put in force against 'Popish opinions' and 'superstitious ceremonies.' 'Severe punishment' was to be inflicted on those who should 'publish either by word or writing anything contrary to orthodoxy.' The books of Montague and Cosin were to be burnt, and 'authors and abettors of those Popish and Arminian innovations,' to be condignly punished. 'Good order' was to be taken 'for licensing of books.' 'Bishoprics and other ecclesiastical preferments' were to be conferred only 'upon pious, learned, and orthodox men.' Parliament was to consider how means might be provided for maintaining 'a godly and able minister in every parish church,' and care was to be taken that the Ecclesiastical Commissioners might be men 'approved for integrity of life and soundness of opinion.'

If the House should adopt these resolutions—and there was slight probability that it would refuse to do so—it would be but to little purpose to allay the strife about the responsibility of officials. Of liberty and of all the treasures which that word conveys there was no thought in the minds of the members of the House of Commons. The idea had not yet presented itself even to the leaders. It would be the merest pedantry to blame them for not anticipating the thought of days to come. Only through suffering does any people enter into rest. To strive ever forwards amidst bewildering entanglements and distracted wanderings from the true path is the law of service, for a nation as truly as for an individual. Happy is that nation which keeps its courage high and its heart pure, that the eyes of its understanding may in due time be enlightened.

The day on which the House was to resume its debates, brought an order of the King commanding an adjournment for another week. Charles fondly hoped that the Commons might be induced to reconsider their position. His agents were busy with the leaders to induce them to desist from their pretensions, in order that, as he afterwards said, 'a better and more right understanding might be begotten between him and them.'[1] It could not be. In the Church the policy of silence imposed on theological disputes and of permission to revert to older ceremonial practices, was met by the policy of the absolute exclusion of opinions and ceremonies to which the existing generation had ceased to be accustomed. In the State, King and Commons were striving for the mastery.

It is hardly likely that under any circumstances the breach could have been long averted. But the conflict in its actual form was distinctly the work of Eliot. He now resolved to urge the House to appeal from the King to the country. When the House met again it would probably only meet to be re-adjourned, and Eliot resolved to take advantage of the claim of the House to adjourn itself in order to move a protest which might go forth to the world before the dissolution which was certain to follow.

Of the leaders who had stood by his side in the

[1] *Parl. Hist.* ii. 502. Contarini's Despatch, March $\frac{6}{16}$.

great struggle for the Petition of Right, Selden alone supported him now. Pym had relapsed into silence ever since the course which he had proposed had been overborne by the torrent of Eliot's eloquence. Phelips and Littleton and Digges, and many another whose voices had once been loud, took no part in his counsels. But there was plenty of indignation amongst members of less repute, and in these he found not a few who were ready to assist him in carrying out his plan.

March 2. The adjournment resisted.

The first difficulty was to obtain a few minutes before the Speaker left the chair, and arrangements were accordingly made to resist the usual hurried adjournment.

As was expected, when the morning of March 2 came, the Speaker, Sir John Finch, declared the King's pleasure that the House should be adjourned to the 10th.[1] He then put the formal question to which, under such circumstances, a negative had never been returned. Shouts of No! No! rose on every side. Eliot rose, as if to speak to the question of adjournment. Finch did his best to check him. He had, he said, an absolute command from his Majesty instantly to leave the chair if any one attempted to speak.

The right of adjournment.

The question of the right of adjournment which was thus brought to an issue was not beyond dispute. The King had again and again directed adjournments.

[1] There are three accounts of the proceedings of this day which throw a much clearer light upon them than anything which has been hitherto published; one in *Nicholas's Notes*, the others amongst the *State Papers, Dom.* cxxxviii. 6, 7. Excepting in the case of one or two unimportant speeches the order in which everything occurred becomes quite clear from the agreement of these authorities. Some valuable information is to be had from Lord Verulam's MS., of which this part was published by Mr. Bruce in *Archæologia*, xxxviii. 237. Mr. Forster's narrative is very incorrect, and the paper printed at p. 244 was certainly not the paper read by Eliot. Consequently the charges which he brings against Heath of distorting facts are founded upon a very imperfect knowledge of the evidence.

The Lords had always considered the command as binding. The Commons had been accustomed to adjourn themselves in order to avoid the appearance of submission to the King's authority, though they had never refused to comply with his wishes.

<small>CHAP. II.
1629.
March 2.</small>

Eliot had made up his mind that the time had arrived when the House ought to make a practical use of the right of self-adjournment which he claimed for it. As Finch moved to leave the chair, Denzil Holles and Benjamin Valentine stepped forward, seized him by the arms, and thrust him back into his seat. May and Edmondes, with the other Privy Councillors present, hurried to his assistance. For a moment he broke away from his captors. But his triumph was short. Crowds of members barred the way, and Holles and Valentine seized him again and pushed him back into his seat. "God's wounds," cried Holles, "you shall sit till we please to rise." Physical force was clearly not on his side, and he made no further effort to escape.[1]

<small>The Speaker held down.</small>

As soon as quiet had been restored Eliot's voice was heard claiming for the House the right to adjourn itself. His Majesty, he went on to say, must have been misinformed, or he had been led to believe that they had 'trenched too far upon the power of sovereignty.' They had done nothing unjust, and as the King was just, there could be no difference between them. A short declaration of their intentions had been prepared, which he asked to be allowed to put to the question.

<small>Eliot claims to be heard.</small>

<small>Proposes a declaration</small>

Eliot spoke from the highest bench at the back of

<small>The Speaker</small>

---

[1] As Finch spoke frequently afterwards, it is probable that Holles and Valentine did not continue to hold him, contenting themselves with watching him. Mr. Forster separated the two seizures, but I have followed Heath's information (*Parl. Hist.* ii. 510), which gives a very probable account of the matter. The theory that the Government was always inventing falsehoods seems to me quite unreasonable.

the House, and he threw the paper forward in order that some one in front might hand it to the clerk to be read if the Speaker refused to allow the clerk to read it. Shouts of "Read! read!" were raised in the midst of a confused struggle. The crowd swayed backwards and forwards around the chair. In the midst of the excited throng, Coryton struck one of his fellow members.[1] The Speaker defended his rights. He knew no instance, he said, in which the House had continued to transact business after a command from his Majesty to adjourn. "What would any of you do," he added plaintively, "if you were in my place? Let not my desire to serve you faithfully be my ruin."

There was no room for the suggestion that the Speaker was not properly authorised to order the adjournment. He had had the command, he said, from the King's own lips. Eliot rejoined that they were quite ready to adjourn in obedience to his Majesty, but the declaration must first be read. Strode in a few words acknowledged the reason for this persistency. "I desire the same," he said, "that we may not be turned off like scattered sheep, as we were at the end of the last session, and have a scorn put on us in print, but that we may leave something behind us." They wished that their voice should be heard as a rallying cry to the nation in the conflict which had begun.

One after another rose to urge upon the Speaker the duty of obeying the order of the House. The order of the House, said Eliot, would be sufficient to excuse him with the King. If he refused obedience, he should be called to the bar.

---

[1] This incident is placed here by Heath, and is made probable by the words used by Coryton soon afterwards, in which he speaks of himself as having been to blame as well as the rest.

At this intimation of defiance of the King's command, some members rose to leave the House. Orders were at once given to the Serjeant-at-Arms to shut the door, that no tales might be carried to those who were outside. The Serjeant-at-Arms hesitated to obey, and Sir Miles Hobart, at his own suggestion, was directed to close the doors. He swiftly turned the lock and put the key into his pocket.[1]

CHAP.
II.
―――
1629.
March 2.
The door locked.

As soon as order was restored, Finch's voice was heard once more. To be called to the bar, he said, was one of the greatest miseries which could befal him. Then, after a few words from others, he begged to be allowed to go to the King, as in the last session. He had done them no ill offices then, and he would do them none now. "If I do not return, and that speedily," he ended by saying, "tear me in pieces."

Finch begs to be allowed to go.

Cries of Ay and No shewed that there was a division of opinion. Eliot again threatened the Speaker with the consequences of persisting in his refusal. No man, he said, had ever been blasted in that House, 'but a curse at length fell upon him.' He asked that his paper might be returned to him. He would read it himself, that the House and the world might know the loyalty of the affections of those who had prepared it. Before the paper was returned, Strode made one more effort to have the question regularly put. "You have protested yourself," he said to the Speaker, "to be our servant, but if you do not what we command you, that protestation of yours is but a compliment. The Scripture saith 'His servants ye are to whom ye obey.' If you will not obey us, you are not our servant."

Renewed appeal to him to put the question.

---

[1] The usual account makes the shutting of the doors consequent upon an attempt of the Serjeant to carry off the mace. But a comparison of the three principal narratives induces me to think that the Serjeant was sent for to bring the mace at a later period.

CHAP. II.
1629.
March 2.
His difficult position.

Finch's position was indeed a hard one. Elected by the Commons, but with a tacit regard to a previous selection by the King, the Speaker had hitherto served as a link between the Crown and the House over which he presided. In Elizabeth's days it had been easy for a Speaker to serve two masters. It was no longer possible now. The strain of the breaking constitution fell upon him. " I am not the less the King's servant," he said piteously, " for being yours. I will not say I will not put the reading of the paper to the question, but I must say, I dare not."

Eliot's speech.

Upon this final refusal Eliot raised his voice. He told his hearers, silent enough now, how religion had been attacked; how Arminianism was the pioneer to Popery; how there was a power above the law which checked the magistrates in the execution of justice. Those who exercised this power had been the authors of the interruptions in this place, whose guilt and fear of punishment had cast the House upon the rocks. Amongst these evil counsellors were some Prelates of the Church, such as in all ages have been ready for innovation and disturbance, though at this time more than any. Them he denounced as enemies to his Majesty. And behind them stood another figure more base and sinister still. The Lord Treasurer himself was the prime agent of iniquity. " I fear," continued Eliot, "in his person is contracted the very root and principle of these evils. I find him building upon the old grounds and foundations which were built by the Duke of Buckingham, his great master. His counsels, I am doubtful, begat the sad issue of the last session, and from this cause that unhappy conclusion came." Not only was

He proposes to impeach Weston.

[1] Eliot began, " I shall now express," &c., as printed by Mr. Forster (ii. 244.) Then followed, "The miserable condition," &c., which Mr. Forster believed to have been spoken at the beginning of the debate (ii. 240.) The concluding phrase, " And for myself," &c. (ii. 245) followed next.

Weston 'the head of all the Papists,' and the root of all the dangers to which religion was exposed, but the course which he had taken in the question of Tonnage and Poundage had been adopted from a deliberate design to subvert the trade of the country, and in the end to subvert the Government. When commerce had been ruined, and the wooden walls of England were no longer in existence, the State would be at the mercy of its neighbours. " These things," cried Eliot, " would have been made more apparent if time had been for it, and I hope to have time to do it yet."

Once more Eliot's highly-kindled imagination had played him false. The charge of deliberate treason was as unfounded as it was improbable. In the wild excitement of that day everything seemed credible to him, and the proud confidence of his bearing stamped upon his listening auditors the firm assurance that he was not dealing his shafts at random. At last, turning to the paper which he held in his hand, he briefly explained its meaning. " There is in this paper," he said, " a protestation against those persons that are innovators in religion, against those that are introducers of any new customs, and a protestation against those that shall execute such commands for Tonnage and Poundage, and a protestation against merchants that, if any merchant shall pay any such duties, he as all the rest shall be as capital enemies of the State, and whensoever we shall sit here again, if I be here—as I think I shall—I will deliver myself more at large, and fall upon the person of that man."[1]

Eliot had made it known what the contents of the

Explains the proposed protest.

The reading of the

---

[1] This last paragraph is from *S. P. Dom.* cxxxviii. 6. It is more lifelike than the words given in *Nicholas's Notes.* " If ever I serve again in Parliament I shall proceed against them as capital enemies of the State." It must be acknowledged, however, that the latter form agrees better with that printed by Mr. Forster (ii. 245.)

1629.
March 2.
protest again urged.

paper were; but unless it could be formally put by the Speaker, it would not go forth as more than the expression of his private opinion. Coryton urged that it would be for the King's advantage that the paper should be read. He had need of help from the House, and those persons that had been named kept it from him. The members had come there with a full resolution to grant not merely Tonnage and Poundage, but all other necessary supplies as well. Shouts of 'All! All!' encouraged Coryton to proceed. "Shall every man," he said, "that hath broken the law have the liberty to pretend the King's commands?" Ought that transcendent Court, highest of all others, to permit the laws to be 'broken.' "Therefore," he ended, "I shall move that his Majesty may be moved from this House to advise with his grave and learned Council, and to leave out those that have been here noted to be ill councillors both for the King and kingdom."

Weston defended by his son.

There was one in that assembly whose ears tingled with shame and indignation. Jerome Weston, the Lord Treasurer's eldest son, stood up to defend his father. "We have here in consideration," he said, "human laws which, as they be many, so there is one eternal law of God, that we should love our neighbours as ourselves. Now, what can be more unjust than, without true grounds, to lay aspersions upon a noble person? Would any of us think it just to be done to ourselves? Let not the Lord Treasurer be prejudged. He has as faithful a heart to Church and Commonwealth as any man sitting here."

Clement Coke's syllogism.

Then, as now, the House of Commons was wisely tolerant of divergence of opinion, especially when it was prompted by domestic affection. Even in that supreme hour of conflict the call was not altogether without effect. The reckless Clement Coke, indeed, struck the blow home. "Whoever," he said, "laid Tonnage and Poundage on the people without the gift of Parliament is an enemy to the Commonwealth, and that this great person has done this, there are not light suspicions only upon him, but apparent proofs." But Eliot was not so entirely thrown off his balance as to assume guilt which had not been proved. He had no intention, he declared, of asking the House to take his assertions as evidence. He hoped to be allowed to produce his proofs when they met again.

_{CHAP. II.}
_{1629.}
_{March 2.}
_{Eliot's explanation.}

The discussion threatened to become endless for want of definite aim. Selden brought it back to the original issue by telling the Speaker once more that he was bound to put the question. If he refused, they had in him a master instead of a servant. He would virtually abdicate his office, and they ought then to proceed to the choice of another Speaker. For the present he would be content with moving that Eliot should take the chair and put the Resolutions to the House.[1]

_{Selden threatens to place Eliot in the chair.}

An unexpected obstacle arose. Eliot having, as it would seem, despaired of obtaining a formal vote upon his Resolutions, had thrown the paper in the fire. "I think," said Holles, reasonably enough, "that gentleman hath done very ill to burn that paper." Eliot gracefully submitted to the correction. "I give that gentleman great thanks for reproving me for the burning of that paper, and of all obligations that have passed between us I hold this for the greatest." With the exception of a formal motion made shortly afterwards, these words of courtesy were the last utterance of the high-souled man within the walls of the House of Commons.

_{Eliot has burnt his paper.}

Whatever was to be done must be done speedily. As Holles rose, a knocking was heard at the door. The

_{The Serjeant sent for.}

[1] *Nicholas's Notes.*

King had sent for the serjeant to bring away the mace. The House would not yet part with the symbol of authority. But after some delay, the serjeant was allowed to go. Hobart let him out, and locked the door after him again.[1]

As soon as order was restored, there was a fresh discussion on the propriety of naming the Lord Treasurer. Sir Peter Heyman turned once more upon Finch: "I am sorry," he said, "that you must be made an instrument to cut up the liberties of the subject by the roots. I am sorry you are a Kentish man, and that you are of that name which hath borne some good reputation in our country. The Speaker of the House of Commons is our mouth, and if our mouth will be sullen and will not speak when we would have it, it should be bitten by the teeth, and ought to be made an example; and, for my part, I think it not fit you should escape without some mark of punishment to be set upon you by the House."

It was easier to speak of punishment than to inflict it. Maxwell, the Usher of the Black Rod, was now knocking at the door with a message from the King. The moments were fast flying, and there was no time for longer deliberation. Charles had sent for his guard to force a way into the House. Not a minute was to be lost in idle recrimination. Holles threw himself into the breach. "Since that paper is burnt," he said, "I con-

---

[1] Heath's information speaks of the serjeant as having been detained a prisoner. On the other hand, *Lord Verulam's MS.* and *Hargrave MS.* 299, fol. 139 b, plainly speak of his being put out. I have tried to reconcile the two. From *Nicholas's Notes* we learn that the knocking was heard when Holles rose, and from *S. P. Dom.* cxxxviii. 6, that the messenger was still at the door after Eliot's reply. This delay would enable Heath to speak of the serjeant as a prisoner. Mr. Forster brings no authority for his statement that the serjeant laid his hand on the mace to take it away, and that 'a fierce cry arose to shut the door.' *Sir J. Eliot,* ii. 244. The door had been shut long before.

ceive I cannot do his Majesty nor my country better service than to deliver to this House what was contained in it, which, as I remember, was thus much in effect :[1]—

"Whosoever shall bring in innovation in religion, or by favour seek to extend or introduce Popery or Arminianism, or other opinions disagreeing from the true and orthodox church, shall be reputed a capital enemy to this Kingdom and the Commonwealth.

"Whosoever shall counsel or advise the taking and levying of the subsidies of Tonnage and Poundage, not being granted by Parliament, or shall be an actor or an instrument therein, shall be likewise reputed an innovator in the government, and a capital enemy to this Kingdom and Commonwealth.

"If any merchant or other person whatsoever shall voluntarily yield or pay the said subsidies of Tonnage and Poundage, not being granted by Parliament, he shall likewise be reputed a betrayer of the liberty of England, and an enemy to the same."[2]

It was hopeless to apply again to Speaker or Clerk. Holles put the question himself. Hearty shouts of Ay, Ay, adopted the defiance which he flung in the face of the King. The House then voted its own adjournment. The door was thrown open at last, and the members poured forth to convey to the outer world the tidings of their high resolve. Eleven years were to pass away before a House of Commons was permitted to cross that threshold again.

[1] *Nicholas's Notes.*   [2] *Parl. Hist.* ii. 491.

CHAPTER III.

PRIVILEGE OF PARLIAMENT BEFORE THE JUDGES.

CHAP. III.
1629.
March 2. Dissolution of Parliament discussed.

IMMEDIATELY after the adjournment a Proclamation for the dissolution of Parliament was drawn up and signed by the King. Charles threw the whole blame upon the insolence of those who had resisted his command to adjourn.[1] Yet it was not without hesitation that the decisive step was taken. Coventry was supported by a considerable following in the Council in asking that a milder course should be adopted. Weston, whose impeachment had been called for by Eliot, argued strongly on the other side. For two days the contending parties strove with one another, and it was only on the 4th that the Proclamation was made public.[2] The day before, Eliot and eight other members of the Commons had been summoned to appear before the Board. Seven of them presented themselves before the Council, and were committed to the Tower and to other prisons. The other two were subsequently captured, and shared the fate of their friends.[3]

March 4 Imprisonment of members.

The dissolution pronounced.

The Houses had stood adjourned to the 10th, and Charles thought it well to go to the House of Lords, that the words of dissolution might be pronounced in

---

[1] Proclamation, March 2. *Rymer*, xix. 29.
[2] Contarini's Despatch, March $\frac{6}{16}$. *Ven. MSS.*
[3] *Council Register*, March 3, 4.

his presence, and that he might take the opportunity of expressing his confidence in the Peers. It was observed that on his return he looked pleased with his day's work, as if he had at last freed himself from a yoke to which he had long submitted with difficulty.[1]

<small>CHAP. III.
1629.
March 10.</small>

Charles's feeling of self-satisfaction was in truth the most ominous element in the political prospect. No candid person can find fault with him for dissolving Parliament. The House of Commons which had just ceased to exist had been elected under circumstances of peculiar excitement, and it had ended by clamouring for stringent measures of repression which would have been fatal to the free development of thought in England. Unhappily Charles had been himself to blame for the explosion by his unwise promotion of men holding unpopular opinions. Yet if he had repented of his mistake, and had merely wished to gain a year or two to recover the confidence of the nation, no one but a constitutional purist would blame him for refusing to abdicate his hereditary authority. A wiser man might well have shrunk from placing himself unreservedly in the hands of a House of Commons which claimed supremacy in the State whilst crying down that essential condition of liberty of thought and speech, without which parliamentary government is only a more crushing form of tyranny.

<small>Charles's self-satisfaction.</small>

<small>Was the dissolution justifiable?</small>

The Declaration set forth by the King[2] to justify the dissolution was an able statement of his case against the House of Commons. In his own mind at least Charles took his stand upon the law. He would carry out, he said, the provisions of the Petition of Right. He would allow no innovations in the Church. But he protested against the new doctrine that the House of

<small>The King's Declaration.</small>

---

[1] *Lords' Journals*, iv. 43 ; Contarini's Despatch, March 13/23. *Ven. MSS.*
[2] Declaration, March 10. *Parl. Hist.* ii. 492.

Commons might erect itself into a supreme tribunal, before which all Ministers of State, and even all Courts of Justice, were bound to give account. As to Tonnage and Poundage, it had always been enjoyed by his predecessors from the first day of their reign. His father had collected it for a year before it had been granted by Parliament. It was clear to him therefore that the Commons had no right to construe a formal and friendly act of acknowledgment into an authority to transfer the whole government of England into their hands.

Of course there was an answer to all this. Formal or not, the grant of Tonnage and Poundage by Parliament signified that the government rested upon the co-operation of King and Parliament. If it was a new thing for the Commons to claim supreme power without the King, it was also a new thing for the King to claim supreme power without consulting the wishes of the nation. The old order had given way. It was not in the nature of things to eliminate the House o Commons from the constitution without effecting corresponding changes in every direction. A King without a Parliament would be quite different from a King with a Parliament. He would glide without a check down the easy path which leads through arbitrary power to despotism, and through despotism to anarchy. No doubt Charles did not distinctly acknowledge to himself that he had resolved never to call a Parliament again. But he had made up his mind to exact conditions which no English Parliament would ever again yield. The time had gone by when a House of Commons could be content with respectfully watching for the word of command from the throne, not because the members were more unruly than they had been fifty years before, but because the King was utterly careless of the course of public opinion. Elizabeth had controlled her Parliaments because she embodied that opinion better than they did. Charles would, in the end, be controlled by his Parliaments because they represented that opinion better than he did. He had indeed a work to do to guide that opinion, to prevent it from degenerating into mob-government either in Parliament or in the streets. It was his misfortune to think it possible to fulfil this duty by placing himself in opposition to the current of contemporary sentiment. He did not appeal to the nation against the House of Commons. He bade the nation to keep silence whilst he moulded it into the shape which seemed best to himself.

On the 17th of March a series of questions was put to the prisoners. It now appeared that they were not all alike prepared to carry their opposition to extremes. Valentine indeed firmly refused to answer any charge founded on acts done in Parliament. Coryton was less firm. He acknowledged that it was 'fit to suffer by paying' Tonnage and Poundage rather 'than to do those things that might be worse.'[1] Before long he made his submission, and was at once released, and Heyman soon afterwards satisfied the Court that he too might safely be allowed his liberty.

Selden, who was examined on the following day, had still less the temperament of a martyr than Coryton or Heyman. Intellectually audacious, he needed the applause of a favouring audience to inspire him to resist authority. He boldly assured his examiners that he was in absolute ignorance of all that had passed on the eventful morning. He had never moved that Eliot's paper should be read by the clerk. He had

---

[1] Interrogatories and Examinations, March 17. *S. P. Dom.* cxxxviii. 87, 88, 89.

only made a motion in order to help on the adjournment of the House in compliance with the King's wishes. If he had understood Eliot's speech, 'he would have absolutely dissented from him.' The falsehood was so unblushing that it can hardly be reckoned as a falsehood at all. He could never for an instant have expected to be believed. All he meant was to intimate that he had no intention of allowing himself to be made a victim for any opinion whatever.[1] He deeply felt his separation from his books and his pen, and he was anxious to recover the use of them as soon as possible.[2]

And of Eliot.

If Eliot was weak where Selden was strong, he was strong where Selden was weak. He never peered forward into the gloom of the future in anxious watching for the new ideas of toleration and liberty. But he was not the man to flinch before danger. To every question put he had but one reply to give. "I refuse to answer, because I hold that it is against the privilege of the House of Parliament to speak of anything which was done in the House."[3]

Charles's feeling towards Eliot.

No wonder the whole wrath of Charles was discharged upon Eliot. To Charles, as his Attorney General expressed himself in a subsequent case, Parliament was 'a great court, a great council, the great council of the King.' But the Houses were 'but his council, not his governors.'[4] Eliot claimed for Parliament an independent position, free except in the

[1] Mr. Forster (*Sir J. Eliot*, iii. 249) doubts the correctness of these answers because 'the alleged result of Selden's examination is not reconcilable either with his former speeches or with his tone afterwards.' Probably Mr. Forster contented himself with the abstract in Mr. Bruce's Calendar. The original examination (*S. P. Dom.* cxxxiv. 8) is signed by Selden, and his signature is attested by the Privy Councillors present.
[2] Selden to Apsley, March 30. *S. P. Dom.* ccxxxix. 78.
[3] *Ibid.* cxxxiv. 7.
[4] Heath's speech against Leighton, p. 9. *Camden's Miscellany*, vol. vii.

specified cases of treason, felony, or breach of the peace, from any authority whatever. The whole conflict between Crown and Parliament appeared to be summed up in this duel between two men, of whom one was armed to the teeth, and the other was a defenceless captive at his feet.

To Charles, Eliot was but an ambitious demagogue who must be punished in order that the Commonwealth might have peace. Eliot, he knew, did not stand alone. Men of the highest rank, the Earl of Lincoln, Lord Rochford, Lord St. John, and many others were flocking to the Tower to express their sympathy with him in his sufferings.[1] A Proclamation issued on March 27th bore the impress of Charles's angry feeling. He spoke of Eliot as 'an outlawed man, desperate in mind and fortune.' "And whereas," he continued, "for several ill ends the calling again of a Parliament is divulged, however we have shewed by our frequent meeting with our people our love to the use of Parliaments; yet the late abuse having for the present driven us unwillingly out of that course, we shall account it presumption for any to prescribe any time unto us for Parliaments, the calling, continuing, and dissolving of which is always in our own power, and we shall be more inclinable to meet in Parliament again when our people shall see more clearly into our intents and actions, when such as have bred this interruption shall have received their condign punishment, and those who are misled by them and by such ill reports as are raised in this occasion, shall come to a better understanding of us and themselves."[2]

The Proclamation breathed nothing but the fiercest indignation. Charles had no thought that amongst

---

[1] Apsley to Dorchester, March 20. *S. P. Dom.* cxxxix. 19.
[2] Proclamation, March 27. *Rymer*, xix. 62.

the wild deeds and wilder words of the past session there might be something which it would be well for him to lay to heart. There was no bending forward to meet his people half way, no sympathetic eye to detect the true causes of their complaints. He alone stood upon the rock. He alone could afford to wait. His subjects might come to him. He would never go to them.

It was Charles's fixed determination to inflict severe punishment upon Eliot. It was the business of the Crown lawyers to consider how he was to be reached in accordance with the forms of the law. In the meanwhile Weston was hard put to it to find a remedy for the emptiness of the exchequer. The subsidies voted in the preceding session were more than swallowed up by the payment of debts contracted in the war. Nor was the war itself at an end. English commerce had long been liable to the ravages of Dunkirk privateers and of French cruisers. Then had come the strife about the customs duties. The refusal to allow the legality of Tonnage and Poundage was met by a prompt order that all persons declining to pay the duties were to be imprisoned until his Majesty should direct otherwise, 'or that they be delivered by order of law.'[1] The Judges were still to be the arbitrators between the King and his subjects. It was easier to enforce obedience than to bring about a revival of trade. Merchants held back from buying and selling, and if any goods were brought into the Custom House at all, the owners were hooted by the crowd outside as traitors to their country.[2] A deputation from the Merchant Adventurers, the great Company which had in its hands the exportation of cloth, was summoned before the Council. The merchants who composed it

[1] *Council Register*, March 7.
[2] Contarini's Despatch, March $\frac{20}{30}$. *Ven. MSS.*

were asked why exportation had ceased. At first they made excuses. They were afraid of pirates. The markets were glutted. At last they spoke plainly. They were afraid of the Protestation of the House of Commons. Personally, at least, they had laid themselves open to a sharp retort. Manchester reminded them that they carried on the most lucrative part of their trade, the exportation of undressed and undyed cloths, in direct defiance of a parliamentary statute which had been suspended in their favour by an act of prerogative. In the end they were told to summon a full Court of the Company, and to submit the King's wishes to its consideration.

The Court was held, and the merchants were asked whether they would ship cloths or not. Not a hand was held up in the affirmative. The Council then turned to the Dutch merchants settled in London, in the hope that they would be less regardful of the Resolutions of an English House of Commons. The Dutch merchants, however, refused to separate their interests from those of their neighbours. "We shall be much degenerate," they replied, "if we go about to betray the liberties of the English nation."[1] In London the resistance was general, and nearly the whole trade of the kingdom was concentrated in London. So angry was the King at this passive opposition, that he thought of dissolving the Merchant Adventurers' Company in order to substitute for it a body composed of noblemen and courtiers who would make no difficulty about paying the duties.[2]

The King's exchequer did not suffer alone. It was calculated that there were in England 200,000 persons depending on the cloth trade.[3] The weavers in Essex

---

[1] *Tanner MSS.* lxxi. fol. 1.
[2] Joachimi to the States-General, April $\frac{2}{12}$, *Add. MSS.* 17,677 M. fol. 336.
[3] *Salvetti's Newsletter*, April $\frac{16}{26}$.

were thrown out of work. The Council interfered to mitigate the worst consequences of the stoppage of trade. The adjoining parishes were ordered to contribute to the relief of the poor in the villages in which distress prevailed. A proclamation was issued forbidding the export of corn, whilst at the same time some rioters who had rifled a vessel laden with grain at Maldon were put down with a strong hand. But the knot of the difficulty was in London, not in Essex, and one body of merchants after another was summoned before the Council, to be entreated or threatened to take the goods off the weavers' hands.[1]

There were indeed some shrewd heads who perceived that men who lived by trade would not persist in ruining themselves for the sake of a principle. But such was not the general feeling. "The obstinacy," said a letter-writer of the day, "lies not only in the merchant's breast, but moves in every small vein through the kingdom."[2] In the beginning of May there was a slight improvement. " I have ever said," wrote Williams, " that the merchants would be weary of this new habit of statesmen they had put on, and turn merchants again by that time they heard from their factors that their storehouses began to grow empty. God send those men more wit who, living in a monarchy, rely upon the democracy."[3]

The soreness caused by this prolonged resistance shewed itself in the punishment inflicted by the Star Chamber upon Chambers. Eight months before, he had told the Council that ' the merchants were in no part of the world so screwed and wrung as in England, and that in Turkey they have more encouragement.' The con-

[1] *Council Register,* April 18, 29; May 12, 22, 23.
[2] *Notes on Trade,* April 6. Lake to Vane, April 20. *S. P. Dom.* cxl. 24; cxli. 10.
Williams to Dorchester, May 5. *S. P. Dom.* cxlii. 19.

stitution of the Star Chamber had been admirably adapted for the purposes for which it had been used in the days of the Tudor sovereigns. Composed of the two Chief Justices and the whole of the Privy Council, it brought the highest legal and the highest political capacity to bear upon cases in which the offenders were too powerful to be reached by the ordinary courts, or in which the evidence was too complicated to be unravelled by the skill of an ordinary jury. It had thus become a tribunal constantly resorted to as a resource against the ignorance or prejudices of a country jury, much in the same way as a special jury is applied to in our own days.[1] In such investigations it showed itself intelligent and impartial. In political trials, however, impartiality could hardly be expected. Every member of the Court, with the exception of the two Chief Justices, was also a Privy Councillor. The persons who were cited as defendants were invariably persons who in some way or another had given offence to the Privy Council, and the great majority of the members of the Court were therefore in reality parties to the dispute which they were called upon to decide.

CHAP. III.

1629. May 6.

Before such a Court, Chambers had no chance of escape. But there was a difference of opinion as to the extent of the punishment to be inflicted. The two Chief Justices, Hyde and Richardson, would have been content with a fine of 500*l*. The two Bishops, Neile and Laud, would not be satisfied with less than 3,000*l*. The fine was at last fixed at 2,000*l*., and to this was added—the Chief Justices alone dissenting—imprisonment until the fault committed had been duly acknowledged.

Sentence of Chambers.

Chambers refused to allow that he had committed

He refuses to acknow-

---

[1] We are so apt to think of the Star Chamber simply as a Court employed upon State Trials, that it requires a strong effort of the imagination to grasp the fact that the great majority of cases before it were owing to the action of private prosecutors.

any fault at all. In vain a form of submission prepared by the Court was offered to him for signature. "All the above contents and submission," he wrote at the foot of it, "I, Richard Chambers, do utterly abhor and detest as most unjust, and never till death will acknowledge any part thereof." Then followed a string of Scripture texts denouncing those who refused to execute judgment and justice, and who were ready to make a man an offender for a word."[1]

CHAP. III.
1629. May 6. ledge his offence.

Chambers was not content with the choice of imprisonment rather than submission. In order to force on a legal decision upon the main point at issue, he brought an action in the Exchequer for the recovery of his goods against the officers of the customs by whom they had been seized.[2] He even made application to the same Court to invalidate the Star Chamber decree against himself on various grounds, of which the most important was that the Court had exceeded the statutory powers conferred upon it in the reign of Henry VII.

Brings an action against the Custom House officers.

The question of the legality of the levy of Tonnage and Poundage by prerogative alone was not one to be decided in a hurry. But there was time before the Long Vacation to reduce the practical grievance of the merchants to the lowest possible point. A quantity of their goods sufficient to serve as a security for the ultimate payment of the duty was retained in the Custom House by order of the Court of Exchequer. The rest of the

June 23. The greater part of his goods restored.

June 25.

---

[1] *State Trials*, iii. 374.

[2] There are two actions traceable, Chambers *v.* Dawes &c., and The Attorney-General *v.* Chambers. The answer of Dawes &c. is dated May 12, and Chambers's answer is dated June 22. I presume, therefore, that Chambers brought his action first. *Exchequer Bills and Answers, Charles I.,* Nos. 264, 236.

property which had been seized was restored to its owners.[1]

The consideration of Chambers's objection to the jurisdiction of the Star Chamber was also postponed. It was not likely that the Barons of the Exchequer would seriously entertain it. It had long been held by lawyers, as it is held by lawyers at this day, that the jurisdiction of the Star Chamber was extended, not created, by the statute of Henry VII. But the decision was thrown over to Michaelmas Term.[2]

Question of the jurisdiction of the Star Chamber.

It is impossible to overrate the service rendered to the nation by such men as Chambers. No doubt faults had been committed on both sides in the political struggle. But when once the wearer of the crown insisted on standing alone without responsibility to anyone, it was necessary to raise a protest against a theory of government which could never be admitted unless Englishmen were to degenerate into that servitude into which most of the nations of the Continent had sunk in order to escape from the still more terrible evils of aristocratic anarchy.

Service rendered by Chambers.

At the time, Chamber's sturdy resolution appeared to be thrown away. But it is not by its immediate result that such conduct as his can be judged. The habit of firm but legal resistance to hardships which are permitted or supported by the opinion of those who hold the reins of government in their hands is one of those precious possessions of a race which every member of it is bound to defend to the uttermost. Chambers had not the tongue or the brain of Selden; but he

---

[1] The amount demanded from Chambers was 364*l*. 2*s*. 2½*d*. on goods valued at 7,282*l*. 0*s*. 8*d*., or almost exactly 5 per cent. *Exchequer Orders and Decrees,* June 23.

[2] *State Trials,* iii. 376.

knew what Selden never learned, that England required those who could suffer for its rights, as well as those who could defend them in argument.

CHAP. III.
1629.

April. Case of Eliot and the other Members of the Commons.

In the main, the position taken by Chambers was the same as that taken by Eliot. But Eliot was for the present concerned not with the general question of parliamentary taxation, but with the special question of the privileges necessary to enable the House of Commons to hold its own against the claim of the Crown to be the originator of taxation. It had been possible for the Star Chamber to make short work with Chambers. It was necessary for the Government to make sure of its ground before it could deal as it wished with Eliot.

Opinion of the Judges.

The first thing to be done was to obtain the opinion of the Judges. The Petition of Right had strengthened the hands of the Judges as arbitrators between the King and his subjects. But it had not converted them into warm admirers of the doctrine of the supremacy of Parliament. The dismissal of Chief Justice Crew had doubtless not been without its effect in lowering the tone of the Bench, and his successor, Chief Justice Hyde, had neither energy nor acquirements to compensate for the irregularity of his elevation. Richardson, Chief Justice of the Common Pleas, had received promotion on account of his connexion with Buckingham, whilst Chief Baron Walter enjoyed a high reputation as a sound lawyer and an honest man. Whether honest or not, the Judges were now under special temptations to look askance upon the House of Commons. In the last session their authority had been called in question as much as the authority of the Crown, and the ruling of the Barons of Exchequer in the case of customs had been treated with special contempt.

The Chief Justice and the Chief

In spite of all this, however, it was not likely that the Judges would act with precipitation. Their legal training would serve to guard them against that, and there is no reason to doubt that they wished to take their position seriously, and to decide as fairly as they were able to do in such a case. It was not without hesitation that the two Chief Justices and the Chief Baron answered a series of questions propounded to them by Heath.[1] The extent of Parliamentary privilege had never been reduced to a fixed rule, and there would naturally be a wide difference of opinion on the subject between the members of the Privy Council and the members of the House of Commons.

The case put by the Attorney General was a double one. In the first place, he held that in the week of adjournment before March 2, there had been a conspiracy to publish false statements against Privy Councillors or, in plain language, against Weston. In the second place, he held that as soon as the King's command to adjourn had been delivered by the Speaker, the House had been legally adjourned, and that all that had taken place afterwards was of the nature of a riot. In this way he did his best to steer clear of an examination of the full extent of Parliamentary privilege. He laid his charges at times when the House was either not actually sitting or might be held not to be legally sitting.

From the answers of the Judges it is evident that they took much the same view of the question as Heath

Chap. III.
1629. April. Baron consulted.

The Attorney General's case.

The answer of the Judges.

---

[1] Two sets of questions have been printed, the one in *Rushworth*, i. 662; the other in the *State Trials*, iii. 235, and 238, *Note*. Mr. Forster treats them as mere variations, and Mr. Bruce seems to have been of the same opinion, as he has calendared the MSS. of both forms under the same date, April 27. I feel no doubt that they are quite distinct. The form in the *State Trials* which is taken from Nalson is said to contain the answer to questions put to 'the three Chief Judges.' From *S. P. Dom.* cxli. 45, we find that the three Judges asked 'that their opinions might not be published 'but by consent and conference with the other Judges.' Rushworth's form contains answers from all the Judges, and is therefore doubtless subsequent to that given in the *State Trials*.

VOL. I. I

had taken. They held that the King's ordinary right of inflicting punishment was limited by the privileges of Parliament. But they did not hold that the House of Commons had the right of declaring itself to be possessed of any privileges it might think good to claim. It was the business of the Judges to examine the precedents upon which such claims were based, and to hinder encroachments upon the authority of the Crown. Hence the answers to the questions put were framed in a spirit of true judicial caution. A conspiracy to publish false and scandalous rumours against the Privy Council or any of its members, 'not to the end to question them in a legal or Parliamentary way, but to bring them into hatred of the people and the Government into contempt,' would be punishable out of Parliament; but it would be necessary to examine the whole of the circumstances of the special case before it was possible to pronounce what the nature of the offence had been. On the second point the Judges were of opinion that the power of adjournment was in the King's hands, but it must be exercised in accordance with the precedents of the House. If, however, any should tumultuously oppose it further or otherwise than the privileges of the House would warrant, it would be a great contempt.

In later times it has been wisely decided that it is not expedient that the Judges should act as legal advisers of the Crown. In Charles's reign they were regarded as the King's counsellors, whose opinions he might obtain in all cases of difficulty. The natural impatience of the King to obtain an answer in accordance with his wishes was likely to come into collision with the natural desire of the Judges to refrain from giving a decisive opinion on a point which had not been fully argued before them.

Charles was anxious, as he afterwards said, that his Judges should not answer him in riddles. He sent two further questions, the replies to which might save him from the terrible disaster of a defeat in open court. He wanted to know at once what would be 'the nature of the offence' if a conspiracy were fully proved. He wanted also to know whether any privilege whatever could 'warrant a tumultuous proceeding.'

CHAP. III.
1629.

The three Judges were not to be beaten from their position; but they suggested that, before their replies were acted on, it would be well that all their brethren should be consulted in a body.

The twelve Judges were therefore convened on April 25. To Heath's questioning they gave much the same answers as had been given before by the Chief Justices and the Chief Baron. They were further of opinion that it would be proper to proceed in the Star Chamber against the prisoners; but the form of proceeding ought to be such as not to deny the incriminated persons the use of counsel. Only after a full argument would it be possible to decide finally what the extent of Parliamentary privilege really was.

April 25-28. All the Judges consulted.

Whilst Heath was making preparations for acting on this advice, he was surprised by an unexpected move on the part of the prisoners. Whether their actions in Parliament were punishable or not, it was clear to the seven prisoners who remained in the Tower after the liberation of Coryton and Heyman that they were fairly entitled to bail. Six of the number accordingly, Selden, Valentine, Holles, Strode, Hobart,[1] and Long applied to the Court of King's Bench for a writ of *Habeas corpus*. Eliot took no part in the demand, thinking, perhaps, that the Judges would be more likely to give fair consideration to the application if he were not concerned in it.

May 6. The prisoners apply for a *Habeas corpus*.

[1] Hobart's name is omitted in the usual accounts of the matter. But the *Rule Book of the King's Bench* shows that he joined the others.

1629.
May 7.
The cause of committal expressed.

The application was made on May 6, the day on which Chambers was being sentenced in the Star Chamber. It was held by the Government that it was not bound by the Petition of Right to express the cause of committal till a *Habeas corpus* had been actually demanded, and the original warrant had therefore given no reason for the imprisonment beyond the King's pleasure. A fresh warrant was now issued, stating the ground of committal to be notable contempts against the King and his Government, and stirring up of sedition in the State. The next step to be taken by the prisoners' counsel would be to convince the Judges that the offence so named was a bailable one.

Heath's information in the Star Chamber.

The cause expressed was somewhat vaguely given. All reference to the existence of such a body as Parliament was carefully avoided. In the information exhibited by Heath in the Star Chamber on the same day, it was impossible to avoid all mention of Parliament. But as little was said about it as possible. Heath took his stand upon the conspiracy to publish slanderous rumours, in order to bring the Government into disrepute. The Attorney General waived, in his public information, the question of the King's right to enforce an adjournment which he had mooted in his private application to the Judges, and he contrived to represent the tumult as an offence against the House as well as against the King, by alleging that, but for the machinations of the prisoners, the majority of the Commons would have been ready to adjourn.

It was possible that when Heath came to argue his case he would find that he had only escaped one difficulty to land himself in another. He would first have to prove that the conspiracy had a real existence. He would then have to prove the falsehood of Eliot's deliberate statement that whatever he had said against

Weston had been said with a view to a formal impeachment. The defendants, however, saved him the trouble of marshalling his evidence. They repudiated the jurisdiction of the Court entirely. Of the pleas put in Selden's was the longest and most comprehensive.[1] The great lawyer was himself again. It was one thing to plead in due professional form. It was another thing to be brought face to face with Privy Councillors in a cell in the Tower. Going to the heart of the question, he asserted boldly, what Heath had abstained from denying, that the Royal command did not adjourn the House, and that all that had been done till the doors were thrown open, must therefore be considered as having been done in full Parliamentary session, and as covered by privilege of Parliament.

There was no avoiding this question any more. It was referred to the two Chief Justices and the Chief Baron for their opinion. The point of law was argued in their presence. But they could not bring themselves to take upon their shoulders the responsibility of giving a hasty decision. When June 6 arrived, the day on which their answer was expected, the Judges asked for further delay. They said that they had still many precedents to consult.[2]

The King was too impatient to be satisfied. He sent for all the Judges, and asked them one by one what their opinion was. The answer made has not been pre-

---

[1] *Parl. Hist.* ii. 507. *S. P. Dom.* cxliii. 4–13.

[2] Heath to Conway, June 4. *S. P. Dom.* cxliv. 37. Gresley to Pickering, June 10. *Court and Times*, ii. 17. I have no doubt that the arguments mentioned in the former letter were delivered before the Judges. Mr. Forster speaks of them as arguments in the Star Chamber. It does not seem that the case was ever argued in the Star Chamber at all. The Judges had to consider whether the prisoners could be made to answer in that Court, 'off de gevangen parlementslieden gehouden syn te rechte te staen in de Sterre Chamber.' Joachimi to the States General, *Add. MSS.* 17,677, M. fol. 358 b.

served, but it seems that seven out of the twelve replied in a way which did not respond to the hopes and wishes of the King.¹

June 5. Littleton demands bail for the prisoners.

Whilst the Judges had been taking time to consider whether the general case came under the jurisdiction of the Star Chamber or not, the Court of King's Bench had been listening to arguments on the prisoners' demand for bail. On the 5th, Littleton urged on behalf of the prisoners, that the sedition and contempt of which they were charged did not constitute treason, and that there was therefore nothing to interfere with the taking of bail in the ordinary course.²

June 9. Selden demands judgment.

The heads of Littleton's argument had been furnished by Selden. It seems to have made great impression upon the Attorney General, as he asked for time to consider his reply. As he was not ready on the 9th, Selden demanded an immediate decision. "Will you bail a seditious priest," said Strode, with bitter reference to the affair of the Clerkenwell Jesuits, "though not seditious Parliament-men, as we be charged to be?"

June 13. Heath's reply.

On the 13th Heath at last replied. He began by casting a slur upon the Petition of Right. The first return, he said, would in former times have been held sufficient 'when due respect and reverence were given to Government.' But though Heath had no praise to bestow on the Petition, he was quite right in arguing that its conditions had been satisfied. A cause had been specified for the information of the Judges. It was for them to decide whether the offence was bailable or not. The Petition was silent as to the nature of

¹ Gresley to Pickering, June 10. *Court and Times,* ii. 19. *Life of D'Ewes,* i. 414. The only names of the seven which have reached us are those of Denham, Yelverton, and Hutton.
² *State Trials,* iii. 241, 252.

a bailable offence, and the Judges would therefore have to decide the point by the law as it had stood before. Heath then proceeded to argue that the Judges had often refused bail to prisoners committed by the King, and that, at all events, the Judges might exercise their discretion, and refuse bail to persons who were likely to do harm by spreading the contagion of sedition in the country. If they doubted whether the release of any particular prisoners would be dangerous or not, they ought to consult the King.

CHAP. III.
1629.
June 13.

The old difficulty which had occupied so large a space in the debates of the previous year cropped up once more in an unexpected manner. Somewhere or another there must exist in every State a discretionary power to modify and even to overrule the precepts of positive law. Parliament in 1628 had snatched that power from the King. Heath now offered it to the Judges on condition that they would exercise it in the maintenance of the King's authority. The judicial instinct of the Judges repelled the dangerous gift. It was the function of their office simply to declare the law. When Littleton asked them to bail the prisoners because the particular offence laid to their charge was legally bailable, he spoke in language which they could understand. When Heath asked them to retain the prisoners in custody because it was inexpedient to set them free, he spoke in language which would be comprehensible in a political assembly, but which was out of place when addressed to the Judges.

Where is discretionary power to be placed?

The Judges felt themselves to be in a great strait. They did not believe that they would be doing right in refusing bail. But they did not wish to fly in the King's face. They wrote to the King, informing him that they were bound by their oaths to admit the prisoners to bail, and suggesting to him that he might

The Judges write to the King.

have the credit of the act by sending them directions to do so. In reply they received a summons to Greenwich, where they were warned not to decide on so vital a point without consulting the Judges of the other Courts. The other Judges naturally refused to give an opinion on a question which had not been argued before them, and as time was slipping away, it was possible that the Long Vacation might come before any judicial decision had been openly pronounced.[1]

Charles had evidently made up his mind that if it came to the worst, he would not allow the scruples of the Judges to stand in his way. Yet it was not in his nature to look fairly in the face the obstacle which had risen in his path. He did not wish openly to trample upon the guardians of the law. He did not wish to fall back upon State expediency as upon something far higher than legal precedent. He was anxious if possible to act through the Judges, and would wrap himself in the proud consciousness that the voice of the Judges was the voice of the law itself.

His first step was to assure himself of the safe custody of three of the prisoners who had not been originally committed to the Tower. Long, Hobart, and Strode were removed to the strong fortress, within the walls of which the King could count on the fidelity of the keeper, Sir Allen Apsley. There they were to remain 'until they were delivered by due course of law.'[2]

By due course of law Long, Hobart, and Strode were to have appeared in court on the following day to receive an answer to their application for bail. When the time came for their appearance, the Court was informed by the keeper of the prison from which they

---

[1] *Whitelocke's Memorials*, 14.
[2] *Controlment Roll, King's Bench*, 5 Charles I. Membr. 65.

had been taken, that it was no longer in his power to produce them.

There have been Judges in England who would have been roused to indignation by the slight cast upon their office. But Hyde was not a Coke, and the Court contented itself with the assertion that the prisoners being absent, they could not be bailed, delivered, or remanded.

Charles felt that some justification was necessary. In an obscure and incoherent letter, which painfully betrayed the uncertainty of his mind, he explained to the Judges of the King's Bench that he had kept back the prisoners because they had behaved insolently on a former occasion. Further, as no decision had yet been come to on the legality of the Star Chamber proceedings, he did not think the presence of the prisoners was necessary. Nevertheless, to shew his respect to the Court, he would allow Selden and Valentine to attend them on the following day.[1]

Scarcely had this strange letter been despatched when Charles was warned by Heath that the Court was not likely to take the hint which it was intended to convey. If Selden and Valentine appeared in court, wrote the Attorney General, they would assuredly be bailed. Apsley must therefore be distinctly ordered not to produce them. Charles at once gave the order suggested, and wrote a second letter to the Judges, telling them that he had changed his mind. None of the prisoners should be produced till he had reason to believe that they would make a better demonstration of their modesty and civility than on the last occasion.[2]

---

[1] The King to the Judges of the King's Bench, June 24. *Rushworth*, i. 680.

[2] Heath to Dorchester; the King to Apsley; the King to the Judges of the King's Bench. *S. P. Dom.*, cxlv. 40, 41, 42.

1629.
June 25.
No bail allowed.
June 26.

When the Court met on the following day no prisoners appeared. The Judges accepted the check without remonstrance. On the 26th the term came to an end, and the Court contented itself with directing that the prisoners should be produced after the Long Vacation. This time Eliot's name is found on the list of applicants for bail. It would seem that though he had taken no steps to share in his comrades' chances of freedom, he was ready to share in their misfortune, now that there was no longer any risk of compromising them by his presence.[1]

Charles's conduct to the Judges.

Charles had been scrupulous to observe the Petition of Right in the letter, but he had not observed its spirit. He had sought to entrust the arbitration between himself and his subjects to the Judges, and on the first occasion that the Judges decided against him, he set aside their decision by a subterfuge. Perhaps it was inevitable that he should refuse to submit. A modern Parliament under similar circumstances would have overruled the Judges by suspending the Habeas Corpus Act. It is a clear gain to the working of the constitution that overwhelming power should be placed in a political and not in a judicial body. It is also a clear gain that it should be placed in a body which is likely to exercise it as seldom as possible. Charles was neither in the position of an absolute King nor of an absolute Parliament. The traditions of the constitution forbade him from claiming to be the source of law. Yet the traditions of the constitution justified him in claiming the supreme regulative power in the nation. True to his nature, he concealed from himself the real meaning of his act by the trick in which it was enveloped. His own position was weakened by the manœuvre. He had humiliated the Judges, and if he

[1] *Rule Book of the King's Bench.*

humiliated the Judges his subjects were not likely to respect them. He could no longer look to them to break the collision between himself and his Parliament, if ever a Parliament should meet again.

CHAP. III.
1629. June.

The arrival of the Long Vacation left every constitutional question unsettled. In Charles's relations with foreign Powers equal uncertainty prevailed. Common sense, it might be thought, would have convinced him that his only chance of success at home lay in complete abstention from entanglements with foreign states. It was impossible for him to lay down the law on the Rhine or the Danube without the support of an united nation. It was equally impossible for him to lay down the law at Westminster if he was engaged in war or in the preparations for war. Weston saw all this clearly. Charles did not see it at all. He fancied that because he was able to send Eliot to the Tower his word would be equally powerful at Paris or Madrid. He did not even perceive the necessity of interesting himself in the objects for which the nations of the Continent were striving, and of waiting patiently till his own special grain could be garnered in the general harvest. To recover the Palatinate was the one object which he had set before him, and it was a matter of indifference to him whether he recovered it by the aid of France or of Spain, of Protestant or Catholic. He was treating more or less openly with Richelieu, with Olivares, with Christian IV., and with Gustavus Adolphus at one and the same time. Was it to be wondered at if he failed to secure the confidence of any of them?

Charles's foreign policy.

The spring of 1629 was a time of crisis in Germany. In the preceding summer Wallenstein had been beaten back from the walls of Stralsund. The assistance given to the citizens by Sweden and Denmark had

German affairs.

enabled them to resist the master of the most numerous and well appointed army which had been seen on the Continent since the days of the Romans. The King of Sweden and the King of Denmark drew near to one another in spite of ancient rivalry and personal jealousy. Yet though Wallenstein had failed at Stralsund, his power still seemed irresistible. Krempe had fallen, and Glückstadt was menaced; and if Glückstadt and Stralsund were overcome, Germany would be at the feet of the Emperor. Ships would be built and equipped, and neither Copenhagen nor Stockholm would be safe.

March 19. The Edict of Restitution.

Then it was that the Emperor and the Catholic Electors committed a fault as portentous in its consequences as the Revocation of the Edict of Nantes was to be in future years. The Edict of Restitution, signed nine days after the dissolution of the English Parliament, swept into the hands of the Catholic clergy the Bishoprics and Abbeys of Northern Germany which had long been in possession of Protestant laymen. The Protestant populations of these ecclesiastical lands knew that their religion was at stake. The Protestant Princes around knew that the provision which they had been accustomed to find in these lands for their younger sons was snatched away from them, and that each one of the lost territories would be turned into a garrison held against them in the interests of the Emperor and his Church.

Charles's negotiations with Sweden and Denmark.

It might be a question whether Charles was able to interfere at all with profit on the Continent. But there could be no question that, if he was to interfere at all, it was only by a close alliance with the German Princes that he could hope to gain his ends.

Such a policy had a warm supporter in Sir Thomas

Roe. As ambassador at Constantinople he had been the constant correspondent of the exiled Elizabeth, had been made the confidant of all her hopes and schemes, and had done his best to carry them out so far as his influence allowed him. "Honest Tom," as she playfully called him, after consulting the Prince of Orange on the way, had returned to England in January, with little understanding of the political strife which had arisen during his long absence from home, but with an overflowing knowledge of Continental politics and a clear belief that England's true place was on the side of the Protestants of the world. At that time a good understanding between the King and the House of Commons was looked forward to at Court, and Roe had no difficulty in persuading the Privy Council to listen with approval to his urgent entreaty that forty ships and 6,000 men should be sent to the aid of the King of Denmark before March was over.[1] As, however, nothing could be finally settled till the result of the Session was known, Roe was allowed to visit the Hague once more to concert measures with his friends in Holland.

In the beginning of March Roe was once more in England. He found there Sir James Spens, the Scotchman who had been so often employed as a negotiator by Gustavus, and who had come to urge upon Charles the necessity of taking an active part in the war. He found, too, Parliament dissolved. Charles professed himself as ready as ever to help the King of Denmark. But at present he had not the means to do it. His uncle must have a little patience till he could put his affairs in order.[2]

---

[1] Contarini's Despatch, Feb. $\frac{6}{18}$. *Ven. MSS.* In publishing *Sir Thomas Roe's Mission* for the Camden Society, (*Miscellany*, vii.) I was not aware of this first visit to England.

[2] Dorchester to Anstruther, March 9. *S. P. Denmark.*

Chap. III.
1629.
Jan. French intervention in Italy.

Gustavus's plan was his old one of a Protestant alliance to hold head against the Emperor in Germany, whilst France undertook the conflict against Spain in Italy. Events appeared to be propitious to his undertaking. A disputed succession in the Duchies of Mantua and Montferrat had brought Spain and France into collision beyond the Alps without an actual declaration of war. Casale was besieged by a Spanish army in the name of the claimant who was favoured by Spain and the Emperor. In the name of the Duke of Nevers, the claimant favoured by France, Richelieu, carrying Lewis with him, scaled the Alps in the depth of winter, compelled the Duke of Savoy to separate himself from Spain, and to place Susa in French hands as a pledge of his submissiveness. The siege of Casale

March 5.

was raised. A limit was placed to Spanish predominance in Italy, as a limit had been placed to Wallenstein's predominance in Germany by the failure of the siege of Stralsund. In Italy as in Germany a centre of resistance was formed to a hard uncongenial domination. The ambassadors of the Italian Princes flocked to the camp of Lewis, proffering their friendship and their services.

April 14. Peace between France and England.

At Susa, the scene of Richelieu's triumph, the treaty was signed which put an end to the war between France and England. The principle that each Sovereign was to be free to settle his relations with his own subjects as he thought fit was tacitly accepted. Lewis put in no claim for the toleration of the English Catholics. Charles put in no claim for the better treatment of the French Huguenots. When Lewis learned from his sister that she was perfectly satisfied with her present household, it was impossible for him to press for the return of her French attendants.

The removal of the difficulties which stood in the

way of the treaty was publicly and deservedly ascribed to the efforts of the Venetian Ambassador Contarini. As might have been expected, he had relied much on the influence of the Queen. At a moment when she was looking forward to becoming a mother for the first time, it would have been hard for the husband to resist the entreaties of his wife. The peace was published in London on May 10. Henrietta Maria, proud of her work, came up from Greenwich to take part in the *Te Deum* which was to be sung at the Chapel at Somerset House in celebration of an event which gave her such peculiar reasons for rejoicing. The fatigue of the journey was too great for her, and soon after her return she was frightened by two dogs quarrelling in her presence. On the morning of the 13th she gave birth prematurely to an infant which lived only for two hours. For some time she was herself in great peril. The King was constantly at her bedside, waiting upon her with the tenderest affection during the time of her trial. If God pleased, he said to the physicians, he might have other children. But let them do all they could to save his wife.[1]

Henrietta Maria had looked upon the treaty of Susa merely as a reconciliation between her husband and her brother. Contarini had regarded it as the first step to an alliance against Spain. Charles was, however, still hankering after the promises which Spain was always ready to dispense. In February he had sent Sir Henry Vane to the Hague to ask the Prince of Orange and the States what they thought of the Spanish offers of peace. As might have been expected, they did not even think them worth listening to. They knew well that Spain was crippled by the loss of the treasure fleet,

---

[1] *Salvetti's Newsletter.* May $\frac{15}{25}$. Contarini to Zorzi, May $\frac{15}{25}$. *Ven. MSS.*

and that a portion of her forces would be diverted to the defence of Italy. Vane was accordingly sent back with an admonition to Charles to take part in the vigorous prosecution of the war.

How could Charles prosecute the war vigorously? The despatch urging the King of Denmark to patience was already on its way. Negotiations had long ago been commenced at Lübeck between Christian and the Emperor. Yet Christian had assured Charles's ambassador Anstruther that, if he could be certain of aid from England, he would continue the war. On May 2 he learned that he was to be fed by hopes, and he knew too well from the sad experience of Lutter that it was useless to depend on promises which Charles had not the means of fulfilling. He angrily told Anstruther that he 'wished of God he had known sooner what he might have expected.'[1] Ten days afterwards a treaty was signed at Lübeck. Christian received back his hereditary dominions, and abandoned the championship of German Protestantism. A small fleet which was being leisurely fitted out in the English ports was equipped too late to be of any avail.

The news which reached Charles from France seemed to be almost as bad as the news which reached him from Denmark. Richelieu was the last man in the world to throw himself into a policy of adventure. He contented himself with the success which he had acquired at Casale, and returned to France to complete the subjugation of the Huguenots. Rohan and the Protestants of Languedoc and the Cevennes were still in arms in the South. The King in person, with the Cardinal by his side, marched against the insurgents. On May 28 Privas was taken and treated with the utmost barbarity by the triumphant soldiery. Charles

[1] Anstruther to Dorchester, June 6. *S. P. Denmark.*

may well be excused if he suspected Richelieu of having taken advantage of his credulity to impose a religious tyranny upon the French Protestants. "I have made peace with France," he said to Contarini, "for the advantage of Christendom and to carry out my original designs for the public good." He added that he could not tell what the French were aiming at. The other day a French gentleman had repeated in his presence a list of the Huguenot towns which his master was assailing. "In short," said Charles, "he seemed to be telling me the best news in the world. I thought at first that he was joking, but when I found that he was serious, I listened with great patience without answering a word."

<small>CHAP. III.
1629.
May.</small>

Of all this the Spaniards were not slow to take advantage. Coloma had written from Flanders to his old friend Weston, holding out vague hopes of the restitution of the Palatinate.[1] He obtained permission for Rubens to visit England on an unavowed mission. No diplomatist could have been personally more welcome to Charles, who was never so happy as when he was arranging his pictures or discussing their beauties. Rubens had many illusions to disperse. He acknowledged that it would not be so easy to restore the Palatinate as Charles seemed to think. Only part of it was held by Spanish garrisons, and if those garrisons were removed, their place would be at once occupied by the troops of the Emperor and the League.[2]

<small>Coloma's letters to Weston.</small>

<small>May 27. Rubens in England.</small>

The statement made by Rubens was not the less disagreeable because it was true, and Charles, doubting whether he had anything to hope from France or Spain, turned once more an open ear to those who were

<small>Charles favours Gustavus and the Dutch.</small>

---

[1] Contarini's Despatch, May $\frac{15}{25}$, $\frac{May\ 29}{June\ 8}$. *Ven. MSS.* Weston to Coloma, $\frac{Feb.\ 24}{March\ 6}$. *Simancas MSS.* 2519.

[2] *Ibid.* June $\frac{5}{15}$. Salvetti's Newsletter, $\frac{May\ 29}{June\ 8}$.

VOL. I.　　　　　　　K

*1629.
June.*

*June 20.
Roe's mission to the Baltic.*

urging him to a strictly Protestant alliance. Gustavus was allowed to levy one regiment in England and another in Scotland.[1] The Dutch were permitted to take into their service soldiers for whom he had himself no further use.[2] He sent Roe on a diplomatic mission to the Baltic. It is true that he bound himself to nothing by it. The ambassador was to mediate a peace between Sweden and Poland, which would set Gustavus free to carry out in Germany the great enterprise which he was already meditating. But Roe carried with him no engagement to provide either men or money.

Course of Rubens's negotiation.

Before Roe left England he obtained a promise from Charles that he would come to no agreement with Spain without the consent of his friends and allies.[3] Charles, in fact, had taken fresh offence at the declaration of Rubens, that he had no authority to surrender any part of the Palatinate. Rubens had afterwards disgusted him by proposing a mutual cessation of arms between England and Spain, whilst each state was left free to assist its allies upon the Continent.[4] The Prince of Orange was at that time besieging the fortress of Hertogenbosch, one of the bulwarks of the Spanish Netherlands. Charles, in the presence of Rubens, expressed a hope that the siege might be successful. "Why," said the painter, "should your Majesty wish the triumph of my master's rebels?" "I found them," replied the King, "a free State. I do not know them as rebels. They are my friends, and I wish them to gain the victory in order that your master may become more moderate."[4] Rubens was told that Cottington would be sent as ambassador to treat for peace at

[1] Salvetti to Sacchetti, $\frac{May\ 29}{June\ 8}$.
[2] Joachimi to the States General, June $\frac{5}{15}$, $\frac{June\ 21}{July\ 3}$. *Add. MSS.* 17,677, fol. 357, 362.
[3] Contarini to the Ambassadors in France, June $\frac{19}{29}$. *Ven. MSS.*
[4] Contarini to Zorzi, June $\frac{8}{15}$, $\frac{11}{21}$, $\frac{June\ 26}{July\ 6}$. *Ibid.*

Madrid, but that the intention of the King of Spain to surrender the fortresses held by him in the Palatinate must first be distinctly declared.¹

CHAP. III.
1629.

Whilst Charles was in this mood the Marquis of Chateauneuf, the new French ambassador, arrived in England. He was able to announce that the Huguenots in the south of France had submitted to the King. No resistance to the Royal authority would be allowed. But toleration was to be the maxim of the State. Catholic and Protestant were to have nothing to fear from one another, that they might devote their energies to the defence, it might be to the aggrandisement, of their common country.

June 28. Pacification in France.

Chateauneuf was empowered to invite Charles to active co-operation against Spain. He soon discovered that nothing of the kind was to be expected. "I have orders," he said to Contarini, "to offer to England *carte blanche* for all that they wish to have done in Germany; but I find them so weak that I do not see how, as things stand, anything of importance can be done."²

June 28. Chateauneuf in England.

The very urgency of the French Ambassador must have startled Charles, and he was still more disgusted when Chateauneuf, at Holland's instigation, recommended him to call a Parliament, in order that he might declare war with some prospect of success. Spain, at any rate, did not ask him to join in a war or to summon a Parliament. Once more he turned to Rubens. "In September or October," he said to the Queen, "you will see a Spanish ambassador here."³ Weston plied him, as ever, with the argument

July. Charles turns to Spain.

---

¹ Rubens to Olivares, June 26/July 6. *Simancas MSS.* 2519.
² Despatch of Contarini and Soranzo, July 3/13. *Ven. MSS.* Chateauneuf's Instructions, May 10/20. *Aff. Etrangères,* xliii. 139.
³ Rubens to Olivares, July 13/23. *Simancas MSS.* 2519.

1629.

that unless he made peace he must summon a Parliament again. At last Charles took the step which he had long hesitated to take. On July 12 Rubens was able to forward the English demands in writing. Charles recognised the necessity of consulting others besides the King of Spain about the Palatinate. He would be content, he said, if Rubens would promise to do all good offices in his power with the Emperor and the Duke of Bavaria, and he hoped that those potentates would send ambassadors to Madrid to treat conjointly with his own. Yet he must have something more than a mere negotiation on which to depend. Philip must distinctly declare that whatever happened he would deliver up the fortresses which he himself held in the Palatinate.[1] Cottington, who had lately been appointed Chancellor of the Exchequer, was accordingly named ambassador to the King of Spain. On July 19 Charles announced his intention to the Council. He invited no opinion, and his tone was such that no one ventured to object.

July 9. Resolves to send Cottington to Madrid.

The immediate cause of the resolution thus taken was a fresh letter from Coloma to Weston. It was now arranged that Coloma should come to England as Philip's ambassador; but the real business of the negotiation was to be left to Cottington at Madrid.

July. Weston's antagonists at Court.

Chateauneuf saw clearly that his real antagonist was Weston. The Lord Treasurer was as unpopular at Court as he was in the country. The close-fisted guardian of the Exchequer kept a tight hold upon pensions, and pleaded in surly tones the emptiness of the Treasury to those who had incurred debts in the service of the King. Many a courtier cried out for a Parliament that he might dip his hand in the stream of

---

[1] Paper given to Rubens by Weston, enclosed in a letter from Rubens to Olivares, July $\frac{12}{22}$. *Simancas MSS.* 2519.

subsidies.[1] Rubens, himself no ascetic, was astonished at the vast expenditure of the Court. Carlisle and Holland distinguished themselves by the splendour of their hospitality. Not a few of the Lords in attendance upon the King followed their example with very insufficient revenues. The necessary result followed. "Therefore," wrote the artist, "public and private affairs are to be sold here for ready money."[2] All this craving discontent Chateauneuf hoped to mould to his uses by making the Queen the centre of an organisation which would receive the word of command from the Louvre.

Everything the ambassador saw led him to believe that with the Queen on his side he could hardly fail of success. Charles was still an ardent lover. He kissed his wife again and again in Chateauneuf's presence. "You do not see that at Turin," he said gaily, referring to the Queen's elder sister. "Nor at Paris either," he added in a lower tone, with a glance at the loveless wedlock of Lewis. Some councillors complained that the King was always in his wife's apartments. Except when he was hunting, it was impossible to speak to him. Yet he was excessively jealous of the supposition that he was under the Queen's influence. "I wish," he said to her one day, "that we could be always together, and that you could accompany me to the Council; but what would these people say if a woman were to busy herself with matters of government?" Chateauneuf thought that if the Queen would play her cards well she might lead her husband where she chose. But he could not persuade her to care for politics at all. She was too happy in the immediate present, too little capable at any time of a sustained

Relations between Charles and the Queen.

---

[1] Chateauneuf to Richelieu, $\frac{July\ 27}{Aug.\ 6}$. *Aff. Étrangères*, xliii. 204.
[2] Rubens to Olivares, July $\frac{10}{20}$. *Simancas MSS.* 2519.

1629.
May 7.
The Queen's priests.

effort, except when some personal object was at stake, to trouble herself with the combinations of statesmen.¹

Chateauneuf now tried to reach the Queen through her religious zeal. He proposed to establish in her household eight French Capuchins and a Bishop, and to get rid of the two Oratorians who had been in attendance since the expulsion of the French, one of whom, Father Philip, an Englishman, had acted as the Queen's Confessor. Chateauneuf found the King ready to give his wife all freedom in the exercise of her religion. He sometimes scolded her for staying in bed so long that she was unable to hear mass before noon. To the eight Capuchins he made no objection. But he would not hear of the Bishop. He would come to England, he said, in his episcopal habit, and would jostle with the bishops of the land. To the Queen he expressed his own personal objection. "Your mother," he said, "is sending you a governor. When he comes, do not let him enter your room as you allowed the Bishop of Mende to do. Let him approach you only at church and at dinner." The King of France, he told Chateauneuf, wanted to have two ambassadors in London, one for himself and another for the Queen.

If the King would not admit a Bishop, the Queen would not part with her confessor. Chateauneuf was forced to give way to her strongly expressed wishes, and to renounce for the present the hope of establishing the Capuchins in England, at least till the two Kings could come to terms on the subject of the Bishop.²

The Queen's need of money.

The Ambassador had therefore to engage the Queen against Weston in some other way. The sore point was at last found. Henrietta Maria was profuse in her

¹ Chateauneuf to Richelieu, July $\frac{19}{28}$, Aug. $\frac{17}{27}$, $\frac{\text{Aug. 31}}{\text{Sept. 10}}$. *Aff. Etrangères*, xliii. 195, 217, 249.

² *Chateauneuf's Despatches* are full of his negotiations on this subject from his arrival till his departure.

expenditure. "She is a bad housekeeper," said Charles of her in her presence. Weston, who found it hard enough to get money for any purpose, was driven to despair by the urgent need of satisfying the Queen's demands. Chateauneuf openly did his best to effect a reconciliation; but the quarrel served his purpose too well to be in reality disagreeable to him.[1]

By this time Charles was looking for an answer from Spain to his demand about the fortresses of the Palatinate. He waited in vain. He was told that when Cottington arrived at Madrid the English propositions would form a fitting subject of negotiation. They could not be discussed in England as a preliminary to his mission. Olivares declined to bind his hands beforehand. Charles struggled hard against this conclusion. He pleaded with Rubens that the places held by the Spaniards were of little importance to them, whilst his own reputation was deeply concerned in their recovery. But Olivares maintained an imperturbable silence, and Charles gave way. Cottington was to go to Madrid without any previous declaration from Philip. If he did not receive a satisfactory answer about the fortresses, he was to come away at once, and Charles was to be free to accept the overtures of France.

In Cottington Rubens had found an instrument ready to his hand. His good faith, he assured Olivares, could not be greater if he had been a Spanish Councillor of State. The minister of the King of England now joined the Fleming in urging Charles to offer a higher price for the Palatinate than a mere treaty of peace. Why should not England request the Dutch to come to terms with Spain by threatening to abandon them entirely to themselves, or even to take part against them if they persisted

[1] Chateauneuf to Richelieu, July 13/23. *Aff. Etrangères*, xliii. 125. Soranzo's Despatch, July 17/27. *Ven. MSS.*

CHAP. III.
1629.
Sept.

in carrying on the war? Charles gave way at last so far as to consent that when Cottington left for Madrid Sir Henry Vane should be sent back to the Hague in order to induce the States General to accept his arbitration.[1] Roe's negotiation, of which so much had been thought a few months before, was now entirely neglected, and Charles even left his ambassador to wander amongst the Baltic States without a single despatch to acquaint him of the turn which affairs were taking in England.

Continued resistance to the payment of Customs.

The treaty with France had done something to revive English trade. But the old difficulties were not at an end. To some extent, indeed, the prediction of those who had declared it impossible for the merchants long to desist from buying and selling had been realised. Many of them were now again passing goods through the Custom House; but there were many who were still obstinate, 'because,' as the new Venetian Ambassador Soranzo expressed it, 'they believe in their conscience that they will commit the greatest sin in surrendering their liberties.' The political struggle was carried on with all the instinctive resolution of a war of religion.

The Star Chamber prosecution of members of Parliament dropped.

The Government wisely resolved to leave the merchants to time and to the allurements of gain. The prosecution of the members of Parliament could not be so lightly abandoned. But the Star Chamber process was dropped in compliance with the wishes of the Judges. The great cause was to be removed to the King's Bench.

The scandal of calling the offending members before a Court mainly composed of Privy Councillors was therefore avoided. Charles would appeal to the ordinary guardians of the law to punish his assailants.

Sept. 9. Difficulties about bail.

He had not much cause to fear. The Judges were ready enough to carry out his wishes. The course to

[1] Rubens to Olivares, $\frac{\text{Aug. 23}}{\text{Sept. 2}}$, Sept. $\frac{11}{21}$. *Simancas MSS.* 2519. Instructions to Vane, Oct. 18. *S. P. Holland.*

be pursued in the question of bail was settled at a conference between Coventry, Manchester, and Dorchester, with the assistance of Heath. The first day of term on which the prisoners would be brought up in pursuance of the rule of the Court was October 9. It was now resolved to anticipate the day, to bring them up as soon as possible, and to take their bail for the remainder of the vacation on condition that they would give security for their good behaviour whilst at liberty; in other words, that they would engage not to make the Government unpopular by recounting their wrongs.[1]

This proposal was adopted by the Judges without difficulty. They were even prepared to go further. Not only would they offer the bail on the King's terms, but they would offer it as a matter of favour, not as a right to which the prisoners were legally entitled.[2] Even with this Charles was not satisfied. He required that if the prisoners once refused the grace offered them, they should not be allowed another chance unless they first asked his pardon. On this point, however, the Judges were firm. Hyde answered that the prisoners would not be so foolish as to reject the favour offered to them, yet, 'if they should be so gross,' and should afterwards repent of their folly, 'bailable they are by law.'

The King insisted. He sent his letter empowering the Judges to offer bail, but accompanied with a warning that if his grace was refused the prisoners should 'neither have their liberty by his letter or by other means till they had acknowledged their fault.'[3] The next morning they were admitted one by one before the Court. The bond for good behaviour was un-

[1] The King to the Judges of the King's Bench, Sept. 9. Heath to Dorchester, Sept. 10. *S. P. Dom.* cxlix. 37 ; i. 37.

[2] Hyde to Dorchester, Sept. 30. *S. P. Dom.* cxlix. 110.

[3] Dorchester to Hyde, Oct. 1 ; Hyde to Dorchester, Oct. 1 ; Dorchester to Hyde, Oct. 2. *S. P. Dom.* cl. 3, 4, 10.

doubtedly in the power of the Judges to demand. By the prisoners it was regarded as a deadly insult, for it was seldom if ever asked, except from keepers of disorderly houses, from women of profligate life, or from turbulent disturbers of the peace. One of the seven, Walter Long, after a quarter of an hour's resistance, accepted the terms at the urgent entreaty of his counsel. Not one of the others followed his example. When he found that he stood alone, he bitterly repented his weakness, complained that he had been circumvented, and entreated in vain to be sent back to share the imprisonment of his comrades.[1]

The Judges were in a difficulty. The 9th would quickly come, when they were legally bound to give bail if it was asked for, though they might persist in coupling their offer with the condition which had been rejected. The King had forbidden them to grant bail after the first refusal, till the prisoners had asked his pardon. Hyde supplicated Charles to revoke his decision,[2] and he and Whitelocke were ordered to wait on the King at Hampton Court.[3] They found him in a good humour. It is possible that he thought the chance that the prisoners would now give way was too slight to be taken into account. He always wished, he said, to comply with the opinion of his Judges as long as they did not speak in riddles. He would raise no further objection to the reappearance of the prisoners on the 9th.

When the 9th came the seven appeared at the bar. This time they all refused the terms offered. Long, his

---

[1] Narrative of Proceedings. *S. P. Dom.* cl. 85.
[2] Hyde to Dorchester, Oct. 4. *Ibid.* cl. 22.
[3] This interview is dated Sept. 30 by Rushworth (i. 682), but the letters which we have on that date and the following days seem incompatible with the date. After the 4th it is quite in its place. Besides, it accounts for the want of any answer to Hyde's letter of that date, all the rest of the correspondence being carefully preserved.

few days of unwelcome liberty having come to an end, briskly placed himself by the side of the others, and thus 'by yielding his body once more to prison, he set his mind at liberty.' The three puisne Judges tried their best to explain away the condition of bail as unimportant. Hyde alone threatened the prisoners with the consequences of their folly. If they did not accept the King's offer now they might, he told them, be left in prison, it might be for seven years.[1]

1629. Oct. 3. behaviour again refused.

Hyde was sick of it all. There was no dignity in the part he was called on to play to sustain him. Why, he asked Heath, impatiently, was any further trouble to be taken? Further proceedings were unnecessary. 'The best way were to dispose of them either where they now are or to other prisons at the King's pleasure, and there leave them as men neglected until their own stomachs came down, and not to prefer any information at all, they being now safe and so shall continue.' Heath would not hear of so high-handed a proceeding.[2] He had confidence in the strength of his own position, and he was not afraid to speak out the arguments in which he trusted in the face of a hostile world. He brought in his information against Eliot, Holles, and Valentine, those who had taken the principal part in the attack upon the Speaker.

Oct. 13. What is to come next?

Hyde might well shrink back. Events had conspired

---

[1] *Narrative. S. P. Dom.* cl. 85. *State Trials,* iii. 288.

[2] Heath to Dorchester, Oct. 13. *S. P. Dom.* cl. 53. Hyde's opinion can only be gathered from Heath's letter, from which the words in the text are given. Hyde's meaning is therefore left in obscurity. I suspect that he meant that as the Petition of Right had been obeyed, the cause of imprisonment had been shewn, and bail had been refused, the prisoners might be left where they were simply on the ground that they had refused to give bail. It seems incredible that a Chief Justice should argue, even in Hyde's position, that the punishment for their action in Parliament ought to be perpetual imprisonment without trial, unless there had been some quibble to fall back upon.

CHAP. III.

1629. Oct.

The Judges have to submit to the King.

to thrust forward the Judges into a position which it was impossible for them to hold. The storm of the political battle raged around them, and they were dragged forth to act as arbiters, where arbitration was impossible.[1] The Commons had spurned their decisions, and now the King, with more outward show of respect, waved away their claims to measure his political authority by the standard of legal precedents and maxims. It was so clear to him that his own position was legal, that he could not understand the scruples of the Judges. At this very moment he was treating one of them with contumely, and was doing his best to present to his subjects the men on whose judgments he wished to rely as the tools of a Government which would tolerate no decision of which it did not approve.

Oct. 12. Chief Baron Walter.

The Chief Baron, Sir John Walter, had every claim to the consideration of the King. He had been his Attorney General when he was Prince of Wales, and was universally respected for his ability and integrity. Up to the Long Vacation his course had been eminently satisfactory to Charles. In the Court of Exchequer he had refused to allow the replevins for the goods seized for non-payment of duties, and he had encouraged the King to proceed against the imprisoned members of Parliament.

He is asked to resign his place.

Soon after the beginning of Michaelmas Term, however, Walter received a visit from Coventry. The Lord Keeper had come to suggest to him that he should petition the King to be allowed to retire from the Bench. His Majesty, it appeared, was displeased with

[1] The notion that the Judges could settle all political quarrels is something like the notion that arbitration can settle all international quarrels. In both cases much can be done when both parties are agreed on the principles of the point at issue, and merely ask for their application. In neither case is there sufficient physical force to compel submission when there is disagreement as to principles.

him on account of his laxity on the circuit from which he had just returned in enforcing the obligation of his subjects to attend musters. Walter protested that there had been no laxity at all. The King refused to accept the explanation. He sent Coventry back to ask the Chief Baron whether he intended to 'submit himself to his Majesty, or stand to his trial.' Walter replied that he would stand to his trial. "I desire," he wrote, "to be pardoned for making a surrender of my patent, for that were to punish myself. I do with confidence stand upon my innocency and faithful service to his Majesty, and therefore will abide my trial."[1]

CHAP. III.
1629.
Oct. 13.
Oct. 14.

Charles was unprepared for such an answer. As always happened, he was disconcerted by firm but quiet opposition. Walter held his office by patent 'as long as he should behave well,' and the scandal of an open investigation, which at the most could only result in proof of negligence, was of all things most to be deprecated at a time when Charles was appealing to the Judges to arbitrate between himself and his people. He shrunk from the Chief Baron's challenge. If, however, he could not deprive Walter of his office, he could suspend him from the exercise of his judicial functions.[2] Walter, therefore, continued to bear the title of Chief Baron of the Exchequer, but during the year of life which remained to him, he never again took his seat upon the Bench.

Oct. 22. He is suspended.

Contemporaries agreed to regard the charge about the musters as a mere subterfuge. The real cause of Charles's displeasure, they held, was that Walter, after having exhorted him to proceed against the members,[3]

Probable reasons for this step.

---

[1] Coventry to the King, Oct 12; Dorchester to Coventry, Oct. 13; Coventry to Dorchester, Oct. 14. *S. P. Dom.* cl. 47, 52, 58.
[2] Gresley to Puckering, Oct. 24. *Court and Times,* ii. 35.
[3] Salvetti dwells upon this point. He says (*Newsletter,* Oct. $\frac{16}{26}$),

now turned round, and expressed himself strongly against the course which had been adopted. If this was the case, Charles might very well have taken offence at so sudden a change of opinion, and might have charged him, as he is said to have done, with 'dealing cautelously, and not plainly, concerning the Parliament men.'[1]

It is possible too that a further consideration was not without weight with Charles. The case of the members of Parliament was to be decided in the King's Bench, and as far as that case was concerned, it was of no practical importance what Walter might think about the matter. But the cases connected with the levy of Tonnage and Poundage would come before the Court of Exchequer, and it would be highly inconvenient for Charles to have them decided before a Chief Baron who was likely to adopt the popular view. If reliance can be placed on a statement which has reached us, it would seem that the Barons of the Court, with Walter at their head, had already remonstrated strongly with the Lord Treasurer for attempting to levy Chambers's

that Walter was suspended, 'per havere da principio consigliato sua Maestà d' agitare contro di questi gentilhuomini come fine ad hora ha fatto, et che dipoi giuditiariamente si fusse gettato alla popularità.' That he had done this judicially is a mistake. Soranzo says that the Judges had been ordered to condemn the prisoners, and that the King had been much disgusted by their refusal to do so. He had accordingly suspended one, 'et dicono lui stato quello che più degl' altri affermo doversi venir alla retentione, perche vi eran leggi che li condannavano.' Soranzo's Despatch, Oct. 32/Nov. 2. *Ven. MSS.*

[1] Whitelocke, *Mem.* 16. He gives as Walter's opinion 'that a Parliament-man for misdemeanour in the House criminally out of his office and duty, might be only imprisoned, and not further proceeded against.' This opinion, if indeed it proceeded from Whitelocke, is so strange as to be unintelligible as it stands. It is possible that we have here a distorted report of the words, whatever they may have been exactly, to which Heath replied on Oct. 13. *See* p. 139.

fine before the question of its legality had been adjudged. After Walter's removal no further difficulty was raised.¹ The three remaining Barons dealt summarily with Chambers's plea questioning the jurisdiction of the Star Chamber. That Court, they informed him, was erected many years before the statute of Henry VII. to which he had appealed as limiting its powers. It was 'one of the most high and honourable Courts of Justice,' and to deliver one who was committed by the decree of one of the Courts of Justice was not the usage of the Exchequer.² The proceedings on the main question of the right to Tonnage and Poundage dragged on for some time longer, apparently without any anxiety on the part either of the Government or the Judges to bring them to an issue.

From these it is pleasant to turn to Eliot and his companions in suffering. On October 29, together with Holles and Valentine, he was transferred from the Tower to the Marshalsea, 'from a palace to a country house,' as he playfully expressed it, in order that he might be in the custody of the authorities of the Court which was to determine his case. It was not long before Holles, worn out by the importunities of his wife and friends, consented to give the security for good behaviour which would set him at liberty till the day of trial.³

Some weeks would have to be passed by Eliot in this

---

¹ The following note occurs on the back of a MS. account of the proceedings in the Exchequer in Chambers's case. "The 2 of July, 1629, a *fieri facias cap.* and extent from the Lord Treasurer and Chancellor of the Exchequer without the consents of the Lord Chief Baron and other Barons, who disavowed the proceedings as being out of the due course of the law." *Add. MSS.* 11,056, fol. 39 b.

² *Rushworth,* i. 676.

³ Gresley to Puckering, Nov. 5 (not 1). *Court and Times,* ii. 36.

new prison before the case was ripe for a hearing. They were spent by him without hope of better times in this life, but in the quiet and cheerful confidence of well doing. He had none of the self-consciousness of the aspirant to martyrdom. He had words of playful and tender affection for his friends, serious thoughts about the prerogative of kings at home, and about new homes for exiled religion in far America. He had not a word of scorn for his adversaries, not a word of regret for his comrades' desertion. Now and then came a friendly letter from Hampden or Luke, with presents of game and country cheer. Selden and Strode came to join him in the Marshalsea before long. Here he was allowed greater liberty than in the Tower, and was permitted under due guardianship to attend the preaching at St. Mary Overies.[1]

At last, on January 26, Eliot, Holles, and Valentine once more stood together at the King's Bench bar. Heath's information now at last went directly to the point. There was no longer any attempt to escape from the full assertion of the jurisdiction of the Court over actions done in Parliament. The Attorney General did not urge that there had been a conspiracy during the adjournment in private houses, or that Parliament was no Parliament after the King's orders had been conveyed. The conspiracy, he now declared, had been formed in Parliament itself, to resist the King's lawful order to adjourn, and to rend asunder the links which bound the King to his subjects by calumniating the ministers of the Crown, and by assaulting the Speaker, an order to compel the House to listen to an invitation to the people to refuse obedience to the King's orders.[2]

[1] Forster, *Sir J. Eliot,* ii. 293.
[2] Information, *State Trials,* iii. 320.

To this the prisoners answered by denying the jurisdiction of the Court over acts committed in Parliament. The Judges tried to limit the issue as much as possible. They declared that on the main question their minds were made up already, and that all the twelve Judges were resolved that an offence committed in Parliament, criminally or contemptuously, might, when Parliament came to an end, be punished in another Court. The only question to be argued was whether the King's Bench was the proper Court to punish it.

CHAP. III.
1630.
Jan. 27.
The Judges try to limit the issue.

Mason, who undertook the defence of Eliot, took no notice of this intimation. He roved over the whole field of enquiry, and was told by the Court that a great part of his argument was nothing to the present question. Calthrop, who followed on Valentine's behalf, was more discreet. He argued that there was no instance of the interference of the King's Bench with cases in which Parliamentary privilege was involved, excepting when a capital offence was alleged to have been committed. If the Court took cognizance of the present charge, it would be impossible to draw the line at which its interference was to stop. If treason or murder were committed in Parliament, they might be questioned out of Parliament. If words were to be called to account on the ground that they had been spoken 'maliciously and seditiously,' then 'all actions of Parliament men' might, 'under pretence of malice,' be drawn within the sphere of the Court. Besides, Parliament was a superior Court to the King's Bench, and as such was not subject to its jurisdiction.

Arguments on behalf of the prisoners.

Heath, in reply, admitted that some actions were covered by Parliamentary privilege. But he drew the line not at capital offences but at criminal offences. If no precedent could be found for calling in question such actions as those of which the prisoners had been

Heath's reply.

VOL. I. L

CHAP. III.
1630.
Jan. 27.

guilty, the reason was that no such offence had ever been committed before. For the present, however, the only question was whether the Court had the right of punishment on the hypothesis that the offence were proved to have been committed. If it had not, there would undoubtedly be a failure of justice whenever, as in the present case, a Parliament came to an end without taking action in the matter. Even if a new Parliament were disposed at some future time to seek out the criminal, it could have no official knowledge of the facts of the case.

Judgment of the Court.

The judgment delivered was a foregone conclusion. The reasons by which it was prompted found their fullest expression in the mouth of Whitelocke, the only one of the Judges on the Bench who had had personal experience of Parliamentary life. The offence charged against the prisoners, he said, was one tending to the destruction of the Commonwealth. It was true that Parliament was a High Court, and the King's Bench an inferior Court. But Parliament itself was not called in question. The issue lay between the King and some private persons. "You have," he said, " in every Commonwealth a power that hath this superiority, that do they right or wrong, are subject unto no control but of God, and that in this kingdom is the King. But no other within the realm hath this privilege. It is true that that which is done in Parliament by consent of all the House shall not be questioned elsewhere ; but if any private member puts off the person of a judge, and puts on the person of a malefactor, becoming seditious, is there such sanctimony in the place that they may not be questioned for it elsewhere? . . . There is no man hath more privilege than a minister, in regard he preacheth the word of God, yet if he fall on matter of slander to the State, his coat shall not

Whitelocke's argument.

privilege him. So, if a Parliament man, that should be a man of gravity and wisdom, shall decline his gravity, and fall on matter of sedition, he hath made himself incapable of that privilege, although I conceive the Parliament to be the best servant the King hath, and the Commonwealth cannot stand without it. I have been a Parliament man almost these twenty years, yet I never observed any inveighing against the person of any great man, but we followed the matter, although we thought that there were as great offenders then as at any time. Suppose a Judge of this Court flies into gross invectives and leaves his office, shall this Judge in Court of Oyer and Terminer plead his privilege? No, for you did this as a defamer, not a Judge."[1]

CHAP. III.
1630. Jan. 27.

But for one consideration, it would be impossible to resist this argument. If Parliament was to be nothing more than the High Court which in technical language it still is, it would be for the public benefit that a power should exist strong enough to impose upon its members the restraints to which every other Englishman submits his language and his actions. It was because Parliament was rapidly becoming more than a High Court that Whitelocke's argument was invalid. It was unconsciously putting in a claim to share in the superiority which, as Whitelocke said, was subject to no control. By and by it would vindicate it entirely to itself. Privileges which might be lightly regarded when the machinery of government was working easily, became matters of life and death when the different powers of the constitution were eyeing one another suspiciously, ready before long to sound the challenge to civil war. Calthrop had said that if malice could bring words within the

Consideration of its weight.

---

[1] *State Trials*, iii. 293. *Harg. MSS.* 25, fol. 2. I have taken extracts indiscriminately from the two reports.

jurisdiction of the King's Bench, malice might be imputed to any one. To surrender the point at issue was to renounce the weapon without which victory in the approaching strife was hardly possible.

<small>CHAP. III.
1630.
Jan. 27.</small>

It was simply impossible that such a view of the case should be taken by the Judges. Even Eliot did not avow it—probably hardly suspected it in the self-communings of his heart. With him resistance proceeded rather from instinctive defiance of wrong than from a deliberate foreknowledge of the path before him. As yet the Court had only claimed its jurisdiction. It had yet to decide whether an offence had been committed. For the rest of the time allowed for the preparation of the defence neither Eliot nor his friends were idle. They seem to have thought it possible to discover some form which would enable them to defend themselves without betraying the privileges of Parliament. They met with unexampled difficulties. Counsel could not be brought together at their summons, either because the lawyers shrunk from embarking further in a cause so displeasing to the King, or because they knew that it would be perfectly hopeless to discover a form of words which would satisfy Eliot and the Judges as well. At last, on February 12, the lawyers were collected, and a paper was drawn up reciting once more Eliot's reasons for declining the jurisdiction of the Court. Struck down by illness, the result of fatigue brought on by his exertions in preparing his case, Eliot was unable to be in Court on the day when judgment was pronounced.[1]

<small>Question of criminality reserved.</small>

<small>Feb. 12.</small>

<small>The judgment.</small>

Holles and Valentine, however, were there, refusing, as he would have refused, to acknowledge the jurisdiction of the Court by pleading to the charge. Jones, who delivered the judgment, took unworthy advantage

---

[1] Forster, *Sir J. Eliot*, ii. 315–322.

of their silence, treating it as an acknowledgment of their fault. Eliot was sentenced to a fine of 2,000*l.*, Holles to 1,000 marks, Valentine, as being less wealthy, to 500*l.* None of them was to be released from prison without acknowledgment of the offence and security for good behaviour.[1]

The ground on which the judgment was based was the generality of the charges brought by Eliot in the House. He might have accused any particular Privy Councillor as a preparation for an impeachment. But on one occasion he had brought a sweeping charge against Privy Councillors in general, and as he could not possibly have intended to impeach the Privy Council as a body, his words must be regarded as malicious.

The distinction was not without ground. But it would be impossible to maintain it in practice. A member out of favour at Court would be sure to let drop some words which might be interpreted as a general accusation, and he would find himself face to face with the Judges. The rough common-sense view of the situation was taken by Dorchester when he said that the object of the trial was " to let the world see that Parliament men must be responsible for their words and actions in other Courts, and so they will be more moderate and circumspect hereafter, and the King, when he finds good, may meet his people with so much the more assurance that they will never transgress in the point of due respect and obedience,"[2] an opinion which fully justified Eliot in refusing submission to a claim which was certain sooner or later to pass into the assertion of a right to control Parliamentary speeches of every kind.

Eliot knew that he had no mercy to expect from

[1] *State Trials*, iii. 309.
[2] Dorchester to Fleming, March 3. *S. P. Dom.* clxii. 18.

CHAP. III.

1630.
March 3.
Treatment of the prisoners.

Charles. The way was made easy for the other prisoners to make their submission, and some of them were even allowed to leave their prisons without any submission at all. It was not so with Eliot. It was from Eliot's lips that the challenge of the King's authority had first come. It was Eliot who presented himself before Charles's eyes as the malignant accuser of Buckingham, who had struck down the minister in order that he might strike down the King. To those who know him for what he was, no caricature could be more distorted than such a portrait. It is indeed no service to historical truth to paint him as a faultless prodigy. It is enough to know him as a man, sometimes mistaken, but never wilfully blind to truth, equally ready to brand with withering scorn the traitor to his country, and to turn his own cheek to the petulant reproaches of those whose blows were only directed against himself. The last trial of his patience was that he was deserted in the hours of watching by those who had stood shoulder to shoulder with him in the excitement of the battle. Yet, even for them he had no word of reproof, as he had no word of regret for his own calamities. He was still in the prime of life—only thirty-eight years of age—when liberty is sweet. But, like Luther at Worms, it was not in him to do otherwise than he did. A word of submission would have set him free to revisit his Cornish home and the dear ones whom it contained. That word he would not speak. He had taken care to relieve his children from the consequences of the King's anger. When the Sheriff's officers enquired at Port Eliot for property on which to levy the fine, they were told that the man whom they believed to be the owner of that fair estate had nothing which he could call his own. Everything had been made over to trustees for the use of his family. It was only with his body that he was able to answer the demands made upon him. "I am now freed," he wrote to a friend, "from the tedious attendance of courts and counsel, and am passing again to the observance only of myself."[1] In the highest sense he belonged to himself alone. In a lower sense he belonged to the King and to the King's officers. "Mr. Lieutenant," said the Marshal of the King's Bench as he delivered him at the Tower, "I have brought you this worthy knight, whom I borrowed of you some months ago, and now do repay him again."[2]

CHAP. III. 1630. March 3.

Eliot's many friends were struck with admiration at his self-devotion. "The judgment upon you," wrote Kirton, "is blown amongst us with wonder attending it. For my own part I can wonder at nothing; but I think that that man who doth not take your judgment as in part a judgment upon himself, doth fail either in honesty or discretion. I will use no more words unto you of it, because I know you are so well composed that things of this nature, although never so high, slack not your resolutions, or move you to be otherwise than you were. The time may come that such virtues may be regarded."[3]

Many years were to pass away before Eliot's principles were fully adopted by the nation. The mass of mankind is never moved by the fear of impending evils. To the farmer as he plodded in his daily rounds, to the trader as he looked for customers in his shop, it was nothing that the power exercised by the King might possibly be put forth at some future time to the detriment of religion or of commerce. The ecclesiastical innovations were as yet confined to a very few localities. The Custom House officers did not as yet exact a single

Yet his views are as yet only partially accepted.

---

[1] Eliot to Kirton, Feb. 20. Forster, *Sir J. Eliot*, ii. 326.
[2] Meade to Stuteville, March 13. *Court and Times*, ii. 66.
[3] Kirton to Eliot, March. Forster, *Sir J. Eliot*, ii. 327.

CHAP.
III.
——,——
1630.
March.

penny more than had been paid without sign of reluctance for many years. On the other hand, the events of the last session had made it plain that the objects at which Eliot aimed could only be attained by defiance of the King; and much as the intelligent classes were dissatisfied with the course which Charles had taken, even they, and still less the bulk of the nation, were not as yet prepared to defy the King.

It was well that it should be so, well that the belief that it was possible for a sovereign to cut himself off from sympathy with his people, and yet to keep free from actual misgovernment, should be slowly accepted. To Eliot belongs the glory of being the first to see plainly that this could not be, that Charles's isolation was a fruitful seed of evil. It was for him to suffer as those suffer who see that which their fellows cannot see. Like the Swiss warrior, he had gathered into his own bosom the spear points of the adverse host. His countrymen would follow by and by through the breach which he had made at the cost of his life.

CHAPTER IV.

LAUD, WENTWORTH, AND WESTON.

THE permanent interest of the judicial proceedings which have just been narrated centred in Eliot's protest. Their importance for the immediate future lay in the tacit renunciation by the Judges of that high authority which the Commons had thrust upon them in 1628. They refused to be arbitrators between the King and the nation. They accepted the position which Bacon had assigned them, of lions beneath the throne, upon whom was imposed the duty of guarding the throne from attack. All that had been gained by the Petition of Right seemed to be lost in an instant. What would it matter that the Judges were ready to enforce the specification of the cause of committal, if they were ready to be satisfied with the cause shown, whatever it might be? The Petition, in truth, had laid down a great principle, which could only be carried out to its logical results by the strenuous efforts of future Parliaments.

<small>CHAP. IV.
1629.
The Judges and the Petition of Right.</small>

Would Parliament ever meet again? The real line of separation between the King and the House of Commons had lain in the religious question. So decided had been the opposition that it seemed hardly possible that a compromise could be discovered which would enable them to meet on friendly terms. At first sight, indeed, it might seem that the policy

<small>The religious question</small>

CHAP. IV.
1629.
March.
Laud's comments on the Resolution of the Commons.

involved in the King's Declaration on Religion was more likely to win general support than the zealous intolerance of the Commons. Laud's comment on the Resolution in which the Lower House had taken its stand upon the Calvinistic interpretation of the Articles, was full of promise. " All consent in all ages," he wrote, " as far as I have observed, to an article or canon, is to itself, as it is laid down in the body of it, and if it bear more senses than one it is lawful for any man to choose what sense his judgment directs him to, so that it be a sense according to the analogy of the faith, and that he hold it peaceably, without distracting the Church, and this till the Church which made the article determine the sense ; and the wisdom of the Church hath been in all ages or the most, to require consent to articles in general as much as may be, because that is the way of unity, and the Church in high points requiring assent to particulars hath been rent."[1]

July 14. His letter to Vossius.

A few words in a letter to a foreign correspondent carry us still more deeply into those inmost feelings of Laud's heart which he usually veiled from the eye of the world. " I have moved every stone," he wrote to the learned Vossius, "that those thorny and perplexed questions might not be discussed in public before the people, lest we should violate charity under the appearance of truth. I have always counselled moderation, lest everything should be thrown into confusion by fervid minds to which the care of religion is not the first object. This perhaps has not given satisfaction, but I remember how seriously the Saviour commanded charity to his disciples, and how cautiously and patiently the Apostle commanded us to treat the weak. If I perish by these efforts of mine,[2] and become, as

[1] Prynne, *Canterbury's Doom*, 163.

[2] I suppose this is the meaning of ' si his artibus peream.' The letter is in Latin.

usually happens, a prey to the victorious litigant, my reward is in my own bosom, nor shall I seek comfort out of myself, except in God. For the present I have little to hope, much to fear. The Reformed Church has no greater reason for regret and precaution than the danger lest, at a time when she is being attacked by the sword amongst other nations, she should here and with you where she dwells more safely, be torn in pieces by her own hands, and so by a cruel rent should first be broken up into fragments, and then, by gradual subdivision, into minute atoms, and should so vanish into nothing . . . . . For my own part, I will labour with the grace of God that truth and peace may kiss one another. If, for our sins, God refuses to grant this, I will hope for eternal peace for myself as soon as possible, leaving to God those who break that kiss asunder, that he may either convert them, as I heartily desire, or may visit them with punishment."[1]

Dislike of arrogant and self-sufficient dogmatists is plainly to be read in these words of Laud. For all that, the true ring of liberty is not in them. There is none of that sympathy with the aspirations of the limited human mind to win by arduous struggle a footing on the outworks of truth which is the sustenance of the spirit of toleration. For speculative thought Laud cared nothing. Not truth but peace was the object which he pursued. Hence the interest which he took in the fortunes of that Dutch Church which came so short of his own episcopal standard gave no warrant of equal liberality at home. He never felt himself to be burthened with faults committed outside his own special sphere of action, and he might therefore be easily moved to treat with extreme severity in England prac-

[1] Laud to Vossius, July 14. *Works*, vi. 265.

1629.
July.
His estimate of external influences.

tices which in a foreign country would cause him no more than a passing annoyance. In England his hand was likely to be heavily felt. The pursuit of peace in preference to the pursuit of truth was certain to be accompanied by an exaggerated estimate of the importance of external influences over the mind. It was characteristic in him to speak of Aristotle, the philosopher who taught that virtue owed its strength to the formation of habits, as his great master *in humanis*.[1] His love of outward observances, of the Beauty of Holiness, as he fondly calls it, was partly founded on a keen sense of the incongruity of dirt and disorder; partly upon the recognition of the educative influence of regularity and arrangement. There was in his mind no dim sense of the spiritual depths of life, no reaching forward to ineffable mysteries veiled from the eye of flesh. It was incomprehensible to him why men should trouble themselves about matters which they could not understand. His acts of reverence had nothing in common with the utter self-abnegation of the great Italian falling as a dead body falls before the revelation of those things which eye had not seen, nor ear heard. If he is called upon to defend his practice of bowing towards the altar upon entering a church, he founds his arguments not on any high religious theme, but upon the custom of the Order of the Garter. To him a church was not so much the temple of a living Spirit, as the palace of an invisible King. He had a plain prosaic reason for everything that he did.

His dreams and omens.

Even those strange entries in his diary which have sometimes been treated as if they contained the key of his mind have nothing imaginative in them. There is no thought of following a heavenly voice when he records the falling down of a picture or the dropping out

[1] *Works*, iv. 59.

of a tooth. "God grant," he writes, "that this be no omen," as if there were just a possibility that the invisible King might have something to tell him in this way. He notices it sufficiently to make him think it worth while to jot it down for future comparison with events. But he never thinks of acting upon it.

CHAP. IV.
1629. July.

To form the habits of Englishmen in order that there might be peace amongst them, was the task which Laud set before him. The Declaration on Religion had been the first great step in this direction. The excitement caused by polemical controversy must be allayed by the prohibition of controversy. It remained to foster a sense of union amongst those whom theological argument had divided. If all men worshipped in the same way, used the same forms and ceremonies, pronounced the same words, and accompanied them with the same gestures, a feeling of brotherhood would gradually spring up. The outward and visible was to be the road to the inward and spiritual. "Since I came into this place," he wrote long afterwards in defence of his conduct, "I laboured nothing more than that the external public worship of God—too much slighted in most parts of this kingdom—might be preserved, and that with as much decency and uniformity as might be; being still of opinion that unity cannot long continue in the Church where uniformity is shut out at the church door. And I evidently saw that the public neglect of God's service in the outward face of it, and the nasty lying of many places dedicated to that service, had almost cast a damp upon the true and inward worship of God; which, while we live in the body, needs external helps, and all little enough to keep it in any vigour."[1]

Policy of the Declaration on Religion.

Uniformity and Unity.

Forming so high an estimate of the value of ex-

[1] *Works,* iv. 60.

ternal influence, he had no difficulty in accepting fully the Royal supremacy. As the task of a Bishop was in his eyes chiefly the enforcement of regulations, he naturally looked with the highest respect to that authority which was able to compel the observance of those regulations. All the thoughts which had led the great ecclesiastics of the Middle Ages to regard the merely external authority of kings as something infinitely inferior to the spiritual power of the guardians of the divinely appointed faith had no place in his mind. What he wanted was force to carry out his ideas, and that force he found in the King. He did not even care to theorise about the source of this authority. The notion of a divine right of kingship hardly assumed any real prominence anywhere till Charles's title to rule was questioned, and it never assumed prominence at any time in the mind of Laud. It was enough for him to accept the Royal supremacy in the Church as it was established by existing law and custom, and to use it for the great ends which he hoped to accomplish by its means.

Laud, therefore, was ready to speak everywhere in the name of the King. Charles was ready to accept the responsibility. He could no more originate a scheme for the reform of the Church than he could originate a scheme for the recovery of the Palatinate. But he would give his confidence to Laud as he had given his confidence to Buckingham. He, too, thought of the outward and visible before the inward and spiritual. To him, too, the fervent individual zeal of Puritanism was an unfathomable mystery, and its fierce dogmatism a hateful annoyance. When it had been driven out of the land, England would be itself again, as loyal and obedient as it had been to its Tudor sovereigns. He took counsel, as Bacon would have said, of the time past, not of the time present.

Hitherto Laud had not occupied the foremost place in the attacks of the Puritans. During the last session Neile and the Durham ceremonialists had almost covered the field of vision. In his own diocese he was regarded more correctly. His name was coupled with that of Weston in the popular imagination of the Londoners. Libels were scattered about the streets, threatening his life. "Laud, look to thyself," was read upon one of these; "be assured thy life is sought. As thou art the fountain of all wickedness, repent thee of thy monstrous sins, before thou be taken out of the world." Weston, to whom similar threats were addressed, was easily frightened. Dread of assassination haunted him to the last. But Laud was absolutely above fear, as he was absolutely above self-seeking and corruption. "Lord," he wrote in his diary, as the only notice fit to take of the insult, "I am a grievous sinner; but I beseech thee, deliver my soul from them that hate me without a cause."[1]

As long as Abbot lived, Laud's sway in the English Church could never be complete. With the King's authority to rely upon there might be no active opposition to his wishes, but there would be a force of inertia at the very centre of the ecclesiastical machinery which it would be impossible to overcome. Yet if he could not do all that he wished, he could accomplish much. Every man who was at issue with Puritanism knew that he could count upon a favourable hearing if he poured his complaints into the ear of the Bishop of London, and that the Bishop of London was sure of a favourable hearing from the King. Eavesdroppers

[1] *Works*, iii. 210.

CHAP. IV.
1629.

July 19.
Smart's case.

July 20.
Yelverton's charge.

1630.
Nov. 18
Smart's sentence.

and talebearers soon discovered how to set at naught the orders of their own Bishops or the commands of laymen in authority.

Laud's influence made itself felt in the disputes by which the Chapter of Durham was distracted. At the Summer Assizes, Smart repeated his charges of the preceding year against the Prebendaries who had deprived him of his prebend. The Judges on this occasion were Yelverton and Trevor. Yelverton at once took Smart's part. He spoke in conversation of Smart's sermon as good and honest. It was quite right, he added, to condemn the singing of the service. When the organ was playing it was impossible to know what was said. One of the Prebendaries asked him how he contrived to sing psalms to the accompaniment of music. Trevor told him that if he would look at his Prayerbook, he would have no difficulty in understanding what was said. Yelverton would hear nothing in favour of the organ. He did not like whistling at the service. He had always been called a Puritan. He thanked God for it, and as such he would live and die.

In this spirit he charged the jury on the following day. Innovations in the Church, he said, were fair matters to be dealt with at the Assizes. The jury accordingly found a true bill against the Prebendaries. Smart and his friends were in high spirits. The next morning they were plunged into bitter disappointment. Yelverton had all his life been accustomed to pass suddenly from blustering independence to servile humility. He now changed his tone, scolded Smart for his conduct, delivered an address in commendation of peace and charity, and refused to allow the proceedings to be carried further.

All this was duly reported to Laud. Smart's own fate might easily be predicted. He was sentenced to degradation from the clerical office by the Northern High Commission, to whose jurisdiction he had been returned. The disputes at Durham did not end here. Bishop Howson was no Puritan, and he had been one of the four Bishops who had supported Montague in 1625. But he had been frightened at the rapid ceremonial changes at Durham, and had come to look upon Cosin as a firebrand whose persistency in his own crotchets was endangering the maintenance of peace. Laud was appealed to, and after a long correspondence the King commanded Howson to carry the dispute no further. Such interference with a bishop tended to bring episcopal authority into contempt by shewing that it might be wielded in one direction or another according to the varying influences which prevailed at Court.[1]

CHAP. IV.
1629.

In the suppression of books in which the predestinarian doctrine was handled, Laud had no need of the King's assistance. A decree of the Star Chamber in Elizabeth's reign had prohibited the printing of books without the license of one of the Archbishops or of the Bishop of London. Printers and authors in vain urged the argument which Selden had supported in Parliament, that the Star Chamber had exceeded its powers. Printers and authors were brought before the High Commission, and were taught to obey the restrictions imposed upon them at the risk of fine and imprisonment.

Suppression of unlicensed books.

In his own diocese, at least, Laud was able greatly to restrict, if not altogether to bring to an end, that diversity of practice which had long been suffered to prevail. The Book of Common Prayer was to be accepted as the complete rule of worship. The

Prohibition of nonconformity.

[1] *Cosin's Correspondence*, i. 155. Acts of the High Commission. Surtees Society. App. A. Much correspondence is scattered through the State Papers. The first letter from the King to Howson is dated Nov. 3, 1631. *Tanner MSS.* lxx. 128.

VOL. I. M

ministers of the Church were no longer to be permitted to omit this or that prayer at pleasure, to stand when they were bidden to kneel, or to kneel when they were bidden to stand.

Laud's chief difficulty lay with the lecturers. The parish clergy could hardly avoid reading Morning or Evening Prayer in a more or less mutilated form. But a lecturer was under no such obligation. He was paid by a Corporation, or by individuals, to preach and to do nothing more. He might remain sitting in the vestry, if he chose, till the service was at an end, when he could come out to ascend the pulpit, and to shine forth in the eyes of the congregation as one who was far superior to the man by whom the printed prayers had been recited. The lecturers were to be found chiefly in towns where there was a strong Puritan element in the population, and they were themselves Puritans almost to a man.

To those who think it desirable that the teaching of a Church should bear some relation with the prevalent opinions of the congregations of which it is composed, the arrangement may seem not to have been a bad one after all. The existence of the lecturers provided a certain elasticity in the ecclesiastical institutions of the country, without which the enforcement of uniformity would in the long run prove impracticable. Laud was not likely to regard the lecturers from so favourable a point of view. Not only were they careless about forms and ceremonies, but they owed their appointment to the private action of the laity. Those who appointed might dismiss as well, and if Laud's eyes were closed to the evils of subjecting the clergy to the word of command from the Court, they were opened widely to the evils of leaving them in entire dependence upon the varying humours of the richer members of their congregations.

In December Laud's meditations on the subject of lecturers took shape in a series of Instructions sent out by the King to the Bishops. Some clauses were applicable to special abuses committed by the Bishops themselves in the administration of the property of their sees. But the clauses of most general importance touched the preachers, and more especially the lecturers. In the first place the King's Declaration forbidding the introduction of controversial topics was to be strictly observed. Further, there were no longer to be any afternoon sermons at all. Catechizing of children was to take their place. In the morning sermons were still permitted, but no lecturer was to be suffered to open his mouth unless he had first 'read Divine Service according to the Liturgy printed by authority, in his surplice.' Nor was any lecturer to receive an appointment in a corporate town unless he was ready to accept 'a living with cure of souls' within the limits of the Corporation. The bishops were to gather information on the behaviour of the preachers, and to 'take order for any abuse accordingly.' Lastly, in order to discourage the entertainment by the wealthier country gentlemen of private chaplains who were dependent entirely upon their patrons, the Bishops were to 'suffer none but noblemen and men qualified by law to have a chaplain in their houses.'

CHAP. IV.
1629. Dec. The King's Instructions.

The King's Instructions were the first step taken in narrowing the limits of Church union. The lectureships were not a very satisfactory provision for meeting the strain of enforced conformity. But at least they permitted diversity of opinion to manifest itself without an absolute breach of religious continuity. They could not be suppressed without suppressing the independent development of religious thought. In some way or another, in spite of Laud, Puritanism would find a voice in England. The silenced lecturer of 1629 would be the triumphant Presbyterian or Independent of 1645, and the excluded Nonconformist of 1662.

The King's resolution to allow no polemics in the pulpit was firmly taken. Davenant, Bishop of Salisbury, a man of mark amongst the Calvinistic prelates, ventured to touch upon the forbidden topic of predestination in a sermon preached at Whitehall. He was at once summoned before the Council Table to answer for his disobedience. He pleaded that he had done no more than explain the Articles. He was told that it was the King's will that 'for the peace of the Church these high questions should be forborne.' He received a sound rating from Harsnet, now Archbishop of York, and only escaped actual punishment by promising a judicious silence for the future.[1]

In their attempt to close discussion for ever, Charles and Laud were at least impartial. In vain Dr. Brooke, the Master of Trinity at Cambridge, implored permission to publish a book which, as he affirmed, would crush the Puritans and reconcile all difficulties at issue. Laud told him coldly that he should have no objection to read his argument, but that he had not changed his opinion that 'something about these controversies' was 'unmasterable in this life.' As the book never reached the press, it is to be presumed that, in spite of a vehement tirade against Puritanism from the author, Laud's objection was insuperable.[2]

An unexpected event brought to Laud an increase of work and an increase of responsibility in

---

[1] *Fuller*, vi. 74.

[2] Brooke to Laud, Nov. 17, Dec. 1. *S. P. Dom.* clxxv. 69; clxxvi. 2; Laud to Brooke, Dec. 9; *Laud's Works*, vi. 292; Brooke to Laud, Dec. 15; Prynne, *Canterbury's Doom*, 167.

a fresh direction. On April 10 the Earl of Pembroke died suddenly.¹ Several times during the past years men had looked up to him hopefully as a possible leader. He was known to be averse to all rash and unpopular measures, and he had a high character for disinterestedness. But his disinterestedness was merely that of a wealthy man with nothing to seek for himself and the solace of an affable and unruffled disposition. He had no force of character to enable him to control events. As Bacon said of him, he was 'for his person not effectual.'² He easily passed from hot opposition to the tamest submission. With an intelligence greater than his power of will, he was the Hamlet of Charles's Court.

<small>CHAP. IV.
1630.</small>

No attempt was made to fill up the office of Steward of the Household, left vacant by Pembroke's death. Charles seemed to think that by leaving such posts vacant he would have a stronger hold upon those who aspired to fill them. But Pembroke had been Chancellor of the University of Oxford as well, and that post, at least, could not be left vacant. The Earl of Montgomery, who now succeeded his brother in the Earldom of Pembroke, was put in nomination by those who were faithful to the traditions of Calvinism. The election, however, fell upon Laud, though only by a majority of nine. The defeated party complained of unfair dealing; whether truthfully or not it is now impossible to say.³

<small>April 12. Laud Chancellor of Oxford.</small>

The University was made to feel that the days of slack government were at an end. Laud at once attacked the riotous and disorderly habits of the place. Academical costume was no longer to be neglected. Undergraduates were no longer to occupy seats destined to Masters of Arts. Above all the King's Declaration

<small>May. Discipline revived.</small>

---

¹ Mead to Stuteville, April 17. *Court and Times*, ii. 71.
² *Works*, vii. 446.   ³ *Laud's Works*, v. 3.

was to be enforced. Even a preacher who ventured to praise Arminianism and to revile the Synod of Dort was severely reprimanded. Another preacher had offended in a different way. He had declared 'directly against all reverence in churches, and all obeisance or any devout gesture in or at the receiving of' the Communion. "If this be true," wrote Laud, "belike we shall not kneel neither."[1]

There was little in common between the bustling energy of the Bishop prying into every corner of the land, and counting nothing too small for his regulative authority, and the ponderous inertia of the Lord Treasurer, to whom it was the highest of arts to leave difficulties alone, and who was well satisfied if he could leave to a future generation the problems which he was himself incapable of solving. There was but one man in England as untiring as Laud, and that man, though long admitted into the King's service, had only recently acquired even a very slight hold upon the King's favour. But little is known of Wentworth for nearly a year after his speech at York.[2] He was in his place in the House of Lords during the short session which followed, and it needs no evidence to prove that the proceedings of the Lower House must have left an indelible impression upon his mind. Whatever distrust he had before of the intolerant predominance of Calvinism; whatever shrinking he had felt for the rule of a dominant House of Commons, was now doubled. In the maintenance and elevation of the Royal authority lay for him now the only path of safety and wisdom. It was impossible for him to be content, as Charles and Weston were content, with the mere suspension of Parliamentary life. He knew too well that the habit of insubordination to authority could not be

[1] Laud to Tolson, May 7. *Ibid.*, v. 15.   [2] See p. 39.

uprooted by mere passive expectation. Like Laud he perceived that it must be met face to face, be wrestled with and overthrown. Yet if he did not despise the remedial measures which seemed all-sufficient to Laud, the training of the mind to obedience by uniformity of external worship, and the silencing of preachers who claimed the right of declaring doctrines which engendered strife, he had too much genius to be content with this. He required active co-operation in the service of the Commonwealth from every man who received protection from the Government. In thought, if not in expression, he anticipated the watchword which the nation was hereafter to accept from the dying lips of her greatest sailor, that England expects every man to do his duty. But he did not see that it is only by enlisting the active sympathies of those upon whose co-operation he depended that he could reasonably hope for the assistance upon which he was forced to depend. Knowing that the mass of men is ignorant and prejudiced, he fancied that they would not merely submit to be guided, but that they would throw themselves heart and soul upon his side, if only he commanded their services in a right direction. Wisdom, simply because it was wise, was to bind folly and slothfulness to its car, and to compel them to bear it swiftly onward on its triumphant path. He could not stoop to the slow and irregular progress which is all that can be expected when a nation guides its own course, nor could he acknowledge that a progress thus made is surer than the most brilliant achievement into which it is dragged panting and gasping for breath in the hands of a master.

There were moments in which Wentworth felt that there was something wrong, though he never dreamt of tracing the mischief to anything in himself. He lamented that his lot had fallen in an age in which he was forced to wish with all his heart that 'men knew less and practised more.'[1]

Its weakness.

No idealist, it has been often said, commits so many errors as the practical man of the world. Eliot, with all his superabundant trust in the wisdom of the House of Commons and his superabundant reliance upon the all-sufficiency of the average religious feeling of his day, never entered upon a course so hopeless as Wentworth did when he set his hand to build up a compact constitutional edifice of which Charles was to be the corner-stone. Nor would he have been likely to achieve permanent success even if Charles had been other than he was. Willing co-operation can never be looked for where there is no sympathy between the governors and the governed, no spontaneousness of action in those whose assistance is required. Experience teaches that such a sympathy and such spontaneousness of action can only be maintained where the government is in one sense or another representative. Either by the election of a controlling assembly or by some less direct means, the nation must be able to make its voice heard, unless a gulph is to open between King and people which nothing short of revolutionary violence could close up.

Eliot and Wentworth.

Eliot and Wentworth indeed were of one mind as to wishing such a catastrophe to be averted. But they differed as to the means to be employed to ward off the danger. For Eliot it was enough that the House of Commons had spoken. That House in his eyes truly represented the nation in the fervour of its religion, in the wisdom and gravity of its political aspirations. In Wentworth's eyes it only partially represented the nation, if it represented it at all. The lawyers

[1] Wentworth to Conway, Oct. 14. *S. P. Dom.* cl. 61.

and country gentlemen of whom it was composed were not to be trusted to govern England. The lawyers with their quirks and formulas too often stood in the way of substantial justice. The country gentlemen too often misused the opportunities of their wealth to tyrannise over their poorer neighbours. Wentworth therefore would appeal to the nation outside the House of Commons, as Chatham afterwards appealed to the nation outside the House of Commons. The King was to do judgment and justice fairly and equally for rich and poor. So would come the day when Parliament would meet again. The King would not have altered his course to put himself in harmony with the nation, but the nation would have grown in intelligence to take hold of the hand which was offered to it by the King.

Thus Wentworth seemed to himself to be contending for the old and undoubted liberties of Englishmen, for their right to freedom from vexatious injustice. He was standing in the ancient paths. His knowledge of history told him how a Henry II. and an Edward I., a Henry VIII. and an Elizabeth, had actually guided a willing people. It told him nothing of a dominant House of Commons reducing its Sovereign to insignificance. What it told him of control from the baronage, or even from Parliament as a body, might safely be set down as irregular and unconstitutional, the deplorable result of misgovernment. That Charles should ever make such violence necessary he could not bring himself to believe. At all events, he did not see that the King had made it necessary by his resistance to the House of Commons. As he had accused Buckingham once, so he might accuse Eliot now 'of ravishing at once the spheres of all ancient government.'

Was there indeed a nation behind the House of

Commons to which Wentworth could give an articulate voice, or had he miscalculated his strength and overestimated his power of raising the inert masses to a level with the effective strength of the nation, in the same way as he undervalued the worth of those religious and moral ideas to which the political classes clung so tenaciously? This was the secret of the future. Others, Charles more especially, would have to contribute to the solution of the problem. But even if all power had been concentrated in Wentworth's hands, it is unlikely that he would have solved it successfully. He had too little attractive force to overcome the difficulties in his path. He was too self-reliant, too ready to leave his deeds to speak for themselves, too haughty and arrogant towards adversaries, to conciliate opposition, or even to be regarded by those whose cause he supported with that mingled feeling of reverence and familiarity which marks out the true leaders of mankind. He might come to be looked upon as the embodiment of force. Men might quail before his knitted brow and his clear commanding voice. They would not follow him to the death as Gustavus was followed, or hasten to his succour as the freeholders of Bucks hastened to the succour of Hampden. Wentworth in his strength and Charles in his weakness were alike lonely amidst their generation. They understood not the voices which sounded on every side, they drew no strength from the earth beneath nor from the heaven over their heads. They set before them the task of making men other than they were, not the task of guiding men to make themselves other than they were. What could come of it but failure, disgrace, and ruin?

In the beginning of November 1629 a paper fell into Wentworth's hands which stirred his indignation to the uttermost. The writer urged the King 'to bridle the impertinency of Parliament' by taking military possession of the country, establishing fortresses guarded by mercenary soldiers in every town, and compelling the payment of new and unheard of taxes to be levied by the sole authority of the Crown.[1] There was just enough resemblance between the course thus recommended and the constitutional position assumed by Wentworth to rouse his resentment at so gross a caricature of his own principles. He took the paper at once to the King, who regarded it as the result of a plot to bring his Government into disrepute, and ordered enquiry to be made for the author.[2]

<small>CHAP. IV.
1629.
places in the King's hands a paper which he has found.</small>

Wentworth, at least, was the gainer by the discovery. Five days after he had placed the paper in Charles's hands he took his seat in the Privy Council. He owed his promotion to his resolution to guard from all attack the prerogatives of the Crown, without infringing upon the outward decencies of English constitutional practice.

<small>Nov. 10. Wentworth a Privy Councillor.</small>

The paper which shocked Wentworth and the King had a curious history. Soon after the dissolution of the Parliament of 1614, Sir Robert Dudley, the illegitimate son of Elizabeth's favourite Leicester, who was living in exile at Florence, fancied that he saw a way of gaining permission to return to his native soil. Together with a proposal to communicate to James certain naval inventions which as he asserted were such as to change entirely the face of maritime warfare, he forwarded to Sir David Foulis, a Scotchman in the King's service, the very paper which was at last brought into unexpected notoriety.[3]

<small>Dudley's paper of advice. It gets into circulation.</small>

Foulis gave the paper to Somerset, and Somerset,

---

[1] A proposition for his Majesty's service. *Rushworth*, i. App. 12.
[2] Rawson to D'Ewes, Nov. 6. *Harl. MSS.*, 383, fol. 90.
[3] Dudley to Foulis, May 8, 1614. *Fortescue Papers*, 6, and note at p. 11.

at that time at the height of his favour, shewed it to James. James would have nothing to say to it, and it was laid aside and forgotten. Some years later it found its way into that great receptacle of manuscript treasures, Sir Robert Cotton's library. Time went on, and Cotton entrusted the care of his books to his librarian, Richard James, a clever, well-informed man, who was not above earning money by lending his master's papers to the curious. In the summer of 1629, when all men were talking about the encroachments upon Parliament, James lent this particular paper to Oliver St. John, a young lawyer who took the popular side, and who showed the copy which he took of it to his client, the Earl of Bedford. Bedford showed it to Somerset, who distinctly remembered that it had once been in his hands. From Somerset it passed to the Earl of Clare, the father of Denzil Holles, and Clare carried it to Cotton. Cotton, who had quite forgotten that the original had long been in his own library, fancying that he had before him a revelation of the immediate designs of the Court, sat down to reply to its arguments, no doubt with the intention of publishing his refutation.

Cotton was not well served. In his house was a youth who passed by the name of Flood, but who was commonly reported to be his own natural son. Like James he saw in the paper a means of making money. He sold copies freely, and in this way the paper had come into Wentworth's hands.[1]

The investigation ordered traced the document through Cotton and the three Earls to St. John. St. John was committed to the Tower, and his chambers were

[1] Harsnet to Vane, Nov. 6. *Court and Times*, ii. 37. Dorchester to Edmondes, Nov. 7, 18. *S. P. France. D'Ewes's Autobiography*, ii. 39. Examinations of Somerset and Bedford, *State Trials*, iii. 396.

searched for incriminatory evidence. He stoutly affirmed that the paper had come to him from Cotton's library, and Cotton who, as well as the Earls, had been committed to private custody, as stoutly declared that he knew nothing about the matter. On November 15, as no further light seemed likely to be thrown on the mystery, Charles protested in the Council that the suggestions of the paper were 'fitter to be practised in a Turkish state than amongst Christians.' Eleven days later, much to Cotton's surprise, the original manuscript was discovered in his own library, and Foulis, who was still living, deposed to the circumstances in which it had formerly come into his hands. The paper thus lost much of its supposed importance. But orders had already been given to prosecute Cotton, St. John, and the Earls in the Star Chamber for concealment of the paper, and these proceedings were allowed to run their course.[1]

Nov. 15. The King renounces the advice of the paper.

Nov. 26. Discovery of the original.

Prosecution ordered.

What Charles wanted was evidently an opportunity of making a protestation of his resolution to abide by the law. He could have had no angry feeling against those who circulated the paper as soon as the circumstances had been explained. The hearing of the cause had been fixed for May 29. The day arrived, and a few words had been spoken when a messenger hastily entered the Court and whispered in the Lord Keeper's ear. Coventry at once interrupted the proceedings. It had pleased Heaven, he said, to bless his Majesty with a son, 'a hopeful Prince, the great joy and expectation both of the King and kingdom.' His Majesty therefore was inclined to think rather of mercy than of justice. Dudley's paper should be burnt, but those who had circulated it might depart unharmed. This was the last appearance of the most notable of the

1630. May 29. The defendants pardoned in consequence of the birth of a Prince.

---
[1] Dorchester to Edmondes, Nov. 26. *S. P. France.*

defendants before the eyes of the world. The fact that an important State Paper which ought never to have passed out of the possession of the Crown had been discovered in Cotton's library, gave rise to the suspicion that other documents of the same kind might be found in his possession. Orders were accordingly given that he should himself prepare a catalogue of the manuscripts, with the assistance of two clerks of the Council, and that he should only enter the library in their presence.[1] The old man felt the grievance deeply. He was not, it is true, excluded from the sight of his beloved books. But it was one thing to be permitted to visit his treasures in the presence of two unwelcome companions. It was another thing to sit at ease as the master of the house, with his friends chatting around him, each more eager than the other to pay court to the dispenser of such stores of knowledge. His death, which was at the time ascribed to his annoyance, took place within the year after his visit to the Star Chamber. The services which he rendered to historical literature will never be forgotten. In his own day the services which he rendered to political controversy were more highly appreciated. His function was to collect materials for others to use. His own antiquarianism was not enlightened by any steady and consistent view of society and life. At one time it led him to associate with Somerset and Gondomar. At another time it drew him to Eliot and Selden.[2]

The child whose birth formed an excuse for dropping a hastily undertaken prosecution was destined to strange vicissitudes. Through the fault of his parents

---

[1] *Council Register*, Nov. 24.

[2] *D'Ewes's Autobiography*, ii. 41. After a decent interval orders were given that the catalogue should be continued in the presence of Cotton's son. *Council Register*, July 23.

he was early to taste the bitterness of exile, and to be recalled after years of apparently hopeless wandering to sit upon his father's throne. To his mother the child, dark and ugly as she playfully acknowledged him to be,[1] was the more welcome after her disappointment a year before. There were others who were very far from sharing her delight. The birth of the infant seemed to be a pledge of the permanence of the existing system of government, even if he were not nurtured in his mother's faith to trouble Protestant England when he came to sit upon the throne. Till now there had been a prospect, however remote, of seeing the golden crown of England encircling the fair brow of Elizabeth, and it was never doubted that if Elizabeth took her seat upon the throne, there would be no place for Laud and Weston upon its steps. No wonder the Puritans hung their heads whilst bells were ringing and bonfires blazing. " God," said one, " had already better provided for us than we had deserved in giving such a hopeful progeny by the Queen of Bohemia, brought up in the Reformed religion; whereas it is uncertain what religion the King's children will follow, being to be brought up under a mother so devoted to the Church of Rome."[2]

It was only by the remonstrances of his ministers that Charles was induced to avoid emphasising in the eyes of all men the risk which would have to be faced at last. On the very day of his son's birth, he announced that the child was to be entrusted to the charge of the Roman Catholic Lady Roxburgh, who, as Jane Drummond, had been the main instrument in attaching the infant's grandmother, Queen Anne, to the religion which

[1] The Queen to Madame de St. George. *Strickland's Lives of the Queens*, v. 252.

[2] Heylyn, *Cyprianus Anglicus*, 198. Soranzo's Despatch, June $\frac{4}{14}$. *Ven. MSS.*

she herself professed. It had doubtless been hard for Charles, at such a moment, to resist the entreaties of his wife. But he gave way at last, and Lady Dorset, an Englishwoman and a Protestant, was finally appointed. Charles, however, continued as usual to mar the graciousness of concession by the coldness of his manner. "This King," wrote the Venetian ambassador, "is so constituted by nature that he never obliges any one, either by word or deed."[1]

<small>Laud's attachment to Charles.</small>

To no one, except to his parents, was the birth of the heir more welcome than to Laud. Wentworth's attachment to Charles, though not without a romantic tinge, was political at the bottom. Laud regarded him with the warmest personal affection. The two men had so much in common. Nor did Laud, like Wentworth, soar into regions in which Charles was incapable of following him. He simply found in Charles's mind the receptive soil in which he might hopefully plant his ideas of external order. Laud joyfully composed a prayer commending the royal babe to its heavenly Protector,[2]

<small>June 27. Baptism of the Prince.</small>

and on June 27 he was called upon to baptise him by his father's name.

<small>Alexander Leighton.</small>

At the time of the Prince's birth, Laud and Wentworth had as yet formed no special tie of friendship. They were brought together by a common dislike of subversive doctrines, and a common resolution to visit with the harshest penalties those who spread them amongst the people. Such a one, at least in the eyes of courtiers and councillors, was Alexander Leighton. A Scot by birth, the father of the gentle and thought-

---

[1] Soranzo's Despatch, July $\frac{2}{12}, \frac{16}{28}$. *Ven. MSS.*

[2] Hacket (ii. 96) records Williams's expression of dissatisfaction with a phrase in this prayer, "Double his father's graces, O Lord, upon him, if it be possible." As printed in *Laud's Works,* iii. 103, it is simply, "And when fulness of days must gather time, Lord, double his graces, and make them apparent in this his heir."

ful student, who became Archbishop of Glasgow in the next generation, had been a minister of his native Church, and had risen to the full height of Presbyterian zeal. Of his reasons for leaving Scotland no record has been preserved, but it is probable that he fled, like Calderwood, to avoid submission to the innovations of James. At Leyden he studied physic, and took the degree of doctor of medicine. Coming to London, he attempted to practise his new profession. But he was soon brought before the College of Physicians, charged partly with being a quack and partly with daring to smuggle himself into a profession from which his orders excluded him. He was subjected to an examination in which he failed to satisfy examiners who were probably not very anxious to detect his knowledge, and he was then interdicted from practising in England. He continued, however, to prescribe clandestinely, and he also reverted to his clerical work, collecting around him, doubtless in the privacy of his own house, a considerable number of disciples. His first book, the *Speculum Belli Sacri*, was launched into the world in 1624, as an incentive to the declaration of war against Spain. It was chiefly distinguished by the furiousness of its intolerance, and by the cool presumption with which, with the help of quotations from the Scriptures and the writers of Greece and Rome, he ventured to give dogmatic opinions on the military art.

His first book.

In 1628, after the Houses had been prorogued and the Remonstrance of the Commons was passing from hand to hand to fan the flame of opposition, the enthusiasts who gathered at Leighton's house began to talk over plans for carrying on the war against the prevalent ecclesiastical system in the coming session. Some talked of abating the authority of the Bishops, others of various minor reforms. Leighton, like a true Scotch-

1628. *Sion's Plea against Prelacy.*

man as he was, went to the root of the matter. His 'opinion was right down for extirpation of the prelates, with all their dependencies and supporters.' This audacious proposal was well received, and he was requested to embody his views in a petition to Parliament. A draft was soon prepared and circulated amongst those whom Leighton described as 'the godliest, learnedest, and most judicious of the land.' Before long he had five hundred signatures to his petition, some of them being those of members of Parliament. Satisfied with the number, he crossed over to Holland, to print the petition without fear of interruption. In its passage through the press it was elaborated into a lengthy treatise, dated, apparently with the object of exciting indignation against the Government, 'in the year and month wherein Rochelle was lost.'

Two early copies were sent over to be laid before the two Houses when they met for their last session. The dissolution came before they had reached those for whom they were intended. In July, Leighton, probably thinking that his work had escaped notice, returned to England. His book, however, though it could not be sold openly, was circulated in private under the title of *An Appeal to Parliament; or, Sion's Plea against Prelacy.* In the following February a copy fell into Laud's hands. The pursuivants were at once put upon the track of the daring author, and, before long, he was arrested by a warrant from the High Commission, and lodged, if his description is correct, 'in a nasty dog-hole full of rats and mice.'[1]

Leighton's treatise was undoubtedly the production of a vigorous understanding. There is an intellectual freshness in its composition which is wholly wanting in the ponderous learning of Prynne. It is, however, the

[1] The evidence on which this narrative is based is collected in the introduction to Heath's speech in the *Camden Miscellany,* vol. vii.

work of a man with a single fixed idea. Whatever evil existed in the world was laid to the charge of the Bishops, the antichristian and Satanical prelacy. If the season was unhealthy, if provisions were dear, if ladies displayed extravagance in dress, it was all the fault of the Bishops. They had poisoned the ear of the late King, telling him that if he would support their authority he might have 'absolute liberty to do what he list.' They had supported Buckingham in his resistance to Parliaments till God cut him off. They were 'men of blood,' persecuting the saints, 'knobs and wens and bunchy popish flesh;' they were the 'trumpery of Antichrist,' by whom the land was filled with swearing, drunkenness, pride, idleness, and all kinds of sin.

Of the King, Leighton spoke respectfully. But he did not shrink from wounding his tenderest feelings. He described Buckingham as 'that great Goliath' who had been made 'to fall unexpectedly' by 'the Lord of Hosts.' Buckingham had set 'all things to sale, and sold the fee-simple of England to Rome, that he might have the tenant-right.' The King's own marriage was not spared. God had 'suffered him to match with the daughter of Heth, though he missed an Egyptian.'

Sion's Plea was more than an ecclesiastical manifesto. It was an appeal to political Presbyterianism to take the sword in hand. " Put the case," wrote Leighton, hypothetically, " that the good harmless King be a captivated Joash by Athaliah's Arminianised and Jesuitical crew, or a misled Henry VI., dispossessed of his faithfullest friends and best counsel by the pride of the French; or a Henry III., overawed by a devilish domineering favourite; or an Edward VI., overpoised and borne down from his good purposes to God's glory and the good of the State by the halting and falsehood of the prelates and their Romish confederacies, so that such a king, though he hold the sceptre, neither can be free himself nor execute his designs, because the sons of the man of sin are too hard for him."[1]

Call upon Parliament to interfere.

Leighton did not shrink from calling upon Parliament to take up the work which had been left undone by the King. "Then," he said, addressing the two Houses, which the book contemplated as still in session, "you, the great Council of State, must remove the wicked from the head, and take away the corrupting and corroding dross from the silver excellency and excellent argentry[2] of the King. ... Strike neither at great nor small, but at these troublers of Israel. Smite that Hazael in the fifth rib."[3] The words were no doubt intended to be taken metaphorically, but they were easily capable of another interpretation.

And to resist a dissolution.

Leighton ended his book with a deliberate invitation to Parliament to resist a dissolution. Its members, he argued, were bound to stay in the ship. "Every dissolution of Parliament without real information is against right, reason, and record."[4] This long indictment of Royalty and Episcopacy was brought to a close with the following suggestive lines:—

'High must you soar, but glory gives thee wings,
No low attempt a starlike glory brings.'[5]

Did Leighton stand alone?

The invitation to Parliament to constitute itself into a permanent body was naturally regarded by the Government as an invitation to revolution. The Attorney General, as might have been expected, was anxious to

---

[1] *Sion's Plea,* p. 207. [2] "ingentrie" as printed.
[3] *Sion's Plea,* p. 240. [4] *Sion's Plea,* 337.
[5] *Ibid.,* 344. I have read a copy in Dr. Williams's Library. I do not understand why former enquirers have failed to discover most of the passages here quoted.

know whether Leighton stood alone. He lavished all his powers of persuasion to draw from him the names of those five hundred persons who had signed the petition. It was all in vain. No offers of forgiveness or liberty could draw a single name from Leighton's lips. The form of his book he distinctly asserted to be entirely his own.[1] The Court of Star Chamber was called to judge his offence.

CHAP. IV.
1630.
Feb.

At the present day Leighton's attack would doubtless be left to the contemptuous indifference of all sensible men. But the conduct which commends itself to a Government so strong as to defy treason to do its worst is hardly to be expected from a Government conscious of weakness. Leighton's attack came too near Eliot's attack to be treated as an isolated occurrence. Unhappily, the contemplation of the danger was not likely to be accompanied by any profitable reflections. That the House of Commons, so loyal and submissive to Elizabeth, should have raised a thinly disguised demand for supremacy in the State; that the forcible introduction of Presbyterianism should be regarded as anything more than a dream; were surely phenomena to induce the King and his counsellors to ask themselves what they had done to make such things possible. No such thought, however, passed through their minds for an instant. All that was thought of was to crush a fanatic who could only be dangerous through their own maladministration. The two Chief Justices, in their place in the Star Chamber, declared that if the King had so pleased, Leighton might have been put on his trial for high treason, and other members of the Court assured him that 'it was his Majesty's exceeding mercy and goodness' which had brought him there. In order to show his Majesty's mercy and goodness, Leighton

June 4. Proceedings against him in the Star Chamber.

His sentence.

[1] Leighton's Answer, *Sloane MSS.* 41.

was condemned to pay a fine of 10,000*l*., to be set in the pillory at Westminster, and there whipped, and after his whipping to 'have one of his ears cut off and his nose slit, and be branded in the face with SS, for a sower of sedition.' At some future time he was to be taken to the pillory at Cheapside. The lash was again to descend upon his back, his other ear was to be sliced off, and he was then to be imprisoned for life, 'unless his Majesty shall be graciously pleased to enlarge him.'

It is not probable that any one of the Judges expected Leighton ever to pay a hundredth part of the fine which had been set upon him. In truth the enormous fines which have left such a mark upon the history of this reign were seldom exacted, and became little more than a conventional mode in which the Judges expressed their horror of the offence,[1] except so far as it may have been intended to bring the offender to an early confession of his fault. But the rest of the sentence was far from consisting of nominal penalties. It is true that, in its treatment of criminals the age was hard and brutal. The constant passing of the deathcart along the road to Tyburn raised no compunction in the minds of Londoners. The pillory

---

[1] Every individual payment of the fines is set down in the Receipt Books of the Exchequer. The only question is whether any of these fines was paid underhand. I think if this had been the case we should have heard something of it. There is, moreover, one instance in which, if ever, concealment would have been maintained. When the heavy fine of 70,000*l*. was set on the City of London in 1635, nothing was heard of any payment for some time. In 1638, however, there is a pardon for the whole sum (*Pat. Rolls*, 14 Charles I., Part 14). About the same time the Receipt Books (June 29) shew a payment of 12,000*l*. from the City. The explanation is found in a Privy Seal of April 23 of the same year (Chapter House Records), in which the King states that he had promised the Queen 10,000*l*. out of this fine, and that he thought fit to make it 12,000*l*. Surely if the Queen's grant passed through the Exchequer, money given to inferior persons would have been dealt with in the same way. See Appendix to Vol. II.

with its accompanying brandings and mutilation, was an ordinary penalty known to the law, and there was nothing in Leighton's sentence which was not authorised by the practice of the Court of Star Chamber.[1] What was really new was that the members of the Court were now virtually parties in the case. They had a personal interest in avenging an insult directed against themselves. If this was true of the Judges and the temporal Lords, it was still more true of the Bishops. If Leighton's account of the proceedings, given many years afterwards, when his temper was soured by cruel sufferings, is to be accepted as at all approaching to accuracy, the Bishops took a leading part in insisting upon the heaviest sentence. Neile opposed the theory of the divine right of Episcopacy to Leighton's theory of the divine right of Presbytery. He had his calling, he

[1] Hudson's *Treatise on the Star Chamber*, being written in James's reign, is good evidence of past practice on this point, as well as on the point of the fines. "The punishment," he writes, "is by fine, imprisonment, loss of ears, or nailing to the pillory, slitting the nose, branding the forehead, whipping; of late days, wearing of papers in public places, or any punishment but death.

"Fines are now of late imposed *secundum quantitatem delicti*; and not fitted to the estate of the person, so that they are rather *in terrorem populi* than for the true end for which they were intended when fine and ransom was appointed. The ransom of a beggar and a gentleman being all one, to the loss of the Crown and the great detriment of the Commonwealth.

"Imprisonment always accompanieth a fine, for if the party be fined he must be imprisoned, and there remain until he find security to pay his fine, and then must pay his fee to the Warden of the Fleet.

"Loss of ears is the punishment inflicted upon perjured persons, infamous libellers, scandalers of the State, and such like.

"Branding in the face and slitting the nose is inflicted upon forgers of false deeds, conspirators to take away the life of innocents, false scandals upon the great, judges, and justice of the realm.

"Whipping hath been used as the punishment in great deceipts and unnatural offences, as the wife against the husband, but never constantly observed in any case but where a clamorous person *in formâ pauperis* prosecuteth another falsely, and is not able to pay him his cost. Then, *quod non habet in ære, luet in corpore.*"

said, 'from the Holy Ghost. If he could not make it good, he would fling his rochet and all the rest from his back.'[1] Laud's speech lasted for two hours, "Until the time of Luther, Calvin, and Beza," he said, "the world heard not of any other government of the Church but by Bishops, and although Calvin and Beza did abjure Bishops and their government, yet he found them to be more proud and imperious in their government than any Bishops in England."[2] According to the same authority, as soon as judgment had been delivered, Laud took off his cap, and raising his hands, 'gave thanks to God who had given him the victory over his enemies.'[3]

Whether this last anecdote be true or false, it illustrates the position into which Laud had come. He looked upon those who opposed his opinions as his enemies, and upon his enemies as the enemies of God.

Leighton to be degraded.

Before the terrible sentence could be carried out Leighton was to be degraded from his ministerial office by the High Commission, in order that he might not appear in his clerical character upon the pillory. As the High Commission was not then sitting, it might be that the names of his supporters might be extracted from him during the vacation. But Leighton was of the stuff of which martyrs are made. Introduced before the Commission at last, he refused to take off his hat to the Court, and declared defiantly that it had no

Nov. 4. His degradation.

---

[1] Leighton's *Epitome*, 75.

[2] *Ibid.*, 70. Leighton, however, does not seem to have been present at this part of the proceedings, as he says, 'I have set down his own words as they were related unto me,' p. 73, misnumbered 65.

[3] *Ibid.*, 78. The part of Laud's speech given above seems just what he would have said. Other things attributed to him seem unlikely, and the story of raising the cap may have been invented or distorted. This book of Leighton's seems to have been entirely overlooked.

authority to touch him. Leighton's clerical dress was stripped from his back, and he was sent back to prison to prepare for suffering.¹ The King, it is said, was meditating the remission of his corporal punishment.² On the night before the day fixed for his appearance in the pillory, however, he contrived to make his escape from prison, with the aid of two of his countrymen named Livingston and Anderson. A fortnight afterwards he was captured in Bedfordshire. His flight put an end to all thoughts of mercy. Leighton went bravely to his suffering, together with two other culprits who had in some way offended against the law. His wife walked before him as if in some triumphal procession. "As Christ," she said, "was crucified between two thieves, so is my husband led between two knaves." His own courage did not fail him. "All the arguments brought against me," he said to the spectators, "are prison, fine, brands, knife, and whip." "This is Christ's yoke," he cried, as his neck was thrust into the pillory. Then, as the sharp knife of the executioner rent away his ear, he exclaimed, "Blessed be God, if I had a hundred, I would lose them all for the cause." But in the opinion of some he marred the simple dignity of these words by others which trenched upon profanity. 'He told the people he suffered that for their sins; and out of the Psalms and Isaiah applied unto himself the prophecies of Christ's sufferings, to the great scandal of many.'³

Leighton was carried back bleeding and fainting to

Margin: CHAP. IV. 1630. Nov. 9. His escape and recapture. Nov. 26. His punishment. Part of it remitted.

---

¹ Leighton's *Epitome*, 83. Meade to Stuteville, Nov. 27, *Court and Times*, ii. 79.

² "For, at the censuring of those that helped him to escape, some of the lords said that, had he not made an escape, his Majesty was graciously inclined to have pardoned all his corporal punishments." Meade to Stuteville, Dec. 5. *Ibid.*, ii. 82.

³ *Ibid.*

his prison, there to endure long years of misery. The second agony at the Cheapside pillory was spared him. One ear was left uncropped. One scourging was not inflicted. So far the mercy of Charles extended.¹

There is no evidence that Leighton met with anything like general sympathy. He had his followers, no doubt, who regarded him as a martyr for the truth; but nothing is heard of any popular movement in his favour round the pillory at Westminster. At the Inns of Court, when search was made for him at the time of his escape, the lawyers 'took it unkindly that they should be suspected for Puritans.'² It may well be doubted whether the feeling of opposition had as yet reached below the political classes. Even amongst them Leighton's subversive Presbyterianism could have found but few defenders. It required many years of misgovernment to convert dissatisfaction with particular acts of the King and the Bishops into the torrent of revolutionary abhorrence which was to sweep away King and Bishops together.

It has been said, and it is by no mean improbable, that Leighton's denunciations were the means of drawing Laud and Wentworth into close communication with one another.³ To them at least they would

---

¹ The infliction of the second part of the sentence is noticed only in the forged entry in Laud's diary (*Rushworth*, ii. 57). It is conclusive against it that Leighton says nothing of it in the *Epitome*. The sentence had not been executed when Meade's letter of Dec. 5 was written. *Court and Times*, ii. 82.

² Meade to Stuteville, Nov. 27. *Ibid.*, ii. 79.

³ Leighton, in his *Epitome*, says that 'a man of eminent quality told me that the book and my sufferings did occasion their combination, for the prelate seeing that the book struck at the root and branch of the hierarchy, and Strafford perceiving that the support and defence of the hierarchy would make him great, they struck a league, like sun and moon to govern day and night, religion and state.' He also says that in the Star Chamber Wentworth 'used many violent and virulent expressions against' him.

contain the same lesson of warning. Presbyterianism in the Church and Parliamentarism in the State would seem to be two forms of one disease, of the error which sought to control the government of the wise few by the voice of the ignorant many.

Governments do themselves little direct harm by the punishment which they inflict upon violent and unreasonable opponents. Indirectly, the temper which encourages harsh and extreme repression leads to an unwise antagonism to the moderate demands of those who are neither violent nor fanatical. Charles might long have treated the claims of the House of Commons with contempt, and might long have bidden defiance to Presbyterian enthusiasts, if he could have understood how to make use of the higher devotional tendencies of the Puritanism of his day. It was of no good omen for the State that by choice or by compulsion men who would have added strength to any government stood aside from participation in public duties, and that some even sought elsewhere than in England for homes in which they might pass the remainder of their lives in peace.

Foremost amongst these latter was John Winthrop. Sprung from an ancient family which had enriched itself by trade, and born at Groton in Suffolk in 1588, he had grown up under the influence of the tide of Protestantism which swept over the nation in the years of triumph which followed upon the ruin of the Armada, and was nowhere so strongly felt as in the eastern counties. His sensitive mind was early racked by the agonies of religious despondency. Self-examination, leading to self-condemnation, became the habit of his daily life, albeit it was chequered by intervals of calm refreshment in the remembrance of his Saviour's mercies. He had 'an insatiable thirst after the word of God,' so as never willingly 'to miss a good sermon, though many miles off, especially of such as did search deep into the conscience.'[1]

To Winthrop the God whom he worshipped seemed to be very near, an invisible presence detecting and bringing to light his faults, and even saving him from bodily harm in the occurrences of daily life, 'crossing him in his delights,' if he fell into idleness, or revealing to his wife a spider in the children's porridge.[2] For many years the consciousness of being unworthy of such favour gave rise to a morbid feeling. He could not attend the sessions as Justice of the Peace without dreading lest he should be entangled in the vanities of the world, or without thinking with self-conscious shyness of the smiles which rose to the lips of his gayer neighbours as they glanced at his plain and unadorned dress.

Domestic trouble came to add its depressing influence. Married at eighteen to an illiterate wife four years older than himself, he accepted his lot without repining. But there was no intensity of love, no tenderness of feeling to soften the rigours of his life. When his wife died after eleven years of wedlock, she had borne him six children. He quickly married again, but it was only to lay his second wife in the grave, after a brief year of happiness. In his third wife, Margaret Tyndal, he found his mate; she it was who made him what he now became. From the day that his faith was plighted to her, nothing more was

---

[1] Winthrop's *Life of John Winthrop*, i. 61.
[2] A spider, it should be remembered, was believed to be poisonous. *Winter's Tale*, ii. 1.

heard of the old moodiness and timidity. He learned to step boldly out amongst his equals, to take his share in the world's work. He became a practising attorney in the Court of Wards, and in his letters of this period there is nothing to distinguish him from any other godfearing Puritan of the time, excepting the almost feminine tenderness and sensitiveness of his disposition.[1]

<small>CHAP. IV.
1618.
His third marriage.</small>

To this life of his the dissolution of Parliament in 1629 sounded the death-knell. The proneness to despondency had been banished from his own religion. But as he looked around him he despaired of his native country. Evil times were coming, when the Church must 'fly to the wilderness.' Where Eliot saw a passing sickness, Winthrop's softer nature turned sadly from the symptoms of mortal disease. Population, he thought, was overtaking the means of subsistence. The rich were vieing with one another in sumptuousness of dress and fare. At the universities men had learned to 'strain at gnats and swallow camels,' to 'use all severity for the maintenance of caps,' but to 'suffer all ruffian-like fashions and disorders in manners to pass uncontrolled.' Winthrop resolved to seek in New England the congenial home which Old England could not afford him.[2]

<small>1629. Determines to go to New England.</small>

---

[1] It is only by inference that the evident change can be connected with Winthrop's marriage. He says (*Life*, ii. 171), "I was about thirty years of age, and now was the time come that the Lord would reveal Christ unto me. I could now no more look at what I had been, or what I had done, nor be discontented for want of strength or assurance; mine eyes were only upon his free mercy in Jesus Christ." Winthrop was thirty on January 22, 1618. His father, writing on March 31, speaks of the marriage as already arranged. I am responsible for this and other conclusions on Winthrop's character, but they are based on the facts as narrated in the *Life*, the memorial which has been raised by the devotion of the Hon. R. C. Winthrop to illustrate the deeds of his ancestor.

[2] Reasons to be considered. *Life*, i. 309.

1629.
State of New England.

Emigration to New England was no longer the service of danger which it had been when Bradford and Brewster crossed the Atlantic in the Mayflower. But it was still a work demanding endurance of hardship. The Plymouth colony had succeeded in establishing its footing, and others had come out in scanty numbers to settle here and there upon the neighbouring coast. Few Englishmen were tempted to leave their native land for a home in the wilderness, and of those who tried the experiment many succumbed to the difficulties of the undertaking.

Settlements of the Dutch and French

It was time that a fresh stream of English emigration should be directed to the coasts of America. The Dutch had already erected Fort Amsterdam at the mouth of the Hudson on the island which was afterwards to bear the great commercial city of New York. The French had settled at Port Royal in Nova Scotia, and had established a trading post for the purchase of furs from the Indians at Quebec. Though Sir William Alexander claimed the whole district under a grant from the Crown, and his emissary, Captain Kirk, had seized Port Royal and stormed Quebec, negotiations were already on foot in Europe for the restoration of the French settlers.

1628. Settlement at Salem.

Religious enthusiasm was to secure the preponderance on the Continent for men of English race. At the close of 1628 about fifty or sixty persons had formed a settlement at Salem in Massachusetts Bay under authority of a company in London which had received a grant of lands from the Council for New England. In the following year fresh members were admitted to the company; and on March 4, two days after the Speaker had been held down in his chair by Holles and Valentine, it was reconstituted by Royal Charter under the name of the 'Company of the Massachusetts Bay in New England.' About two hundred persons were despatched in April, and Charlestown rose by the side of Salem. They carried with them two clergymen who were dissatisfied with the state of things in England, and they immediately on their arrival constituted themselves into a church after the Separatist model. Bradford came over from Plymouth to offer them the right hand of fellowship. "That which is our greatest comfort," wrote one of them, " is that we have here the true religion and holy ordinances of Almighty God taught among us. Thanks be to God, we have here plenty of preaching and diligent catechizing, with strict and careful exercise, and good and commendable orders to bring our people into a Christian conversation."

CHAP. IV.
1629.
The Company of Massachusetts Bay.

In setting up their worship these men had no idea of admitting the principle of toleration. Two brothers who attempted to worship apart, using the English Common Prayer, were at once placed on board ship and sent back across the Atlantic. It may be that the rulers of the little community were wise in their resolution. Their own religious liberty would have been in danger if a population had grown up around them ready to offer a helping hand to any repressive measures of the home government.

Toleration not allowed.

It was in this settlement that Winthrop proposed to find his new home. But neither he nor those who were ready to join him were willing to go if they were to be merely the subjects of a trading company in London liable to be controlled by the King. An unexpected way was found to meet the difficulty. On July 28, Cradock, the governor of the company, proposed that the government of the Corporation should be trans-

July 28. Transfer of the Massachusetts Company to America.

ferred to America, 'for the advancement of the planta-
tion, the inducing and encouraging persons of worth and
quality to transplant themselves and families thither.'
He did not say, what he must have been clearly understood to mean, that in this way the King would
have some difficulty in laying his hand upon the
governor. On August 26 Winthrop and eleven other
gentlemen signed an agreement to emigrate if this condition were fulfilled. Two days later the transference
was voted by the company, and on October 20 Winthrop was elected governor in Cradock's place.

In April, 1630, Winthrop was on his way to Massachusetts. His name was a powerful magnet to draw
his friends and neighbours to associate their fortunes
with his own. Either in the fleet in which he sailed or
in vessels which shortly followed, a thousand persons
were added to the struggling settlements on the New
England coast.[1] It was not the love of democratic
equality which led these men—many of them gentlemen of wealth and position—to wrestle with the hardships of an unkindly soil, and of a harsh and rigorous
climate. If they had their share with Bradford and
Brewster and Winslow as the founders of a nation, it
was because these temporal blessings were added to
them who first sought the Lord and his righteousness.
They had set an ideal before them which they strove to
realise upon earth, and in spite of human shortcomings
in its conception, and of human errors in its embodiment in action, their life and the life of those around
them was ennobled by their high spiritual earnestness.
The old world, they believed, was growing very old,
falling swiftly into corruption and decay. The im-
moralities around them, they thought, would be

---

[1] *Life of Winthrop*, i. 305. Palfrey, *Hist. of New England*, i. 283.

strengthened, not weakened, by the ecclesiastical ceremonialism which was in favour in high places in England. Winthrop and his friends believed thoroughly in the Calvinistic system of theology, but to him, as for every noble nature, that theology was clothed in the heartfelt appreciation of the personal nearness of his Saviour to his heart. It was this which to him and to so many others rendered a ceremonial worship so hateful. It was a mere distraction from the burning self-sustained passion of devotion. All that was needed to impose a check upon the intense individuality of his creed he found in the study of the Scriptures, in which he recognised the voice of his heavenly guide. To his soul, hungering and thirsting after righteousness, the Bible was a code of moral law perfect and complete. Earthly life, as those Massachusetts settlers held, was to be the expression of the heavenly life. No man who had no part in the greater could be entrusted with control over the less. By their charter, which they carried with them to America, the members of the company who formed the governing body were empowered to admit freemen to share in their privileges, and they used this power to establish a Commonwealth into which none were to enter as masters who did not fully share in the religious conceptions of the existing members. "The only way," wrote Winthrop, " to avoid shipwreck is to do justly, to love mercy, to walk humbly with our God."[1] Church membership was declared to be the indispensable condition of admission to the governing body. A religious oligarchy was thereby established, round which gathered hundreds of persons who were unable or unwilling to satisfy the test imposed. But for the mingled firmness and gentleness of the rulers, such an arrangement could not have lasted

[1] *Life of Winthrop*, ii. 18.

CHAP. IV.
1630.

1631.
Severe rule.

Toleration rejected.

for a month. The year after Winthrop's arrival only 126 freemen were admitted, and it took ten years of immigration and selection to add 1,200 more.[1]

Massachusetts was not a place where men might do as they liked. Those who gave signs of proving troublesome to the colony were simply placed on shipboard and sent back to England. Those who were guilty in any special way were condemned to harsher penalties. A quack doctor was fined 5*l.* Captain Stone, for assaulting a member of the community 'and calling him a just ass,' was fined 100*l.* and banished. Edward Palmer, who made the Boston stocks and charged too highly for the wood, had to sit in them himself. Swearers had to stand with their tongues fixed in cleft sticks. Philip Ratcliff, the Leighton of the colony, was ordered to 'be whipped, have his ears cut off, fined 40*l.*, and banished' out of the limits of the 'jurisdiction,' for uttering malicious and scandalous speeches against the government.[2]

In proportion as the student of the history of the seventeenth century perceives clearly that religious toleration was the goal to which it was tending, and that in it alone could its difficulties find their appropriate solution, he is tempted to think hardly and bitterly of those men who turned their backs upon such a benefit. Eliot and Winthrop would hear as little of it as Laud and Wentworth, Even the intellectual perception of the value of toleration had not yet dawned upon the world. The obstacle was, however, not purely intellectual. The real difficulty was to know who was to begin. The problem as it presented itself to the men of that generation was not whether they were to tolerate others, but whether they were to give to others the opportunity of being intolerant to them-

[1] *Lowell Institute Lectures*, 237.   [2] *Ibid.*, 86.

selves. Was Laud to allow Leighton to gather strength to sweep away the whole Church system of England? Was Winthrop to allow the dissidents to gather strength to sweep away the whole Church system of New England? It is only when a sentiment of mutual forbearance has sprung up which renders it improbable that the spread of any given opinion will be used to repress other opinions by force, that the principle of toleration can possibly commend itself to a wise people. Even in these days we are tolerant because we believe that freedom of thought, besides being a good thing in itself, is not likely to be turned against ourselves; not because we feel bound in principle to give to the holders of one particular doctrine a chance of establishing their own authority on the ruins of the rest.

It was the glory of England that she had approached more nearly than other nations to the condition of mutual forbearance which renders toleration possible. It was the misfortune of the reign of Charles I. that the tacit compact between the two great parties in the Church was broken. The Puritan demanded exact conformity with the doctrine which he professed. Laud demanded exact conformity with the practices of which he approved. The largeness of view, the power of concession, the recollection on the one hand that personal and individual religion need not throw off regard for the demands of external authority and ceremonial, and on the other hand that the devotees of external authority and ceremonial need not reject the demands of personal and individual religion, was being lost sight of. Each party was coming to look upon the other as something to be repressed and extirpated. Yet each party regarded itself, not without excuse, as standing on the defensive. Winthrop explained his refusal of the use of the Common Prayer-book by calling to mind the persecution to which the emigrants had been subjected in England. Cosin preached on the text, "Pray for the peace of Jerusalem." "Those other men," he said, "have but little to do, it seems, who are finding fault with the public prayers of the Church when, according to the prophet's rule here, we pray for the continuance of our peace, and desire to be kept from battle and persecution. . . . 'Pray for the peace of Jerusalem,' saith the prophet here; pray that you may live a peaceable and a godly life under your king, saith St. Paul. No; pray for no peace, pray not against any battle, saith our Puritan, directly against the text; and for so saying, let us ever think what spirit governs the sect, we shall be sure to find that it is none of the Spirit of peace. They are all for contentions and brabbles, both at home and abroad, and He everywhere against them, as we also ought to be."[1]

The tendency of these words is unmistakable. To Cosin disputatiousness was not the mere waste thrown off in the process of maintaining intellectual vigour. It was a sheer evil, without any compensating good whatever, from which it was the duty of the governors to protect the helpless mass of the population. Something of the same idea lies at the root of the action of the Privy Council in social matters. It would be a great mistake to attribute to Wentworth at this time anything like the influence which he subsequently acquired. In the general direction of the Government he had, as far as we know, no hand whatever, and his name was not even thought worthy of mention by those who chronicled the doings of the King and his ministers. But it can hardly be by accident that his accession to the Privy Council was followed by a series of measures aiming at

[1] Sermon vii. *Cosin's Works*, i. 115.

the benefit of the people in general, and at the protection of the helpless against the pressure caused by the self-interest of particular classes. No doubt much was done which in later days would be regarded as injudicious. But there can be no doubt of the existence of a tendency to find a sphere of action in the pursuance of the common good.

The aid of the Council was first invoked by a visitation against which the science of that age afforded little or no protection. The plague, which had committed such devastations in 1625, reappeared in England in the spring of 1630.[1] The Council sounded the alarm. Magistrates were ordered to stop the passage of rogues and vagabonds who might carry the infection. Houses in which the disease already prevailed were to be closed. Householders were to refuse relief to wandering beggars, and to cause them to be apprehended by the nearest constable. On the other hand, the deserving poor were to be protected against want and suffering, and the laws on their behalf were to be strictly put in force.[2]

Three months later an attempt was made to deal with the evil in London, where its consequences were most to be dreaded. There is no doubt that our forefathers were indebted for the existence of this as well as of other forms of disease to the overcrowded habitations in which they dwelt, and to the neglect of the most elementary sanitary precautions. In such a city as London, growing from year to year, it seemed hopeless to cope with the evil in any other way than by strictly controlling the influx of population to the city. An Act of Parliament in Elizabeth's reign had prohibited the building of new houses, and the recep-

[1] Meade to Stuteville, March 20. *Court and Times*, ii. 68.
[2] Proclamation, April 23. *Rymer*, xix. 160.

CHAP. IV.
1630.
July 14.

tion of an increased number of lodgers in the old ones, but had been passed for a limited period of seven years, and when the term came to an end it had not been renewed. In James's reign, however, the same difficulty had been felt. Recourse had been had to the Judges, who had declared that the excessive building of houses was illegal as a nuisance, and could therefore be dealt with whether the Act of Parliament were renewed or not.[1] James had accordingly proceeded to execute the powers thus acknowledged to be his, and Charles followed in his father's steps. All previous orders on the subject were reinforced by a fresh proclamation not long after the outbreak of the plague. Injurious as the intervention was, there is no reason to doubt that it was well intended, and the prohibitions against building new rooms under a certain height, and against erecting houses with the upper stories overhanging the streets deserve unqualified praise.[2]

Deficient harvest.

June 13. Measures to avert famine.

Sept.

This time the pestilence was accompanied by an extraordinary drought which caused a failure in the harvest. As early as in June the alarm was taken, and the exportation of corn was prohibited.[3] In September a proclamation was issued which sounds strange at the present day. The observance of Lent and other special days by abstinence from meat had been a practice handed down from the mediæval Church. Elizabeth's Parliaments had sought to find an economical basis for that which had ceased to be acknowledged by most persons as a religious duty, and had enjoined abstention from meat at those seasons as a means of encouraging the fisheries. The Elizabethan statutes,

---

[1] "About 6 *Jacobi* the Judges resolved in the Star Chamber and declared that these buildings were nuisances and against the law." Notes in the hand of Secretary Coke, February (?) 1632. *S. P. Dom.* ccxi. 92.

[2] Proclamation, July 24. *Rymer*, xix. 177.

[3] Proclamation, June 13. *Ibid.*, xiv. 175.

with some alteration in details, had been re-enacted in the last Parliament of Charles, and the proclamation which now demanded the observance of the law only carried out the views which had been accepted by that House of Commons which had risen up in indignation against Laud and Weston. The fast, as was stated in the proclamation, was observed in his Majesty's household, in the houses of the greater part of the nobility, at the Inns of Court, and at the Universities. But it was treated with contempt at taverns and other places of entertainment. More meat was eaten there on fasting nights than on any other day. Private persons were therefore to be admonished to use abstinence, and the City companies to suspend their festivities, devoting the money thus saved to the starving poor, unless they wished the King 'to remember the hardness of their hearts.'[1]

More direct measures were taken at the same time. The Lord Mayor and Aldermen were ordered to prevent the price of corn from rising in the London market. Directions were sent to Ireland, which had not been reached by the dearth, to transmit to England all the grain which was not absolutely required to meet the wants of its own population. Justices of the Peace in counties where corn was by any accident plentiful were to supply the wants of less fortunate neighbourhoods. No one was to venture to ask more than seven shillings a bushel for wheat, about two shillings more than the highest ordinary price, nor was more than a limited quantity to be purchased, or the storing of grain permitted for resale. It was not in the nature of things that such directions should be submitted to without opposition. Again and again the Council complained of resistance. In spite of threats, corn was

[1] Proclamation, September 28. *Rymer*, xix. 116, 195.

held back from the market, and prices continued to rise. Justices had to be reminded that it was their duty to visit the markets week by week. Starchmakers had to be reminded that their work was not absolutely necessary to human existence. Maltsters were told to limit the quantity of barley consumed by them. Here and there there were riots and disturbances. But on the whole order was maintained. Fortunately the next harvest proved to be a good one, and in the summer of 1631 prices fell as rapidly as they had risen.[1]

Dec. 31. Commission for the relief of debtors.

It was perhaps the experience gained in this struggle with famine which suggested to the Council the propriety of more permanent intervention on behalf of the poor. The class of bankrupt debtors was one which met with but little pity from the prosperous tradesman, and it had been one of the charges against Bacon before his fall, that he had been inclined to stretch his authority in their favour. A body of Commissioners was now appointed to mediate with the creditors of prisoners whose debts were under 200*l.*, and whose cases were reported by the Judge by whom they had been committed as worthy of commiseration. The mediation of Privy Councillors would be apt to express itself in language difficult to resist, and was sure to be regarded by the creditors as an attack upon their legal rights. "What care I," said one who was summoned to give account of his harshness, " for the King or his Commissioners, for they have no power to give away my debt? ... Unless the Commission be confirmed by Act of Parliament, I will go when I list and come when I list, nor never a messenger in England shall make me come but when I list."[2]

[1] The whole course of the proceedings can be traced in the *Council Register*.
[2] Commission, December 31. *Rymer*, xix. 228. Affidavit of R. Steevens, August 28, 1632. *S. P. Dom.* ccxxxi. 48.

Still more sweeping was the appointment of Commissioners to see that the laws for the relief of the poor were duly carried out. The country Justices of the Peace were charged, doubtless with truth in many instances, with neglecting their duties where their interests were concerned. Few, it was said, dared complain of the great landowners of their neighbourhood. 'Poor people' had once been better relieved than now they were. Such abuses were to continue no longer. Money bequeathed for charitable uses was to be applied to the purposes for which it had been given. Rogues and vagabonds were to be punished, alehouses to be kept in good order, children without visible means of subsistence to be put out as apprentices, and those who had fallen into distress to be provided with support. The Justices were ordered to report from time to time the result of their labours; and in this way a check was put upon the tendency of the local powers to slacken in their efforts for the public good.'[1]

Such measures on the part of the Government may serve as an indication that there were some at least in the Council who were anxious to fall back upon an alliance with the people in their quarrel with the aristocracy. It was hardly likely that their good deeds in this direction would weigh very heavily in the balance. When the whole state of society is rotten, when the upper classes use the superiority of their position freely for oppression, a Government may deservedly rise to power by substituting the despotism of one for the tyranny of many. Such had been the cause of the extraordinary powers acquired by the Tudor sovereigns at the beginning of the sixteenth

[1] Commission, January 5, *Rushw.* ii. App. 82. There is a copy of the orders in Lord Verulam's Library, apparently printed for general circulation. The *State Papers* are full of the Justices' Reports as long as Charles maintained his authority.

century. But it was only by the grossest exaggeration that anything of the kind could be apprehended in the reign of Charles. If Justices of the Peace were sometimes ignorant or harsh, if country gentlemen were sometimes violent or oppressive, the evil was not sufficiently widely spread to call for so drastic a remedy. There was nothing to shew that the propertied classes would fail as a body to respond to a demand from the Government that justice should be done.

July 10. The Huntingdon Charter.

One instance had not long before occurred in which all the efforts of the Government would have proved futile to avert injustice without local co-operation. In the summer of 1630 a new charter was granted to the borough of Huntingdon.[1] A dislike of popular action prevailed at Court, and at the petition, it was said, of the burghers themselves, the rule of the town was handed over to a Mayor and twelve Aldermen appointed for life, in the first instance by the King himself, and authorised to fill up all future vacancies in their own body. The change seems to have been made with Cromwell's consent,[2] and he himself was named one of the three Justices of the Peace for the borough. But if Cromwell did not care much for democratic theories, he was easily moved to anger by injustice, especially by injustice to the poor. He saw that under the new charter the Aldermen might deal as they pleased with the common property of the borough, and in pointing out the hardship thus entailed upon the less prominent members of the community, he spoke roughly to Robert Barnard, the new Mayor, who had been the prime instigator of the change. A complaint

Cromwell's objections.

---

[1] Huntingdon Charter, July 10. *Patent Rolls,* 6 Charles I., Part ii.

[2] This seems placed beyond doubt by Dr. Beard's certificate, printed in the Duke of Manchester's *Court and Society from Elizabeth to Anne.*

was quickly carried to London, and Cromwell was summoned before the Council. In the end the matter was referred to the arbitration of the Earl of Manchester, whose brother was now the owner of Hinchinbrook. Manchester was not likely to be prejudiced in Cromwell's favour, but he sustained his objections in every point, and ordered that care should be taken to guard against the risk which he had pointed out. On the other hand, Cromwell acknowledged that he had 'spoken in heat and passion,' and begged that his angry words might not be remembered against him.[1] A few weeks later Cromwell withdrew from Huntingdon, selling his property, and renting lands near St. Ives. It is possible that some very prosaic motive may have influenced him in making the change. But it may be that he found that his influence was at an end in a town the governors of which he had successfully opposed.

CHAP. IV.
1630.
Nov. 26. He is summoned before the Council.

Dec. His objections admitted.

It is hardly possible for a government to break loose from popular control without falling into financial difficulties. Sooner or later it is certain to engage in enterprises the expenses of which the nation is unwilling to meet, and which necessitate the imposition of taxation the levy of which gives rise to discontent out of all proportion to the burthen imposed. In Weston, however, Charles had a minister who would put off the evil day as long as possible. He had no fancy for bold and startling remedies, and would rather submit to a deficit than resort to new and unpopular schemes. Yet even Weston was unable to avoid doing something. Ever since the dissolution, he had been engaged in meeting the most pressing debts of the Crown with the help of the subsidies which had been voted in 1628. Still the creditors cried for more. There were claims

Financial difficulties.

---

[1] See the whole story in the Preface to Mr. Bruce's *Calendar*, 1629-31, xiii-xiv.

1630.

arising from the expedition to Rhé, from the expedition to Stade, and even from the Cadiz voyage. A debt of 40,000*l.* was owing to the Earl of Holland. A debt of 42,000*l.* was owing to the Earl of Carlisle. Carlisle was put off by a grant of fines to be paid by persons who had encroached upon the King's landed property,[1] and which would bring him in a few hundred pounds annually for some time to come. Holland was contented with promises[2] which several years after were not fulfilled. But the mass of creditors could not be dealt with so, and it was absolutely necessary, if Charles was not to acknowledge himself a bankrupt, that either Parliament should be summoned, or that resort should be had to some unusual mode of obtaining money.

Jan. 28. Composition for knighthood.

Of all men Charles was the least likely to perceive the risk attending upon the revival of obsolete but technically legal forms of levying money. If, however, recourse was to be had to any such measures, the one which was actually adopted was probably open to fewer objections than any other. No lawyer doubted that the King had the right to summon such of his subjects as were owners of an estate worth 40*l.* a year to receive knighthood. No lawyer doubted that he had the right of fining them if they neglected or refused to obey the summons, and though this right had not been put in force for more than a century, it could not be said that the King was asking for anything illegal. The first demand was made in January 1630.[3] It was some time before those who were asked to pay could be convinced that Charles was in earnest. In

---

[1] Commission for Defective Titles, February 24. *Rymer*, xix. 123. The payments appear from the Receipt Books of the Exchequer.

[2] *Inrolment of Privy Seals*, April 9. No. 11, p. 167.

[3] Commission, January 28. Proclamation, July 13. *Rymer*, xix. 119, 175. The King to Mildmay, August 4. *S. P. Dom.* clxxii. 16. Proceedings in the Exchequer, February 5, 7. *Add. MSS.* 11,764, 53.

July it was thought necessary to appoint commissioners to receive compositions. Up to Michaelmas, however, only 13,000*l.* was thus brought in. The Judges then came to the aid of the Government. In August the Barons of the Exchequer pronounced the King's right to be undoubted, and in the following February they overruled a series of special objections on points of form. Payment could no longer be avoided. By Michaelmas 1631, 115,000*l.* was collected, and much more was still to come.[1]

1630. July 13.

1631. Feb. 7.

Charles was evidently determined to put in force his legal rights, and he doubtless persuaded himself that nothing more could be demanded from him than conformity to the requirements of the law as interpreted by the Judges. To the Court which vindicated his right to the compositions for knighthood he was indebted for a support which was at least practically sufficient for him in his claim to levy Tonnage and Poundage. It is true that Chambers pleaded in vain for a day to be fixed on which the wide issues which he had raised might be determined by the Court of Exchequer. There was less difficulty in meeting the case of Vassall, who had refused to pay the imposition on currants. He was told that in the preceding reign the Court had decided that imposition to be due, and its decision was not to be departed from. He was therefore to pay the duty. Vassall sturdily replied that he would have nothing to do with the currants under such circumstances. 'The order did not constrain him to fetch them away, and he would let them lie where they were.' He was at once committed to custody for contempt of the Court; and the Judges were at last obliged to order the sale of the currants

Tonnage and Poundage.

June 5. Vassall's case.

---

[1] *Receipt Books of the Exchequer.*

General resistance dies out.

without the intervention of their owner.[1] Payment was enforced in the other cases in a somewhat similar way.

Those who continued to resist payment, however, were no longer assured of the support of their fellow merchants. Before the year 1630 came to an end, a treaty of peace was signed with Spain. Trade revived with the cessation of hostilities, and the mass of persons engaged in commerce was indisposed to hold back from the pursuit of wealth for the sake of a political principle.

[1] *Exchequer Decrees and Orders*, viii. 269, 309 b; ix. 204 b; xi. 466 b.

CHAPTER V.

ENGLISH DIPLOMACY AND SWEDISH VICTORIES.

On the whole Charles's treatment of his home difficulties had been tolerably straightforward. He had been under no temptation to act otherwise than he had done. He had cast upon the Judges the duty of defending his position, and as there was no general disposition to resist their decisions he was able to maintain his ground without much effort of his own.

The moment that Charles cast his eyes beyond his own dominions these conditions were reversed. He could not cite the Kings of France or Spain before the Court of Exchequer. He could not persuade the citizens of the Dutch Republic to submit the interests of their State to technical argument. Whatever he wanted he must achieve by wise foresight and by the confidence inspired by honesty of purpose and by readiness to postpone considerations of his own welfare to considerations of the general good. Nothing of the kind was to be expected from Charles. His knowledge of foreign nations was most elementary. With their aims and struggles he had no sympathy whatever. James had made many mistakes, but at least he had a European policy. Charles had no European policy at all. The one thing for which he cared was the

CHAP. V.
1629.

re-establishment of his sister in the Palatinate. His object was merely dynastic. How it would affect Germany, even how it would affect England, were questions which he never thought of proposing to himself. The result was what might have been expected. Whatever tendency to duplicity was in him was fostered by the effort to cajole those who had it in their power to give him what he required. Regarding himself as the one just man in the midst of angry and interested combatants, he began by offering aid to one or the other, regardless of the intrinsic merit of the quarrel which for his own purposes he offered to espouse. The habit of looking out for the highest bidder quickly grew into the habit of making profuse and often contradictory offers to each bidder in turn.

Nov.
Vane at the Hague.

1630.
Jan.

When, in the autumn of 1629, Vane started for the Hague and Cottington for Madrid, Charles was probably full of the most beneficent designs. If he could mediate a peace between Spain and the Netherlands at the same time that he was negotiating a treaty for himself, he would at least be quit of the obligations of the Treaty of Southampton, which bound him to assist the Dutch against their enemies. Vane now discovered that his message of peace found no favour in the eyes of the Prince of Orange. The campaign of 1629 had been eminently successful. Wesel and Hertogenbosch had fallen. The Prince was informed by the English ambassador that if his master failed to recover the Palatinate by his treaty with Spain, he would be ready to enter into a fresh agreement with the Republic on condition that the restitution of the Palatinate was distinctly provided for. He replied that the States would never consent to bind themselves to a stipulation which would bring them into direct collision with the Emperor. Charles thought it very hard that the

Dutch were unwilling to run the risk in his sister's service.[1]

Coloma's reception in England.

Was it likely that the chivalrous self-renunciation for which Charles had sought in vain in Holland would be found at Madrid? When Don Carlos de Coloma arrived in England, the Banqueting Hall at Whitehall was crowded with spectators. The ruffs of the ladies were torn in the struggle which ensued,[2] but there were very few who gave the new ambassador a hearty welcome. The Queen paid him no compliment. It was only with difficulty that a house had been found for his reception.[3] But he had Weston on his side, and Weston's word was all-powerful with Charles.

Cottington at Madrid.

It was to Cottington, however, not to Coloma, that the business of the negotiation was entrusted. Cottington soon found that Olivares would make no positive engagement for the restitution of the Palatinate. German ambassadors were expected, and when they came the whole subject might be discussed.[4] Nothing need be done at once. "We well know," said the Spanish minister, "that the King will be contented with a promise from hence." Cottington had to inform his master that if he expected anything more decisive he had better order his return.[5]

Feb. Charles dissatisfied.

When Charles heard of the difficulty, he was much annoyed, and the Queen took good care to heighten his displeasure. One morning he sent her in jest a white hair which he had discovered in his head. "Don

---

[1] Vane to Dorchester, Nov. 20. The King to Vane, Jan. 5. Vane to Dorchester, Feb. 4. *S. P. Holland.*

[2] Dorchester to Cottington, Jan. 10. *S. P. Spain.*

[3] Soranzo's Despatch, $\frac{Oct. 23}{Nov. 2}$. *Venice MSS.*

[4] The Spanish Government had been urging the sending of these ambassadors in order to find some means of accommodation. Philip IV. to Aytona, July $\frac{6}{16}$, 1629. *Add. MSS.*, 28,474, fol. 184.

[5] Cottington to Dorchester, Jan. 29. *S. P. Spain.*

VOL. I.   P

Carlos," she replied, "will give you many such before the Emperor restores the Palatinate." In spite of his disappointment, however, Charles ordered Cottington to await the coming of the ambassadors from Germany.[1]

With one diplomatist, at least, Charles was on good terms. When Rubens left England he received the honour of knighthood. During his stay his brush had not been idle. The picture of Peace and War, which formed one of the glories of Charles's gallery, is the memorial of the painter's abode here. After wandering to the shores of the Mediterranean, it has once more found a fitting resting-place in the National Collection.[2]

Between peace and war Charles had, in reality, no choice. But it pleased him to think that he had a choice. In March fresh news came from Madrid that the German ambassadors were not coming after all, and that all negotiations must be carried on in the Diet which was expected to meet shortly at Ratisbon. At the same time Philip insisted that if a peace was to be treated of it must be treated of independently of the cession of the Palatinate. He would do all that lay in his power to induce the Emperor to take off the ban. Frederick would then be capable of holding the towns occupied by Spanish garrisons, and it might then be hoped that the rest would follow. To this reasoning Charles succumbed. He would not ask for any promise about the Palatinate as a condition of peace, but he must have for his own satisfaction a written declaration stating what the King of Spain intended to propose at the Diet, and he must have a document conferring on him powers to mediate with the Dutch. Whatever firmness still remained in Charles's mind was explained away by Weston. The Lord Treasurer told Coloma

---

[1] The King to Cottington, Feb. 14. Gerbier to Cottington, Feb. 17. *Ibid.* [2] Sainsbury's *Rubens*, 147.

that his master was ready to make peace, whatever was done about the Palatinate, and that his demand for a declaration had only been made to stop the mouths of the wretches who were trying to sow discord between himself and Spain.¹

Cottington, in fact, had private orders to hold out hopes that if his master's mediation were not accepted by the States General, England would interfere in a far more decisive manner. On May 10, Olivares and Oñate were authorised to listen to a proposal which the English ambassador had made for a league offensive and defensive against the Dutch.² Of course the Spaniards were delighted. Powers were at once sent off to enable Charles to mediate conjointly with the Infanta Isabella as soon as his own peace was made with Spain. He would offer his mediation to the Dutch as satisfaction in full of all demands which might be made upon him for assistance in accordance with the terms of the Treaty of Southampton. If the Dutch refused to accept it, he might consider himself free from all obligations to them. At the same time Philip himself wrote to assure him that not only would he support the claims of his brother-in-law at the approaching Diet, but that, if the exiled Frederick were rendered capable of holding territory in Germany by the revocation of the ban, he would at once surrender into his hands the fortresses in the Palatinate which were garrisoned by Spanish troops.³

---

¹ Cottington to Dorchester, March 3. Dorchester to Cottington, March 21. The King to Cottington, April 7. *S. P. Spain.* Dorchester's answer to Coloma, April $\frac{5}{15}$. Coloma to Olivares, April $\frac{7}{17}$. *Simancas MSS.* 2519.

² Consulta of Olivares and Oñate, Jan. $\frac{2}{12}$, 1631 (misdated 1632). *Simancas MSS.* 2520.

³ Rojas to Cottington, May $\frac{11}{21}$. Philip IV. to the King, May $\frac{13}{23}$. *Simancas MSS.* 2574.

CHAP. V.
1630.
June.
Missions of Anstruther and Vane.

July 5.

Charles and Richelieu.

It was a strange revolution of events. The days of James and Gondomar seemed to have returned. Charles expressed himself content with offers which six years before had at his instigation been indignantly rejected. Anstruther was to go to Ratisbon to negotiate with the Emperor. Vane, who had returned to England, was to go back to the Hague to ask the Dutch to accept the proposed mediation. But he was also to hold out hopes of what might happen if the negotiation with Spain proved unsuccessful. "We may then," Charles expressed it in Vane's instructions, "make this virtue of necessity. We shall have leisure to rectify our affairs at home, to make friends abroad, and by a joint quarrel with those who have equal if not more interest in the restitution of the Palatinate, work better effects than by the course we have hitherto continued of diversion by the war upon Spain; for experience hath shown us that to beat the King of Spain until he bring the Emperor to reason is not the next way to gain our desires; besides, it is impossible for us alone to effectuate this great work, except our friends and allies join with us more heartily than hitherto they have done."

A league with Spain against the Dutch, or a league with the Dutch against Spain, was to Charles but means to an end. He was perhaps right in thinking that Richelieu's professions of interest in the public welfare were hollow. Richelieu cared for the national aggrandisement of France and for the humiliation of the House of Austria, and he was ready to seek any allies who would help him to attain his object. But he did not, like Charles, fancy that allies could be gained without definitive action on his own part, or without a resolution to associate himself with those great currents of popular feeling in which strength is ultimately to be found.

Affairs in Germany were rapidly approaching a crisis. On the one hand, the resolution of the Emperor and the Catholic States to carry out the Edict of Restitution exasperated the Protestants. On the other hand, the ravages and oppressions of Wallenstein and the Imperial army exasperated the Catholic States. At the Diet of Ratisbon, Ferdinand was compelled to dismiss Wallenstein at the demand of the Elector of Bavaria and the Catholic Princes. The great military instrument which had hitherto overpowered all resistance was shattered. Before it could be reconstructed a fresh enemy appeared to attack that Empire which was outwardly so strong, but which had grown so weak through its inward distractions. In June, Gustavus Adolphus landed on the Baltic coast.

CHAP. V.
1630.
June.
Dismissal of Wallenstein.

Landing of Gustavus.

Richelieu had been ready to profit by every circumstance. All through the year French troops had been fighting in Italy. French emissaries had been busy at Ratisbon, hounding on the angry Princes against Wallenstein. A French envoy, in conjunction with Roe, had patched up the truce between Sweden and Poland which set Gustavus free for his great enterprise. Charles was strongly urged to seize the opportunity, and to strike for the Palatinate in the only way in which he had a chance of regaining it, by placing himself on the side of Gustavus.

Charles could neither accept nor reject a policy so promising and yet so hazardous. He listened to appeals from every side. He offered both to the Dutch and to the French to join them on some future occasion, if his negotiation with Spain should fail. For the present he adopted his father's favourite device for freeing

Aug.
Hesitation of Charles.

himself from responsibility. He gave permission to the Marquis of Hamilton to levy six thousand volunteers for the service of Gustavus, a course which would not implicate himself, whilst it gave him, as he fancied, a title to the gratitude of the King of Sweden.[1]

Roe, who had by this time returned from Germany, was amongst the most active supporters of a more warlike policy. Charles proposed to send him back as his ambassador to Gustavus. Roe told him plainly that unless he could carry with him a large sum of money the mission would be useless, and he soon found that his master ceased to care to listen to his advice.[2]

If Charles had held aloof from the German war on the ground of his own inability to take part in war at all, no reasonable objection could be raised to his inaction. Almost at the moment when the Swedish army was crossing the Baltic, a story was going the round of the English Court, telling how the Queen, in receiving a French lady who came to see her and the infant Prince, had been obliged to direct that the shutters should be closed lest the visitor's critical eye should detect the signs of poverty in the ragged coverlet of the bed. It is possible that the tale was untrue or exaggerated; but how was a King to go to war of whom such a story could be credited for an instant?[3]

No difficulties of this kind, however, could restrain Charles from meddling with Continental affairs. At Madrid, indeed, no further obstacle was placed in the way of the negotiation for peace, and on November 5

---

[1] Dorchester to Vane, Aug. 16. *S. P. Holland.* Undated secret negotiation in *S. P. France*, dated approximately by a letter from Montague to Richelieu, Aug. $\frac{11}{21}$. *Aff. Etr.* xliv. 96. *Salvetti's newsletters*, Sept. $\frac{13}{23}$.

[2] *Salvetti's newsletters,* $\frac{\text{Aug. 30}}{\text{Sept. 10}}$.

[3] Soranzo's despatch, June $\frac{16}{26}$. *Venice MSS.*

a treaty was signed which reproduced with a few unimportant modifications the treaty which had been concluded in 1604. Charles received the news with the liveliest satisfaction, and ordered bonfires to be lighted in the streets. The Queen, on the other hand, took care to note her displeasure by appearing at a banquet given to Coloma in her soberest attire, and it was observed that there was but little enthusiasm in the public demonstrations. The unofficial partisans of peace were mostly to be found amongst the merchants who looked forward to the prospect of enriching themselves, now that the fear of the Dunkirk privateers was removed.[1]

On December 7 Coloma swore to the peace in his master's name. At the same time he placed two papers in Charles's hands. The one contained the King of Spain's promise to do his best for the restoration of the Palatinate. The other contained the authority to Charles to mediate with the Dutch.[2]

The Prince of Orange, at least, did not form a high opinion of the value of either of these papers. "Whenever," he said to Vane, "either the Upper or the Lower Palatinate is restored by treaty, I will give his Majesty my head, which I should be loath to lose." Nor did he think more of Charles's capacity for war than he thought of his capacity for negotiation. "The Emperor," he added, "is powerful and great, and to think of the recovery of the Palatinate by the sword may be as full of difficulty as by treaty." Besides, the King's treasure was exhausted, and he was 'in dispute with his people.' If he wished the States to bind themselves to make no peace without the restitution of the Palatinate, he must 'be pleased timely to

[1] *Salvetti's newsletters*, Dec. $\frac{10}{20}, \frac{17}{27}$.
[2] Soranzo's despatch, Dec. $\frac{10}{20}$. *Venice MSS.*

CHAP. V.
1631.

Jan. 2.
Secret Treaty with Spain.

Feb. 15.
Coloma's leave-taking.

consider of the way and means' of maintaining the undertaking 'upon solid grounds.' Vane replied that his master was thinking of some way to provide money. Frederick Henry shook his head. Only by a Parliament, he said, could money be readily obtained.[1]

The Prince little thought what a price Charles was prepared to offer for the Palatinate. On January 2 a secret treaty was signed at Madrid by Cottington and Olivares for the partition of the independent Netherlands. The two Kings were to make war upon the Dutch by land and sea till they were reduced to submission. In the part which was to be ceded to England, the Roman Catholic religion was to be freely tolerated. No corresponding stipulation was inserted on behalf of Protestantism in those lands which were to be handed over to the King of Spain.[2]

No doubt everything was not settled by this nefarious instrument. It still needed Charles's ratification. It seems, too, that there was no more than a general understanding upon the order in which each Government was to take the steps to which it was bound. In Spain there was a tendency to think that the promise of an intervention with the Emperor would be fulfilled by a few formal words. In England there was a tendency to think that nothing short of the complete restitution of the Palatinate was intended. Charles, at all events, took the engagements of Spain as being worth far more than they really were. Upon taking leave, Coloma asked for certain favours which had been granted to former ambassadors. Charles replied that the cases were different. In his father's time there had been friendship between England and

---

[1] Vane to the King, Jan. 14. *S. P. Sweden.*
[2] Secret Treaty, Jan. $\frac{2}{12}$. *Clar. St. P.*, i. 49. Drafts of this treaty, as well as the treaty itself, are at Simancas. Dorchester refers to a different document altogether in *Clar. S. P.* ii. App. xxxiv.

Spain. Now there was only a 'peace barely and simply concluded, with promise of further satisfaction.'[1]

Pending Charles's resolution on larger questions, there was one way in which he hoped to reap a profit from his new ally. Cottington brought home with him 80,000*l*. in Spanish silver, to be made over in bills of exchange to Brussels for the payment of the troops in the Netherlands. So much bullion, to the simple economists of the day, was a mine of wealth. London would become the Exchange of Europe when the precious metals were received, and nothing but paper was to be given in return. The Dutch might grumble if they pleased.[2] The ambassador received his reward on his elevation to the peerage by the title of Baron Cottington.

Early in March instructions were sent to Anstruther to set out for Vienna, that he might put the Spanish professions to the test. The mission was hopeless from the beginning. Gustavus had been establishing himself in Pomerania during the autumn and winter. It was impossible that either the Emperor or the Catholic States should listen to a demand for the re-establishment of a Calvinistic Prince in Southern Germany. Charles, too, had given offence by his permission to Hamilton to levy volunteers for Gustavus. The explanation with which he had accompanied the act was not likely to be considered satisfactory at Vienna. Coloma had been told before he left, that he was not to be surprised if Charles should think fit to assist Gustavus, 'engaging himself in the public cause of the liberty of Germany,' which 'hitherto,' he added, 'we have not done, but only permitted our subjects to serve him; yet it may be that shortly we shall, of which we judge the Spanish

CHAP. V.

1631. Feb. 15. Money brought for the Netherlands.

March 5. Anstruther sent to Vienna.

Hamilton's levies.

---

[1] Memorial, Feb. 19. *S. P. Spain.*
[2] Joachimi to the States General, April 6. *Add. MSS.* 17,677 K. fol. 163.

ministers should not be very sorry, for that by that means we shall have a tie of that King not to go further than for the liberty of Germany.'[1] Hamilton's levies, in short, were to serve as a threat to the Emperor to drive him to the surrender of the Palatinate, whilst they might also be used as a check upon the ambition of Gustavus if that end were once obtained.

Roe's comment.

Charles's designs were far too complicated to prosper. He thought he had done much when he granted Hamilton 11,000*l.* for his levies, leaving him to depend afterwards upon Gustavus for support. Roe's comment was the utterance of common sense. "I fear nothing," he wrote, "but the greatness of the design, not laid low enough in the foundations to build so high." He wished that the King had himself taken the design in hand.[2]

Richelieu's designs.

Whilst Charles was attempting to stand well with the House of Austria and its enemies at the same time, Richelieu was aiming at the less difficult object of uniting the two branches of the opposition to that House. In January, by the Treaty of Bärwalde, he engaged to provide Gustavus with money, whilst Gustavus promised to leave the Catholic religion unmolested where he found it established, and to allow the Elector of Bavaria and the Catholic League to enter into a treaty of neutrality if they chose so to do. Four months later, on May 10, a secret treaty was signed between France and Bavaria, by which they mutually guaranteed to one another the territories which they respectively possessed. The Upper Palatinate was therefore placed by this treaty under French protection.

Jan. 13. The Treaty of Bärwalde.

May 10. Treaty between France and Bavaria.

To substitute political opposition to the House of

---

[1] The King to Anstruther, March 21. *S. P. Germany.*

[2] Roe to Elizabeth, March 22. *Ibid.* Hamilton subsequently received a grant of 15,015*l.* See Appendix to Vol. II.

Austria for the religious conflict between Catholic and Protestant was Richelieu's object. His plan was simplicity itself when compared to the airy imagination of Charles. But even Richelieu had aimed at more than he could accomplish. The Edict of Restitution stood in the way. The Elector of Bavaria wished to preserve it intact. Gustavus had not only come to destroy it, but he saw in the terror which it produced a lever by which the German Protestant Princes, more especially the Elector of Saxony, might be driven to throw in their lot with his own.

As yet John George of Saxony held aloof, hoping that the Emperor would yet abandon the Edict, and spare him, as a German Prince, the odious necessity of joining a foreign invader. Tilly, who had succeeded Wallenstein at the head of the Imperialist armies, was assailing Magdeburg, which had prematurely declared in favour of Gustavus. John George barred the way against the Swedish succours, and on May 10, the very day of the signature of the treaty between France and Bavaria, the city was taken by storm. Amidst blood and flame the citadel of North German Protestantism perished with a mighty destruction. The next day the cathedral alone stood untouched amidst the blackened ruins.

In all probability the fire was the work of a few desperate citizens.[1] The whole Protestant world believed it to be the deliberate work of Tilly.

The future course of the war depended on the Elector of Saxony. John George had placed himself at the head of a league which was ready to support the Emperor if only the Edict of Restitution were abandoned or even modified.

John George's request received support in an un-

---

[1] Wittich, *Magdeburg, Gustav Adolf, und Tilly.*

expected quarter. Olivares deserves a place amongst the most tragic figures in history. He was not one of those blind guides who, like Charles of England, rush headlong into danger from sheer incapacity to discover its existence. No physician was ever more skilful in forming the diagnosis of physical disease than Olivares was in fathoming the diseases of the State. He was perfectly aware that Spain was sinking under the strain to which it was subjected. He never blinded himself to the absolute necessity of cutting short the demands upon the blood and treasure of the country. For all that, he knew well that he could not stay his hand. His shrewd words were never followed by wise deeds. The monarchy which he served was bound by its past history, and he was not the man to cut loose the ties. With the heroism of calm and impassive courage he guided Spain as wittingly into the valley of death as he who rode at the head of the six hundred Englishmen to the muzzles of the guns of Balaclava foresaw that the sacrifice would be made in vain.

The Spanish Government now gave wise counsel to the Emperor. Alliance with the Elector of Saxony against France and the Elector of Bavaria on the basis of the suspension of the Edict of Restitution was the policy recommended by Olivares.[1] Ferdinand would

[1] "Mucho conviene en el estado presente de las cosas en que el movimiento contra la casa de Austria es casi universal que el Emperador mire por si y ponga el hombro a su propria defensa y conservacion por todos los medios permetidos á la religion Catholica que se pudieren disponer, y siendo cierto que el mundo tiene hoi al Duque de Baviera por el enemigo mayor de la casa de Austria, y el que mas va machinando su ruina con ligas y negociaciones secretas (quando no lo sea) es licito al Emperador hazer un partido por el daño que despues seria irreparable. El camino es quietar y dar satisfacion al Duque de Saxonia a condicion de que con sus armas y poder, y con el de sus parciales asista al Emperador contra qualesquier enemigos suyos publicos y secretos; y esto no parece difficil de encaminar, per ser el de Saxonia Principe constante y que se mueve tarde y se halla obligado de la casa de Austria,

not listen. He insisted on the maintenance of the Edict. He spoke contemptuously of the Saxon armaments. John George was arrogantly bidden to dismiss his troops, and to submit to the head of the Empire.

With a whole world crashing about his ears, Ferdinand had no time to listen to the pleadings of the English ambassador. Anstruther turned to the Spanish ambassadors, urging upon them the wisdom of revoking the Edict and satisfying the dispossessed Princes. He got but little comfort from them. "Acts," he was told, "so solemnly done, upon mature deliberation, could not be undone or revoked without a world of difficulty."[1]

Neither the King of Spain nor the Emperor would mould their policy in accordance with Charles's wishes. They knew well that from him they had nothing to fear or to hope. Months had passed away, and the secret treaty against the Dutch had not been ratified in England. In March, Hamilton had been sent to Scotland to levy volunteers for Gustavus.[2] It was enough to irritate the Catholic Powers, not enough to compel their respect. He found that in Scotland, at least, the name of the half-hearted King was not a tower of strength. There was plenty of enthusiasm for the Protestant cause, and many a younger son had already carried his stalwart arm and his ill-lined purse to the

y siendo hoi el edicto de la restitucion de los bienes ecclesiasticos la causa porque se inquieta, en la qual persiste el Emperador llevado du su zelo, o persuadido de los que con pretexto de piedad quieren irritar contra el a los hereges, es facil y justo suspender la execucion del edicto a mejor sazon, y grangear al Duque de Saxonia y sus confederados, y asegurar con el la propria defensa, y estorvar una guerra de religion en el imperio, que si comienza a creer sera de gravisimos daños á la causa Catholica." Philip IV. to Cadereyta, May 18/28. *Simancas MSS.* 2547.

[1] Anstruther to Dorchester, July 5. *S. P. Germany.*

[2] Articles by the King of Sweden, May 31, 1631. Articles by Hamilton, March 1, 1631. Burnet, *Memoirs of Hamilton,* 7.

1631.
May.

service of Gustavus. Four hundred men only could be induced to follow Hamilton's standard.[1] Amongst the volunteers in Germany the vacillations of Charles formed a frequent topic of the rough soldiers' talk around the camp fire or the mess table. To these hardy adventurers it was as incomprehensible as it was in more polished circles how the King of England could hope to regain his brother-in-law's inheritance by negotiation.

Lord Reay's charge against Hamilton.

Some of this talk came to the ears of Donald Mackay, Lord Reay, who commanded a regiment in the service of Gustavus. Either in the mouths of his informants or in his own brain, the gossip of the camp assumed a formidable shape. He told a friend, Lord Ochiltree, that Hamilton never intended to go to Germany at all. He meant to rely on his levies, to seize the King, execute Weston and the partisans of Spain, and make himself King of Scotland, to which, after the descendants of James, he was the nearest heir. Ochiltree, who had reasons of his own for disliking Hamilton, passed the tale on to Weston.

Charles disbelieves it.

Where Charles placed his confidence he placed it wholly. "He does not trust many," wrote the Venetian ambassador, "and when he conceives a good opinion of any one, he does not let it fall. He is accustomed to say that it is necessary to grant his favour to a single person, and to maintain him in it, as he would be attacked on all sides with calumny."[2] But his resolution to support Weston's political authority did not stand in the way of his personal friendship with Weston's enemies. Holland and Pembroke and Hamilton were the constant companions of his leisure hours, and he was the last man to believe a slanderous accusa-

[1] Beaulieu to Puckering, May 25. *Court and Times,* ii. 122.
[2] Soranzo's despatch, Jan. $\frac{8}{18}$. *Venice MSS.*

tion against one with whom he was in the habit of daily intercourse. When Hamilton returned from Scotland he received him with open arms. He told him of the charges which had been brought against him, and insisted upon his sleeping in the same room with himself as the best evidence in his power to give of his entire disbelief in the alleged conspiracy.[1]

The accusers paid the penalty for their rashness. Ochiltree was put upon his trial at Edinburgh as a sower of sedition. He was condemned to perpetual imprisonment, from which he was only liberated twenty years later by Cromwell. Lord Reay named David Ramsay, an officer in Hamilton's service, as his informant. Ramsay denied the truth of the accusation, and as no sufficient evidence could be produced on either side, the two Scotchmen demanded the right of settling the question by combat. A Court of Chivalry was formed, and trial by combat was awarded. The King, however, interfered, and sent both parties to the Tower, till they consented to give securities against breach of the peace.[2]

Charles no sooner heard of Hamilton's ill success in Scotland, than he gave him permission to try his fortune in England. In London his drums attracted even fewer volunteers than in the Northern kingdom.[3] The experience of those who had gone forth at Charles's bidding to the war in Germany was not encouraging. At Hamilton's entreaty, the Lords Lieutenants of the Counties were ordered to give every assistance in filling his ranks, pressing only excepted. There were always vagabonds and rogues enough in England, of whom the official people were anxious to be rid, and Hamil-

---

[1] *Burnet*, 13.
[2] *State Trials*, iii. 425–520.
[3] *Salvetti's newsletters*, $\frac{June\ 24}{July\ 4}$.

ton, as Mansfeld had done before him, at last gathered round him a force of which the numbers were more imposing than the quality. On July 16 he sailed from the Downs with 6,000 Englishmen. The Scottish levies had by this time reached 1,000, and with the whole force he started for the Baltic.[1]

It was probably the knowledge that Charles had given his support to Hamilton which induced Richelieu to make overtures to Weston for the establishment of a better understanding between them. Weston replied, doubtless by his master's direction, that no such understanding was possible unless France were honestly resolved to assist in the recovery of the Palatinate.[2]

There was something not very dissimilar in the position of the two ministers. Both of them were possessed of the fullest confidence of their respective Sovereigns. Both of them found their most vigorous assailants in the family circle of their Sovereigns. In France, the two Queens, Anne of Austria and Mary de Medicis, the wife and mother of Lewis, joined with his only brother Gaston, Duke of Orleans, in an attempt to overthrow the Cardinal. It was an opposition directed not against the weak points of the Cardinal's government, but against his strongest. If it had been successful, it would have substituted plunder and waste for orderly finance, the despotism of the aristocracy for the despotism of the King, and subservience to Spain for a national policy. In November 1630, the clique had almost succeeded in overthrowing Richelieu by taking advantage of a moment of weakness in the King. But Lewis recovered himself in an

---

[1] *Salvetti's newsletters*, July $\frac{3}{11}$, $\frac{15}{25}$. Dorchester to Carleton, June 22. S. P. Holland.

[2] Wake to Weston, July 25. Weston to Wake, Aug. 14. S. P. France.

instant, and the Day of Dupes, as it was called, left the Cardinal more firmly seated in power than before.[1]

Great as was the sullen indignation of all who had taken part in the plot, that of the Queen Mother was justly regarded as the most dangerous. She had once ruled France as Regent, and her proud spirit could ill brook the disgrace of being supplanted by one whom she had herself assisted to office. In February it was found necessary to place her in confinement at Compiègne. The next month the weak and cowardly Gaston fled across the frontier to the Duke of Lorraine, and in July Mary de Medicis herself escaped from her prison and took refuge in the Spanish Netherlands.

It was no secret that the Queen Mother and Gaston would offer the aid of their influence in France to the Spanish Government. A gentleman had come from Gaston immediately after his flight, to urge Charles to make common cause with Spain and Lorraine against the detested Cardinal. Gerbier, who had lately gone to Brussels as Charles's resident minister, was carried off his balance by the enthusiasm of the place. He retailed to his master all the tattle of the fugitive Queen; told how the lustful Cardinal had offered his hateful love to his master's wife, and had attempted to poison her when he found his overtures rejected. The King of Spain, he said, had sent money to aid the good cause. There were to be levies in Alsace, in Lorraine, and the Spanish Netherlands. The Papal Nuncio, accompanied by the ambassadors of the Queen Mother's sons-in-law, the King of Spain and the Duke of Savoy, was formally to adjure Lewis to hear what his mother had to say in her own defence, and it was

---

[1] For the relations between the King and Richelieu, see Topin, *Louis XIII. et Richelieu.*

expected that Charles, as the third son-in-law, would follow the example.[1]

Charles had no inclination to take the part assigned to him by the Queen Mother. Still less was he willing to risk a war in order to restore her to her country. Gaston, who talked of leading an army into France, asked for the loan of some English ships. His mother urged that Rochelle and Rhé were without fortifications and would easily be taken. She forgot that the names must sound somewhat ominously in the ears of her son-in-law.

The fact was that Spain was not quite so ready to assist her as she hoped. Olivares, with his usual good sense, had seen the arrival of the Queen in his master's dominions with the greatest displeasure, and only wanted to be quit of her as soon as possible. He had no wish to add an open war with France to his other difficulties.[2]

The Queen Mother was growing impatient. Through Lord Chaworth, who was returning from Spa, she sent a pressing message to Henrietta Maria, begging her to grant her a refuge in England.

Henrietta Maria had other motives than that of filial affection for supporting her mother's demand. The strife between the Cardinal and Mary de Medicis had found an echo in the English Court. Early in 1630 Chateauneuf had returned to France, to occupy the post of Keeper of the Seals. His successor, the Marquis of Fontenay-Mareuil, had come into collision with the Queen by insisting on the dismissal of her confessor.[3] By this time Chateauneuf had been

---

[1] Dorchester to Wake, March 30. *S. P. Savoy.* Gerbier to Weston, June 29; Gerbier to the King, July 1, 11, 30. *S. P. Flanders.*

[2] Henrard, *Marie de Médicis dans les Pays Bas*, 99.

[3] *Salvetti's newsletters*, June $\frac{10}{20}$, $\frac{17}{27}$. Fontenay to Richelieu, $\frac{May\ 26}{June\ 5}$, June. *Aff. Etr.* xliv. 274, 276.

drawn into the opposition against Richelieu by the influence of the bright eyes of the Duchess of Chevreuse, who was the soul of the Spanish party in France. Chateauneuf, whose influence was strong with the Frenchmen and Frenchwomen who still remained in the Queen's Court, placed himself at the head of an intrigue for the overthrow of Weston, who was led by his desire of peace to avoid an open breach with Richelieu. Chateauneuf's chief instrument was the Chevalier de Jars, a witty adventurer, who chatted with the Queen and played tennis with the King. At last the contest between the Chevalier and the Ambassador broke out into an open scandal. Fontenay employed a housebreaker to enter the window of De Jars, and to carry off the cabinet in which his correspondence with Chateauneuf was contained. The Queen demanded justice. Fontenay declared proudly that he had a right to use any means he chose to discover the disloyal manœuvres of his master's subjects, and Charles refused to press the matter further. He saw that there was a common bond between the intrigue against Richelieu and the intrigue against Weston, and, like Lewis, he sustained his minister against his wife.

CHAP. V.
1631.
Sept. Chateauneuf's intrigues.

June. Theft of his correspondence.

It was not a moment in which Charles was likely to listen to the Queen's pleadings for her mother. He consented to send Sir William Balfour to the Low Countries on a complimentary mission to Mary de Medicis, but he shut up Lord Chaworth for a few days in the Fleet, for presuming to bring a political message to the Queen without his sanction. Hesitating as he was in more important matters, he was unalterably firm in his resolution not to admit of a visit from his mother-in-law.[1]

Visit of the Queen Mother forbidden.

[1] Gerbier's despatches, Aug. and Sept. *S. P. Flanders.* Soranzo's despatches, Aug. 19/29, Sept. 6/16, Sept. 23/Oct. 3, Oct. 7/17. *Venice MSS.*

1631.
Aug.
Difficulties of the Spanish monarchy.

Olivares might well strive to avoid a collision with France. Sooner or later it would be unavoidable. That huge Spanish monarchy, without geographical or political cohesion, was at once a menace to the weak and a prey to the strong. It had interests everywhere but at home, and at every point there were those who understood those interests otherwise than they were understood at Madrid. At Brussels the Infanta Isabella and her ministers were giving encouragement to the French refugees in spite of Olivares. At Vienna the Emperor welcomed gladly the support of the Spanish Government, whilst he turned a deaf ear to its counsels.

Sept.
Anstruther learns the Spanish demands.

Amongst those counsels, the recommendation to restore the Palatinate can hardly be seriously reckoned. Anstruther, weary of delays at Vienna, applied to Quiroga, a friar in close connection with the Spanish embassy. The Friar told him frankly that the King of Spain would not even surrender the towns garrisoned by his own troops for nothing. He must have either a general peace, or assistance against the Dutch. The statement was confirmed by the ambassadors themselves. They had no other instructions, they said, than a paper which had been shown to Cottington in Spain.[1]

What this paper was is not exactly known. It seems, however, to have been unsigned, and to have contained a proposal that the restitution of the Spanish part of the Palatinate should be conditional on the carrying out of the secret league against the Dutch.[2]

[1] Vane, the younger, to Sir H. Vane, Sept. 13. *S. P. Germany.*
[2] A comparison of the extract from Dorchester's letter printed in *Clar. St. P.* ii. App. xxxiv. with Olivares' Consulta of Nov. $\frac{19}{20}$ (*Simancas MSS.* Est. 2519) makes this probable. The paper was certainly not the secret treaty itself, as it is described by Olivares as unsigned. Ranke (Engl. transl. ii. 22) seems to confound 'the paper given to Lord Cottington' with the secret treaty.

The unsatisfactory nature of the news which reached Charles from Vienna induced him at last to open negotiations with Gustavus. Sir Henry Vane had long been designated for the mission, but it was not till the end of September that he was allowed to cross the sea. As a friend and dependent of Weston he could be trusted not to engage his master too precipitately in war, but so great had been the pressure put upon Charles to throw himself into the cause of Gustavus, that even Weston's friends had thought it prudent to associate themselves with the popular cry. Parliament, they said, would soon be summoned in order to provide means for reinforcing Hamilton.[1]

CHAP. V.
1631.
Sept. Vane sent to Gustavus.

When Vane landed in Holland on his way to Germany, shouts of victory rung in his ears. A Spanish attempt to land a military force on the coast of Holland had been signally defeated. Almost at the same time news arrived that Tilly had been struck down by Gustavus at Breitenfeld.

Sept. 7. The victory of Breitenfeld.

Richelieu's calculations had proved abortive. He had hoped to hold back Tilly from attacking the Swedes, through his influence with the Elector of Bavaria, whilst he launched Gustavus against the hereditary dominions of the House of Austria.[2] The refusal of Ferdinand to admit the slightest modification of the Edict of Restitution cleared away these diplomatic cobwebs. He ordered Tilly to attack the Elector of Saxony, and Tilly obeyed. John George, loath as he was to abandon his loyalty to the Empire, took his stand with Gustavus. Maximilian took his stand once

---

[1] Soranzo's despatches, Aug. $\frac{19}{29}$, Sept. $\frac{9}{19}$. *Venice MSS.*

[2] It is clear from Wake's despatches (*S. P. France*) that Richelieu expected that Tilly would leave Gustavus alone. I must leave it to German enquirers to clear up the secret history of Maximilian's conduct in this year.

more with Ferdinand. Catholic and Protestant were again fairly face to face.

The victory of Gustavus was complete. His success at Breitenfeld decided once for all that North Germany was to be essentially Protestant. The Edict of Restitution was swept away at a blow. Ferdinand's system, like that of Charles, was one which rested on technical legality, and which took no account of the feelings and aspirations of the populations over which he ruled. Guarded by the most numerous and well appointed armies which the world had seen since the days of the Roman Empire, that system had been dashed to the ground through its own inherent weakness. Could Charles hope to escape a like calamity? In Breitenfeld lay the promise of Marston Moor and Naseby—of the ruin of a cause which rested on traditionary claims in the face of the living demands of the present hour.

Gustavus pushed on for the Rhine to lay his hand on the Ecclesiastical States of the League, to gather round him the scattered forces of the Southern Protestants, and to drive home the wedge which he had struck in between France and Bavaria. Vane had hard work to come up with him. On November 6 he found him at Würzburg. He had been sent, he explained, to 'treat of an alliance . . . the ground whereof was to be the restitution of both Palatinates and the liberty of Germany.' Gustavus naturally enquired what help Charles purposed to give. If he would send him ten or twelve thousand men in the spring, and a large sum of money besides, he was ready to give the undertaking he required. The German Princes, he said, had made no stipulations for the Palatinate. It concerned his Majesty to look about him, for unless he gave a Royal assistance, the proposal could not be entertained. Vane thought all this very unreasonable. "If this King," he wrote, "gets the Palatinate," it will be hard fetching it out of his hands without satisfaction." It would be far better to get it in a peaceable way by negotiation at Vienna.¹

Few in England would have echoed Vane's opinion. The news of Tilly's defeat had been received with an outburst of enthusiasm. Sir Simonds D'Ewes, the plodding antiquary, raised his head from his plea-rolls and genealogies to record how 'the sole honour and glory of this victory, next under God—to whom the religious King of Sweden gave the only glory—redounded to the Swedes and Scots and other nations in the Evangelical army.' By Gustavus, he added, 'the bloody robbers, ravishers, and massacrers of Tilly's army were not only executed, but infinite comfort afforded to the distressed and persecuted and oppressed Protestants in Germany, so as all men hoped he in the issue would assert fully both the true religion and the ancient liberties of Germany.'² Eliot, from his prison in the Tower, awoke to new delight. 'If at once,' he wrote, 'the whole world be not deluded, fortune and hope are met.'³

To Charles the great deliverance brought no pleasant thoughts. When the news reached England he was planning a closer alliance with the Emperor and Spain. The Abbot of Scaglia had come to England to revive the negotiation about the Palatinate. Weston and Cottington had already agreed with him that the Emperor should be allowed to levy 12,000 volunteers in England, and on October 7 the Abbot was able to write that Charles was ready to enter into a league with the Emperor and the King of Spain against their enemies in Germany, and to induce his brother-in-law

---

¹ Vane to Dorchester, Nov. 12. *S. P. Germany.*
² D'Ewes. *Autobiography,* ii. 59, 60.
³ Eliot to Luke, Oct. 3. Forster, *Sir J. Eliot,* ii. 438.

to do the same as soon as justice was done him in respect to the Palatinate.¹

<small>1631.
Nov.
Hesitation of Charles.</small>

Weeks passed away, and there was no sign that either Spain or the Emperor would pay any attention to these lavish offers. The Friar, who had been in England in 1624 under the name of Francesco della Rota, returned to throw the blame upon Anstruther's zeal for the interests of the King of Sweden. Then came bad news from Hamilton. His troops had melted away as Mansfeld's had melted away before, and he had only 500 men left. Charles could not make up his mind one way or another. He did not like to give up hope of an agreement with the Emperor till he heard again from Spain. He was not ready to send reinforcements to Germany. He ordered Dorchester to write to Vane that 'His Majesty felt Hamilton's losses like a father of his people to whom their blood is precious,' and he would risk no more of their lives.² Yet when Vane's despatch announcing the offer of Gustavus arrived, it seemed incredible that Charles should reject it, if he really cared for the Palatinate. The rumours of an approaching meeting of Parliament acquired fresh consistency.³ With the thought of a Parliament men's minds turned instinctively to the prisoner in the Tower who would once more become a power in the land. A message, the purport of which is now unknown, was sent to Eliot from some persons about the Court. By popular rumour it was magnified into a visit paid to him by men high in place to bespeak his goodwill in

<small>Dec.
Hamilton's misfortunes.</small>

<small>Fresh rumours of a Parliament.</small>

---

¹ Consulta on the Abbot of Scaglia's despatches, Nov. $\frac{10}{20}$. *Simancas MSS.* 2519.

² Joachimi to the States General, Dec. 3. *Add. MSS.* 17,677. N. fol. 243. Soranzo's despatch, Dec. $\frac{2}{12}$. *Venice MSS.* Dorchester to Anstruther, Nov. 29. *S. P. Germany.* Dorchester to Vane, Dec. 19. *S. P. Sweden.*

³ Roe to Hepburn, Dec. 12. *S. P. Dom.* cciv. 34.

the days when their doings were likely to be called in question. Eliot knew better than to trust such rumours. He declined to answer the message he received. Yet he was by no means insensible to the critical position of affairs. In a sketch of the doings of the first Parliament of Charles which he drew up about this time, he spoke enthusiastically of Gustavus as 'that person whom fortune and virtue had reserved for the wonder of the world.' For himself he had no hope in this life. He knew better than Holland or Roe that no earthly consideration short of absolute necessity would induce Charles to summon another Parliament. Yet he never doubted that some day or other that necessity would arise. His historical sketch he named *Negotium Posterorum*. His own example and the example of those who had been his fellow workers he bequeathed to generations coming, nothing doubting that the spirit of England would not be extinguished for ever by the heavy weight of silence under which the voice of his country was smothered for a time.

1631. Dec. Their effect upon Eliot.

If Eliot had little hope that his own voice would again be heard in Parliament, he could not deny himself the satisfaction of setting down upon paper the thoughts which burned within him. If opportunity were by any strange freak of fortune to be allowed him, he would not be the counsellor of compromise. He held that the things which had been done were worse than all the misgovernment which had called forth the Petition of Right. "The one was an act of oppression against liberty and the laws; but the design of the other is to put at once a conclusion to the work of darkness, and to depress and ruin law and liberty itself. For it is not in any stream, in any branch or derivative of our freedom, in some one particular of the laws, but it is in the spring and fountain from whence all the streams flow,

Eliot's Notes of a speech.

that the attempt has been made, not to trouble and corrupt it for a time only, but wholly to impeach its course, to make the fountain dry, to dam and stop it up for ever." Parliament, he added, was the sanctuary of liberty, the guardian of 'the rubrics of the law.' In harmony with Parliament Kings had ruled happily; in discord with Parliament success was impossible.[1]

Such was Eliot's last word on politics, such was the standard which he set up round which his countrymen might gather. In him spoke the voice of a mighty nation, conscious of its powers and impatient of the tutelage under which it had been thrust. What if folly had mingled with wisdom in the last Parliamentary session? What if the leaders of the Commons, Eliot himself included, had been hasty and impatient where quietness and confidence would have been the higher wisdom? We at least have been admitted within the closed doors of Charles's Cabinet. We at least have seen the value of that statesmanship to which he appealed as giving him a claim to guide the nation in its onward course. There was no educative power in a ruler who set before himself low and poor objects, and who strove to gain those objects in the manner in which Charles was striving to recover the Palatinate. If there were errors and follies in the House of Commons, they were far exceeded by the errors and follies of the Court.

The time would come when Charles's misgovernment would bear its appropriate fruit. The mass of men rise up against the consequences of misgovernment, not against misgovernment itself. Those who, like Eliot, see too clearly into the future, have to bear the burthen of the coming generations. The rumour which told of consultations with Eliot pointed him out

[1] Forster, *Sir J. Eliot*, ii. 445.

for Charles's vengeance. On December 21 came an order from the Council restraining access of persons of several conditions to Sir John Eliot. Nor was this all. "My lodgings," he wrote on the 26th, "are removed, and I am now where candle-light may be suffered, but scarce fire."[1] This, too, was in the cold Christmas weather. Here are no traces of that generosity with which Hamilton was welcomed home from Scotland. Charles could cling to the friend with whom he had associated from his youth up. It required some imagination to picture to himself the sufferings or the nobility of the man whom he had known but as an enemy, and had looked upon as a traitor to his beloved Buckingham.

Charles had no intention of allowing Eliot ever again to raise his voice in opposition. He called upon the Privy Council to advise him upon the means of satisfying the demands of Gustavus. There was but one answer to be made. If 200,000*l*. or 300,000*l*. were to be expended upon the German war, it would be necessary to summon Parliament. Such counsel found no favour with the King. The very mention of a Parliament, he said, was derogatory to his authority. The King of Sweden must be helped, but not in such a way as that. Any other plan, even if it presented greater difficulties, would be more opportune. The Council was thus driven back upon projects similar to those which had ended in so signal a failure before the session of 1628. One proposed a general collection in the churches. Another thought that all pensions should be stopped, and the expenses of the Court cut down. Nothing serious could have come of a discussion thus commenced.[2]

[1] Forster, *Sir J. Eliot,* ii. 448.
[2] Soranzo's despatch, Dec. 30 / Jan. 9. *Venice MSS.*

CHAP.
V.
1632.
Feb. 15.
Dorchester's death.

Those who took an interest in the fortunes of German Protestantism at Charles's side were fast falling. Conway had died a year ago, and he had soon been followed by May. It was Dorchester's turn now. On February 15 he died, 'Christianly and manly,' expressing, 'as well in his latest words as in his life, that his affections were right to God, to his master, and the good cause.' His master cared little for the good cause, and even amongst those who were not so indifferent, there were many who, as Roe said, were ready to 'enquire curiously what the King of Sweden doth, and censure him for doing too much or too little, but who did not consider that they themselves were doing nothing.'

Further negotiation with Gustavus.

In his perpetual oscillation Charles was now tending, or thought he was tending, to the side of Gustavus. He was dissatisfied with the coolness with which his overtures for a league had been received at Madrid.[1] Before the end of the year he had given permission to his brother-in-law to betake himself to Germany, and to place himself at the disposal of the Swedish King.[2] Then came fresh offers to Gustavus. But the negotiation was rapidly degenerating into a mere bargain, like the negotiations with Parliament and army which fifteen years later were to prove to the world that no political reconstruction was possible of which Charles was an element. Gustavus was as little to be bargained with as Cromwell. The constant harping upon the string of the Palatinate, to the disregard of larger objects, was an offence to him. How could he bind himself to the restitution of a province which France and Bavaria were leagued to keep? Was the great cause of the political and religious independence of

[1] *Salvetti's newsletters*, Feb. $\frac{17}{27}$.
[2] Dorchester to Vane, Dec. 31. *S. P. Sweden*.

Germany to be postponed to make way for a petty dynastic interest? He was ready enough to do the best for the Palatinate that circumstances would permit. Charles wanted him to act as if the one question of pre-eminent importance to the world were the question whether an incapable and headstrong Prince were to rule again over the dominions which he had inherited from his father. What hearty co-operation could there be between two men so differently constituted?

Gustavus had need to walk warily. In the midst of his triumphant progress, when all Protestant Europe was shouting applause, he was weighing the difficulties before him—above all, the difficulties which were likely to arise from France. When he kept Christmas at Mentz, a French army was not far off. Richelieu had fallen upon the Duke of Lorraine, and had frustrated the hopes of Gaston and the Queen Mother. It was not, however, merely to crush the Duke of Lorraine that he had brought Lewis with him. The Cardinal cherished hopes which were not as yet destined to be fulfilled. He hoped that the German Princes and Cities on the left bank of the Rhine—the Ecclesiastical Electorates especially—would take refuge from the storm of Protestant conquest beneath the lilied banner of France. The great German river would form the boundary, if not of French territory, at least of the French confederation, whilst Gustavus would be thrust on to the work for which Richelieu had originally destined him—the work of crushing the House of Austria for the benefit of France.

Richelieu's schemes were premature. As yet the German Princes showed no disposition to revolve as satellites round the throne at Paris. The Elector of Bavaria drew closer and closer to the Emperor. Before the end of January, Lewis, sick and disappointed, hurried home from the army, leaving the affairs of Germany to be disposed of by Gustavus. He was not anxious to remain as a looker on, when he had expected to step forth as the arbiter of Europe.[1]

Involved as he was in a diplomatic struggle with France, Gustavus was not likely to bind himself as Charles desired that he should be bound, without securing the absolute co-operation of England in his great designs. He told Vane, with perfect frankness, of his difficulties. He thought it by no means improbable that by raising the Protestant standard he would bring upon himself a combined attack from France and Spain. He therefore asked for the aid of an English fleet to assure his communications with Sweden and his position on the Baltic coast. He asked, too, that if the Palatinate were recovered, the restored Elector should tolerate the Lutheran religion in it, and should place at his disposal the military strength of the country during the remainder of the war. Eight regiments of foot and 3,000 horse were to form Charles's contingent, of which he was himself to have the absolute military direction. He would then do his best to recover for Frederick his lands and dignities, and if any towns in the Palatinate fell into his hands, he would at once place them in the hands of the Elector.

Charles, in short, was to have perfect confidence in Gustavus, and was to resign himself to the fusion of his own particular interest with the larger interests of German Protestantism. The great majority of the Privy Council spoke strongly for the acceptance of these terms.[2] Charles would not hear of them. The request that in

---

[1] Wake's despatches (*S. P. France*) contain minute information on all this, and shew the tone prevailing from day to day in the French camp.

[2] Soranzo's despatch, Feb. $\frac{3}{13}$, $\frac{\text{Mach 30}}{\text{April 9}}$. *Venice MSS. Salvetti's newsletters*, March $\frac{16}{26}$.

certain eventualities he should oppose the fleets of France and Spain seemed to him to be totally inadmissible. A league for general co-operation he did not need. By such a course he 'must change his settled quiet state, or else desert that party to which he doth adhere.' There were, however, 'other two kinds of leagues, one of amity and alliance, the other of aid and assistance, and neither of these breaketh peace nor giveth just offence to any.' For either of these he was prepared. He would give Gustavus 10,000*l.* a month, in return for which the King of Sweden was to endeavour by all means possible, whether by arms or treaty, to 'effect the restitution of the Palatinate, delivering up to the Elector the places in it which were recovered.' As Charles omitted to stipulate that his contribution should continue for any definite number of years, he, in reality, bound himself to nothing beyond the first month's contribution.[1]

CHAP. V.
1632.
April 26. Charles's counter propositions.

Before Charles's proposal reached Gustavus, the south of Germany was at the feet of the Swedish conqueror. On March 21 he entered Nüremberg. On the 26th he was at Donauwörth. On April 4 he came up with Tilly on the Lech, and forced the passage of the river after a sharp fight, in which the veteran commander of the Imperialist forces was mortally wounded. Gustavus pressed on. He liberated Augsburg, and entered Munich in triumph.

March. Fresh victories of Gustavus.

The news of victory was received in England with indescribable emotion. It had come, wrote Roe, like rain in a dry May. 'We will not give the King of Sweden leave to conquer like a man by degrees nor human ways, but we look he should fight battles and take towns so fast as we read them in the Book of Joshua, whose example indeed he is.' The Papist, he added, hung his head like a bulrush. The offer of 10,000*l.* a month

Reception of the news in England.

[1] Articles. April 26. Coke to Vane, May 2. *S. P. Sweden.*

was not all which Gustavus had a right to expect, but a wise Prince would accept of less than he wished to obtain.'[1]

In drawing near to Gustavus, Charles had taken some steps to draw near to Richelieu as well. On March 10 a treaty was arranged to put an end to the commercial disputes which had arisen with France since the peace. Four days afterwards, Charles's ambassador, Sir Isaac Wake, presented to Lewis a letter from his master, formally proposing a joint action in Germany. Like Ferdinand and Gustavus, Lewis had views and objects of his own which were not absolutely identical with those of Charles. He was ready, he said, to do anything for Frederick which would not tend to the ruin of the Catholics of Germany.[2] For the moment Richelieu had work enough to do at home. The party of Gaston and the Queen Mother caused him continual disquiet. He struck hard and pitilessly. Marillac, the political chief of the opposition, died in prison. His brother, a Marshal of France, perished on the scaffold. Gaston prepared an invasion from the Spanish Duchy of Luxemburg, whilst the Duke of Lorraine, eager to avenge his defeat of the previous summer, permitted Gaston's troops to enter his territory. Richelieu treated the act as a declaration of war, entered Lorraine, and compelled the Duke to sign a treaty by which he surrendered three of his strongest fortresses as a pledge of his enforced fidelity.[3] This time Richelieu's hand stretched over Germany itself. The Elector of Treves, failing to obtain support from the Emperor, invoked French protection. The lilies of France floated over the fortress of Ehrenbreitstein.

[1] Roe to Horwood, May 28. *S. P. Dom.* ccxvi. 92.
[2] Wake to Coke (?) March 11. Wake to Weston, March 16. Treaty signed, March 19. *S P. France.*
[3] Instructions to St. Chaumont, May $\frac{10}{20}$. *Aff. Etr.* xlv. 215.

Before commencing the attack upon Lorraine, Richelieu had thought fit to despatch the Marquis of St. Chaumont as a special envoy to prevent Charles from taking offence. He did not promise himself much from England. But if Spain should attack France in consequence of its interference in Germany, it was just possible that Charles might be roused to give some kind of assistance. "Although," wrote Lewis in his instructions to St. Chaumont, "the English should not keep any of their promises, it is important to bring about some sort of union between the two crowns." St. Chaumont was also charged to effect a reconciliation between the French Ambassador, Fontenay, and Henrietta Maria, in order to bring the Queen's influence to bear in the interests of France.[1]

Charles received St. Chaumont coldly; talked about his good intentions, but went no further. The Queen refused to be reconciled to Fontenay. He had done her no special injury, she said, but she did not like him.[2]

The views of those who advocated an alliance with Sweden, independently of France, may best be taken from an argument in its favour forwarded by Roe to the Earl of Holland whilst St. Chaumont was still in England. He did not agree with those who feared danger from the ambition of Gustavus. "The King of Sweden," he urged, "is not to be considered in his branches and fair plumes of one year's prosperity, but in his root, and so he is not at all to be feared; and it hath been a false and a feigned suspicion in those who from his sudden growth have augured that he might prove dangerous to the public liberty.

[1] Instructions to St. Chaumont, May $\frac{16}{26}$. *Aff. Etr.* xlv. 215.
[2] Fontenay to Richelieu, $\frac{May\ 30}{June\ 9}$. St. Chaumont to Richelieu, May? *Ibid.*, xlv. 111, 112.

That kingdom of itself can do no more than Bœotia without Epaminondas. If this King had a foundation, ancient dependence, and a settled posterity, it were great wisdom to stay his career and limit it; but when we see he doth embrace more than he can hold, and is rather a torrent than a live spring, that all his glory and greatness depends upon his own virtue and life; and that in case of sure mortality it is certain that all this inundation will dry up and return to the first channel of moderation, it is mere folly to object him, mere malice and envy to make the seeming care of the future hinder that course of victory which God hath chosen by him, not to set up a new monarchy, but to temper the fury of tyranny and to restore the equality of just government."

From France or Spain, Roe thought there was nothing to be hoped. Neither of these States cared for anything except the gratification of its own ambition, and they were therefore 'best employed like millstones to grind themselves thin.' The true alliance for England was with the Dutch. It was true that the States had been ungrateful and insolent. But they had not been kindly treated, and if the English Government would meet them in a friendly spirit, it would obtain their friendship in return. "I confess," he continued, "they abuse their liberty, deceive us in trade, cosen us of our money, but I cannot be angry with them that they prove cunning friends when we prove slothful and improvident of our own advantages. One settled treaty would at once stop all these breaches and limit them."

Roe's policy was an immediate alliance with Sweden and the Netherlands, with a view to a general Protestant alliance to be independent of both the great Catholic monarchies. Roe, as was well known, was the candidate of the party opposed to Weston for the vacant

secretaryship. Charles was not likely to give the post
to one who held opinions so different from his own. If
Wake had lived, he would probably have been Dorchester's successor.[1] But Wake died of a sudden attack
of fever. The new Secretary was Francis Windebank,
Clerk of the Council, a man utterly unknown in the
world of politics. But he was an old friend of Laud,
and Laud's friend was not likely to frighten Weston
by urging the King to a breach with the House of
Austria. Roe concealed his disappointment as best he
might. "That there is a new Secretary brought out of
the dark," he wrote to Elizabeth, "is no news; preferred
by my Lord of London,—not my Lord Mayor—whose
sufficiency may be great for anything I know. In other
things he is well spoken of, and if he please my master,
he loves himself better than he ought that is displeased.
These are the encouragements we receive that have
laboured abroad; but for my own part I protest I envy
not; I can make my own content as fit as a garment,
and if the State be well I cannot be sick. We cannot
say there is any faction in England. All goes one
way, and I know not the wit of it."[2]

Truly there was no faction in England. The voice
of Parliament was silent. If words of opposition rose to
the lips of private men they were seldom expressed
loudly enough to reach the Government. The party at
Court, with Holland at its head, to which for want of
better support, Roe looked for help, had neither moral
earnestness nor intellectual power to recommend it.
The taunts and allurements with which it sought to
draw Charles to break with Weston have left scarcely an
echo behind them. Their views must be sought in two
plays in which Massinger made himself the exponent

[1] Gussoni's despatch, March $\frac{2}{12}$, June $\frac{8}{18}$. *Venice MSS.*
[2] Roe to Elizabeth, July 1. *S. P. Germany.*

of a more daring foreign policy than that which was acceptable to Charles. In *Believe as you List*, licensed for the stage in January 1631, the dramatist reproduced under fictitious names the refusal of Charles to grant assistance to his brother-in-law, and satirised the mastery which Weston himself, seduced, as it was alleged, by the gold of the Spanish Ambassador, exercised over the mind of the King. Under the feigned name of Flaminius, the Ambassador of Rome, Coloma is made to point out to Charles the material advantages of an inglorious peace:—

> Know then, Rome,
> In her pious care that you may still increase
> The happiness you live in; and your subjects,
> Under the shadow of their own vines, eat
> The fruits they yield them—their soft musical feasts
> Continuing, as they do yet, unaffrighted
> With the harsh noise of war—entreats as low
> As her known power and majesty can descend,
> You would retain, with due equality,
> A willingness to preserve what she hath conquered
> From change and innovation.

In the play the Ambassador requires not merely the abandonment, but the actual surrender of Antiochus, who stands for Frederick. From this, King Prusias, who stands for Charles, recoils.

> Shall I, for your ends
> Infringe my princely word? or break the laws
> Of hospitality? defeat myself
> Of the certain honour to restore a king
> Unto his own? and what you Romans have
> Extorted and kept from him? Far be't from me!
> I will not buy your amity at such loss,
> So it be to all after times remembered
> I held it not sufficient to live
> As one born only for myself, and I
> Desire no other monument.

This, Massinger would seem to say, is the real Charles, generous and high-minded. It is only the low, coarse-minded minister who stands in the way. Coloma points to Weston—

> Here's a man,
> The oracle of your kingdom, that can tell you,
> When there's no probability it may be
> Effected, 'tis mere madness to attempt it.

Then comes a stinging comparison between the weakness of Bithynia and the strength of Rome, in other words, of England and Spain. The power of the former, the Ambassador allows—

> Is not to be disputed, if weigh'd truly,
> With the petty kings, your neighbours; but when balanced
> With the globes and sceptres of my mistress Rome,
> Will but—I spare comparisons, but you build on
> Your strength to justify the fact. Alas,
> It is a feeble reed, and leaning on it
> Will wound your hand much sooner than support you.
> You keep in pay, 'tis true, some peace-trained troops,
> Which awes your neighbours; but consider, when
> Our eagles shall display their sail-stretched wings,
> Hovering o'er our legions, what defence
> Can you expect from yours?

The Ambassador has his way. The King, on the plea of 'necessity of State,' submits.

In *The Maid of Honour*, printed in 1632, and probably written in the beginning of that year, or in the end of the year before, James I. and his dealings with the Palatinate are brought upon the stage in order to censure, indirectly, Charles's abandonment of Hamilton. Under the name of Roberto, King of Sicily, we see James arguing that he is not bound to support his ally if he made the first attack upon others. He had only engaged to send him support if he were himself attacked. Then, as if to draw attention to those parts of his father's policy which Charles was imitating, the King is made to boast of his peaceful rule—

CHAP. V.
1632.

> Let other monarchs
> Contend to be made glorious by proud war,
> And with the blood of their poor subjects purchase
> Increase of empire, and augment their cares
> In keeping that which was by wrongs extorted,
> Gilding unjust invasions with the trim
> Of glorious conquests; we, that would be known
> The father of our people, in our study
> And vigilance for their safety, must not change
> Their ploughshares into swords, and force them from
> The secure shade of their own vines, to be
> Scorched with the flames of war; or, for our sport
> Expose their lives to ruin.

To this Bertolo answers in words which bear the impress of the fierce love of adventure and prowess which sways alternately with more peaceful energies the breasts of Englishmen.

> Here are no mines of gold
> Or silver to enrich you : no worm spins
> Silk in her womb, to make distinction
> Between you and a peasant in your habits:
> No fish lives near our shores whose blood can dye
> Scarlet or purple ; all that we possess
> With beasts we have in common : nature did
> Design us to be warriors, and to break through
> Our ring, the sea, by which we are environed,
> And we by force must fetch in what is wanting
> Or precious to us.

The King will hear nothing of his counsels. Think not, he answers,—

> Think not
> Our counsel's built upon so weak a base
> As to be overturned, or shaken with
> Tempestuous winds of word. As I, my lord,
> Before resolved you, I will not engage
> My person in this quarrel; neither press
> My subjects to maintain it ; yet to shew
> My rule is gentle, and that I have feeling
> O' your master's sufferings, and these gallants, weary
> Of the happiness of peace, desire to taste
> The bitter sweets of war, we do consent
> That, as adventurers and volunteers,
> No way compelled by us, they may make trial
> Of their boasted valours.

In another speech Charles himself is brought before us as his language to Hamilton appeared to those who were dissatisfied with the course which he had taken.

> 'Tis well, and, but my grant in this, expect not
> Assistance from me. Govern as you please
> The province you make choice of; for, I vow
> By all things sacred, if that thou miscarry
> In this rash undertaking, I will hear it
> No otherwise than as a sad disaster,
> Fallen on a stranger; nor will I esteem
> That man my subject, who in thy extreme
> In purse or person aids thee.[1]

So great was the strength of the feeling which gave rise to these two plays that even Weston himself bowed before it. In expectation of the reply of Gustavus, preparations were made for a more active intervention on the Continent. Jerome Weston, the Treasurer's eldest son, was sent on a mission to France and Italy. He was to pave the way to a better understanding with France, and to urge Lewis to a direct declaration for the restitution of the Palatinate. He was to say that Charles hoped that the French were by this time 'sufficiently disabused' of the notion that anything could be effected as long as attention was paid to the 'interests of Bavaria.' "The King," wrote the Treasurer himself to his son, "hath left no way untried, nor lost any opportunity in uniting his counsels or aids with Princes that be interested, as to the King of Sweden, both by the Marquis of Hamilton and his Ambassador, with large offers of monies and other kinds of aids, which we hear now by our Ambassador are likely to

---

[1] See a paper on *The political element in Massinger* in the *Contemporary Review* for Aug. 1876. It had been previously read before the New Shakspere Society, when Mr. Hales pointed out that the suggestion in *Believe as you List* (iii. 1), that Antiochus should fly to Parthia to Egypt, or to *the Batavian*, is evidence that Massinger's thoughts were travelling in the direction which I had assumed.

be accepted, and that by this that friendship is concluded."[1]

Weston expects the alliance with Gustavus to be concluded.

Weston was not the man to speak so strongly unless he had believed that the alliance with Gustavus was practically concluded. It was his first object to be on the winning side, and no man had better opportunities of ascertaining the direction in which his master was drifting. It was not long before he learned that he had overestimated the pliancy of Gustavus. When the draft treaty from England was placed in Vane's hands, the King of Sweden could no longer afford to despise any genuine offer of assistance. Bavaria and the League had been crushed, and it seemed for a moment as if no further opposition could be offered to the conqueror. But in the hour of supreme danger Wallenstein was recalled to the command, and entrusted with unheard of powers. His old veterans flocked round his standard at his call, and in a few weeks he was at the head of an imposing army. His first work was to manœuvre the Saxons out of Bohemia. Then he turned sharply round and pinned Gustavus to the defence of Nüremberg. Yet, even in his mortal duel with the great strategist, Gustavus would not hear of accepting Charles's offers. Doubtless he had a keen recollection of the treatment to which Christian of Denmark had been subjected, and he may well have doubted whether Charles's engagement to pay 10,000*l.* a month was in reality worth as many pence. At all events, he knew that Charles had refused him the naval aid for which he had asked, and had fixed no time during which the payment was to be continued. The aid now offered, he said, was useless, 'and for the indefiniteness of the time it was against all form of proceeding in alliances.' Charles's overtures

[1] Instructions to Jerome Weston, July 24. Weston to Jerome Weston, Aug. 10. *S. P. France.*

CHAP. V.

1632.

were absolutely rejected. Vane had nothing more to offer. He took his leave, and returned to England. Anstruther's position at Vienna had already become untenable, and he too had been ordered home. To Charles's unfeigned surprise neither of the belligerents considered his alliance worth purchasing.[1]

July. Recall of Vane and Anstruther.

Aug. Failure of Charles's diplomacy.

Charles's failure was one more illustration of the truth which Bacon was wont to urge upon James in his dealings with his Parliaments. Success is to be had not by sharp bargaining, but by sympathy tempered by prudence. Of this system Roe was now the spokesman. "If his Majesty," he wrote to Holland, "take not care of the King of Sweden, not so much by money, or that only, as by countenance and reputation of unity and colligation, though an enemy may beat him out of Germany, cold and jealous friends may undermine and undo him." Very different was the thought of Weston's friends when the tidings came from Nüremberg. "You have given," wrote Cottington to Vane, "great satisfaction to his Majesty, and to those his ministers by whom he manageth his foreign affairs. Through your wise and dexterous carriage of that great business you have saved his Majesty's money and his honour, and yourself from any kind of blame, as I understand it."[2]

Sept. 29.

Oct. 17. Silence imposed upon the gazettes.

Whether abstention from interference in Germany were wise or not, it was impossible to represent Charles's diplomacy in a favourable light. The public appetite for news had called forth swarms of pamphlets and gazettes, which told all who could read how Gustavus had forced the passage of the Lech, and how Maximilian, the oppressor of the Palatinate, had abandoned his own capital to the invader. The mere news that such successes

[1] Vane to Coke, July 19. *S. P. Sweden.* Curtius to Vane, Sept. 14. *S. P. Holland.*

[2] Cottington to Vane, Sept. 29. *S. P. Dom.*, ccxxiii. 56.

CHAP. V.
1632.
Sept. 29.

had been achieved without the help of England would easily be regarded as a tacit reproach to Charles, and the authors of the gazettes were sternly bidden to refrain from 'all printing and publishing of the same.'[1]

Nov. 5.
Gustavus and Frederick.

The Swedish King was not long to cross Charles's path. If he was not defeated at Nüremberg, at least he had ceased to be victorious. In his train was the exiled Frederick, who had come to beg his inheritance of the disposer of power. Earlier in the year he had wearied the King of Sweden with his obstinate refusal to submit to reasonable conditions. Gustavus had not, however, given up hopes of numbering him as an active member of the great Protestant alliance. "I will let my brother of England know," he said, "that my intention is more generous towards the King of Bohemia than that I should have any mercenary dealing with him, as Vane would have me."[2] The time was fast passing when words or acts of his would avail anything. Wallenstein had marched northwards and was ravaging Saxony. Gustavus hastened to the succour of his ally.

Nov. 6.
Battle of Lützen and death of Gustavus.

On November 6 the victory of Lützen was won by the Swedish army. But the soul of that army expired on the field in the death of its heroic King.

In England the death of Gustavus was felt as keenly as if he had been a national commander. "Never," wrote D'Ewes, "did one person's death in Christendom bring so much sorrow to all true Protestant hearts,—not our godly Edward's, the Sixth of that name, nor our late heroic and inestimable Prince Henry,—as did the King of Sweden's at this present." The general sorrow was

Charles proposes that Frederick shall

not shared by Charles. He had already found out a successor to Gustavus in the helpless, headstrong Frederick. 'He conceived hope,' he said, 'in God's good-

---

[1] *Council Register*, Oct. 17.
[2] Durie to Roe, Nov. 11. *S. P. Germany*.

ness that as He hath taken away him whom He had exalted, so He may restore him whom He hath humbled.' It was said of Henry VIII. that he knew a man when he saw him. It was evident that this quality had not descended to his successor. Charles at once despatched a messenger with 16,000*l.* in ready money to enable Frederick to levy an army of 10,000 men. He prepared to ask the Dutch to transfer to his brother-in-law the contribution which they had hitherto paid to Gustavus. Around the Elector Palatine, he hoped, would gather the German Princes and the German Cities, so 'that the body which was kept together by the power and credit of the King of Sweden' might 'not by his death be dissolved and broken.'

CHAP. V.
1632.
lead the German Protestants.

Frederick never heard of the great expectations which had been conceived of him in England. A merciful fever snatched him away from one more bitter disappointment. Thirteen days after Gustavus fell, the candle of his restless unsatisfied life died away in the socket at Bacharach, by the side of the eddying Rhine.

Nov. 19. Frederick's death.

The death of Gustavus and the death of Frederick were alike welcome to Weston and his clique. In their detestation of war there was nothing noble, no preference of higher objects to be gained in peace, no wise conception of international duties. To them material prosperity had become an idol, and the habit of regarding the accumulation of wealth as the sole test of greatness was accompanied by a contemptuous indifference for the trials and sorrows of other nations, of which the hot Protestant partisan of earlier days had never been guilty. Flatterers found their account in praising the skill with which Charles had preserved England from the scourge of war. The low and debased feeling which had been fostered by men in high places found full expression in the lines in which Carew,

Boast of material prosperity in England.

himself a royal cupbearer, commented on the death of the Swedish King.

> "Then let the Germans fear, if Cæsar shall
> On the United Princes rise and fall;
> But let us that in myrtle bowers sit
> Under secure shades, use the benefit
> Of peace and plenty which the blessed hand
> Of our good king gives this obdurate land.
>
> . . . . . .
>
> Tourneys, masques, theatres better become
> Our halcyon days. What though the German drum
> Bellow for freedom and revenge? The noise
> Concerns not us, nor should divert our joys."

Perish Europe, if only England may fiddle in safety! Already the sword was sharpening which should chastise the men by whom such things were said.

Charles's first thought on receiving the news of the death of his brother-in-law was to solace his widowed sister. Laying aside for the moment his fear that her presence in England would serve as an encouragement to his own Puritans, he despatched Arundel to offer her a refuge at his Court. At first in her loneliness she was inclined to accept the offer. But she very soon changed her mind. She told Arundel that her duty to her family required her presence in Holland. It is probable that she shrank from exchanging a dwelling-place amongst a sympathetic people for the daily annoyance of the companionship of a brother who promised so much and performed so little.[1]

With the death of Gustavus the question of the relations between England and France assumed increased importance. If, as was only too likely, jealousies broke out amongst the Princes who had with difficulty been kept in harmony by the genius of the Swedish King, it

---

[1] Gussoni's despatch, Dec. $\frac{7}{17}$, $\frac{21}{31}$, Feb. $\frac{1}{11}$. *Venice MSS.* Goring to ——? Jan. 5. *S. P. Holland.*

would be absolutely necessary that Richelieu should take a more prominent part in the conflict than he had hitherto done. And at this time circumstances were occurring in the Netherlands which forced Charles to consider how his alliances would affect the national interests of England as well as how they would affect the dynastic interests of his family.

The weight of the war fell heavily upon the Spanish Netherlands. The King of Spain was no longer able to protect them as of old. Every year was now marked by some fresh defeat, and unless the course of the Prince of Orange could be stopped the whole country would sooner or later be at his disposal. The nobility echoed the lamentations of the common people. The proud Belgian aristocracy complained that military and civil employments alike were in the hands of Castilians. Meetings were held, and in the spring of 1632 many of the nobles banded together and made overtures to Richelieu for assistance to enable them to shake off the authority of Spain. When Frederick Henry took the field, he found but cold resistance. Venloo and Ruremonde quickly surrendered, and the Prince proceeded to lay siege to Maestricht. Count Henry de Bergh, a Netherlander who had been replaced by a Spaniard in the command of the army, passed over to the Dutch, and called upon his countrymen to free themselves from the foreign yoke.

The country was not disposed to follow the interested counsels of a malcontent nobility. It was afraid of being brought under the sway of the Dutch Calvinists. It was equally afraid of incorporation with the French monarchy. The Belgians looked down with well-grounded pride upon a country where municipal liberties and the administration of justice itself were in a far more backward state than in the old provinces of the

House of Burgundy.[1] But though the country did not wish for revolution, it wished to be rid of the intervention of Spaniards in its own internal affairs. Above all it wanted peace.

The wish was a natural one. But it was impossible that the Provinces could remain attached to the Spanish monarchy without continuing to share its fortunes. They must shake off the yoke or submit to their fate.

July. The States General summoned.
Aug 4. The nobles ask for Charles's support.
Aug. 21.

The Infanta was obliged to temporise. In July she summoned the States General to meet in the end of August. Before the day of assembly came the discontented nobles applied to Charles's agent, Gerbier, to know if they could count on his master's help. Charles was at first startled by the proposal. "Since," he replied to his minister, "I am in friendship with the King of Spain, it is against both honour and conscience to give him just cause of quarrel against me, I being not first provoked by him, and a juster he cannot have than debauching of his subjects from their allegiance. But since I see a likelihood—almost a necessity—that his Flanders subjects must fall into some other King's or State's protection, and that I am offered, without the least intimation of mine, to have a share therein; the second consideration is that it were a great imprudence in me to let slip this occasion whereby I may both advantage myself and hinder the overflowing greatness of my neighbours, so that my resolution must depend upon the agreement of these two considerations."[2]

Views of Charles.

It is no blame to Charles if, believing the overthrow of the Spanish power in the Netherlands to be inevitable, he sought to avert the absorption of the Provinces by the King of France and the States General. The es-

[1] See on all this M. Henrard's book, *Marie de Médicis dans les Pays Bas.*
[2] Gerbier to the King, Aug. 4. The King to Gerbier, Aug. 21. *Hardwicke St. P.* ii. 55, 79.

tablishment of an independent Belgian State would have best served the interests of England, and would have best served the real interests of the population. What was characteristic of Charles and his ministers was that they fancied that this could be effected with the concurrence of Spain, and that they did not see that in order to promote a settlement which would be distasteful to the French and the Dutch, it would be necessary scrupulously to avoid any appearance of self-seeking on the part of England. At a conference held at the Lord Treasurer's, it was resolved to offer the help of the navy to convey the Spanish soldiers home as soon as they were ready to evacuate the Low Countries, and to ask Philip to make over a large part of Flanders to Charles, to be held under the Spanish crown. The nobility were to be persuaded that the protection of England would be far more agreeable than that of the Dutch Republic. The English Church was as well ordered as their own, and there would be no risk of the introduction of a system under which every burgher might claim a share in the direction of the State.[1]

On August 14 Maestricht surrendered to the Dutch. On the 30th, the States General were opened at Brussels. They at once demanded permission to treat for a peace or truce with the Northern States without the intervention of the executive government, and this demand was accorded by the Infanta. At the same time the Prince of Orange issued a manifesto promising the alliance of the Dutch States to the obedient Provinces if they would declare themselves independent of Spain. The Spanish troops would then be forced to quit the country, and the Brussels States would become the rulers of the Southern Provinces, as the Northern

[1] Conference at the Lord Treasurer's. *S. P. Flanders.*

Provinces were governed by the States which assembled at the Hague.

CHAP. V.
1632. Sept. Refusal of the Brussels States.

Against this incitement to revolution the Brussels States stood firm. They would treat for a truce on the basis of the arrangement of 1609, but they professed their intention to remain the subjects of the King of Spain. Their resolution seriously compromised the chances of an arrangement. Doubtless there were large numbers in the Northern Provinces who were weary of war, and who would have welcomed a cessation of hostilities at almost any cost. But a large party, with Frederick Henry at its head, was by no means inclined to give way to peace or truce so long as the Spaniards retained a threatening position on their southern frontier. It was true that for five years the Dutch armies had been victorious. Grol, Hertogenbosch, Wesel, Venloo, Maestricht, had fallen in rapid succession. But the Spanish monarchy was not crushed. A few seasons of peace might enable it to restore its dilapidated finances and to reorganise its military resources.

Oct 22. Charles's intervention.

With this divergency of feeling, it is not likely that an agreement would have been come to in any case, and it is therefore doubtful whether Charles could have intervened with good effect. The course which he actually took was pitiable. The tendency to intrigue which was rooted in his character had been growing during the last few years. He instructed Boswell, his Minister at the Hague, to be present at the conferences between the deputies of the two States General. He was to do his best, in an underhand way, to make any arrangement impossible. He was to press the Northern States to include the restoration of the Palatinate in the negotiation. He was to hold up to the Southern States the advantage which they would gain by an open trade with England, and to 'show them what near and powerful protection

His instructions to Boswell.

they may have from his Majesty's dominions to support them in their freedom and liberties, if they resolve to make themselves an entire and independent body; what indignity and prejudice they may suffer if they submit themselves to those neighbours upon unequal conditions, under whom neither their clergy, their nobility, nor their burghers can expect those honours, that profit, and that continual defence which from his Majesty upon reasonable and equal terms they may be assured of.'[1]

CHAP. V.
1632.
Oct. 22.

Assuredly Charles did not stand alone amongst the rulers of the world in resorting to intrigue. Richelieu was quite as ready to veil his intentions in a cloud of words, and to cover his self-seeking with an appearance of disinterestedness. But whilst Charles had absolutely no perception of the facts of the world, Richelieu surpassed all his contemporaries, except Gustavus, in the skill with which he mastered events by adapting his course to the currents of opinion around him. He had just brought to a close the long internal struggle with the French aristocracy. Gaston had at last summoned up courage, and had crossed the French border to make his way to the South, where Montmorency, the dashing cavalier, the flower of the French nobility, was ready to rise at his bidding. On the field of Castelnaudary that conflict was brought to an issue. Richelieu stood up for national unity and religious toleration against those who would have made France their prey, who would have stooped their heads to the foreigner abroad, and relighted the flames of civil war at home. The better side prevailed. The gay chivalry which followed the banner of the insurgents was no match for the steady discipline of the Royal army. Montmorency bowed his head as a traitor on the scaffold, whilst Gaston

Aug. 21 Defeat of Montmorency.

---

[1] Instructions to Boswell, Oct. 22. *S. P. Holland.*

slunk home, like a poltroon as he was, to accept a contemptuous pardon from his brother.

Richelieu turned his attention fixedly abroad. He did not build his hopes much upon the uncertainties and the oscillations of the States of Brussels. Charles might dream of thrusting the wedge of English power into Flanders by the expenditure of a few soft words. Richelieu knew that strength was to be found amongst the burgher counsellors of the Hague and the tried veterans who had reduced the proud citadel of Maestricht to surrender. If the obedient Provinces chose to throw off the yoke of Spain, it would be easy to satisfy them on all secondary points. If not, an alliance with the independent States against Spain was the policy imposed by circumstances upon France.

By the middle of November, Charles had learned that he had no prospect of effecting his object with the assent of Spain. He had directly asked for the surrender of Dunkirk, or of some other strong place in Flanders, as the price of his co-operation. The Spanish Government was not yet reduced to extremities, and returned a peremptory refusal.[1]

Charles then turned to France. This time he held language which, if he had been strong enough to support his words by action, would have been worthy of an English Sovereign. Jerome Weston, who was at the French Court, was directed to assure Lewis that though the King of England was ready to concur in any step for the liberation of the discontented Provinces from Spain, he would not hear of the increase of Dutch or French territory at their expense. He had 'better reason to maintain the Spaniards there than to let the French in.' At the same time the Lord Treasurer was

---

[1] Windebank's Notes, *Clar. S. P.*, i. 61. *Salvetti's newsletters*, Sept. 23/Oct. 3, Nov. 30/Dec. 0.

profuse in his expressions of attachment to Richelieu, and in his assurances of a wish to see France and England united on the great questions of the day, the recovery of the Palatinate being naturally included.[1]

Two days after these instructions were sent, the Deputies from the States General of both fractions of the Netherlands met at the Hague. Before the end of the year, it was evident to all that the negotiation would end in nothing. The Southern States persisted in regarding themselves as the subjects of the King of Spain. The Northern States were unwilling to come to terms unless the King of Spain's authority were declared to be at an end. The negotiation dragged on, neither party being willing to give up hope of a satisfactory conclusion. But no clear-sighted bystander could think it at all likely that such a conclusion would be reached.

Richelieu, at all events, saw plainly how matters stood. On January 3 he instructed Charnacé, the French Ambassador at the Hague, to offer to the Dutch increased subsidies and a military force. If Richelieu could succeed in establishing French influence in Germany, he would be ready to engage in open war with Spain, with the object of effecting a partition of the Spanish Netherlands between France and the States General.[2]

Charles could not make up his mind what to do. In November he had instructed Jerome Weston to protest against such a partition. But there was a large party at his Court which regarded the scheme with favour, though no one in England had any knowledge that the proposal had actually been made. If, it was argued, the Dutch frontier became conterminous with

---

[1] Coke to Weston, Nov. 22, *S. P. France.* Fontenay to Father Joseph, Nov. 17. Fontenay to Richelieu, Nov. 26. *Aff. Etr.* xlv. 143, 145.

[2] Richelieu to Charnacé, Avenel. *Lettres de Richelieu,* iv. 421.

the French, the Dutch would speedily become as jealous of France as they had hitherto been of Spain. Necessity would thus drive them into the arms of England, and they would be forced to make concessions to English commerce as the price of political support. To these representations Charles was for a moment inclined to give ear. Even Weston, either because he thought it prudent to agree with his master, or because, as Philip's agent Necolalde fancied, the Spanish Government had not bribed him highly enough, talked in the same strain. Even Cottington declaimed on the approaching downfall of the Spanish monarchy.[1] Charles, however, soon repented of his momentary weakness. Necolalde had an interview with him, and won him back to his old jealousy of France and the States.[2]

Charles was now engaged in a fresh diplomatic intervention in Germany. His nephew, Charles Lewis, the eldest surviving son of Frederick and Elizabeth, was a boy of fourteen. Anstruther was ordered to betake himself to the Chancellor Oxenstjerna, who had succeeded to the conduct of affairs after the death of Gustavus. He was to offer assistance in money, though, if possible, he was to promise a sum smaller than the 10,000*l.* a month which had been proposed to the late King. In return he was to ask that the Swedes and the German Princes should acknowledge his nephew's right, and should at once make over to him the strong places which they had conquered in the Palatinate.[3] Jerome Weston was directed to ask the French Government to support this demand, and to join if necessary in carrying on the war in Germany. But he was to add with respect to the Low Countries a repetition of the message which

---

[1] Intercepted letters of Necolalde to Olivares, $\frac{\text{Dec. 26}}{\text{Jan. 5}}$, Jan. $\frac{9}{19}$. *Aff. Etr.* xlv. 166, 176.

[2] Necolalde to Olivares, $\frac{\text{Jan. 23}}{\text{Feb. 2}}$. *Simancas MSS.* 2520.

[3] Anstruther's instructions, Dec. *S. P. Germany.*

he had conveyed in November. He was to say 'that if they shall agree to erect those interjacent countries into free and independent States, his Majesty will give no interruption. But if they pretend to share or divide them without any consideration of his Majesty's interests, he will to his uttermost oppose them.'[1]

CHAP. V.
1633.
Jan.

How far Charles was guided by Weston in this determination it is difficult to say. At all events it was quite in accordance with Weston's character to keep an eye upon the dangers likely to arise from the increase of the material forces of his opponents, without any comprehension of the moral and spiritual movements by which the world was pervaded. Charles seized this moment to testify his approbation of the Treasurer's services. He conferred upon him an earldom, a dignity which he dispensed with a far more sparing hand than his father had been accustomed to do. From henceforward his favourite minister would be known as the Earl of Portland.

Feb. 17.
Weston created Earl of Portland.

When Jerome Weston, now by his father's promotion Lord Weston, returned to England in March, he brought with him Richelieu's terms. They were very different from those which had been expected by Charles. The French asked for a defensive alliance against the House of Austria. In other words Charles was to bind himself to protect France from a Spanish attack in the impending war. An end was to be put to the assistance which he had given to Spain by convoying money and men to the Flemish ports. Lewis, in return, would assist in recovering from the Spaniards any part of the Palatinate which might fall into their hands.[2]

March.
Terms brought by Lord Weston from France.

---

[1] Coke to J. Weston, Jan. 22. *S. P. France.*
[2] Draft Treaty, March. Memoir of Fontenay, Apr. 16. *Aff. Etr.* xlv. 222, 233, 235.

<small>CHAP.
V.

1633.
March.
Discrepancy between the two Governments.</small>

The discrepancy between the two Governments was thus plainly brought to light. Charles expected the King of France to make war for the recovery of the Palatinate, and to refrain from satisfying his ambition whenever his objects might clash with English interests. Richelieu asked Charles to take some part, if it was but a subordinate one, in his meditated attack upon Spain. With a Prince more resolute and more powerful than Charles, such a divergency of view would probably have led soon to open war. But Richelieu knew his man. He was prodigal of assurances of good will. He was firmly resolved to give no unnecessary offence. He knew well that Charles's threats would end in words. The busy diplomacy of the English Government had been absolutely wasted, and it was not likely that failure in the past would be compensated by success in the future.

<small>A letter of the Queen's seized by Lord Weston.</small>

If Richelieu had a political interest in maintaining friendly relations with the English Government he had also a personal interest in maintaining friendly relations with the Lord Treasurer. The enemies of both were still in close correspondence with one another. On his return through France Lord Weston had met an English messenger bearing a packet addressed in Holland's hand to a French minister. The fact was enough to awaken suspicion in a Weston, and using the privilege of an ambassador he opened the parcel. Inside he found a cyphered letter from Holland, and another letter from the Queen, which he did not attempt to read. He brought both back to England, and placed them in Charles's hands.

The letters proved harmless. Richelieu had discovered that Chateauneuf and his instrument, De Jars, had joined in the never-ceasing intrigues against him, and had sent them both to prison. According to the most consistent accounts, Henrietta Maria's letter was written to intercede in their favour.¹ If Chateauneuf was the enemy of Richelieu now, he had been Portland's enemy before, and Charles, who looked with well-founded suspicion upon the clique with which his wife was surrounded, warmly declared his approbation of Weston's conduct, and, guessing what was likely to follow, ordered him to refuse any challenge which might be sent him.

_{CHAP.
V.
1633.
March.}

The King's prevision was justified by the event. The whole of the Queen's Court took up their mistress's quarrel. Holland challenged Weston. Charles interfered with decision, and ordered Holland, who sent the challenge, and Henry Jermyn, who carried it, to be placed in confinement. The Queen's followers turned savagely upon Weston. Only a coward, they said, would accept a duel, and then give notice of it. The gallant young Lord Fielding, Denbigh's son, who was just about to marry Weston's sister, stepped forward to vindicate the honour of the family into which he was about to enter, and challenged George Goring as the noisiest of the offenders. Once more the King interfered, and stopped the duel. A new way was then discovered of showing dislike of the Lord Treasurer. Crowds of persons of every degree flocked to the house in which Holland was confined, to express their sympathy, till this, too, was angrily stopped by Charles. Holland was then summoned before the Star Chamber. It was commonly believed that he would hardly escape without the loss of his offices. But Charles could not resist the tears and entreaties of his wife. The birth of the Prince of Wales in 1630 had been followed in 1631 by the birth of the daughter who was one day to bring William of Orange into the world. The Queen

_{April.
Weston is
challenged.}

¹ Brasser to the States-General. *Add. MSS.* 17,677, Q.fol. 41.

CHAP. V.
1633.

Understanding between Richelieu and Portland.

was now looking forward to becoming a mother again, and Charles was too tender a husband to deal harshly with her preferences at such a time. Holland escaped with a reprimand from the Lord Keeper delivered in the Privy Council.[1]

A common danger drew Richelieu and Portland together. The Cardinal had seized from De Jars a correspondence in which the intrigues of some of the Queen's Court against the Treasurer were unveiled. He sent the compromising letters to England, that Portland might have evidence before him that he was himself attacked by those who sought to effect a change in the Government of France.[2] In this way Richelieu hoped to secure an ally against the suggestions of the Queen on behalf of her mother, which were in reality suggestions made in the interests of Spain.

[1] Kilvert to Lambe, April 4. Noy to Windebank, Apr. 11. Act of Council, Apr. 13. *S. P. Dom.*, ccxxxvi. 14, 43, 47. *Council Register*, April 5. Fontenay to Bouthillier, Apr. 14. *Aff. Etr.* xlv. 229.

[2] Memoir for Boutard. *Ibid.*, xlv. 336.

CHAPTER VI.

DIVERGENT TENDENCIES IN POLITICS AND RELIGION.

It is impossible to pass from the foreign to the domestic politics of 1631 and 1632 without being conscious of the immense gulf between them. On the Continent great problems were presented to the human mind, and great intellects applied themselves to their solution with the pen and with the sword. Gustavus, Richelieu, and Frederick Henry tower above ordinary men. At home all things appear tame and quiet. English life seems to be unruffled by any breeze of discontent. It is only here and there that some solitary person puts forth opinions which, read in the light of subsequent events, are seen to be the precursors of the storm, only here and there that the legal action of the Government is put forth to settle controversies which, but for those subsequent events, would not seem to possess any very great importance. It was a time of preparation and development for good or for evil, which Charles, if he had been other than he was, might have guided to fruitful ends, but in which it was impossible for the man whose diplomatic helplessness has just passed before us to act with forethought or decision.

<small>CHAP. VI.
1631.
Contrast between foreign and domestic politics.</small>

One great advantage Charles had. The lawyers began to rally to his side. In August 1631 Chief Justice Hyde died little regretted, and his place was

<small>Aug. Legal promotions.</small>

taken by Richardson. The Chief Justiceship of the Common Pleas thus vacated was deservedly allotted to Heath.

Oct. Noy Attorney General.

To the surprise of all men the new Attorney General was William Noy. His long Parliamentary opposition was remembered. His differences with the leaders of that opposition, like the differences of Wentworth, were forgotten. In 1628 he had supported Wentworth's conciliatory policy. In 1629, though he had declared strongly for the Parliamentary view of the question of Tonnage and Poundage, he had opposed Eliot's mode of action, and had expressed his dislike of the interference of the Commons with the Law Courts and of their claim to make the ministers of the Crown responsible to themselves. A link too between him and the Government was probably found in his dislike of Puritanism. He had never had pretensions to any grasp of constitutional law, and to one whose brain was a mere storehouse of legal facts, it may have seemed as easy to quote precedents on one side as on the other. Contemporaries appear rather to have amused themselves with the oddity of seeing a man so rugged and uncourtly in such a situation, than to have censured him as a turncoat. They told how he replied to the King's offer of the post by asking bluntly what his wages were to be, and how when Coventry, seeing him proceed unattended to Westminster Hall like an ordinary lawyer, directed a messenger to accompany him, he drove the man away, telling him that 'people would take him to be his prisoner.' [1]

Dec. 7. Littleton Recorder.

Two months later, Littleton, who had also distinguished himself on the popular side, accepted the Recordership of the City. Though the office was not directly in the King's gift, it was virtually at the dis-

[1] Gresley to Puckering, Oct. 27. *Court and Times,* ii., 136.

position of the Crown. Other lawyers less distinguished were not long in following his example in desisting from an apparently hopeless opposition.

The acceptance of Charles's claims by the principal lawyers of the day may no doubt be ascribed to a great extent to the hope of professional advancement. But other causes may also have been at work with them. Revolutionary as Charles's government in reality was, it did not profess to have broken with the old constitutional system. He took its stand upon rights which had been possessed by English Kings for centuries, and if he disregarded other rights which had been possessed by English Parliaments, he could argue that these rights were necessarily in abeyance till the Commons consented to resume their proper place in the State. In truth there was much to induce a lawyer to cast in his lot with Charles rather than with the House of Commons. If only the Judges could make up their mind to avoid challenging the King's claim to supreme headship of the nation, and the consequences which he deduced from it, they were certain to be treated with the highest respect. Charles's attack upon the independence of the Bench was directed against individuals. In the persons of Crewe and Walter the whole legal profession had in reality been assailed. But no other member of the profession need feel personally insulted. The House of Commons, on the other hand, had proceeded much more undisguisedly. They had openly found fault with a judicial declaration solemnly pronounced in the Court of Exchequer. They had summoned the Barons to give account of the reasons by which they had been guided. It is not strange if many lawyers preferred the silken chains of the Court to the iron yoke of a popular assembly not yet conscious of the necessity of submitting to those restraints which it

CHAP. VI.
1631.
Dec.
Legal position of the Government.

1631.
Sir Simonds D'Ewes.

was one day to impose upon itself in the hour of victory.

How far the lawyers who now took the side of Charles were led by these considerations we have no means of knowing. But in Sir Simonds D'Ewes we are able to examine the feelings of a man who without being a practising lawyer himself, had received a legal education, and whose Puritanical turn of mind would lead us to expect a decided antagonism to the King. A prim and acrid young man in his twenty-eighth year, he had made the study of legal antiquities the delight of his life, though he kept a human corner in his heart for his wife, the little lady who possessed, as he boasted, the smallest foot in England. As a proof of the tenderness of his affection, he tells how at the time of his courtship, he 'could not find leisure once to visit the Court of Common Pleas, or continue' his 'course of reporting law cases, but devoted mornings and afternoons to the service and attendance of' his 'dearest.' Happily his two passions coalesced into one. The lady had so many ancestors that his 'very study of records grew more delightful and pleasant than ever before,' as he 'often met with several particulars of moment which concerned some of those families to which she was heir, both of their bloods and coat-armour.' The happiness of the antiquary's domestic life was sustained and permeated by an abiding sense of religious duty and of religious sympathy, not the less real because it ran in narrow and sectarian channels. A Protestant victory on the Continent called up a triumphant outburst of thanksgiving. A Protestant defeat thrust him into the depths of despair.[1]

His religious sympathies.

His view of the late dissolution.

That such a man should not have sided with Eliot's resistance to the Crown may indeed to some extent be

[1] D'Ewes. *Autobiography,* i. 321.

accounted for by the smallness of his nature; but it is also some evidence of the amount of support on which Royalty was still able to reckon. The day of the late dissolution indeed, he pronounced to be 'the most gloomy, sad, and dismal day for England that had happened in five hundred years,' but he added his opinion that 'the cause of the breach and dissolution was immaterial and frivolous, in the carriage whereof divers fiery spirits in the House of Commons were very faulty and cannot be excused.' They ought never, he says, to have attempted to summon the King's officers to their bar. The quarrel, he thinks, was the work of some 'Machiavellian politics, who seemed zealous for the liberty of the Commonwealth,' but who sought to 'raise dispute between the King and his people, as they verily feared that their new Popish adorations and cringes would not only be inhibited but punished.'[1]

The explanation was ridiculous enough, and looks like the suggestion of personal vanity or dislike. What is worthy of notice is the decision which the man of precedents and records gives against the claim of the House of Commons to seize the supreme power into its own hands. As yet the lawyers and the antiquaries are on Charles's side. A few years later he will have alienated both.

It is no wonder that the lawyers and antiquaries did not venture as yet to justify this claim. Even Eliot himself, who had done more than any man living to give it prominence, hid from his own mind the full significance of his actions. In the *Monarchy of Man*, the political and philosophical treatise which was the

Eliot's Monarchy of Man.

---

[1] Selden and Noy seem to be aimed at, Selden as an Arminian, or at least an anti-Calvinist; Noy as an anti-Puritan. The whole passage displays complete want of intelligence, and should put the reader on his guard against attaching too much importance to D'Ewes's opinion.

result of his enforced leisure in the Tower, Eliot drew a picture of government as he conceived that it ought to be. Of all governments he pronounced monarchy the best. The King was to rule for the good of his subjects, not for his own private advantage. He was to conform his actions to the law. But beyond this there was a sphere particularly his own. He had to look to ' the safety and preservation of the whole.' In this was ' involved a higher care and providence for prevention of those evils which the law by power or terror cannot reach, . . . the practice and invasion of their enemies, or sedition and defection in the subjects, as also for the operation of all good which industry and wisdom shall invent for the benefit and commodity of the kingdom, wherein, though the notions flow from others, Princes only can reduce them into act.' To all this Charles might fully have subscribed. Even when Eliot speaks of the way in which this power is to be exercised, the difference between his view and Charles's is rather suggested than expressed. Charles had once said, that he was ready to allow to Parliament the right of counselling him, not the right of controlling him. Eliot here asks for no more. He dwells, indeed, upon the wisdom of Parliaments, and upon the safety which lies in taking advice. But he distinctly argues that it is ' the true explication of a Senate and the duty it sustains, to conceive and form all actions and designs,' ' to give them preparation and maturity, but no further, the resolution and production resting wholly in the King.'[1]

Such an argument was no contribution to practical politics. The King's case was that Parliament had come persistently and hopelessly to a wrong conclusion, and that it threatened to make all government impossible till its own errors had been carried into practice.

[1] *Harl. MSS.* 2228. Mr. Forster, in his extracts, took no notice of these important words.

Eliot held that the conclusion come to by Parliament had been right, but he did not touch the question whether in such a case Parliament might in any way force its opinions upon the King.

If, however, Eliot had no particular medicine to offer for the sickness of the Commonwealth, he could lay his hand, as Bacon had laid his hand before him, on the true source of the disease. It had all come, he held, because there had been no sympathy between the King and his people, because the King had not striven to understand their thoughts, or to feel for their grievances. To the misfortunes of the State he declared the art of government must now be applied, 'so to dispose the several parts and members that they may be at peace and amity with each other, reciprocally helpful and assistant by all mutual offices and respects as fellow-citizens and friends, brethren of the same mother, members of one body, nay individually one body, one consolid substance; . . . and likewise to compose them to that concord and agreement as they may be at unity in themselves, rendering that harmony of the heavens, that pure diapason and concent,[1] and in that strength to encounter all opposition of the contrary for the public utility and good, the conservation and felicity of the whole. For these, because no single ability is sufficient, helps and advantages are provided,' laws, 'which are a level and direction,' and a council 'to be aiding and assistant . . . a supply of that defect which may be in one person by the abilities of more, that by many virtues so contracted one *Panaretus* might be formed, an all-sufficiency in virtue and fulness of perfection, the true texture and concinnity of a King.'[2]

[1] Had Eliot seen a copy of Milton's lines *At a Solemn Music*, supposed to have been written in 1630?   [2] P. 67.

Eliot had not many more months of life before him. "I have these three days been abroad," he wrote to Hampden in March, "and as often brought in new impressions of the colds, yet both in strength and appetite I find myself bettered by the motion. Cold at first was the reason of my sickness, heat and tenderness by close keeping in my chamber has since increased my weakness. Air and exercise are thought most proper to repair it. As children learn to go, I shall get acquainted with the air. O the infinite mercy of our Master! Dear friend, how it abounds in us that are unworthy of His service! How broken, how imperfect, how perverse and crooked are our ways in obedience to Him! How exactly straight is the line of His providence unto us, drawn out through all occurrents and particulars to the whole length and measure of our time! . . . What can we render; what retribution can we make worthy of so great a Majesty, worthy such love and favour! We have nothing but ourselves, who are unworthy above all; and yet that, as all other things, is His. For us to offer up that is but to give Him of His own, and that in far worse condition than we at first received it, yet,—so infinite is His goodness for the merits of His Son,—He is contented to accept. This, dear friend, must be the comfort of His children; this is the physic we must use in all our sickness and extremities; this is the strengthening of the weak, the enriching of the poor, the liberty of the captive, the health of the diseased, the life of those that die, the death of that wretched life of sin! And this happiness have His saints. . . . Friends should communicate their joys; this as the greatest, therefore, I could not but impart unto my friend."

For six months the curtain drops on Eliot's sufferings and upon his abounding joyfulness. Then he petitioned the Court of King's Bench for leave to go abroad for the benefit of his health. Richardson, the new Chief Justice, referred him to the King. Charles answered that the prisoner's request was not sufficiently humble. Eliot would not save his life by an acknowledgment that he had erred. 'Sir,'—this was the utmost to which he could be drawn,—'I am heartily sorry I have displeased your Majesty, and having so said, do humbly beseech you once again to set me at liberty, that when I have recovered my health I may return back to my prison, there to undergo such punishment as God hath allotted unto me.' It was not in Charles's nature to listen to such a petition. No hope in this life remained for Eliot. The dying patriot had no harsh words for him who was causing his death. Anger on account of his own sufferings was not a feeling which found entrance into his mind. What he had endured was to him but part of the great purpose of God working out the deliverance of His Church and of the English nation. His enforced leisure, as the motto prefixed to *The Monarchy of Man* testified,[1] had proceeded from the hand of God. The misery in the Tower, as the last petition testified, had been a punishment allotted by God. He had fought a good fight, he had wrestled hard for his fellow countrymen, for generations yet unborn. As a testimony to those coming generations who would take up his work he had prepared his *Negotium Posterorum*, the unfinished record of his unfinished labours. One thing remained, to bequeath to his own family the memorial of his great struggle. When his descendants one after another took their place at Port Eliot they must not be allowed to think of him only as he was represented in the portrait taken in the days of early manhood. The dying man sent for a painter, bidding him to reproduce upon

[1] *Deus nobis hæc otia.*

1632. Nov. 27. Eliot's death.

canvas the wan, emaciated features which were all the reward of his heroic persistency. Then a few days later came the end. On November 27 that noble and unconquered spirit passed away from amongst living men.

Eliot and Gustavus.

The life of Gustavus had ended in far other fashion but three weeks before. In the main the task of the two men was the same, to defend the living spirit of nations against the pressure of misinterpreted legal obligations. Charles had heard of the death of Gustavus with a feeling of relief. When Eliot died the feeling of relief was tinged with rancorous animosity. To Charles, Eliot was but a factious and unprincipled rebel who had murdered Buckingham with his tongue, and who would have pulled down the throne itself if it had been in his power. He drily refused a request from the son of his deceased prisoner that he might convey his father's mortal remains to rest at Port Eliot, where he had been loved and honoured in his life. 'Let Sir John Eliot,' wrote the King on the petition, 'be buried in the church of that parish where he died.'

Charles refuses leave to transport the body to Port Eliot.

The dust of the first of England's Parliamentary statesmen lies unnoticed and undistinguishable amongst that of so many others, none more noble than himself. The idea for which he lived and died was the idea that the safest rule of government was to be found in the free utterance of the thoughts of the representatives of the people. He was the martyr, not of spiritual and intellectual, but of political liberty. He had confidence in the common sense of ordinary citizens, not indeed to govern directly, but to call in question those who were guilty of crime or mismanagement, and to insist that the direction of affairs should be entrusted to purer or abler hands.

What the House of Commons was to Eliot, the King's authority was to Wentworth. He had no confidence in the common sense of ordinary citizens. With him, government was a question of ability and authority. "It is a chaste ambition if rightly placed," he said afterwards when he was put upon his defence, " to have as much power as may be, that there may be power to do the more good in the place where a man lives."[1] When his enemies brought him to bay, they had much to say about the illegality of the Court over which he presided, and of its incompatibility with the ordinary legal system of the country. They had no charge to bring of personal injustice against Wentworth, except so far as masterful dealing with those who resisted his own authority and the King's might count for injustice.

It was perhaps not altogether a matter of accident that whilst the West and South of England produced the warmest defenders of the predominance of Parliament, the warmest defender of the King's authority should come from the North. Beyond the Trent, government by the strong hand was far more needed than it was in Hampden's Buckinghamshire or Eliot's Cornwall. Old men could still remember the day when the Northern Earls burnt the Bibles in Durham Cathedral and laid siege to Elizabeth's representative in Barnard Castle. Those northern shires were still the stronghold of recusancy, and, except in the south of Yorkshire, where a scanty manufacturing population gathered in Leeds and Bradford and Sheffield, poverty was great, and the power of the gentry was great in consequence. The gentry themselves were far less politically advanced than in the South of England, and they banded themselves together from the consideration of social ties and the memory of ancient feuds rather than from any difference of ideas on affairs of State. In looking upon the rule of the gentry as synonymous with the predomi-

[1] Rushworth. *Trial of Strafford*, 146.

nance of faction, Wentworth was but transferring to the whole of England an inference which might fairly be drawn from the condition of his native county. He knew well enough how little of public virtue had given him the victory over his rival Savile in the electoral conflicts of his earlier life.

Wentworth insulted by Bellasys.

In returning to Yorkshire, therefore, as Lord President of the North, Wentworth had to encounter a personal as well as a political opposition. One of those who grudged him his new honours was Henry Bellasys, the son of Lord Fauconberg, a young man of haughty disposition and uncontrollable temper. Coming one day into the hall in which Wentworth was sitting in full council, he neglected to make the customary reverence to the King's representative, and when at the close of the business the President left the room, he alone of all who were present, kept his head covered.

He is brought before the Privy Council.

Bellasys was sent for by the Privy Council to answer for his offensive conduct. He shewed as little good breeding in London as he had done at York. He appeared before the Council with a large stick in his hand, and omitted to kneel as the custom then was. He passed his rudeness off lightly. He asserted that he had no intention of showing disrespect to the President. He was in the midst of an interesting conversation, and he had not noticed that he was leaving the hall.

The Privy Council took him at his word. All that was asked of him was that, in their presence, and again before the Council of the North, he should acknowledge that he had not intended any disrespect to Wentworth. He refused to make any public declaration of the kind.

May 6. He makes his submission.

He was sent to the Gatehouse. After a month's imprisonment, he expressed himself ready to make the required submission if it was clearly understood to be offered to the Lord President's place, not to his person.

Wentworth, who was present, repudiated the wish to take cognizance of any personal offence. He had even asked his Majesty, he said, to excuse Bellasys from repeating the acknowledgment at York. But as the young man had chosen to draw the distinction, he could interfere no further on his behalf. Bellasys accordingly had to make the submission at York as well as in London, and received, at some cost to himself, a lesson in politeness.[1]

Oct. Death of Lady Wentworth.

It would be interesting to know how far Wentworth was rewarded by the affection of the poor at the time when he was flouted by this unmannerly youth. But only very indirect evidence exists of the feelings of those who had most to gain by a prompt and vigorous execution of justice. The year 1631 was a year of sorrow to Wentworth. In September one of his children died. In October, his dearly-loved wife, the sister of Denzil Holles, 'that departed saint now in heaven,' to whom his heart turned in his hour of trial long afterwards, was taken from him. His affections were as strong as his passions, and the stern demeanour which he bore in the presence of the many melted into the tenderest attachment to the few whom he really loved and respected. His grief was the more abundant as he was himself the innocent cause of his wife's death. One day, when she was in an advanced stage of pregnancy, he stepped from the garden into the room in which she was. A large fly, which had settled on his breast, spread its wings and frightened the weakly, delicate lady. She was prematurely brought to bed of a daughter at the cost of her own life. The widower had many companions in his grief. 'The whole city' had ' a face of mourning, never any woman so magnified and lamented even of those

---

[1] *Council Register*, Apr. 6, May 6. *Rushworth*, ii. 88.

that never saw her face.'[1] Such an expression of feeling would hardly have been manifested if Wentworth himself had been generally unpopular in York.

CHAP. VI. 1631.

1632. Jan. Wentworth appointed Lord Deputy of Ireland.

Whether Wentworth had succeeded or not in securing the regard of the lower and middle classes in the North, he had undoubtedly succeeded in securing the regard of the King. In January 1632 he was called upon, as Lord Deputy of Ireland, to face difficulties infinitely more alarming than any which he was likely to encounter in the North of England. But he did not leave England for eighteen months, and he had yet time to arouse and to bear down opposition amongst the gentry, whose submission to his authority he was resolved to enforce. Sir David Foulis, a Scotchman who had received a large estate in Yorkshire from the liberality of James, was one of those who chafed against the strong hand which held him down. He had lately been compelled by Wentworth to pay a sum of money which he owed to the Crown, but which he had long retained in his own possession. Though he was himself a member of the Council of the North, he seized every opportunity of opposing its President. Wentworth's zeal in exacting the compositions for knighthood enabled Foulis to make common cause with the gentlemen with whom that exaction was naturally unpopular. He said that the people of Yorkshire 'did adore the Lord Viscount Wentworth, and were so timorous and fearful to offend his Lordship, that they would undergo any charge rather than displease him;' and that 'his Lordship was much respected in Yorkshire, but at Court he was no more respected than an ordinary

July. Case of Sir D. Foulis.

He attacks Wentworth.

---

[1] Ferdinando Fairfax to Lord Fairfax, Oct. 8. *Fairfax Correspondence*, ii. 237. Sir G. Radcliffe gives the birth of the child and the death of the mother as both occurring in October, and as the mother died before the 8th, and was on her feet when the accident occurred, the order of events follows as given above, though they are nowhere clearly stated.

man;' and that, as soon as his back was turned for Ireland, his place of Presidentship of the Council would be bestowed on another man. Then came a direct attack upon Wentworth's personal honesty. Foulis publicly asserted that he had put the knighthood fines into his own pocket. A few days later he took a fresh opportunity of aspersing the character of the President. Sir Thomas Layton, the Sheriff of Yorkshire, received orders from the Exchequer to levy the fine on the goods of a Mr. Wyville, who had already compounded with Wentworth. Wentworth interfered on Wyville's behalf. He sent for the sheriff to come to him at York. Foulis urged him to refuse obedience. The President's Court, he argued, had no authority over him in the execution of his office. It owed its authority simply to the King's Commission. A mere Justice of the Peace held office under an Act of Parliament.[1]

These words touched the weak point in Wentworth's position. The Court over which he presided was not established by any law. It had come into being by an act of prerogative in the days of Henry VIII. after the suppression of the Pilgrimage of Grace. Its powers had increased gradually till there was little room left for the ordinary execution of the law by its side.

It may be that such a tribunal was needed in the North. A case occurred in Yorkshire in this very year which seems to carry us back to the Norfolk of the days in which the Paston Letters were written. Lord Eure, the possessor of an ancient barony, had fallen into debt, and had executed a deed surrendering his estate to feoffees in order that they might be sold for the benefit of his creditors. When the feoffees, fortified by an order from the Court of Chancery, attempted to

CHAP. VI.

1632.

The Council of the North without Parliamentary authority.

Lord Eure's case.

July.

---

[1] *Rushw.,* ii. 215.

take possession of the family mansion at Malton, he peremptorily refused them admission, garrisoned the house, and stood a siege. Layton, who was still sheriff, discovered that he was absolutely helpless without Wentworth's aid. Wentworth at once ordered cannon from Scarborough Castle to be brought up. It was not till a breach was made by these guns that Lord Eure submitted to the authority of the law.[1]

In consequence of the language used by Foulis, Wentworth had taken occasion at the Summer Assizes to point out that the King's demand from those who willingly paid a composition for omitting to take up their knighthood was only a third or a quarter of the sum which would be exacted as a fine by the Court of Exchequer from those who refused to compound. The little finger of the law was heavier than the loins of the King.[2]

Foulis was left to feel the weight of the loins of the King. He tried to curry favour with Charles by offering to bring the gentry of the county to a better temper. He was ready, he said, 'to lead and persuade others.' He would 'by his example much better the King's service,' whereas much harm might be done 'by his disgrace.' Wentworth's indignation blazed up at once. With a

---

[1] *Dominus Arundel c. Dominus Eure. Chancery Order Books.* Wentworth and the Council of the North to the Privy Council, Oct. 14. Mason's affidavit, Nov. 20. *S. P. Dom.* ccxxiv. 28 ; ccxxv. 47.

[2] *Rushw.*, viii. 150. This is Wentworth's account of the matter. It is corroborated by other evidence, and this is exactly what he might have been expected to say under the circumstances. At his trial, he was charged with having said that the little finger of the King was heavier than the loins of the law. On the whole, I rather think he made use of both expressions at different times, the latter perhaps on some occasion when obedience had been refused on the ground that some demand was not warranted by law. The theory of a repetition of words is not usually a desirable one to adopt, but Foulis's evidence at the trial reads as if it referred to a different occasion from these Assizes, and Wentworth was so fond of Scriptural expressions that he might easily have repeated this one.

grand impetuosity he swept away the pretensions of any single man to offer terms to his Sovereign. "Lord," he wrote scornfully to Carlisle, "with Æsop's fly upon the axletree of the wheel, what a dust he makes! Where are those he can lead or persuade? . . . Surely if he leave it to be considered by the best affected, their verdict will be, his Majesty shall contribute more to his own authority by making him an example of his justice than can possibly be gained by taking him in again. But this is an arrogance grown frequent now-a-days which I cannot endure. Every ordinary man must put himself in balance with the King, as if it were a measuring cast betwixt them who were like to prove the greater losers upon the parting. Let me cast then this grain of truth in, and it shall turn the scale. Silly wretches! Let us not deceive ourselves. The King's service cannot suffer by the disgrace of him, and me, and forty more such. The ground whereupon government stands will not so easily be washed away; so as the sooner we unfool ourselves of this error, the sooner we shall learn to know ourselves, and shake off that self-pride which hath to our own esteem represented us much bigger, more considerable, than indeed there is cause for."[1]

The best, the highest side of Wentworth's character stands here revealed. It had been the crowning evil of the days of anarchy which preceded the establishment of the Tudor Monarchy, that wealth and high position had enabled men to bargain with the King and to grind the faces of the poor by terrifying or influencing juries. It was one day to be the evil attendant upon the victory of the Parliamentary system, that the territorial aristocracy were to make use of the forms of the

[1] Wentworth to Carlisle, Oct. 24. Printed in the Preface to Bruce's *Calendar* of *S. P. Dom.*, 1631-33.

constitution to fill their own pockets at the expense of the nation, and to heap honours and rewards upon their own heads. Against such a degradation of the functions of the State, Wentworth struggled with all his might. The depository of the national authority, he held, must be above all persons and all parties, that he might dispense justice to all alike. Unhappily for the great cause which Wentworth represented, Charles's course was running counter to those national instincts upon which alone national authority can be securely based. It is not on Charles alone that the blame of failure must be laid. Wentworth himself had too little sympathy with the religious and political feelings of the prosperous and orderly South to be entitled to speak in the name of the whole of England, or to comprehend what a basis of order and authority might be gained by the admission that the complaints which had found so revolutionary an expression in the last Parliament were not without serious foundation.

Foulis was left to his fate. In the following year a sentence in the Star Chamber stripped him of the office which he occupied under the Crown, fined him 500*l.*, and imprisoned him in the Fleet. He remained in confinement till the Long Parliament came to set him free. Wentworth himself had urged the members of the Court to show no mercy in a case in which his own personal quarrel perhaps seemed to him to be merged in the public interest.

In addition to his conflict with the country gentlemen, Wentworth had to do battle with the Courts of Law at Westminster, which naturally regarded the special jurisdiction of the Council of the North with a jealous eye. On one case which arose he felt himself on particularly strong ground. Sir Thomas Gower insulted the King's Attorney in open Court and then took refuge in London. Wentworth's officers met him in Holborn, and attempted in vain to arrest him. The Lord President appealed to the Privy Council. "Upon these oppositions," he wrote, "and others of like nature, all rests are up, and the issue joined, as we conceive. A provincial Court at York, or none? It is surely the state of the question, the very mark they shoot at; all eyes are at gaze there, and every ear listening here what becomes of it: so as it behoves us to attend it, and clearly to acknowledge it before your Lordships, that unless this Court have in itself coercive power, after it be possessed justly and fairly of a cause, to compel the parties to an answer and to obey the final decrees thereof, all the motions of it become *bruta fulmina*, fruitless to the people, useless to the King, and ourselves altogether unable to govern and contain within the bounds of sobriety a people sometimes so stormy as live under it, which partly appeared in the late business of Malton, where, we dare without vanity speak it, had it not been for the little power and credit that is yet left us here, the injunction of the Chancery itself had been as ill obeyed, as little respected, as either our commission or sergeant in Holborn."

Other questions than that of jurisdiction arose between the Council of the North and the Courts of Westminster. Persons worsted in their suits appealed to the Judges of the King's Bench, who welcomed their complaints and issued prohibitions to stop the execution of their sentences. Wentworth utterly refused to pay any attention to these prohibitions. 'As for the question of jurisdiction of Courts,' he wrote, 'which indeed little concerns the subject, much more the Crown, and which it may restrain or enlarge from time to time as shall in his Majesty's wisdom seem best for the good government of his people and dominions,' he was well able to give satisfaction to the Council.[1]

Wentworth was clearly right in holding that it was not fit to leave such matters to be settled by the Judges at Westminster. Whether exceptional jurisdictions were to be created or maintained was a question to be determined on broad political grounds rather than upon legal arguments. It was one moreover upon which the Judges had clearly their own interests at stake, whilst it might very well happen that the interests of the community lay on the other side. At the present day new Courts are created and their functions defined, not by the Judges, but by Parliament, acting as the supreme political authority of the nation.

The real objection to Wentworth's course lay elsewhere. Was the King, acting alone, the proper depository of that power? In other words, was he capable of acting in the real interests of the community, or not? Did he maintain the claims of the Council of the North as an exceptional jurisdiction, suitable to exceptional circumstances, or was his support of it merely a part of an impatience of control, of a desire to cast himself loose from the necessity of deferring to the ideas and opinions of his subjects. If the latter was the case, the Court at York would stand or fall with the good or ill success of Charles's aims in the more populous and wealthy parts of the kingdom.

For the moment, Wentworth secured his wish. In January 1633 he left the North to prepare for his removal to Ireland. He retained his title of Lord President, and continued to exercise a general supervision over the affairs of the North. The particular question at issue was decided in his favour. Gower

[1] Wentworth and the Council of the North to the Privy Council, Dec. 1. *S. P. Dom.* ccxxvi. 1.

was sent back to York, and expiated his offence by an imprisonment of eighteen months. In March a new set of instructions was issued to the Council of the North, giving it the widest and most undefined authority, more especially by clothing it with all the powers of the Court of Star Chamber at Whitehall.[1] Wentworth afterwards declared that these powers were affirmed to be in accordance with the law by the legal advisers of the Crown. But it was evident that they would provoke discussion and resistance if ever the existence of the great parent Court of Star Chamber at Westminster were seriously attacked.

CHAP. VI.
1633.
March 21.
The new instructions.

In the North, Wentworth had far more to do with the opposition of the country gentlemen than with the opposition of the Puritans. In the South, the Government found more resistance from the Puritans than from the country gentlemen. The spirit of submission to the King's authority was widely spread even amongst those who shared the feelings of the Parliamentary opposition. It is true that the system of expecting men to assist in carrying out the orders of the Government whilst no pains were taken to consult their wishes or to conciliate their prejudices, was one which was likely to break down if any strain were put upon it. But as yet no strain had come, and it seemed as if Charles had no danger to fear in this direction.

1632.
Action of the Government in the South.

An illustration of the bearing of the Government towards the gentry is to be found in a proclamation issued in the summer of 1632, directing all gentlemen to leave London and to return to their houses in the country.[2] The Judges were expressly ordered by the Lord Keeper to enforce obedience to it at the Assizes. The King, said Coventry, had power by ancient precedents to send the gentlemen to their homes. They

June 20.
Proclamation for leaving London.

June 22.

[1] Instructions, March 21. *Rymer*, xix. 410. [2] Proclamation. *Ibid.* xix. 374.

formed the principal part of the county organisation. In their absence there would be no one to preside over musters or suppress rebellions, no one to perform the duties of the Justices of the Peace, or to supply a higher element in the composition of juries. In London they only wasted their time. "Themselves," said the Lord Keeper, "go from ordinaries to dicing-houses, and from thence to play-houses. Their wives dress themselves in the morning, visit in the afternoon and perhaps make a journey to Hyde Park, and so home again." As the exhortations of the Judges did not produce the desired effect, a Mr. Palmer, who had remained in London during the summer, was brought before the Star Chamber. He pleaded in vain that his house in the country had been burnt down, and that he had nowhere to live except in London. A fine of 1,000*l.* was the only answer vouchsafed to his reasoning.[1]

If the feeling of the country gentlemen was one of dissatisfaction, that of the Puritan clergy was far more bitter wherever the hand of Laud reached. As yet, indeed, it did not reach very far. In his own diocese and in the University of Oxford he was supreme. To the rest of England he was able to issue mandates in the King's name, but he could not personally see to their execution, nor could he engage other Bishops to be very zealous in carrying his theories into practice. Practically, therefore, the Puritan was safe, excepting in certain localities. But those localities, the University of Oxford, the City of London, with the counties of Middlesex and Essex, were precisely those where Puritanism was exceptionally strong, and where a defeat would be most ruinous to it.

If the settlement at which Charles aimed by the issue of his Declaration, had been less onesided

[1] D'Ewes. *Autobiography,* ii. 78.

than it was in reality, it could not have secured peace for more than a very short time. Even if the contending parties had agreed to forget all about predestination, some other question would of necessity have arisen about which they would contend as bitterly. When men are divided by opposing tendencies of thought, it matters little what is the actual point round which a storm of discussion gathers. Such a discussion is not to be judged worthy or unworthy according to the subject by which it is provoked, but according to the temper in which it is conducted, and the intellectual and moral problems which are raised by it. There have been times when opposite views of the deepest problems of human nature have been called out by a dispute about the colour of a vestment, as there have been times when questions of infinite importance to mankind have been approached by men of the meanest intellects and the most wrangling temper.

In his anxiety to carry out the directions of the Church to the letter, Laud soon gave positive offence even to those of the Puritan clergy who had submitted with more or less willingness to the King's Declaration. The Canons of 1604 had enjoined upon congregations the duty of expressing reverence by bowing their heads whenever the name of Jesus was uttered. Laud, however, went further than this. He held it right that every one who entered a church should bow in like manner, not, as he explained it, to the altar, but towards the altar, as to the throne of the invisible King in whose house he was. No general law enjoined this practice, but it was inculcated by the special statutes of certain churches, and Laud was able to commend it by exhortation and example.[1]

[1] This was the line taken by him at the censure of Bastwick, Burton, and Prynne in 1637. "The Government," he then said, "is so moderate

1631.
Jan.
The consecration of churches.

In January 1631 attention was publicly called to Laud's views on the subject by his proceedings at the church of St. Catherine Cree, in the City of London. It had been lately rebuilt by the liberality of the parishioners. The Church of England had provided no form for the consecration of churches. In Elizabeth's time there had been but little church building,[1] and when the practice again came into favour, individual Bishops seem either to have omitted the ceremony altogether, or to have introduced a form of their own devising. In 1616 Abbot set apart by a special form of prayer a chapel at Dulwich.[2] In 1620 Andrewes consecrated another chapel near Southampton after a more ornate form of his own composition. With Laud, the authority of Andrewes was conclusive. He had recently been engaged, with the assistance of Buckeridge, in issuing to the world a collected edition of Andrewes' sermons, and his whole life was an effort to carry out in a hard practical way the ideas which cast a gleam of

Precedents of consecration.

.... that no man is constrained, no man questioned, only religiously called upon, *Venite adoremus*, Come, let us worship." *Works*, i. 56. This would not, however, apply to officials of a church in which the practice was enjoined by the statutes.

[1] "Wherein the first thing that moveth them thus to cast up their poison, are certain solemnities usual at the first erection of churches. Now, although the same should be blameworthy, yet this age, thanks be to God, hath reasonably well forborne to incur the danger of any such blame. It cannot be laid to many men's charge at this day living, either that they have been so curious as to trouble bishops with placing the first stone in the churches they built, or so scrupulous as, after the erection of them, to make any great ado for their dedication. In which kind notwithstanding as we do neither allow unmeet, nor purpose the stiff defence of any unnecessary custom heretofore received; so we know no reason wherefore churches would be the worse, if at the first erecting of them, at the making of them public, at the time when they are delivered, as it were, in God's own possession, and when the use whereunto they shall ever serve is established, ceremonies fit to betoken such intents and to accompany such actions be used, as in the present times they have been." Hooker, *Eccl. Pol.* Book v. xii. 1.

[2] Wilkins, *Conc.* iv. 455.

poetry over the unworldly Bishop. On January 16, accompanied by his official attendants, he appeared in full canonicals in Leadenhall Street before the church of St. Catherine Cree, which had just been rebuilt. He adopted the form which had been prepared by Andrewes. After two Psalms had been sung by all who chose to join in them, he entered the church, and kneeling in the doorway, offered the building to be set apart to the worship of God. Passing from one end to the other he pronounced the church with all its distinctive parts to be consecrated.[1] Then followed other prayers and the Communion Service, Laud doubtless bowing low 'towards the altar' on the appropriate occasions.

No contemporary account has reached us to tell what impression was made upon the bystanders. Eight years before an almost similar ceremony had taken place when Bishop Montaigne consecrated the neighbouring parish church of St. James' in Aldgate, in the presence of the Lord Mayor and Aldermen.[2] Arch-

---

[1] The general consecration was as follows:—"God the Father, God the Son, and God the Holy Ghost, accept, sanctify, and bless this place to the end whereunto, according to His own ordinance, we have ordained it, to be a sanctuary to the Most High, and a church for the living God. The Lord with His favour ever mercifully behold it, and so send upon it His spiritual benediction and grace, that it may be the house of God to Him and the gate of heaven to us." The consecration of the Communion-table was, "Grant us that all they that shall at any time partake at this table the highest blessing of all, Thy Holy Communion, may be fulfilled with Thy grace and heavenly benediction, and may, to their great and endless comfort, obtain remission of their sins, and all other benefits of Thy passion." Andrewes. *Minor Works*, 316.

[2] A sketch of the ceremony is preserved in Strype's edition of Stow's *Survey of London*, Book ii. 60. One point objected to in Laud is to be found here. The Lord Mayor and Aldermen presented the keys of the church to the Bishop, praying him to proceed to consecration, 'which the Bishop receiving, he unlocked and opened the doors which before were locked, and entered with the Archbishop, etc., and took possession.' Then 'in the very threshold at his entrance' he 'blessed the place.' Then 'going a little forward, with bended knees, and hands towards the

bishop Abbot himself had taken part in the service, and there is no rumour of any objection being made by any one. A London crowd in 1631, however, was not in quite the same temper as a London crowd in 1623, and it may be that if it were now possible to examine some of those who were present at St. Catherine Cree, better evidence than that of the two witnesses who drew so largely on their imagination before the Long Parliament might be found to shew that some feeling of disapprobation was evinced.[1]

Laud's buildings at St. John's.

In all matters connected with the construction and repair of ecclesiastical buildings Laud is to be seen at his best. In our time he would have been in his place as

East, lifted up to heaven, he made a devout prayer, thereby devoting, dedicating the place from that day for ever unto God.'

[1] Prynne (*Cant. Doom*, 113) merely gives the story as it was told to the Long Parliament, and Rushworth (ii. 77), whom most modern writers have followed like sheep, does the same. When it is remembered that they both adopted the forged entry in Laud's diary about Leighton's punishment, it is plain that they add nothing to the credit of the witnesses. Laud (*Works*, iv. 247) not only denied the statements made, but asserted that he had used Bishop Andrewes' form. It is intelligible that the Long Parliament should have neglected to send for a copy of that form, but modern historians might have been expected to take the trouble of looking at it. No part of the charge has been so often repeated as that which relates to Laud's mode of consecrating the sacrament. "As he approached the Communion-table," we are told, " he made many several lowly bowings, and coming up to the side of the table, where the bread and wine were covered, he bowed seven times, and then after the reading of many prayers, he came near the bread, and gently lifted up the corner of the napkin wherein the bread was laid, and when he beheld the bread he laid it down again, flew back a step or two, bowed three several times towards it, then he drew near again and opened the napkin and bowed as before," etc. Laud did not contradict the statement in particulars, thinking perhaps that he had already said enough to discredit the witnesses. But it is altogether incredible, and is worthless except as an illustration of the sort of stuff that men were prepared to believe about Laud twelve years afterwards. He was not given to histrionics. His observance of formalities was of a more sober cast. Besides, if he had done anything like this once, he would have been sure to do it again, and Prynne would not have neglected to inform us of his follies.

the Dean of a Cathedral in need of restoration. His works at his own College of St. John's at Oxford were forwarded with ungrudging but measured and business-like liberality which have to this day kept his memory green amongst a generation of students which has drifted far from his principles in religion and politics. No surveyor of works was a better judge of the execution of a contract or the correctness of an account than the Bishop of London. To such a man the ruinous condition of St. Paul's was an eyesore not to be borne. He was scarcely settled in his See before he called upon the King to carry out the plans for the restoration of the church which had been made and abandoned by his father. In 1631 Charles visited the Cathedral and appointed commissioners to gather money for the repair of the fabric. The money of the citizens did not flow in very freely. After two years only 5,400*l.* had been collected.[1] Laud, however, was not the man to allow the undertaking to sleep. He brought his own personal influence to bear upon the wealthy. He caused the Privy Council to put in motion the whole machinery of the Justices of the Peace to gather contributions from every county in England. The clergy were the special object of his appeals, and few liked to risk their chances of promotion by refusing to carry out his wishes.[2] Something, however, must be allowed for the growing zeal for the building and adornment of churches, which was only encouraged by the jeers of such Puritans as thought it seemly to speak of the grand

[1] *Heylyn*, 208. Jones, Carter, and Cooke to the Commissioners, May 22, 1633. *S. P. Dom.* ccxxxix. 20.
[2] The existence of this motive is distinctly admitted by Heylyn. "Some men," he says, "in hope of favour and preferment from him, others to hold fair quarter with him, and not a few for fear of incurring his displeasure, contributing more largely to it than they had done otherwise, if otherwise they had contributed at all."

old fabric as 'a rotten relic,' and to argue that 'it was more agreeable to the rules of piety to demolish such old monuments of superstition and idolatry than to keep them standing.'[1]

1632. Houses removed.

Already preliminary steps had been taken. Houses built up against the walls not only concealed the architectural proportions of the great Cathedral, but threw obstacles in the way of a searching investigation into the causes of its decay. The houses had been raised, if Laud is to be trusted, on land belonging to the church in defiance of legal right. The Privy Council therefore issued orders for their speedy demolition. But they offered at the same time sufficient compensation for their value. Some of the owners resisted the order. But the Council stood firm, and before the end of 1632 the long nave stood exposed to view in all its unrivalled proportions.[2]

Complaints were afterwards made that the action of the Council was a violation of the law. None of the complainants, however, seem to have thought of submitting their grievances at the time to a Court of law, and indeed it would hardly have been prudent for a private person to contest the King's authority in a case so manifestly for the public advantage. In our own day powers would easily be obtained from the legislature to treat the owners of these houses precisely as they were treated by Laud and the Privy Council.

1631. Jan. Puritan feeling about bowing.

It was only occasionally that churches required consecration or repair. The practice of bowing towards the East gave daily annoyance to the Puritan. The idea of God having a throne at all except in the hearts of men was abominable to him, and it was still

---

[1] *Heylyn,* 209.
[2] *Council Register,* Oct. 28, 1631. March 7, 16, May 9, Aug. 9, Aug. 24, 1632. Windebank to the King, Oct. 20. *S. P. Dom.* ccxxiv. 40.

worse to be told that that throne was an altar, a name which he directly associated with idolatry and superstition. Prynne, as usual, was at once in the thick of the fight. His first antagonist was a certain Giles Widdowes, who had written in defence of the practice of bowing, and whom he scornfully attacked in a book characteristically entitled *Lame Giles his haltings*. In one place Widdowes argued that men ought to take off their hats on entering a church, because it was 'the place of God's presence, the chiefest place of His honour amongst us, where He is worshipped with holy worship; where His ambassadors deliver His embassage; where His priests sacrifice their own and the militant Church's prayers, and the Lord's Supper to reconcile us to God, offended with our daily sins.' 'Ergo,' rejoined Prynne, triumphantly, 'the priests of the Church of England—especially those who erect, adore, and cringe to altars—are sacrificing priests, and the Lord's Supper a propitiatory sacrifice, sacrificed by those priests for men's daily sins.'[1]

Prynne was not allowed to have the last word. An Oxford writer named Page commenced a reply. It was evident that a controversy about gestures was impending which was likely to prove as bitter as the controversy about predestination. Abbot imagined that he would be allowed, as Archbishop of Canterbury, to say something on the matter, and that the principle of abstinence from disputation which had been used against his own side would hold good against the other. "Good Mr. Page," wrote Abbot's secretary, "my Lord of Canterbury is informed that you are publishing a treatise touching the question of bowing at the name of Jesus, an argument wherein Mr. Widdowes foolishly,

---

[1] Widdowes, *The lawless, kneeless, schismatical Puritan*, 33. Prynne, *Lame Giles his haltings*, 34.

and Mr. Prynne scurrilously, have already, to the scandal of the Church, exercised their pens." To keep this question on foot would be to foment 'bitterness and intestine contestations.' If Page had not been a mere theorist, living in a cell of his own, he would never have touched a subject 'wherein the governors and chief pilots of the Church discern more harm and tempest to the Church than' it was possible that one who was 'unacquainted with ecclesiastical estate and the well-ordering of it' could 'any way attain unto.'

Abbot forgot that he had to reckon with Laud, and that Laud had the King at his back. The University of Oxford had power to license books for the press whether the Archbishop approved of them or not; and at that University Laud was now supreme. Page was therefore encouraged to continue his work. His Majesty, wrote Laud, was unwilling that Prynne's ignorant writings should be left unanswered.[1]

The encouragement to carry on the controversy was likely to be more bitterly felt, as Laud was at the very time engaged in enforcing the King's Declaration at Oxford with the utmost strictness. Party feeling was running high in the University. Preachers, not content with asserting their own views on the forbidden topic of predestination, proceeded to vilify their antagonists as wantonly promulgating heretical opinions for the sake of Court favour. The Vice Chancellor's authority was openly set at naught, and he found no support in Convocation, which was still predominantly Calvinistic. Charles himself intervened, and summoned the offenders before him at Woodstock. He ordered the preachers whose sermons had been complained of to be expelled from the University, and the proctors

[1] Baker to Page, May 31. Laud to Smith, June 22. *Laud's Works*, v. 39.

who had failed to call them to account to be deprived of their offices.[1]

Silence on controverted points of doctrine combined with encouragement to argue on one side alone of ceremonial dispute was the arrangement favoured by the Government. It is easy to see how Charles and Laud came to approve of such a solution of their difficulties. On the one hand, they regarded speculative theology as a mere intrusion on religion, and they had no confidence in the attainment of truth by the hot conflict of thought with thought. On the other hand, they were unable to understand that a ceremony which conveyed to their own minds an innocent or pious impression might be associated in the minds of others with thoughts which were neither pious nor innocent. The result was none the less deplorable. All that had been gained by opposition to the doctrinal intolerance of the Commons was thrown away. Under the show of impartiality, and doubtless with the firm conviction that impartiality had been actually attained, Charles had deliberately assumed the position of a partisan. Whatever vantage ground he possessed in 1629 was surrendered in 1631.

Partial, however, as Laud's administration was, he justified it to himself as an appeal to law against caprice. On a subject the most difficult to confine within legal restrictions, the most spiritual and undefinable of all objects of human thought, he appealed simply to the strictest possible interpretation of the law of the Church. Even when the Prayer-book had been drawn up, and still more when the Canons had been voted, the ecclesiastical legislature had been very far from representing the currents of opinion which swept over the ecclesiastical body. It was notorious that in

CHAP. VI.

1631. Meaning of the course taken.

Laud's view of conformity.

[1] *Laud's Works*, v. 49-70.

Laud's own day the contrast between the opinion of Convocation and the opinion of the religious laity was still more striking. It was no matter to Laud. It was no part of his belief that law ought in any way to conform itself to opinion. It was enough for him that it existed. The Canons and the Common Prayer-book were to be accepted by all the clergy. Those who objected had no such resource as they have at the present day. They could not pass from the church to the chapel. They could not address their countrymen on religious subjects even in private houses. They must conform to the least tittle, or abandon their position as teachers.

Laud and the Puritan clergy.

The utmost that can be said is that if Laud's pressure was unremitting, it was not spiteful or violent. "Concerning some ministers," wrote a Puritan clergyman who had complied with Laud's demands, "I am a witness of your patient forbearing them, giving them time again and again to consult thereabout with what conformable ministers they themselves thought best."[1] Others, however, complained bitterly at the sudden tightening of the string. "It is no easy matter," wrote the despairing Vicar of Braintree, "to reduce a numerous congregation into order that hath been disorderly this fifty years, and that for these seven years last past hath been encouraged in that way by all the refractory ministers of that country... If I had suddenly and hastily fallen upon the strict practice of conformity, I had undone myself and broken the town to pieces. For upon the first notice of alteration many were resolving to go to New England, others to remove elsewhere, by whose departure the burden of the poor and charges of the town had grown insupportable to those who should have staid behind. By my moderate and slow pro-

[1] Baker to Laud, Oct. 19. *S. P. Dom.* ccii. 3.

ceeding I have made stay of some, and do hope to settle their judgment and abode with us, when the rest that are inexorable are shipped and gone."[1]

Laud, in short, was a lawyer in a rochet, and that not a lawyer of the highest sort. He could understand the necessity of conducting life in accordance with fixed rules. He could not understand that all existing rules were but the product of fallible human intelligence perpetually needing correction, perpetually halting after the infinite life and diversity of nature.

Above all, the ill-feeling which his proceedings aroused was unintelligible to Laud. He could not endure to be misunderstood, or perceive that it was in the nature of things that his own misrepresentations of others should be returned in kind. One of those who paid the penalty for his too vivid indignation was Nathaniel Bernard. He was not a man of either reticence or prudence. Three years before he had startled his congregation by praying, " O Lord, open the eyes of the Queen's Majesty, that she may see Jesus Christ, whom she hath pierced with her infidelity, superstition, and idolatry." He now, in preaching at Cambridge, attacked those who went about to deprive the nation of God's ordinances for his public worship; "whereby," he added, "we may learn what to account of those amongst ourselves—if any such be, which is better known to you than me—who endeavour to quench the light and abate the glory of Israel by bringing in their Pelagian errors into the doctrine of our Church established by law, and the superstitions of the Church of Rome into our worship of God; as high altars, crucifixes, and bowing to them, that is, in plain English, worshipping them, whereby they symbolise with the Church of Rome very shamefully, to the irre-

[1] Collins to Duck, Jan. 18, 1632. *S. P. Dom.* ccx. 41.

parable shipwreck of many souls who split upon the rock."¹

Bernard was fined and imprisoned by the High Commission. Of that Court Laud was the ruling spirit. Yet it must not be forgotten that Abbot was constantly in attendance, and was almost as energetic as Laud in his enforcement of conformity. In the only case affecting ceremonial in the records which have been preserved, and which reach from October 1631 to June 1632,² Abbot declared his opinion to be strongly against the right of certain parishes in London to place seats above the Communion-table. In questions relating to marriage the Court struggled, against every kind of opposition, to uphold the standard of a high morality. The case of Sir Giles Alington, who married his niece, was doubtless exceptional. But it needed all Laud's firmness to put an end to the scandal. Alington appealed to the Court of Common Pleas, and the Judges of that Court issued a prohibition to stay proceedings. The High Commissioners set the interference at naught. "If this prohibition," said Laud at the Council table, "had taken place, I hope my Lord's Grace of Canterbury would have excommunicated throughout his province all the Judges who should have had a hand therein. For mine own part, I will assure you, if he would not, I would have done it in my diocese, and myself in person denounced it both in Paul's church and other churches of the same against the authors of so enormous a scandal to our Church and religion." In clerical circles the Bishop's firmness gave the highest satisfaction. "I know not," wrote Meade from Cambridge, "what you will say in the country, but we say here it was spoken

---

¹ Prynne, *Canterbury's Doom*, 363.
² Harl. MSS. 4130, and Rawlinson MSS. 128.

like a Bishop indeed."[1] Alington's fine was 12,000*l*., with a bond of 2,000*l*., to be forfeited if he ever lived again with his niece as his wife. But the object of the Court was to prevent rather than to punish offences, and as soon as Alington made it understood that he had forsaken his evil ways for ever, a pardon wiped away the fine which had been imposed upon his previous misconduct.[2]

The Court shewed a special consideration for the misfortunes of injured women. "The law of England," as an advocate pleading before it said, " is a husband's law," and many a time the Commissioners interfered to enforce a separate maintenance for the victim of infidelity or brutality.

Excepting so far as the suppression of lectureships was concerned, there does not seem to have been any thought at this time of treating ordinary Puritanism as a crime. But anything approaching to Antinomianism was put down with a strong hand. No man was to preach the doctrine of free grace in such a way as to lead his hearers to suppose that the commission of sin was a matter of indifference. A fanatic named Richard Lane was imprisoned for saying that through Christ's grace he was above sin and needed no repentance, and clergymen who maintained the same opinion were deprived of their livings. Private meetings for prayers or preaching were strictly forbidden. "We took another conventicle of separatists," wrote Laud, merrily, "in Newington Woods on Sunday last, in the very brake where the King's stag should have been lodged for his hunting the next morning."[3] Those who were captured were sturdy representatives of a sturdy sect. Brought before

---

[1] Meade to Stuteville, May 20. *Court and Times*, ii. 119.
[2] Pardon to Alington, July 14. *Sign Manuals*, xiii. 32.
[3] Laud to Windebank, June 13. *S. P. Dom.* ccxviii. 46.

CHAP.
VI.
───
1632.
June 14.

the High Commission, they refused to take the *ex-officio* oath to answer whatever questions might be proposed to them. They said that they owed obedience to none but to God and the King, and those who were lawfully sent by him. "You do shew yourselves," said Abbot, "the most ungrateful to God, and to his Majesty the King, and to us the fathers of the Church. If you have any knowledge of God, it hath come through or by us or some of our predecessors. We have taken care, under God, to give milk to the babes and younglings, and strong meat to the men of understanding. You have the word of God to feed you, the sacraments to strengthen you, and we support you by prayer. For all this what despite do you return us. You call us abominable men, to be hated of all; that we carry the mark of the Beast, that we are his members. We do bear this patiently, not because we have no law to right us, but because of your obstinacy. But for the dishonouring of God and disobeying of the King, it is not to be endured. When you have reading, preaching, singing, teaching, you are your own ministers. The blind lead the blind, whereas his Majesty is God's Vicegerent in the Church. The Church is nothing with you, and its ministers not to be regarded; and you run into woods as if you lived in persecution. Such an one you make the King, to whom we are so much bound for his great care for the truth to be preserved among us, and you would have men believe that he is a tyrant; this, besides your wickedness, unthankfulness, and ungraciousness towards us the fathers of the Church. Therefore let these men be put, two and two, in separate prisons."

Difficulties of Church government.

The idea of tolerating separate worship had not occurred to either party in the Church. Until that idea had made its way, the difficulties of governing the Church were almost insuperable. If the rule of the law were strictly enforced, many earnest and conscientious preachers would be put to silence. If it were laxly enforced, congregations would suffer from the mere vagaries of eccentric clergymen. It is noticeable that the only important case of irregular teaching, not Antinomian, which was brought before the Court during the eight months over which the report extends, was that of John Vicars, Vicar of Stamford, prosecuted, not by the Bishop of the diocese, but by the inhabitants of the parish, with the Town Clerk at their head. Vicars had invited persons from other parishes to attend his sermons in words not complimentary to their own clergy. 'They must have a care,' he said, 'to hear that minister that preached the word, and not those that brought chaff.' His own preaching seemed very like chaff to many of his congregation. He had a theory that Christmas Day ought to be kept in September. He had peculiar views about married life, which he enunciated with such plainness of speech as to give offence even in that plain-spoken age. He held meetings of preparation before the administration of the Communion, and in his sermons he spoke scornfully, with irritating emphasis, of those who abstained from attending them. He told his congregation that it was a sin to receive the Sacrament except upon the Sabbath-day. He had warned them that persecution was at hand. A specimen of the objurgations with which he ventured to interlard the exhortation in the Communion Service was given. "Thou son of the devil," he cried out to one who presented himself before him, "thou art damned and the son of damnation. Get thee to the devil. Take hell for thy portion." The High Commission does not deserve blame for removing this man from his ministry at Stamford. He was, however, subsequently reinstated upon promise of obedience.[1]

On the whole, it would seem that as long as Abbot

[1] *S. P. Dom.* cclxi. fol. 5, b.

lived there was nothing done by the Court of High Commission likely to give offence to moderate men of either party. We must look elsewhere for the two great ecclesiastical processes of the day, and even those processes aimed not so much at the suppression of any particular opinions as at the gathering up of all authority in the Church into the hands of the central Government. Laud was rather sharpening the instrument of power than making use of it in any special direction.

In 1629 Henry Sherfield returned home to Salisbury from the Parliament in which he had represented the city, with no kindly feeling towards Bishops or ceremonies. He was Recorder of the borough, and a member of the vestry of the parish of St. Edmund's. Like the great majority of the laity of his day, he had no objection to bring against the services of the Church as he had been in the habit of seeing them carried out, that is to say, with some omissions. He had, however, been accustomed to kneel at the reception of the Communion, and had been active in punishing separatists. Together with his fellow-vestrymen, he had a special grievance to complain of. The windows of the church were of painted glass, and one of them contained a representation of the First Person of the Trinity as an old man measuring the world with a pair of compasses, and raising Eve out of the side of Adam.

It was easy to take offence at such a picture; and though to most persons entering the church it was probably a mere piece of coloured glass and nothing more, there were relics of old mediæval superstitions still floating about under the shadow of the most graceful of English Cathedrals. One Emily Browne bowed before the window as she passed to her seat. "I do it," she replied to Sherfield's remonstrance, " to my Lord God." " Why," said the Puritan lawyer, "where is He?"

"In the window, is He not?" was the answer he received. In February 1630 Sherfield brought the matter before the vestry, and the vestry directed him to remove the painting and to replace it by plain white glass. They did not, however, care to place on record the real motive of their decision. "The said window," they explained, "is somewhat decayed and broken, and is very darksome, whereby such as sit near the same cannot see to read in their books."[1]

<small>CHAP. VI.
1630.
Jan. 16.
The vestry give orders to remove it.</small>

The affair was not long in reaching the ears of Davenant, the Bishop of the See. He was regarded as the theologian of the Calvinistic party in the Church, and had been one of the representatives of the King of England at the Synod of Dort. But he at once sent for the churchwardens of St. Edmund's, and forbade them to carry out the order of the vestry.

<small>The Bishop objects.</small>

Accordingly no action was taken in the matter. About Michaelmas, Sherfield was called by business to the neighbouring village of Steeple Aston. The Vicar showed him over the church. The windows glowed with 'painted images and pictures of saints.' Not far off a knight lately dead had left in his will a sum of money to put up windows representing 'works of mercy.' The mischief, as Sherfield considered it, was plainly spreading. "For my part," he said to the Vicar, "I do not like these painted windows in churches. They obscure the light, and may be a cause of much superstition." He then spoke of the window at St. Edmund's, and complained of the Bishop's interference.[2]

<small>Sept. Sherfield's visit to Steeple Aston.</small>

Sherfield returned to Salisbury with his mind made up. He had personally received no official notice of the Bishop's inhibition, and he resolved to set it at defiance. Obtaining the key of the church from the

<small>Oct. He breaks the windows.</small>

---

[1] Order of the Vestry in Hoare's *History of Wiltshire*, vi. 371.
[2] Webb's Deposition, Jan. ? 1631. *S. P. Dom.* clxxviii. 58.

sexton's wife, he went in alone, locked the door behind him, climbed up on the back of a seat and dashed his stick through the glass. In his vehemence he lost his balance and fell to the ground.

A Star Chamber prosecution was the result. The case was postponed till February 1633.[1] It was Noy's first appearance as Attorney General in an important State prosecution. He said something to show that Sherfield had acted independently of the vestry's order. But the main scope of his argument went to urge that a vestry had no power to make such an order at all. It might make or mend seats, or place a reading-desk in a more convenient position. But it was not in its power to carry out a change which implied a special religious view without the Bishop's consent. If every vestry could deal at pleasure with the fabric of the building in its charge, one church might be pulled down because it was in the form of a cross, another because it stood East and West. One man might hold that to be idolatry which was not idolatry to another. These differences of opinion would engender strife, and strife would lead to sedition and insurrection.

The Star Chamber unanimously concurred in Noy's view of the case. But there was much difference of opinion as to the penalty to be inflicted. The lawyers, Coventry, Heath, and Richardson were on the side of leniency. The Bishops, Laud and Neile, were on the side of harshness. The sentence was at last fixed at 500l. and a public acknowledgment of the fault. Sherfield duly made the acknowledgment before the Bishop of Salisbury; but he died not very long afterwards, leaving the fine to be paid by his relatives.[2]

[1] The date 1633/2, which even Mr. Bruce accepted (*S. P. Dom.* ccxi. 20) is clearly wrong. The fact that Windebank took part in the sentence is decisive against it.

[2] *State Trials*, iii. 519. Nicholas to E. Nicholas, written early in

On the general question Noy's argument was unanswerable. But the objections of the lawyers in the Court went deeper than the lowering or raising of a fine by a few hundred pounds. It was well that the authority to remove such a window as had been removed by Sherfield should be in the hands of persons of larger views than the members of a parish vestry were likely to be. But it would be to little purpose to assign this authority to the Bishops, if the Bishops were to have as little sympathy as Laud had with the dominant religious feelings of the country. Works of art are worth preserving, but the religious sentiments of the worshippers demand consideration also. It was evident from the language employed by Coventry and the Chief Justices, that though they objected to the way in which Sherfield's act had been done, they shared his dislike of the representation which had given him offence. Laud was so occupied with his detestation of the unruly behaviour of the man, that he had no room for consideration whether his dislike was justifiable or not. He treated the reasonings of the lawyers as an assault upon the Episcopal order. He told them that the authority of the Bishops was derived from the authority of the King, and that if they attacked that, they would fall as low as Bishops had once fallen.

CHAP. VI.
1633.
The Bishops and the lawyers.

A few days afterwards, a case of still greater importance was decided by the Court of Exchequer. In the beginning of the reign, four citizens of London, four lawyers, and four Puritan clergymen of note, had associated themselves for the purpose of doing something to remedy the evil of an impoverished clergy. They established a fund by means of voluntary contributions, from which they bought up impropriate

1625.
The feoffees for impropriations.

1634, not in 1632, as calendared. *S. P. Dom.* ccxiv. 92. Narrative, March 15, 1633. *S. P. Dom.* cxxxiii. 89.

tithes, and were thus enabled to increase the stipends of ministers, lecturers, and schoolmasters. Naturally the persons selected for their favours were Puritans, and Laud had early marked the feoffees for impropriations, as they were called, for destruction.

1630. July 11. Heylyn's sermon.

The first to lift up his voice publicly against them was Peter Heylyn, Laud's chaplain and future biographer. In a sermon preached at Oxford, in 1630, he said that the enemy had been sowing tares. The feoffees were 'chief patrons of the faction.' They preferred those who were 'serviceable to their dangerous innovations.' In time they would 'have more preferments to bestow, and therefore more dependencies, than all the prelates in the kingdom.'[1]

1632. Noy's information.

Laud took the matter up warmly. At his instigation, Noy exhibited against the feoffees an information in the Exchequer Chamber, a Court of Equity in which the Lord Treasurer and the Chancellor of the Exchequer sat as judges by the side of the Barons. The charge against the feoffees was that they had illegally constituted themselves into a body holding property without the sanction of the King. An argument of more general interest was that, instead of employing the money collected in the permanent increase of endowments, they had paid the favoured ministers or schoolmasters by grants revocable at their own pleasure. They had already diverted the tithes of Presteign in Radnorshire to provide lectures for a church in the City of London, and the lecturers here and elsewhere would be obliged to conform their teaching to the opinions of their paymasters. The Court decreed the dissolution of the feoffment, and directed that all the patronage in their hands should be placed at the King's disposal.[2]

1633. Feb. 11. The sentence.

[1] Heylyn, *Cyprianus Anglicus*, 199.
[2] *Exchequer Decrees*, iv. 88. The decree is carefully deleted by pen-

If it were possible to look upon this sentence apart from the circumstances of the time, it would not be difficult to adduce arguments in its favour. Of all modes of supporting a clergy yet invented, their maintenance by a body of capitalists living for the most part at a distance from the scene of their ministrations, is, in all probability, the worst. But there are times when the most irregular manifestations of life are welcome, and in making his attack upon the feoffees Laud was not merely assailing the special system under which they acted, but was taking one more step in the work of suppressing a form of belief which was deeply rooted in the heart of the nation, and of setting aside the life and energy of individual initiative in favour of the cold hard pressure of official interference. The action of Charles, of Laud, and of Wentworth, was all of a piece. Instead of finding their work in the control and guidance of the irregular and often ignorant action of individuals and corporations, they sought to substitute their own ways of thought for those of the generation in which they lived. They forgot that they too were but fallible mortals, and that if they had been possessed of infallibility itself, they would have been the first to learn that the path to excellence lay in the struggle and the aspiration, not in mute and unresisting obedience to the word of command.

CHAP. VI.
1633. Feb. 11.

The first two names on the list of the feoffees, those of William Gouge and Richard Sibbes, offered sufficient guarantees that no destructive influences were here at work. Gouge's sermons at Blackfriars were preached in the presence of an overflowing auditory, of very varying character. It was from his church that Leigh-

William Gouge.

strokes by order of the Lords in Parliament, March 3, 1648. See *Bills and Answers, Charles I. London and Middlesex*, No. 533. The receipts had been 6,361*l*. 6*s*. 1*d*.

ton had stepped forth when he was seized by the pursuivants. It was in his church that Lord Keeper Coventry learned to do judgment and justice. Merchants, lawyers, scholars, flocked to hear him. Strangers did not consider their business in London to be finished till they had heard the lecture at Blackfriars. Gouge's life was a constant stream of benevolent labour. Many a man in the next generation could bear witness that the first seeds of godliness and virtue had been sown in his mind by one of Gouge's sermons.[1] He did his best to satisfy Laud. He received his admonitions on account of some irregularities in the administration of the Communion with meekness. He detested, as he declared, those who despised authorities.[2]

Sibbes was a still more notable personage in the ranks of the moderate Puritans. The son of a Suffolk wheelwright, he had been sent to a neighbouring school. But his father grudged the expense, and fetched him home. He would rather see him hammering at the forge than conning his book. But the village clergyman and the village lawyer had their eyes upon the hopeful boy, and sent him to Cambridge to be educated, making up by the help of friends the scanty sum which they had shamed the wheelwright into allowing him.

Ever since the days of Cartwright there had been a strong Puritan element at Cambridge. Perkins had handed on the torch of religious oratory to Bayne, and Bayne was the spiritual father of Sibbes. He early became a preacher in London. Then he returned to Cambridge. In 1609 he was chosen College preacher of St. John's, and in the next year he was invited to undertake the weekly lecture at Trinity parish church. In his hands Trinity lecture became a great power in

---

[1] Clarke, *Lives of ten eminent divines*, 95.
[2] Gouge to Laud, Oct. 19, 1631. *S. P. Dom.* ccii. 3.

Cambridge. Men like Cotton, afterwards the light of New England, and Goodwin, the noted Independent divine, traced their spiritual generation to Sibbes. "Young man," he said to Goodwin, "if you ever would do good, you must preach the gospel and the free grace of God in Christ Jesus."

CHAP VI.
1610.

The free grace of God, the lovingkindness of a merciful Saviour looking down in pity upon each individual soul, and bidding it be of good cheer, was the message which Sibbes delivered to men. In 1615, for some unexplained reason, he was deprived of his lectureship.[1] In 1617, at Yelverton's suggestion, he was chosen preacher to Gray's Inn. There, men bearing the first names in England, Bacon, it may be, himself dropping in amongst his old companions, flocked to hear him. If the worth of a man is to be known by those who combine to honour him, Sibbes needs no further testimony. In 1626 he was chosen, at Usher's recommendation, Provost of Trinity College, Dublin. Almost at the same moment he was elected Master of Catherine Hall. The choice between his old University and a removal to Ireland was soon made, and he took his place once more at Cambridge.[2] By the statutes of Gray's Inn his preachership was vacated by the acceptance of office elsewhere. But the lawyers would not spare him, and he was allowed, by a special Act, to hold both preferments at once. Cambridge submitted once more to the charm of his fervid eloquence. St. Mary's pulpit was thrown open to him. The church was so thronged that the parishioners had to draw up

1615.

1617.
Preachership of Gray's Inn.

1626.
Sibbes returns to Cambridge.

---

[1] Mr. Grosart, from whose biography, prefixed to his edition of *Sibbes's Works*, I extract these particulars, suggests that Laud had something to do with it,—an evident anachronism.

[2] Trinity College chose Joseph Meade to succeed him, and then upon his refusal, William Bedell, afterwards the celebrated Bishop. *Sir J. Ware's Diary. Crowcombe Court MSS.*

regulations to prevent their being thrust out of their seats by strangers.

1627. Collects for the Palatinate.

Such a man was sure to come into collision with the Court. In 1627, together with Gouge and two others, he issued a circular letter asking for alms for the exiles from the Palatinate. The four were summoned to the Star Chamber, and were reprimanded for this act of invitation to charity, which seemed likely to be more favourably received than the forced loan had been.

1633. Becomes Vicar of Trinity.

Then came the trouble about the impropriations. Though Laud and the King might look askance at Sibbes's work, they could not charge him with being a disturber of the peace. In November, Charles, anxious perhaps to show that he had no personal grudge against him, presented him to the Vicarage of Trinity, and about the same time the grateful Master of Catherine Hall contributed some glowing lines to a collection of Latin verses written in honour of the birth of the King's second son, the future James II.

His letter to Goodwin.

Such words were not mere flattery. Doubtless there were many things in the Church which Sibbes regarded with grave dissatisfaction. But he had no more wish than Gouge to cast off the ties which bound him to his countrymen. He dissuaded Goodwin from separating himself from the Church of which he was a minister in the most urgent terms. That Church, he wrote, had all the marks of a true Church of Christ. It had ' begot many spiritual children to the Lord.' As for ceremonies, even if it were admitted that they were evil, it would be a remedy worse than the disease to tear the Church in sunder on their account. He begged his correspondent to forsake his ' extravagant courses, and submissively to render ' himself ' to the sacred communion of this truly evangelical Church of England.'

That Church would never remain united unless its

rulers knew how to conciliate such moderate opponents. They would have to conciliate others too, whose minds were cast in a very different mould. They would have to find room by the side of Gouge and Sibbes for Nicholas Ferrar and George Herbert.

CHAP. VI.
1633.
Necessity of conciliation.

Nicholas Ferrar was the younger son of a wealthy London merchant. Having received the rite of confirmation when only five years old, as the custom then was, the child slipped in unnoticed on a second occasion, and was twice confirmed. "I did it," he said, "because it was a good thing to have the Bishop's prayers and blessing twice, and I have got it." He was a studious youth, loving above all other books the Bible, and Foxe's Martyrs. After a course of study full of promise at Cambridge, he travelled on the Continent, where he attracted attention by the quickness of his observation and the retentiveness of his memory. At his return he found employment under the Virginia Company, and drew upon himself the notice of the leading statesmen of the day by the vigour and ability with which he defended its charter when it was called in question in 1623. Elected to Parliament in the next year, he took part in the impeachment of Middlesex, who had roused his indignation by his attack upon the Company.

Childhood of Nicholas Ferrar.

1623.
Defends the Virginia Company.

It was Ferrar's last appearance in public life. He took no pleasure in the political and religious conflict which was evidently impending when Charles ascended the throne, and the plague which devastated London in that year gave the final impress to a determination which had long been floating in his mind. His widowed mother bought the manor of Little Gidding, in Huntingdonshire. The once smiling fields had been long ago converted into pasture land, and the cottages of the tillers of the soil had disap-

1625.
Purchase of Little Gidding.

peared. A single shepherd's hut contained all the inhabitants of the estate. The manor house was in ruins. The church was used as a hay-barn and a pigsty. Here mother and son met after a long separation. The young man invited his aged parent to take the rest which she needed in the house, ruined as it was. She refused to follow him. First, she said, she must give thanks in the house of God for his preservation from the plague during his stay in London. The church was full of hay. She pushed her way in as far as she could, knelt down and prayed with many tears. She would take no rest till all the available labourers had been summoned to clear the building.

As soon as the church was cleared, the old lady invited all her children and grandchildren to share her home. Nicholas was ordained deacon by Laud. Preferment in the Church was at once placed at his disposal; but he had made up his mind to live and die at Little Gidding. Nothing would induce him even to take priest's orders. All he wanted was to be the chaplain to the community, some forty persons in all, who had devoted themselves to a special life in the service of God. There were prayers in the church twice a day, and four times in the house. Two of the inhabitants watched all night to read the Psalms through from beginning to end. Ferrar drew up a Harmony of the Scriptures, and this, together with narratives of history and adventure, more especially his old favourite, Foxe's Martyrs, was read from time to time. Besides those who lived in the house, he had his Psalm-children, as he called them, who came in from the neighbouring parishes to receive, in addition to a breakfast, a penny or every Psalm that they could repeat by heart. He had schoolmasters for his nephews and nieces, and the children who lived near were welcome to share in the instruction given. Everyone there was obliged to learn some useful work, and the art of bookbinding was carried to great perfection. Once a month, on Communion Sunday, the servants of the establishment sat down at table with the other members of the community. Two of Ferrar's nieces devoted themselves to perpetual virginity, and all were obliged to remain celibate as long as they continued at Little Gidding. But there was no compulsory injunction on the subject, and not a few who passed many years with the Ferrars, left them without reproach to enter into marriage.

Such an institution naturally gave rise to strange reports. Ferrar, it was said, was a Roman Catholic in disguise. He repelled the charge with energy. One day he was asked what he would do if mass were to be celebrated in his house. "I would build down the room, and build it up again," was his reply. To another who told him that his proceedings 'might savour of superstition and popery,' he answered, quietly, "I as verily believe the Pope to be antichrist as any article of my faith."

Visitors brought nothing but good reports away. Williams, in whose diocese Little Gidding was, expressed his warm approbation, more especially perhaps as the Communion-table was placed east and west, and not along the wall.

In Ferrar the devotional spirit of the age reached the extreme limits possible within the bounds of Protestantism. Life at Little Gidding was preserved from all moral questionings by submission to external rule and order. Those who were always praying or working, had not much time left for thought. Each day passed away as like the last as possible. Ferrar sought but a harbour from the changes of life. There was no striving after an ideal perfection, no fierce asceticism or self-torture in him. His life was the application to himself of that dislike of mental and moral unrest which was at the bottom of Laud's disciplinarian efforts. That which existed acquired a sacredness in his eyes merely because it existed. He was once asked why he did not place a crucifix in his church. "If there had been any when we came," he answered, "I would not have pulled it down except authority had commanded; so neither will I set up anything without command of authority." He at least would be free as long as possible from the responsibility of decision.[1]

It was not by such negative virtues that the old monasticism had gained a hold on the mediæval world. Men came to look at Ferrar's community, wondered, admired, and turned away to their own activities. George Herbert had much in common with Ferrar. But he never could have arrived at this perfect quiescence of spirit. A younger brother of that Edward Herbert who had been created by Charles Lord Herbert of Cherbury, he was fired, at an early age, with an ambition to rise in the service of the State. At Westminster and Cambridge he was noted for industry and intelligence, wrote lines, like so many others, to the memory of Prince Henry, and flashed before the University as the author of a series of Latin poems in defence of the ceremonies of the Church against Andrew Melville. If the reader misses in these sarcastic poems any manifestation of high spiritual devotion, they need not, on that account, be set down as a mere offering upon the altar of courtiership. Herbert was a ceremonialist by nature. The outward sign was to him more than to most men the expression of the inward fact. His religion fed itself upon that which he could handle and see, and that quaintness which

[1] *Two Lives of Nicholas Ferrar.* Edited by J. E. B. Mayor.

strict criticism reprehends in his poetry, was the effect of his irresistible tendency to detect a hidden meaning in the most unexpected objects of sense.

In these Cambridge days Herbert's mind was distracted between two different aims, which yet appeared to him to be but one. Marked out by his character for a peaceful devotional life, and absolutely unfitted for the turmoil of political controversy, his youthful spirits were too buoyant to allow him to acknowledge at once his inability to play a stirring part in the world. One day he was writing religious poetry. Another day he was canvassing for preferment, and he contrived to persuade himself that preferment would enable him to help on the cause of religion still better than writing poetry. In 1619 he succeeded Nethersole as Public Orator of the University. The position delighted him as giving him precedence next to the doctors, 'and such like gaynesses, which will please a young man well.' On the other hand, he reminded himself that progress in the study of divinity was still to be his main object. "This dignity," he wrote, "hath no such earthiness in it but it may very well be joined with heaven; or if it had to others, yet to me it should not, for aught I yet know."

Herbert's efforts after worldly distinction ended in failure. He had good friends at Court. Hamilton, Lennox, and James himself, loved him well. But he was too honest to sink to the lower arts of a courtier's life, and he had not the practical abilities of a statesman. The oration with which he welcomed Charles on his return from Spain was an evidence of the sincerity with which he could not help accompanying flatteries neither more nor less absurd than those which flowed unmitigated from the pens of so many of his contemporaries. It was no secret that the Prince had come back bent upon war. Herbert disliked war, and he could not refrain from the maladroit compliment of commending Charles for going to Madrid in search of peace. All that he could bring himself to say was that, as war was sometimes necessary, he would be content to believe any war to be necessary to which James should give his consent. If Herbert bowed down, it was not to the Prince whom it was his interest to captivate, but to the peaceful King who had maintained the ceremonies of the Church against their assailants.

A change came over Herbert's life. His three patrons, Hamilton, Lennox, and James, died. From Charles, rushing headlong into war, the lover of peace had no favour to expect. His health, always feeble, broke down. In this time of depression he formed a resolution to take orders, to become, as he said, one of 'the domestic servants of the King of heaven.' The clerical office was not in those days held in very high esteem. A friend dissuaded him from entering upon 'too mean an employment, and too much below his birth and the excellent abilities and endowments of his mind.' "Though the iniquity of the late times," he answered, " have made clergymen meanly valued, and the sacred name of priest contemptible, yet I will labour to make it honourable by consecrating all my learning and all my poor abilities to advance the glory of that God that gave them, and I will labour to be like my Saviour by making humility lovely in the eyes of all men, and by following the merciful and meek example of my dear Jesus."

Nevertheless, Herbert hesitated long. He was still a layman when Williams presented him to the prebend of Leighton Ecclesia in the diocese of Lincoln. The church was in ruins, and Herbert signalised his connection with it by collecting money from his wealthy friends for its repair. As in Cosin's church at Brancepeth and Ferrar's at Little Gidding, the reading-desk and the pulpit were placed side by side, and both were made of the same height, in order that it might appear that 'they should neither have a precedency or priority of the other; but that prayer and preaching, being equally useful, might agree like brethren and have an equal honour and estimation.'

Four years after his acceptance of preferment in the Church, Herbert was still a layman. In 1630, at the request of the head of his family, the new Earl of Pembroke, he was presented by the King to the Rectory of Fugglestone and Bemerton, two hamlets lying between Salisbury and Wilton. Stories were afterwards told of his reluctance to undertake a duty which he held to be too high for his powers, and it is said that he only gave an unwilling consent on Laud's representation 'that the refusal of it was a sin.' It was doubtless at this time that he received ordination, either from Laud, or from Davenant his diocesan.[1]

The charm of Herbert's life at Bemerton lies in the harmony which had arisen between the discordant elements of his Cambridge life. The love of action, which was wanting in Ferrar, is still there. "A pastor," he declares "is the deputy of Christ for reducing of man to the obedience of God." But it has blended with a quiet meditative devotion, and out of this soil spring the tenderest blossoms of poetic feeling. His own life was a daily sacrifice, but it was a sacrifice, made not

---

[1] Walton's well-known story that the Court was at Wilton, and that the tailor was sent for from Salisbury to provide a clerical dress, is certainly untrue. The Court was at Whitehall, and the presentation, printed from the Patent Rolls in Rymer (xix. 258) is dated from Westminster. It also describes Herbert simply as a master of arts. The omission of the usual *Clericus* shows that he was still a layman at this time.

by the avoidance, but by the pursuance of work. For him the sacraments and observances of the Church had a fellowship with the myriad-sided sacrament of nature. As the bee hummed and the tree sent forth its branches, they conveyed to his pure and observant mind the inward and spiritual grace which was to him a comfort and a strength. The things of nature formed a standing protest against idleness. "Every gift of ability," he said, "is a talent to be accounted for." There was to be no mere crucifying of the flesh for its own sake, no turning of the back upon the world as evil. His sermons were filled with homely illustrations, and he took good care to explain to his parishioners the meaning of the prayers which they used. His own life was the best sermon. His predecessor had lived sixteen or twenty miles off, and had left the church in need of repair, whilst the parsonage-house was in ruins. The congregation was that of an ordinary country parish, long untaught and untended, and accustomed to regard their rector as a mere grasper of tithe corn. The change produced by Herbert's presence was magical. Wherever he turned he gathered love and reverence round him, and when his bell tolled for prayers the hardworked labourer, weary with the toils of the day, would let his plough rest for a moment, and breathe a prayer to heaven before returning to his labour.

Pathos of his poetry. The dominant note of Herbert's poetry is the eagerness for action, mingled with a sense of its insufficiency. The disease which wasted his body filled him with the consciousness of weakness, and he welcomed death as the awakening to a higher life. Sometimes the sadness overpowers the joy, as in those pathetic lines :—

> "Life is a business, not good cheer,
> Ever in wars.
> The sun still shineth there or here ;
> Whereas the stars
> Watch an advantage to appear.

> Oh that I were an orange tree,
>   That busy plant!
> Then should I ever laden be,
>   And never want
> Some fruit for him that dressed me.
>
> But we are still too young or old;
>   The man is gone
> Before we do our wares unfold;
>   So we freeze on,
> Until the grave increase our cold."

To Herbert the life of the orange tree was the best; the life of strenuous restfulness which brings forth fruit without effort. He lived less than three years at Bemerton. When he died he left behind him a name which will never perish in England. *Herbert's death.*

Herbert and Ferrar were instinct with the feminine tendencies of spiritual thought. The masculine energy of life is to be sought elsewhere. The self-reliant strength is with the Puritan. The voices of Sibbes and Gouge are raised in great cities. Wherever men are thickest, their prevailing eloquence is heard. Herbert and Ferrar allow the waves of change to pass over them, glad if they can find a refuge at last where they may, if but for a little time, be hidden from the storm. From them comes no note of the abounding joyfulness, the calm assurance of success, which breathes alike in the sermons of the Puritan divine, and in the firm conviction of the dying Eliot. *Tendencies of thought.*

Even where there was much similarity in thought and expression, the two influences which were passing over England are immutably distinguished by the passive or active part assigned to the individual human soul. Herbert dearly loved music. Twice a week he would shake off his daily cares by a walk along the banks of the river to Salisbury, to drink in delight by listening to the Cathedral choir. It was for him a *Herbert and Milton on music.*

medicine against the monotony of life and the pains of irresistible disease, healing by the charm of self-forgetfulness.

> "Sweetest of sweets, I thank you; when displeasure
> Did through my body wound my mind,
> You took me thence, and in your house of pleasure
> A dainty lodging me assigned."

From this height of rapt abstraction, those upon whom the burden of the world rested were but objects of distant pity.

> "Now I in you without a body move,
> Rising and falling with your wings,
> We both together sweetly live and love,
> Yet say sometimes, 'God help poor kings!'"

Another singer, quickening in the first flush of youth to the consciousness of poetic power, loved music as dearly as Herbert. John Milton, the son of the London scrivener, had the open ear for—

> "That undisturbed song of pure concent
> Ay sung before the sapphire-coloured throne."

The earthly music lifted Herbert to heaven; the heavenly music sent Milton forth to perform his duties upon earth. The lesson of Puritanism stands as clearly written here as on the last page of *Paradise Regained*:—

> "That we on earth with undiscording voice
> May rightly answer that melodious noise;
> As once we did till disproportioned sin
> Jarred against Nature's chime, and with harsh din
> Broke the fair music that all creatures made
> To their great Lord, whose love their motion swayed
> In perfect diapason, whilst they stood
> In first obedience, and their state of good.
> O may we soon again renew that song,
> And keep in time with Heaven, till God ere long
> To his celestial comfort us unite,
> To live with him and sing in endless morn of light."

To Milton, God was ever 'the great Taskmaster'

who had set him to cultivate the field of his own mind that he might afterwards hold out help to others. Early in life he had perceived that 'he who would not be frustrate of his hope to write well hereafter in laudable things, ought himself to be a true poem—that is a composition and pattern of the best and honourablest things; not presuming to sing high praises of heroic men or famous cities, unless he have in himself the experience and practice of all that which is praiseworthy.' Thus he grew up in his father's house in Bread Street, and amongst the thoughtless, scoffing, Academic youth of Cambridge, breathing the highest life of Puritanism, its serious thoughtfulness, its love of all things good and honourable, its pure morality and aversion to low and degrading vice, yet with nothing exclusive or narrow-minded in him. If he drank deeply of the Bible, he drank deeply of the writers of Greece and Rome as well, and the influence of the philosophers and poets of Greece and Rome was as marked upon his style as that of the Prophets and Psalmists of Jerusalem. Even in the great religious controversy of the day, the voice of the future assailant of Episcopacy and ceremonies gives as yet no certain sound. The tone is Puritan, but there is nothing there of the fierce dogmatism of Prynne. At the age of seventeen he not only joined in the praises of Andrewes, the prelate whom Laud most reverenced, but described him as entering heaven dressed in the vestments of the Church.[1] A few years later, in *Il Penseroso*, he shewed a power of entering into the thoughts of men with whom he was soon to come into deadly conflict, in the well-remembered lines:—

"But let my due feet never fail
To walk the studious cloisters pale,

---

[1] "Vestis ad auratos defluxit candida talos,
    Infula divinum cinxerat alba caput."

    And love the high embowed roof
    With antic pillars massy proof,
    And storied windows richly dight,
    Casting a dim religious light.
    There let the pealing organ blow
    To the full-voiced choir below
    In service high, and anthems clear,
    As may with sweetness through mine ear
    Dissolve me into ecstasies
    And bring all heaven before mine eyes."

The intellectual opposition not yet complete.

To the historian these early poems of Milton have the deepest interest. They tell of a time when the great intellectual disruption of the age was still capable of being averted. Between Herbert and Milton there is a difference in the point of view which may lead to absolute opposition, but which has not led to it yet. It is the same with men so unlike as Ferrar and Gouge. When Ferrar was asked whether 'he thought the chapel more holy than his house,' he replied, 'that God was more immediately present when we were worshipping Him in the temple.'[1] "Though the Lord," wrote Gouge, " in His infinite essence be everywhere present, yet the special presence of His grace and favour abideth in those places where He is truly and duly worshipped."[2] The one lays stress upon the place where the worshippers meet, the other upon the temper of those who meet in it. But there is no breach of continuity, no violent opposition making a conflict necessary.

1633. Civil war apparently far off.

Never, in spite of all that had occurred, had civil war appeared farther off than in the spring of 1633. Never did there seem to be a fairer prospect of overcoming the irritation that had prevailed four years before. If only the rulers of England could comprehend the virtue of moderation, and could learn the strength which is to be gained by conciliation, all might yet be

---

[1] Mayor's *Two Lives of Ferrar*, xxxiv.
[2] Gouge, *The Saint's Sacrifice* (1632), 259.

well. Unhappily, Charles was still at the helm, and Charles had promised the Archbishopric of Canterbury to the most conscientious, the most energetic, and the most indiscreet man in his dominions. Abbot's death would be the signal for violent changes, followed by a still more violent reaction. Abbot had yet a few months of life before him. During those months, Charles, with Laud in his company, paid a visit to his northern kingdom.

CHAPTER VII.

THE KING'S VISIT TO SCOTLAND.

CHAP. VII.
1612.
James's victory over the Presbyterian clergy.

THE act of Parliament which in 1612 confirmed the establishment of episcopacy in Scotland, closed one chapter of Scottish ecclesiastical history. It gave the King a legal mode of keeping the clergy in subjection. In accomplishing his object, he had had the effective strength of the nation on his side. The powerful aristocracy, the lawyers, and part at least of the growing middle classes, had been alienated by the harsh and intolerant spirit of the clerical assemblies which were now silenced. It remained to be seen whether James would be content with providing for some elasticity of speech and thought, without attempting to mould the belief and the worship of his subjects according to his own ideal.

His use of the victory.

James, it is true, was far more prudent than his son was afterwards to be. He disliked extremes, and he shrunk from the exertion needed to overcome serious opposition. But he was fond of theological speculation, and he had the highest confidence in his own conclusions. At the same time his residence in England threw the burden of maintaining the ground which he had taken up on others rather than on himself, and thus rendered him less sensitive to the action of opinion in Scotland.

In the spring of 1614 James issued an order that all persons should partake of the Communion on April 24; the day which to the south of the Tweed was known as Easter Day. In 1615, a second order appeared directing the administration of the Communion 'on one day yearly, to wit, Pasch day.'[1]

1614. The Communion to be received at Easter. 1615.

Further changes were in contemplation. An Assembly was gathered at Aberdeen, and Aberdeen was the centre of a reaction which was growing up against Presbyterianism, even amongst the Scottish clergy. The few southern ministers who made their way to so distant a place of meeting found themselves in a scanty minority. The Bishops and their supporters mustered strongly, and many of the temporal Lords had come in to give them their countenance. Most of those who had come to protest returned in despair to their homes in Fife or the Lothians. As soon as they were gone, the real business of the meeting commenced. The Assembly authorised the preparation of a new Confession of faith, and of a Liturgy which was intended to supersede Knox's Book of Common Order. Children were to be examined by the Bishop or his deputy before they were admitted to the Communion, an administration of which was always to take place on Easter Day.[2]

1616. The Assembly at Aberdeen.

Such a decision ran counter to the feelings of that energetic part of the clergy which had been thrust aside from the management of affairs. But if the composition of the new Liturgy had been left in the hands of the Bishops, it is not likely that it would have caused any widespread dissatisfaction. They had not

Character of the Bishops.

---

[1] *Calderwood*, vii. 191, 196. Act of Scottish Privy Council, March 3, 1614. Botfield's *Original Letters*, i. 448.

[2] *Calderwood*, vii. 222. Compare a paper by Spottiswoode in Botfield's *Original Letters*, iii. 445.

floated to the surface on the tide of ecclesiastical reaction. Their opinions, so far as they had pronounced opinions at all, were very much like those of the clergy around them, only held with an increased sense of the value of quiet and of the duty of submitting to the Royal authority. But James was too impatient to await the slow process of discussion and preparation. In reply to the letter in which the Bishops communicated to him the resolutions of the Assembly, he sent down five Articles of his own which he required them to adopt. These Articles directed that the Communion should always be received in a kneeling posture; that in case of sickness or necessity the Lord's Supper should be administered in private houses; that Baptism should under similar circumstances be administered in the same way; that days of observance should be appointed for the commemoration of the Birth, Passion, and Resurrection of the Saviour, and of the Descent of the Holy Ghost; and that children should be brought to the Bishop for a blessing.

It was not much to ask according to the notions which surrounded James in England. But it would be a severe shock to the religion of Scotland. There is not the slightest reason to suppose that the first Article, which was certain to be more violently opposed than the other four, had the support of any party whatever in the Scottish Church. In England the custom, though sometimes neglected, was in possession of the field. It was in accordance with the law of the Church, the observance of which had never been interrupted. In Scotland it was a pure innovation.

To the Archbishop of St. Andrews, on whom would fall the brunt of the conflict, the news of the King's resolution was most unwelcome. Archbishop Spottiswoode knew his countrymen well enough to be aware that he would have no peace if the Articles were to be enforced, and he would have been glad to avoid a conflict in which his own sympathies were not enlisted. He did not, however, think it wise to oppose the King's peremptory command. But he begged James not to issue the Articles by the Royal authority alone. It would be safer, he argued, to procure for them the sanction of an Assembly—an Assembly doubtless after the fashion of that of Aberdeen ; and he offered, if the question were postponed for another year, to do his best to procure the assent of such a body.[1]

It may be that the Archbishop was not entirely disinterested in wishing so unpopular a change to be discussed in the following year. For James had given out that in that year he intended to visit the country of his birth, and Spottiswoode's work would doubtless be easier if the King were at his side.

James, however, was not desirous of engaging once more in a personal dispute with the clergy. He wrote to the Scottish Council that, though he should have been glad to see the proposed reforms carried out during his visit, he would not at such a time bring forward anything which was unlikely to meet with universal acceptance.[2]

It was not from any wish to consider the feelings or prejudices of his subjects that James threw over the realisation of his hopes to another year. He had resolved at least to shew them what English worship was. In October the citizens of Edinburgh were scandalised by the strange apparition of an organ which

---

[1] *Spottiswoode*, iii. 236.
[2] The King to the Scottish Privy Council, Dec. 15, 1616. Printed with a wrong date in the Abbotsford Club edition of *Letters and State Papers of the reign of James VI.*, 202.

CHAP. VII.
1617.

The carvings for the chapel.

had just been landed at Leith for the King's chapel at Holyrood. Two or three months later it was followed by some English carpenters, who brought with them figures of the patriarchs and apostles, carved in wood for the same chapel. All Edinburgh was immediately in an uproar. Popish images, it was confidently said, were to be set up at Holyrood, and the Popish mass would follow soon. So alarming were the symptoms of the public discontent, that the Bishops begged the King to withdraw his order for the erection of the obnoxious carvings. James yielded, but as usual, he yielded with no good grace. He told the Bishops that he had not been in the slightest degree influenced by their arguments. But he had heard from his master of the works that it would be difficult to complete the proposed arrangements in time. "Do not, therefore," he proceeded to say, "deceive yourselves with a vain imagination of anything done therein for ease of your hearts, or ratifying your error in your judgment of that graven work, which is not of an idolatrous kind, like to images and painted pictures adored and worshipped by Papists, but merely intended for ornament and decoration of the place where we should sit, and might have been wrought as well with figures of lions, dragons, and devils, as with those of patriarchs and apostles. But as we must wonder at your ignorance and teach you thus to distinguish between the one and the other, so are we persuaded that none of you would have been scandalised or offended, if the said figures of lions, dragons, or devils had been carved and put up in lieu of those of the patriarchs and apostles, resembling in this the Constable of Castile, who being sent here to swear the peace between us and Spain, when he understood that this behoved to be solemnly performed in our chapel, he foresaw likewise that then some anthems would be sung, and therefore protested before his entry of our chapel that whatever were sung, God's name might not be used in it."[1] It was all very shrewd. But if the Bishops needed to be reasoned with in this fashion, what hope was there of carrying conviction to the heart of the mass of Scotchmen?

On May 13 James crossed the border. On the 16th he entered Edinburgh, and for the first time since his mother's dethronement the voice of choristers and the pealing notes of the organ were heard in the chapel of Holyrood.[2] But James was not satisfied with the display of the forms of Church worship which he had learned to admire in England. He gave peremptory orders that all the noblemen, the Privy Councillors, and the Bishops who were in Edinburgh should receive the Communion on their knees in the chapel on Whitsunday. Of those who were thus summoned, many complied at once. But there were some who absented themselves from the service, and of those who appeared, some abstained from presenting themselves at the table. A second mandate was then issued, commanding the recusants to appear on the following Sunday, and, in some cases at least, the King's persistency was not without its effect.[3]

James's resolution was the more ill judged as he had before him in Scotland a task which would require all the popular support which he could contrive to rally round him. The conflict which the Crown had waged with the clergy had ended as he had wished it to end mainly because he had entered upon it with the

---

[1] The King to the Bishops, March 13. Botfield's *Original Letters*, ii. 496.
[2] *Calderwood*, vii. 246.
[3] *Calderwood*, vii. 247, 249.

nobility on his side. But for all that, a conflict with the nobility was looming in the future. Though the Scottish nobles were no longer the fierce rebels and murderers which they had been in the days of James's infancy, they exercised powers which were ill-befitting to subjects in a well-ordered state, and they knew how to hold with a strong hand lands and goods which they had acquired by fraud or rapine. Old feudal rights long ago swept away in England were still exercised in Scotland. On their own lands the nobles handed down from father to son their heritable jurisdictions, the right of judging criminals. Men were put to death, not by the sentence of a Royal Judge, but by the sentence of the Lord's Court. James, in his desire to put an end to a system such as this, was acting for the true interests of the Scottish nation.

His mode of setting to work was eminently characteristic. In his speech at the opening of Parliament he told his countrymen that they were a barbarous people. He only hoped that they would be as ready to adopt the good customs of their Southern neighbours as they had been eager to become their pupils in the arts of smoking tobacco, and of wearing gay clothes.[1] If he meant by this that the nobles were to strip themselves of their jurisdictions, he might as well have lectured a gang of smugglers on the propriety of respecting the interests of the revenue. All that was yielded to him was the appointment of a commission empowered to compound with any nobleman who might be inclined to voluntarily surrender his authority to the Crown. It is needless to say that the office of the commissioners was all but a complete sinecure.[2] It was not till the next reign that the Earl of Huntly

---

[1] —— to Bacon, June 28. *Bacon's Works*, ed. Montagu, xii. 320. *Spottiswoode*, iii. 240.

[2] *Acts of the Parl. of Scotland.* iv. 549.

sold his jurisdictions in Aberdeen and Inverness. No other Scottish lord followed his example.

In carrying another point James was more successful. The Scottish clergy were miserably poor. Lands, possessions, and tithes, by which the earlier Church had been supported, were held by the iron grip of the dominant nobility. A miserable stipend, irregularly paid, was all that was assigned to those whose work it was to uphold the standard of religion and morality in an age of chicanery and bloodshed. James now asked for some small increase of this stipend, and for its assignment upon local sources, instead of its being relegated, as had hitherto been the case, to the uncertainty of a general fund. With some difficulty he carried his point, and from the visit of James to Edinburgh dates the possession by the Scottish ministers of a modest competence.[1] But though the King had his way, there were symptoms, for the first time for many years, of resistance amongst the nobility.

Even with the support of the clergy and the middle class it would not be an easy task to reduce the nobles to surrender their special privileges on behalf of the general interests of the State. James, however, had not relinquished those proposals which were likely to offend the clergy and the middle classes most deeply. An act was brought forward in Parliament decreeing that 'whatever His Majesty should determine in the external government of the Church, with the advice of the Archbishops, Bishops, and a competent number of the ministry, should have the force of law.' The more independent of the clergy at once took fright.

---

[1] The minimum was to be 27*l*. 15*s*. 6½*d*., the maximum 44*l*. 9*s*. 0*d*. This in England would imply in modern value an income varying between about 110*l*. to 180*l*. at least. But I suppose that on the scale of living in Scotland it would imply much more than such an income would imply in England now. See Connell, *A treatise on the law of Scotland respecting Tithes*, i. 180.

As many as could be got together at a moment's notice protested warmly against the measure, and James shrunk from encountering the opposition which he had raised.

The act was withdrawn. But the manner in which James withdrew it was justly regarded as an aggravation of the offence. The right, he said, of making changes in the external government of the Church was already inherent in the Crown. It was therefore unnecessary to pass a new act to give him what he possessed already. In these words he asserted in the baldest way his claim to regulate forms of worship as he chose, whilst renouncing his right to decide upon doctrine. As if it were possible to separate between the external observance which is the expression of the doctrinal opinion, and the belief which recommends the use of any given form to those who have attached themselves to it.

James vented his anger upon the protesters. Two of them were imprisoned. A third, David Calderwood, persisted in maintaining that he had been in the right, and was banished.[1] He took refuge in Holland, where he employed his pen in vindicating the cause to which he had sacrificed his worldly prospects. The history in which he embalmed the sufferings and the constancy of the Church of Scotland has become to those who revere the memory of Melville and Henderson all that Foxe's *Book of Martyrs* was to the Elizabethan Protestant, and all that Clarendon's *History of the Rebellion* became to the Tory of the reign of Anne.

That a rigorous Presbyterian like Calderwood should have fallen into disgrace was only to be expected. But it is significant of the state of opinion in Scotland that one of the two imprisoned protesters was

[1] *Calderwood*, vii. 257.

Thomas Hewat, to whom had been committed by the Assembly of Aberdeen, the most episcopal of Scottish assemblies, the task of compiling a Liturgy for the Church. The Liturgy which he prepared is drawn upon the lines of Knox's Book of Common Order, and differs from it chiefly in its greater fulness, and in the introduction of a considerable number of prayers for special occasions.[1] There is nothing in it to give offence to the most zealous Presbyterian. If James was to make any change of importance in the service of the Church it would be his own doing. No Scottish ecclesiastical party was likely of its own accord to go so far as he wished to go.

James, however, persisted in his intention. On July 13 he convened at St. Andrews a special meeting, at which the Bishops and a select number of ministers were present. He told them that he merely wished to introduce a more decent order into the Church. If they had anything to say against his five Articles, he was ready to listen. But they must remember that his demands were just and religious, and that he was not to be resisted with impunity. In conclusion, he reminded them that it was the special prerogative of Christian kings to order the external polity of the Church, after taking the advice of the Bishops. They might approve of his proceedings, or they might disapprove of them. But they must not imagine that anything they might choose to say would have the slightest influence with him unless they could support their opinions by arguments which he found himself unable to answer.[2]

It is not surprising that no one present thought it possible to find an argument which James would acknowledge himself to be unable to answer. Postpone-

---

[1] Hewat's Liturgy is printed in Sprott's *Scottish Liturgies of the reign of James VI.*

[2] *Spottiswoode*, iii. 246.

ment of the difficulty was all that could be hoped, and it was finally arranged that an Assembly should meet at St. Andrews in November to discuss the Articles. James returned to England, trusting that there would be no further difficulty on the subject.

Of the five Articles, three would probably have been accepted without difficulty, though the Assembly might perhaps have wished to fence round with some precautions against abuse the permission to administer Baptism and the Lord's Supper in private houses, and the introduction of the rite of Confirmation. The article which related to Church festivals was more unpopular. Not only was there a disinclination to adopt customs which could not plead the direct authority of the Scriptures, but there was a vague impression that the observance of these days was in some way or another Popish, and a belief that these holidays would serve to many as an excuse for riot and debauchery. But it was to the Article which prescribed kneeling at the reception of the Communion that the most decided opposition was to be expected. It was absurd to speak of the question raised by it as a mere matter of external discipline. Such actions as this are intimately connected with the innermost beliefs and feelings of the heart, and it is impossible to interfere with them without intruding upon the sanctuary of the conscience. To one man, to kneel at the reception of the Communion is a simple act of self-humiliation in the presence of Him in whose worship he is engaged. To another the same action would carry with it an acknowledgment of the doctrine of transubstantiation, or at least of the Real Presence in the consecrated elements. No doubt rules of some kind are necessary in every place where men meet together, and when members of the same congregation differ on matters of importance,

Marginalia: CHAP. VII. 1617. — Two only of the articles unpopular. — Special objection to kneeling at the Communion.

there will be considerable difficulty in keeping them on good terms with one another. But it was not even pretended that any single Scotchman had asked for the change, though Scotch Presbyterians were in those days in the habit of kneeling at the ordinary prayers. No doubt, when James had once declared his resolution, he would meet with plenty of support. But it would be support of that kind which is valueless in the end. He would have the assistance of those amongst the clergy who thought it dangerous to quarrel with him, and of those amongst the laity who bore a grudge against the clergy, and who would have come to his help with equal readiness if he had proclaimed that standing upright or reclining on a couch was the fitting posture for the reception of the Communion.

Nov. The Assembly at St. Andrews.
The Assembly at St. Andrews gave no satisfaction to James. It agreed to the administration of the Communion to the sick, but it postponed consideration of the other Articles to a more convenient season.

1618. Jan. Patrick Forbes, Bishop of Aberdeen.
To all who had ears to hear the opposition of the Assembly conveyed a serious warning. Of all men living in Scotland there was probably none whose advice was better worth taking on ecclesiastical matters than Patrick Forbes of Corse. Sprung from an ancient Scottish family, and himself a landed proprietor in Aberdeenshire, he had attached himself in youth to the high Presbyterian party of Andrew Melville. Circumstances changed in Scotland, and the decline of the combative spirit which made James's alterations possible was not without its effect upon him. Secluded in his Aberdeenshire home from the main current of ecclesiastical pretensions, he grew more earnest in his zeal for the spread of morality and piety, less careful to keep up distinctions of outward ceremonies. The country around him was in a sad state of spiritual

destitution. The great land owners, the Earls of Huntly and Errol, had remained faithful to the Church of Rome, and whilst priests and Jesuits were favoured by the landed aristocracy, the more vehement Presbyterian ministers had been hurried off to prison and banishment by the King. Though Patrick Forbes's own brother, John Forbes of Alford, had been banished for his part in resisting the introduction of Episcopacy,[1] he himself took no share in these conflicts. At the request of the neighbouring clergy he consented to occupy the pulpit, layman as he was, in an empty church near his home, and though he was silenced by the King's directions, he does not appear to have taken offence at the interruption. In 1612, in the forty-seventh year of his age, he received ordination, and when the See of Aberdeen was vacant in January 1618, he was appointed Bishop at the unanimous request of the clergy.

His letter to Spottiswoode.

The letter in which Forbes explained to Archbishop Spottiswoode the reasons of his reluctance to accept the office is most valuable as an expression of the opinion of one so high-minded and so honest. His hesitation, he said, did not proceed from any 'disallowing the office and degree of a Bishop.' Episcopacy, if Bishops were 'rightly elected and defined with such moderation of place and power, as' might 'put restraint to excessive usurpations, was not only a tolerable, but even a laudable and expedient policy in the Church, and very well consisting with God's written word.' Nor was he influenced by any fear of giving offence to others. He even thought it would be right for an honourable man who did not entirely approve of Episcopal government, to accept the office of a Bishop when it had once been determined that the chief

[1] *Hist. of Engl. from the accession of James I.* i, 530-537.

authority in the Church should be entrusted to Bishops, rather than to run the chance of seeing their places filled 'with the offscouring of the world, and the dregs of men.'

Forbes's real difficulty lay elsewhere. "This is that, my good Lord," he writes, "which maketh all my scruple, the present condition and course of things—and we cannot tell how far a farther novation in our Church is intended—so peremptorily and impetuously urged on the one part, and so hardly received on the other; as betwixt these extremities, and the undertaking of a Bishopric, I see no option left to me, but either to incur his Majesty's displeasure, which is the rock under Christ I am loathest to strike on ; or then to drive both myself and my ministry in such common distaste, as I see not how henceforth it can be any more fruitful. I dispute not here of the points themselves; but I am persuaded if so wise, so learned, and so religious a King as God hath blessed us with, were fully and freely informed, or did thoroughly conceive the sad sequel of inforcing our Church, that neither in the points already proposed, nor in any which we fear yet to ensue for this intended conformity, would his Majesty esteem any of such fruit or effect as therefore the state of a quiet Kirk should be marred, the minds of brethren who for any bygone distraction were beginning again to warm in mutual love should be of anew again and almost desperately distracted, the hearts of many good Christians discouraged, the resolution of many weak ones brangled,[1] matter of insulting ministered to Romanists, and to profane epicureans of a disdainful deriding of our whole profession. . . . If wherein our Kirk seemeth defective, his Majesty would so far pity our weakness, and tender our

[1] *i.e.* 'shaken.'

peace, as to enforce nothing but which first in a fair and national Council were determined, wherein his Highness would neither make any man afraid by terror, nor pervert the judgment of any with hope of favour, then men may adventure to do service. But if things be so violently carried as no end may appear of bitter contention, neither any place left to men placed in rooms, but, instead of procuring peace, and reuniting the hearts of the brethren, to stir the coals of detestable debate—for me, I have no courage to be a partner in that work. I wish my heart-blood might extinguish the ungracious rising flame in our Kirk. But if I can do nothing for the quenching of it, then I would be heartily sorry to add fuel thereto.'[1]

Forbes's objections were not insuperable. He became Bishop of Aberdeen. He was one of those Bishops who justify episcopacy in the eyes of men. There was no man in the diocese who was not the better for his acceptance of the office. He was a true overseer of the Church. Parishes were filled under his direction with pious and earnest ministers. Learning was encouraged at the Universities of Aberdeen. The Bishop's justice and gentleness gave him the highest place in the estimation of his fellow citizens, and he was frequently employed as an arbitrator in disputes which a generation before would have led to deadly feuds, to be extinguished only in blood. If, when the day of trouble came, there was a Royalist party in Scotland at all, it was mainly owing to the impression produced by the life and labours of Patrick Forbes.

If his advice had been taken by James and by his son, there would have been no civil war in Scotland. But James was resolved to force on the Articles, and in

---

[1] P. Forbes to Spottiswoode, Feb. 13 [?]. *Calderwood*, vii. 291. For date, see *Funerals of P. Forbes* (Spot. Soc.) lx.

Spottiswoode he found an instrument fitted for the work. For Spottiswoode, who, like Forbes, was a lover of peace, and an opponent of the absolute assertions of the Presbyterians in matters which he believed to be indifferent, was ready for the sake of peace to stoop to work with which Forbes would never have defiled his fingers. James, when he heard of the resolution taken by the Assembly which had met at St. Andrews, told its members that they should now know what it was to draw upon themselves the anger of a King, and to give point to his denunciation, threatened those who refused to accept the Articles[1] with the loss of their stipends. Spottiswoode prevented the immediate execution of the threat, but he made use of the King's letter to overawe the reluctant ministers into submission.[2]

CHAP. VII.
1617. Dec.
James threatens the ministers.

Such were the disgraceful means by which the new religious observances were to be forced upon the Church. Many a man who conscientiously believed the Articles to be Popish and antichristian drew back from an opposition which threatened to reduce to beggary himself and those who were dearer to him than himself. When the Bishops met in Edinburgh in May they were able to inform the King that he might summon an Assembly with every prospect of success.[3] The observance of the festivals had already been enjoined by Act of Council.[4] But for the other Articles it was thought advisable to obtain at least the semblance of ecclesiastical authority. Attempts had been made by the Bishops

1618. Preparations for an Assembly at Perth.

May.

---

[1] The King to the Archbishops, Dec. 6. Botfield's *Original Letters,* ii. 522.

[2] " Which letters being shewed to the ministers of Edinburgh and others that happened to repair to that city for augmentation of stipends, did cast them into great fear; and, repenting their wilfulness, as they had reason, became requesters to the Archbishop of St. Andrews to preach, as he was commanded, upon Christmas Day." *Spottiswoode,* iii. 250.

[3] Lindsay, *The Proceedings of the Assembly at Perth,* 19.

[4] Botfield's *Original Letters,* ii. 540.

to enforce kneeling at the Communion. But these attempts had met with but indifferent success. It was accordingly resolved that on August 25 an Assembly should meet at Perth.

The King was to be represented at Perth by three Commissioners, of whom Lord Binning was the most prominent. As Sir Thomas Hamilton he had been noted for the violence with which he had upheld the Royal authority against all clerical claims to independence. He was now Secretary of State, and his presence at Perth would bring with it the certainty that no unnecessary scruples would be allowed to stand in the way of the King's wishes.

Even Binning, however, was disconcerted as he rode into the streets of Perth. His practised eye told him that many of the black gowns he saw were worn by his old enemies the ministers of the thoroughly Presbyterian districts of Fife and the Lothians. Hurrying to the Archbishop, he confided to him his fears. Spottiswoode quickly reassured him. In the early days of the Reformation, Knox, full of confidence in his country, and wishing to make the General Assembly the ecclesiastical Parliament of the nation, had welcomed the presence of the nobility as well as that of the elected representatives of the clergy and laity. The noblemen were flocking to Perth in large numbers, and were ready, almost to a man, to vote for the King. If only thirty clerical votes were cast for the Articles, failure was impossible; and it would be strange if, with all the means at his disposal, the Archbishop could not secure thirty clerical votes for the King.

The sermons at the opening of the Assembly were preached by Forbes and Spottiswoode. Forbes seems to have contented himself with recommending the members of the Assembly to act according to their consciences, at the same time that he pointed out that if the Articles were themselves indifferent, the effect of the anger of the King upon the Church was an element of the situation which might well be taken into consideration.[1]

CHAP. VII.
1618.
Aug. 25.

Spottiswoode's sermon disclosed more naively still the only ground on which the Articles seemed worthy of recommendation to any one in Scotland. "Had it been in our power," he said, "to have dissuaded or declined them, we certainly would." But they were matters of indifference, and in such matters the danger of disobedience was greater than the danger from innovation. All that he could adduce in support of the Articles was that they were neither impious nor unlawful. "And surely," he continued, "if it cannot be shewed that they are repugnant to the written word, I see not with what conscience we can refuse them, being urged as they are by our Sovereign Lord and King; a King who is not a stranger to divinity, but hath such acquaintance with it as Rome never found, in the confession of all men, a more potent adversary; a King neither superstitious nor inclinable that way, but one that seeks to have God rightly and truly worshipped by all his subjects. His person, were he not our Sovereign, gives them sufficient authority, being recommended by him; for he knows the nature of things and the consequences of them, what is fit for a Church to have, and what not, better than we do all."

Spottiswoode's sermon.

It is easy to imagine what must have been the effect of so absolute a self-surrender on the minds of such of the ministers present as retained a spark of independence. But a glance at the Assembly would have been sufficient to show that the hour of the independent ministers was not yet come. By accident or

Order of the Assembly.

[1] *Calderwood*, vii. 305. Binning to the King. Botfield's *Original Letters*, ii. 573.

design the place in which it was convened was too small to afford decent accommodation to all who were present. Seats were provided for the nobility, for the Bishops, and even for the representatives of the boroughs. The ministers were left to stand huddled together in a crowd behind the backs of those who were seated at the table. As soon as order was established the proceedings were commenced by the reading of a letter from the King.

The king's letter.

James's missive was couched in his usual style. He hoped, he said, that the Assembly would not allow the unruly and ignorant multitude to bear down the better and more judicious. They must, however, understand that nothing that they could do would be of any real importance. It would do them no good to reject the Articles, as they would be imposed at once by the Royal authority, which was all that was really needed. Those who denied this called in question that power which Christian kings had received from God.

Aug. 25.

As soon as the letter had been read, the Archbishop enforced its advice by a recital of the various miseries which would befal those who were unwise enough to brave the King's displeasure.

Aug. 26. Preliminary conference.

A conference was then held in which a number of ministers, selected by Spottiswoode, took part. They had taken care that the majority of these should be on the side of the King. There was a sharp debate on the form in which the question should be put to the Assembly. The independent ministers thought it should be, " Whether kneeling or sitting at the Communion were the fitter gesture?" Spottiswoode was too good a tactician to admit of this, and he carried a motion that the question should be, " His Majesty desires our gesture of sitting at the Communion to be changed into kneeling. Why ought not the same to be done?" The burden of proof was thus thrown upon his opponents.

The next morning Spottiswoode confronted the full Assembly. Everything was done to harass the opponents of the Court. They were not allowed to discuss the ecclesiastical question on its own merits. They were told that the only question before them was, "Is the King to be obeyed or not?" They were repeatedly warned of the penalties awaiting their obstinacy. When at last the vote was taken, Spottiswoode reminded each man of the consequences of his decision. "Have the King in your mind" he said; "Remember the King," "Look to the King." Under this pressure eighty-six votes were given for the Articles, only forty being secured to the opposition.[1]

CHAP. VII.
1618. Aug. 27. The full Assembly.

The articles accepted.

The majority thus obtained was, if the twelve Bishops' votes be set aside as already acquired for the King, almost entirely derived from the laity. Of the ministers present there was a bare majority of seven in favour of the Articles, a majority which, under the circumstances in which the vote was taken, indicates a very large preponderance of clerical opinion against the change. On the other hand, out of thirty lay votes only two were given in opposition.[2] If indeed the divergence between lay and clerical opinion had indi-

Composition of the majority.

---

[1] Calderwood, *Perth Assembly*, and *History*, vii. 304. Lindsay, *A true narrative of all the passages at Perth*. Binning to the King. Botfield's *Original Letters*, ii. 573. Calderwood and Lindsay do not differ more than might be expected from men taking opposite sides. Lindsay admits quite enough against his own party, and Binning's letter, written a few hours after the occurrence, agrees substantially with Calderwood as to the form in which the vote was taken. Calderwood gives the words thus: "Whether will ye consent to these articles, or disobey the King?" Lindsay positively denies that this form was used. It is possible that in the formal question the King's name was omitted; but that Spottiswoode's language left no doubt what was intended.

[2] The following calculation is founded on Lindsay's statements:—

	Bishops.	Ministers.	Laity.	Total.
Affirmative	12	46	28	86
Negative	0	39	2	41
	12	85	30	127

cated a real desire on the part of the laity to alter the ceremonies of the Church, it might have been said that James had only given effect in a hasty and indecorous manner to the voice of the country. But in truth there is everything to show that this was not the case. The laity of Scotland, and especially the nobility, gave no signs of any ardour on behalf of the new ceremonies. They were glad enough to worry the ministers, still more glad, if it were possible, to plunder them of their scanty revenues. But there were no convictions firm and strong behind the votes which they had recorded.

The articles enforced.

The moral weight of high purpose and fixed resolve was on the other side. The Bishops had enough to do in sentencing those who refused to conform, and who declared that the meeting at Perth was no lawful Assembly. In Fife and the Lothians, at least, the recalcitrant ministers had their congregations at their backs. In Edinburgh large numbers of the inhabitants poured out of the city to the country churches where the new orders were less strictly enforced. That a fitting example might be set, the officers of state and the nobles of the land were marshalled to church like unwilling recruits, whilst the poor who lived upon the charity dispensed by the clergy were threatened with starvation if they refused to conform. Ministers were cited before the Bishops, and the examination usually ended in an unseemly wrangle. A man like Spottiswoode could only at the last appeal to the orders of the King.[1] Even Forbes was the worse for the unhappy contest in which he was engaged. "Will you," he said, when some of the Bishops were induced to forward to the King a petition for a dispensation to the recalcitrant ministers, "will you justify the doctrine

[1] *Calderwood*, vii. 370.

of these men, who have called the reverent gesture which we use idolatry, and raised such a schism in our Church? Till they be brought publicly to confess their error, or heresy rather, I shall never be yielding for my part. It was before indifferent, now I esteem it necessary, in regard to the false opinions they have dispersed, to retain constantly the form we have received."[1]

1620.

The activity of the Bishops called up the first signs of resistance in a quarter in which the ministers had hitherto not had much to hope. An order from the King to the Privy Council directed that body to banish four citizens from Edinburgh. The Earl of Dunfermline, the Chancellor of Scotland, with a lawyer's jealousy of the domination of Bishops and Presbyters alike, objected that it was illegal to punish without form of trial. A few months later the Council was directed to send for one of the incriminated ministers. "It is not our part," said the Chancellor, "to judge in Kirk matters. The Bishops have a High Commission of their own to try these things." "Will ye reason with the King," cried Binning, who had been raised to the earldom of Melrose for his services at Perth. "We may reason," replied Dunfermline, "whether we shall be the Bishops' hangmen or not." The old lawyer carried the Council with him, and the case was referred to the High Commission.[2]

April. Objections of Dunfermline.

Oct.

In the following year Parliament was summoned to give the force of law to the Articles. In a House of 120, a majority of twenty-seven pronounced in their favour. The minority amongst the laity was far more imposing than it had been at Perth. An analysis of the division list shows where the King's strength lay.

1621. Aug. The Articles confirmed by Parliament.

---

[1] Spottiswoode to Dr. John Forbes, Apr. 2, 1635. *Funeral Sermons on P. Forbes*, 218.   [2] *Calderwood*, vii. 383.

After the Bishops and the Privy Councillors, his supporters were mainly taken from amongst the high nobility, that is to say, from the men who had the largest hold upon the Church lands.[1]

Long afterwards, zealous Presbyterians loved to tell how at the moment when the Bills of this session were being converted into law by the touch of the sceptre, a blinding flash of lightning burst forth from the lurid sky, giving the first warning of the terrific thunderstorm which followed. The air blackened as in the night, and the crashing hail was followed by torrents of rain. As the Lords, instead of riding home in state, hurried away on foot, or in their coaches, not a few of the citizens gazed upon the spectacle with ill-concealed satisfaction, and muttered that the storm was a visible sign of God's anger. "Nay rather," was the reply made by some one of the opposite party, "it is to be taken for an approbation of Heaven, like that given at Sinai."[2] It was long before the memory of 'Black Saturday' died out in Edinburgh.

The true portents of coming evil were to be sought, not in the sky, but in the bitterness of indignation awakened by the King's action. James, as soon as he heard the result of the Parliamentary campaign, hounded on the Bishops to increased severity. "Hereafter," he wrote, "that rebellious and disobedient crew must either obey, or resist both to God, their natural King, and the law of their country. . . . The sword is now put into your hands. Go on therefore to use it, and let it rest no longer till you have perfected the service trusted unto you. For otherwise we must use it both against you and them."

---

[1] Melrose to the King, Aug. 3. Ratification of the Articles, Aug. 4. Botfield's *Original Letters*, ii. 656, 658. *Calderwood*, vii. 488-501.

[2] *Calderwood*, vii. 505. *Spottiswoode*, iii. 262.

During the remainder of James's reign there was a perpetual effort to enforce the Articles. In 1623 Melrose reported that at Edinburgh 'the number of communicants was small,' and of those 'sundry of the base sort, and some women not of the best, did sit.'[1] James was for ever exhorting and threatening in vain. Unruly ministers were imprisoned without effect. It is no wonder that when such resistance was offered to the Articles, James would hear nothing of giving his sanction to further innovations, and that he turned a deaf ear to Laud's 'ill-fangled platform to make that stubborn Kirk stoop more to the English pattern.'[2]

CHAP. VII.

1623. Difficulty of enforcing the Articles.

Charles's accession was the signal for the opening of that controversy with the nobility on which his father had not ventured to enter. In securing a permanent income for the clergy, James had done nothing to obviate the grave social and political evils attendant upon the vast absorption of Church revenues by the high nobility in the preceding and earlier generations. The possession of a right to tithes, where the tithes were levied in kind, placed the owner of the soil at the mercy of the owner of the tithes, when, as was then the case in Scotland, the latter was not under the control of a strong central authority. The land-owner might be compelled to keep his harvest ungarnered till it pleased the tithe-owner to take possession of his share.[3] Even if such extreme

1625. The Church property of the nobles.

---

[1] Melrose Papers, ii. 637.

[2] Mr. Sprott, in his Introduction to the *Scottish Liturgies of the reign of James VI.*, xxxvii, points out that the story of James's conversation with Williams about Laud cannot possibly have taken place at the date assigned to it by Hacket. But it is probably true in the main.

[3] This is distinctly stated in Charles's Large Declaration issued in 1639, and may be taken as a true representation of the law of the case, even if the practice was more moderate. Compare, too, Lithgow's Scotland's Welcome. *Poetical Remains*, ed. Maidment, sig. O, 2 :—

"For, Sir, take heed, what grief is this and cross?
To my poor Commons, and a yearly loss;

CHAP. VII.
1625.

Oct. 12.
Charles's act of revocation.

rights were seldom put in force, they created a feeling of dependence in those who were subjected to them, which must have gone far to strengthen the power of the nobles against the State, and which would stand in the way of that distribution of equal justice which it was the business of the King's government to enforce.

Charles was therefore evidently in the right in desiring to change an arrangement so fraught with mischief. But his mode of interference was at once harsh and impolitic. Acting, as he usually did, on the supposition that his legal rights were identical with his moral rights, he issued an act of revocation by which the mass of Church property in the hands of laymen was reannexed to the Crown on the ground of technical flaws in the original concession.[1] Not only was the extreme form in which the act was couched certain to raise up enemies of no despicable kind, but it sinned against the principle that long possession is entitled to consideration for the sake of persons totally innocent of the original wrong, whose interests have grown up around it.

1626.
Feb. 9.
Explanatory proclamation.

A proclamation issued to explain the King's intentions did nothing to remove this fundamental objection.[2] The nobility, with the greater part of the Privy

> That when their corns are shorn, stouked, dead, and dry,
> They cannot get them teinded; nay, and why?
> Some grudge or malice moves despight to wound
> The hopeful harvest, and rot their corns on ground.
> This is no rare thing on their stowks that's seen,
> Snow-covered tops, below their grass-grown green."

Scotland entreats Charles not to farm the tithes to the Lords:—

> " Then let my tithes be brought to money rent,
> For thee, from landlord and the poor tenent;
> So may they shear, and lead and stack their corn,
> At midnight, midday, afternoon or morn,
> Which shall be their advantage and my gain,
> When barns and yards are filled with timely grain."

[1] Acta Parl. Scot. v. 23.
[2] Proclamation, Feb. 9, 1626. Connell's *Treatise on Tithes*, iii. 58.

Council, were up in arms. The Earl of Nithsdale, a Roman Catholic peer, who had married one of Buckingham's many kinswomen, and was occasionally employed on delicate negotiations, had been sent to Scotland to carry the revocation into effect. He was met by a storm of opposition. If later report spoke truly, the leading tithe-owners resolved, if nothing else would serve, to 'fall upon him and all his party in the old Scottish fashion and knock him on the head.'[1] Another account charges the interested lords with exciting the people by spreading rumours that Nithsdale was coming to revoke, not the grants of tithes, but the laws establishing the Protestant religion, whilst they frightened Nithsdale by informing him, before he had completed his journey, that the people of Edinburgh had cut in pieces the coach which he had prepared for his entry into the city, had killed his horses, and were quite ready to do the same to himself.[2]

CHAP. VII.

1626. Feb. 9.

It was not often that worldly wisdom entered into the counsels of Charles. But the decision which he took upon hearing of the difficulties raised was admirably suited to meet the danger. On the one hand, whilst laying stress on his intention to relieve the burdens of the land-owners, he offered such of the tithe-owners as would make voluntary submission a reasonable compensation for their loss. On the other hand, he suspended

July 11. Charles offers compensation.

---

[1] Mr. Burton (*Hist. of Scotland*, vi. 358) expresses doubts, in which I fully share, of the 'savage story' told by Burnet of the blind Lord Belhaven intending to murder the Earl of Dumfries. It may be added that the date given by Burnet, of the third year of the King, becomes 1628 in Mr. Burton's history, which is too late, and that the names Belhaven and Dumfries point to the late origin of the story. There were no such titles till 1633. Burnet's statement that the King purchased lands for the Archbishoprics from Hamilton and Lennox ought to have been referred to a later date, as is shewn by the English Exchequer Books, though there is a Privy Seal for 2,000*l.* for the purpose in 1625.

[2] *Heylyn*, 237.

the operation of the Articles of Perth, so far as those ministers were concerned who had been ordained before the new rules had been admitted, on the understanding that they would refrain from arguing against the existing system. At the same time there was to be a general amnesty for the ministers who had been arrested and imprisoned. In this way, whilst the attack upon the high nobility was softened, Charles might hope to rally round him the mass of the nation in support of a wise and justifiable policy.[1] On August 26 the King's Advocate took the first steps to bring the legal question to trial.[2] The blow was followed up by an order to Sir George Hay, the Lord Chancellor of Scotland, a testy and stubborn old man, who had made himself the centre of resistance, to come to London to justify his conduct.[3]

This decided step was at once successful. Envoys were sent from Scotland to treat with the King, and, after considerable discussion, Commissioners were appointed to examine the whole subject.[4] After a long and minute investigation, a compromise was effected. The Church lands were to remain in the hands of those who held them, upon payment of certain rents to the King. Tithes, on the other hand, were dealt with in a more complicated fashion. The land-owner was to be at liberty to extinguish the right of levying tithes on his property by payment of a sum calculated at nine years' purchase. If he did not choose to exercise this option, the tithe in kind was to be commuted into a rent-charge, from which was to be deducted the stipend payable to the ministers, and an annuity reserved for

[1] The King to the Council, July 11. *Connell*, iii. 64. Balfour's *Hist. Works*, ii. 142.
[2] *Connell*, iii. 68.
[3] Contarini's Despatch, Oct. $\frac{6}{16}$.
[4] Commission, Jan. 7, 1627. *Connell*, iii. 71.

the King.¹ Special regard was paid to the circumstances of the minister, and in many instances they received an augmentation of their stipends. In its final shape the arrangement thus made is worthy of memory as the one successful action of Charles's reign. In money value it did not bring anything to the Scottish exchequer, as the King disposed of his annuity in perpetuity in payment of a debt of 10,000*l*.² But it weakened the power of the nobility, and strengthened the prerogative in the only way in which the prerogative deserved to be strengthened, by the popularity it gained through carrying into effect a wise and beneficent reform. Every land-owner who was freed from the perpetual annoyance of the tithe-gatherer, every minister whose income had been increased and rendered more certain than by James's arrangement, knew well to whom the change was owing.

CHAP. VII.
1629.
Nature of the compromise.

To object to the change thus effected because it favoured the growth of the prerogative is mere constitutional pedantry. The stage of civilisation at which Scotland had arrived was one in which it still was desirable that the prerogative should be extended. The nobility were still, with some brilliant exceptions, self-seeking and unruly,³ and the time for the development of a full Parliamentary system only arrives when all members of a State are equally submissive to the laws of the State.

The Crown against the aristocracy.

In Scotland therefore Charles had but to persevere in the course upon which he had already entered. If he could satisfy the temporal requirements of the mass

¹ Connell, Book iii.-iv. Forbes. *A Treatise of Church Lands and Tithes*, 258. See also the observations of Mr. Burton (vi. 353-368).
² Forbes, 264.
³ The beginning of Spalding's *History of the Troubles*, and the latter part of Mr. Burton's sixty-fourth chapter, headed 'Sufferings of the Bishops' (vi. 246) should be studied by all who doubt this.

of the nation, if he could avoid irritating their religious sentiments or their religious prejudices, he might still grasp firmly the nettle of aristocratic discontent.

Aristocratic discontent there was sure to be. It is hard to say that the nobility had any real ground for dissatisfaction. They had exchanged an income irregularly gained, and obtained by oppressive means, for one which was indeed less in amount, but which was to be secured not only by an indefeasible title, but by the cessation of the irritation caused by their former proceedings. But large bodies of men are never very reasonable in their view of changes which cause them apparent damage, and the circumstances under which the original confiscatory act of revocation had been issued were such as to make them suspicious of Charles's future action. The withdrawal of the means of indirectly influencing the conduct of the land-owners, which was a pure gain to the community, naturally left them sore, as the English land-owners were left sore by the destruction of the rotten boroughs.

Question of heritable jurisdiction.

Nor were the nobles without apprehension that Charles would take a further step in the same direction. The question of the heritable jurisdictions had been again mooted in the course of the controversy, and though the King had restricted himself to the expression of a wish to buy them up whenever he was rich enough to do so,[1] it was always possible that a blow might be struck against them as sudden and unexpected as the act of revocation.

Charles invited to Scotland.

It was therefore certain that for some time to come Charles would have to confront the tacit hostility of the Scottish nobility. For the present, however, it was certain to be no more than a tacit hostility. Now that the legality of the act of revocation had been acknow-

[1] Contarini's Despatch, Jan. $\frac{12}{22}$, 1627. *Heylyn*, 238.

ledged, they were anxious that the compromise to which they had consented should receive a Parliamentary sanction, which would save them from a more extreme danger in the future. Charles was therefore entreated to visit Scotland to be crowned, and to hold a Parliament in which the sanction of law might be given to the late arrangements.

CHAP. VII.
1633.

Various circumstances delayed the Royal visit, and it was not till 1633 that Charles crossed the border. On June 15 he entered Edinburgh amidst a storm of loyal welcome. On the 18th he was crowned at Holyrood.

June 18. The King's coronation at Edinburgh.

As a political ceremony there can be little doubt that Charles's coronation was greeted with genuine enthusiasm. But it was a religious ceremony as well, and the form which it took would therefore go far to indicate whether Charles meant to make the ideas of his letter for the suspension of the Perth Articles the leading principle of his ecclesiastical policy, or whether that suspension was only extorted from him by the immediate necessities of the situation, to be revoked as soon as the danger appeared to be at an end. It was a momentous question for Charles, for the decision of it in the wrong way would throw the whole force of popular religious enthusiasm on the side of the nobility if they should at any time find it advisable to renew the struggle which they had for the moment renounced as hopeless.

The Prayer-book, the preparation of which had been enjoined by the Assembly which had met at Aberdeen three years before, was completed early in 1619. Hewat's version had been thrust aside, and another, of which the chief part of the composition has been ascribed to Cowper, Bishop of Galloway, was revised by Spottiswoode and the Dean of Winchester, a Scotch-

1619. The Prayer-book of the Scottish Bishops.

man of the name of Young. But it was not brought into use. James was alarmed at the outburst of resistance to the Perth Articles, and in 1621 he allowed his Commissioners to promise the Scottish Parliament that if those Articles were confirmed there should be no further innovation in matters of religion.

The question of a Liturgy was allowed to sleep for eight years. In 1629 the proceedings of the English Parliament had rivetted the ascendancy of Laud upon Charles's mind, and his success in the business of tithes in Scotland may have induced him to think that he had no reason to keep terms with Puritanism in that kingdom. Whatever the motive may have been, he sent for the draft of the Prayer-book. It was brought to England by Dr. James Maxwell, one of the Edinburgh ministers, a man unlikely to give offence from any undue sympathy with Puritanism, and was by him submitted to Laud, in obedience to Charles's orders.

Laud's judgment could hardly be doubtful. In itself uniformity was delightful to him as the prop and stay of spiritual unity, and the mere fact that the proposed draft for Scotland differed from the existing English version would dispose him unfavourably towards it. In itself, too, the new Prayer-book must have seemed to him to differ for the worse from the forms to which he was accustomed. Though it followed to a great extent the Book of Common Prayer, it had large portions inserted from Knox's Book of Common Order, and was, on the whole, such a recension of the Prayer-book as would commend itself to the feelings of an English low churchman of the present time.[1] Laud therefore declined to give his approbation

[1] Thus, in the Baptismal Service, the use of the sign of the cross, and the declaration after baptism 'that this child is regenerate,' were omitted. At the Communion Service, the table was to stand 'in that part of the church which the minister findeth most convenient.' The double form

to the liturgy which was stamped with the recommendation of the Scottish Bishops. "I told him," he said long afterwards, in giving an account of his conversation with Maxwell, "I was clear of opinion that if his Majesty would have a liturgy settled there, it were best to take the English liturgy without any variation, that so the same Service Book might be established in all his Majesty's dominions." Maxwell's reply was a warning of coming evil. That the Scotch were Puritans was only one side of the danger. They were also Scotchmen proud of their ancient nationality, and jealous, as only small communities are jealous, of any invasion of their special modes of action at the dictation of foreigners. "To this," says Laud, "he replied that he was of a contrary opinion, and that not only he, but the Bishops of that kingdom thought their countrymen would be much better satisfied if a liturgy were formed by their own clergy, than to have the English liturgy put upon them; yet, he added, that it might be according to the form of our English Service Book." Even the hope held out of large modifications did not satisfy Laud. He reported the conversation to Charles, and Charles, as blind as Laud to the dangers in his

derived from the two Prayer-books of Edward VI. was preserved in the administration of the Communion to the people on their knees. But it was prefaced by a short address adopted from Knox:—"Let us lift up our hearts unto the Lord, and by faith lay hold upon Jesus, whom God the Father, by his Spirit, offereth to us in this holy sacrament, that we may draw virtue from the Lord to quicken and conceive our souls and bodies unto eternal life." The whole subject is treated of at length in Mr. Sprott's Appendix to the *Scottish Liturgies of the reign of James VI.* One point which confirms his argument that the Prayer for the Queen was introduced in the autumn of 1629 has escaped his notice. The petition to 'make her a happy mother of *successful* children' must, almost certainly, have been written, not only before the birth of Prince Charles, but after the Queen's miscarriage of her first child. I have not quoted the original authorities for this part of my narrative, as the reader will find them all referred to in Mr. Sprott's excellent Introduction.

CHAP. VII.
1629.

Position of the Scottish Bishops.

path, approved Laud's proposal for the introduction of the English Prayer-book.

The Scottish Bishops were reaping in their humiliation the seed which they had sown in their apparent triumph at Perth. They had preached the acceptance of an order of things which they themselves held to be unadvisable, in order to please the King, and they now found that that King's successor cast aside their advice and their warnings as unworthy of a moment's notice. It is not required of those whose work it is to govern that they should be possessed of the highest spiritual insight, or that they should be constantly promulgating some new discovery in politics or theology. But if they are to retain the respect of contemporaries or of posterity, it is absolutely necessary that they should place some reasonable limits upon the extent to which they allow their own judgments to be overruled by considerations of expediency. It was not mere obsequiousness or ambition which had dictated the readiness of the Bishops to accept, against their better judgment, the Articles of Perth. It was owing to the kingly authority that the Scottish clergy were able to carry out the work of their ministry in the face of the hungry and grasping owners of the soil, and it may well have seemed to the Bishops that to oppose the King, except upon some question on which their own conscience was at stake, would throw back the Church into the clutches of the nobility. Since the Articles at Perth had been put in practice, however, some experience had been gained. The risk of placing the King's rule in opposition to the religious consciousness of the nation was becoming plain to all who had eyes to see. To withstand the King at Perth in 1618 would have been, if they had only known it, the best service that the Bishops could have rendered to James. To withstand the King at Edinburgh in 1633 would be the best service that they could render to Charles. It was because the Scottish Bishops had no word to speak in the great contest which was arising, because, being neither strong partisans nor wise mediators, they drifted helplessly like logs on the current of affairs, that the very name stank in the nostrils of the Scottish nation, and they were credited with all the mischief which they had done nothing to remedy. The great Italian poet would have condemned them without appeal to an endless comradeship with those who were alike displeasing to God and to His enemies. The moral strength which is based on the conviction that a man ought to think and speak independently of the dictation of the King was passing over, if it had not already passed over, to their opponents.

What the Bishops did not say was said by William Struthers, one of the Edinburgh ministers, himself a conformist, though a most unwilling conformist, to the Articles of Perth. "There is some surmises," he wrote in a letter intended for the King's eyes, "of further novation of organs, liturgies, and such like, which greatly augments the grief of the people." The Church, he said, lay groaning under two wounds, the erection of bishoprics and the order to kneel at the reception of the sacrament. If a third were added, and the congregations were 'forced to suffer novelties' in 'the whole body of public worship,' nothing short of general confusion would be the result.[1]

Charles had, when at last he visited Scotland, come with the resolution to override such remonstrances. By his side was Laud, prepared to renew at Edinburgh the recommendations which he had given in London.

[1] *Balfour*, ii. 181. The Earl of Airth, to whom the letter is said to have been addressed, was known at that time as Earl of Menteith.

CHAP. VII.

1633.
June 18.
Ceremonies at the coronation.

On the day of the coronation the final decision had yet to be taken. But the ceremonies observed in Holyrood chapel were not such as gave hope that much regard would be paid to the feelings of Scotchmen. The Archbishop of St. Andrews and the other four Bishops who took part in the service were attired in 'white rochets and white sleeves, and copes of gold having blue silk to their foot.' The Communion-table was prepared after a fashion which must have recalled to all educated Scotchmen the famous epigram of Andrew Melville. One who was by no means a stickler for extreme Puritanism remarked that a table was placed in the church 'after the manner of an altar, having thereupon two books, with two wax chandeliers, and two wax candles which were unlighted, and a basin wherein there was nothing.' At the back of this altar, " covered with tapestry," he added, " there was a rich tapestry wherein the crucifix was curiously wrought; and as these Bishops who were in service passed by this crucifix they were seen to bow the knee and beck, which, with their habit, was noticed, and bred great fear of inbringing of Popery."[1]

The work of exasperating the religious feelings of

---

[1] *Spalding*, i. 36. Mr. Grub, in his *Ecclesiastical History of Scotland*, ii. 345, throws doubt on the usually accepted story told by Rushworth, that the Archbishop of St. Andrews being placed on the King's right hand, and the Archbishop of Glasgow on the left, Laud 'took Glasgow and thrust him from the King in these words:—" Are you a churchman, and wants the coat of your order." ' He argues that 'in Sir J. Balfour's minute narrative of the coronation it does not appear that any special place was assigned to Archbishop Lindsay,' and that Spalding says that ' the Archbishop of Glasgow and the remanent of the Bishops there present, who were not in the service, changed not their habit, but wore their black gowns without rochets or white sleeves.' It may be added that the details of the ceremony must have been arranged beforehand, and if the Archbishop objected to appear in a cope, the question would not have been left to be settled in the church. It should be remembered that during this period Rushworth is no safe authority.

THE PARLIAMENTARY OPPOSITION.

CHAP. VII.
1633.

the greater part of those who had any religious feeling at all in Scotland was thus successfully begun. The pressure put upon congregations to kneel at the Communion was only felt once or twice a year. The offence given by the white garment and the reverence paid in passing before the crucifix would be an offence of weekly, if not of daily repetition, in the eyes of men who were sensitive above all other Protestants to the danger of relapsing into a system which they counted irreligious and antichristian.

That which had been done in the King's chapel was not without its effect upon Parliament. On June 20 that body met for despatch of business. Unlike the English Parliament, it was not divided into two Houses. Out of 183 members, the non-official lords present in person or by proxy could number only sixty-six votes, and resistance to the King was therefore too hopeless to be attempted on a question in which, as in that of the compromise on tithes, he would have at his disposal the ninety-six votes of the representatives of the boroughs and of the untitled gentry. The ecclesiastical bills offered a better rallying ground for opposition. It would be invidious to bring a charge of deliberate insincerity against those of the lords who perceived this. Some of them perhaps may have looked upon the opportunity offered them as merely an occasion for a clever piece of political tactics. Others were doubtless inspired with a conscientious dislike of the new ceremonies. But it is probable that there were many whose eyes were opened to the duty of opposing the ceremonies by the attack made on their own property and interests by the now withdrawn act of revocation.

June 20. Meeting of Parliament.

Opposition to the Crown, however, was never very easy in a Scottish Parliament excepting when the whole of those present were substantially agreed. A

Difficulties of an opposition.

CHAP. VII.
1633.
June 20.

The Lords of the Articles.

Committee named the Lords of the Articles was possessed of the exclusive right of examining and amending Bills, the whole House being compelled to accept or reject in their entirety the Bills which came down to them from that Committee. By a series of changes, permitted or condoned by the Scottish Parliament, never so alive as the English Parliament to the value of forms, the Lords of the Articles were so constituted as to represent as far as possible the wishes of the King. The nobility had first of all to select eight of the twelve Bishops, and it would have been hard to find a single Bishop opposed to the Crown. The Bishops had then to choose eight out of the sixty-six nobles, and it would have been strange if eight nobles could not be found to vote as the King wished. The Bishops and nobles together then chose eight of the untitled gentry and eight of the commissioners for boroughs, and even if every one of these sixteen had joined in opposition, they would be helpless to turn the scale. For the King had the further right of adding eight officers of state to the Committee thus constituted,[1] and of appointing his Chancellor as its president. As if this were not enough, he might himself be present at the deliberations of the body thus formed.

June 28.
The sitting of the whole House.

When at last the Bills were laid before the whole House, there was found to be one which confirmed all acts of the late reign relating to the Church, and another which mixed up the confirmation of an act made in 1606 in acknowledgment of the Royal prerogative with another act giving power to the King to settle the apparel in which judges, magistrates, and the clergy were to appear in public. It would thus be impossible for any one to vote against the latter clause without declaring himself the opponent of the King's

---

[1] *Burton*, vi. 369. *Acts of Parl. of Scotl.* v. 10.

prerogative.¹ Nor was any one left in doubt that the Bill, if carried, would be used by Charles in a way very different from that in which the former Act had been used by James. Hitherto the use of English forms had been confined to the Royal chapel at Holyrood. But on the Sunday before the day on which the vote was to be taken, Charles had attended St. Giles's 'and after he was set down in his own place, the ordinary reader being reading the word and singing psalms,—as the ordinary custom was then,—before sermon, Mr. John Maxwell . . . came down from the King's loft, caused the reader remove from his place, set down there two English chaplains clad with surplices, and they with the help of other chaplains and Bishops there present, acted their English service. That being ended, in came Mr. John Guthrie, Bishop of Moray, clad also with a surplice,' or rather a rochet, 'went up so to pulpit, and taught a sermon.'² Another authority bears witness to the results. "The people of Edinburgh, seeing the Bishop preach in his rochet, which was never seen in Giles' kirk since the Reformation, and by him who was sometime one of their own town's Puritan ministers, they were grieved and grudged hereat, thinking the same smelt of Popery."³

The leaders of the opposition had already prepared a petition which showed that they knew how to meet the King with his own tactics. In complaining against the acts relating to the Church they took care to complain also of a proposed new taxation which weighed upon all land owners in Scotland.⁴

---

[1] The powers conferred on James had been to the effect that 'every preacher of God's word shall hereafter wear black grave and comely apparel,' and that as the King was 'godly, wise, and religious, hating all erroneous and vain superstition,' he might settle what the apparel of the clergy was to be.

[2] Row, 363.   [3] Spalding, i. 20.
[4] Row, Hist. of the Kirk of Scotland, 364.

*1639.
June 28.
The bills accepted.*

Charles refused to receive the petition. In all the opposition which was surging up suddenly around him, he doubtless saw nothing else than a factious and unprincipled attempt to take vengeance upon him for the act of revocation. He threw himself into the struggle with all the heat of a party leader. When the Earl of Loudon stood up to question the propriety of joining the confirmation of two acts in one bill, the King sharply told him that 'the orders of the house' were 'not to dispute there but to vote.'[1] The whole assembly felt the importance of the contest which the King had challenged. When the division was taken there was scarcely a man present who did not anxiously note down the votes as they were given. Charles was too much interested in the result to maintain a dignified bearing; he too jotted down the names, not without expressions of dissatisfaction with those who voted in the negative. This time he was saved from defeat. A majority, probably only a slight majority, was on his side.[2]

Rothes and Loudon.

The names of those who composed the minority are lost to us with scarcely an exception, and rumour has been so busy in swelling the original grain of truth till it is no longer distinguishable from falsehood, that it is impossible to reproduce the scene with any distinctness. But it can hardly be doubted that the Earls of Rothes and Loudon took a leading part in the opposition, and Rothes and Loudon were two of three commissioners who had come to England in 1626 on behalf of the tithe-holding nobility.

---

[1] *Sanderson's History,* 194. That discussion was stopped is stated in the *Humble supplication* for connection with which Balmerino was afterwards tried.

[2] Mr. Napier (*Montrose and the Covenanters,* i. 521) seems to me to have completely disposed of the story that there was a real majority the other way, concealed by Charles. Its antecedent improbability is glaring. But it was believed soon after the time.

How was this opposition to be met by Charles? On June 30 Laud preached at Holyrood on the blessings of conformity, and a meeting of Bishops and other ministers was held to discuss with Laud and the King the proposed introduction of the English Prayer-book. Some of those present, Lindsay, Bishop of Brechin, the historian and defender of the Articles of Perth, Maxwell, who had just become Bishop of Ross, Sydserf, an Edinburgh minister, and Wedderburn, a Scotchman who had been a professor at St. Andrews, and was now a beneficed clergyman in the English Church, gave their voices in favour of Laud's unwise proposal. The mass of the Bishops were still of the same mind that they had been in in 1629. Yet so far as information reaches us, they did not speak plainly out. They did not say that they could not go one step further than the liturgy which they had prepared. They talked of the objection which would be taken in Scotland to a liturgy precisely similar to that used on the south of the Tweed. They complained of a few unimportant errors, mistakes in the translation of the Psalms, and the like. Every Scotchman knew that the real objection did not lie here. Charles did not care to see it. He gave way so far as to agree that some of the Scotch Bishops should set to work 'to draw up a liturgy[1] as near that of England as might be.' The Book of 1619 was tacitly allowed to drop out of sight. It had itself been more obnoxious than the Book of 1617. Its successor might well be more obnoxious still.

The next day Charles set out for a progress in the country, which he enjoyed extremely. In spite of all that had passed, he was received with every demonstra-

---

[1] *Laud's Works*, iii. 278. Crawford, *Lives of the Officers of the Crown*, 177. He founds his narrative on MSS. of Spottiswoode which have been lost, and upon Clarendon, who had doubtless a good opportunity of hearing what passed. Crawford anticipates by calling Sydserf and Wedderburn Bishops.

tion of affection. In the whole course of his wanderings he met with only one mishap. On his way back to Edinburgh he was nearly drowned in crossing from Burntisland, and on July 18 he left his northern capital on his journey home.

The composition of a Prayer-book was for the present suspended. But Charles had not long been in England before he discharged a Parthian shot upon Scotland. In virtue of the powers conferred on him by the recent Act, he directed that at the time of service the clergy should appear in 'whites.'[1] Such an order could not be enforced. But Charles had thrown up one more barrier between himself and the hearts of his loyal subjects in Scotland.

Another step taken in the same direction showed whither Charles was tending. During his visit he arranged for the establishment of a new Bishopric of Edinburgh, the city and the country around having up to that time formed part of the diocese of St. Andrews. The first Bishop appointed by Charles was William Forbes, a distant cousin of the Bishop of Aberdeen. A man more worthy of respect for wide theological learning, for gentleness of spirit, and for earnestness and simplicity of life, it would have been difficult to find. And yet a more indiscreet selection could hardly have been made. In his dislike of contention and strife, Forbes was inclined to overlook the realities which divided the Church into parties, and his theology, derived from a study of the Fathers, led him to admit possibilities of reconciliation by which the most radical diversities of opinion were to be merged in the white light of undefined and impalpable truth.

Least of all were the citizens of Edinburgh likely to give ear to a teacher who placed his ideal in a

---

[1] *Acts of Parl. of Scotl.* v. 21.

scheme of Christian thought which should enable the disciples of a Protestant Church to join hands with the disciples of the Pope. Even in Aberdeen, where a school adverse to the Puritan ideas of the South had arisen in the University, Forbes stood to a certain extent alone. In James's reign he had been settled as one of the Edinburgh ministers. But he had found the place uncongenial, and he had shrunk back to Aberdeen from the atmosphere of strife into which he had been plunged. But if Forbes did not satisfy the Scotch, he satisfied Charles. In a sermon preached before the King he had taken for his text, " My peace I leave with you." As disturbers of peace he arraigned before his pulpit on the one hand the Pope as the claimant of infallibility and the promulgator of new doctrines, and on the other hand the Protestant theologians who contentiously proclaimed that which was not fundamental to be fundamental, and who took needless offence at ecclesiastical rites which were anciently in use with the universal consent of the Christian Church. Three things he, said, were needed to restore order; 'one liturgy, one catechism, one confession of faith.' The Church too needed external protection as well as inward unity. There were those who had stripped God of his portion, the Church of her patrimony, the pastors of their necessary food, the people of God of their spiritual bread, the poor of the maintenance of their bodies. When will the good Samaritan come to relieve the Scottish Church which had fallen among thieves?[1]

CHAP. VII.
1634.

1633.

Charles was encouraged to come forward as the good Samaritan. Forbes himself was not long to be exposed to the contentions of the world. After an episcopate of three months he passed away, and gained

1624.
April 12.
Death of Forbes.

[1] Sermon preached June 25, 1633, in Garden's Life of J. Forbes, 290, prefixed to *J. Forbesii Opera*.

CHAP. VII.
1634.

that peace which was not to be found in the Scotland of his day. His successor was Lindsay of Brechin, who was in turn succeeded by Sydserf. Lindsay and Sydserf had been two of the four who had advised the introduction of the English liturgy. A third was already a Bishop, and the fourth, Wedderburn, would not have long to wait.

A new element was thus introduced into the Scottish episcopate. The old Bishops who had followed falteringly in James's steps would soon die out, and others whose thoughts answered to those of Laud would take their places. The life, the vigour of Puritanism was to be repressed, and a scholarlike uniformity was to smother all rude and violent clamour. Religion and morality were expected to flourish when zeal and the disorders which accompany zeal had been put to silence.

The old and new Bishops.

It was terribly dangerous. The old Bishops at least represented a movement in the Scottish mind, a weariness of ecclesiastical janglings and of clerical domination. The new Bishops represented Laud and Charles and England, or what seemed to be England to those who did not know where the heart of England was. The moral instincts which refused to be smothered by a catechism, a liturgy, and a confession prepared without reference to the beliefs of those for whom they are intended, would combine with the national indignation at those who sought to forge in a foreign country the bonds which they were preparing for their own.

Charles and the opposition Lords.

Till difficulties actually stared Charles in the face, he did not know that they existed. Still less did he perceive how much he was doing to increase them. He did not know that his Church policy was raising such men as Loudon and Rothes from insignificance. He fancied that to overwhelm those selfish and unprincipled adventurers, as he regarded them, he had but to testify his displeasure. Before his arrival in Scotland he had created some new peers, and had raised many Barons to a higher rank. He now gave orders that the grants which had not been formally made out should be suspended in the cases of those who had joined in the opposition in Parliament. When he returned to England, he heard to his annoyance that untrue rumours were floating about, and that Scotchmen were whispering to one another that the majority for the ecclesiastical acts had been a fictitious one, and that he had himself interfered to conceal the fraud.

Charles had thus gone back to England in no good temper with the opposition. Treating it as altogether factious, he had refused, whilst yet in Scotland, to look at a paper which had been drawn up by a certain William Haig, as embodying the sentiments of those who had voted against the acts. This paper had been approved of by Lord Balmerino, and had been passed on by him to Rothes to be shown to the King as a 'supplication of a great number of the nobility and other commissioners in the late Parliament.' Rothes knew what the King's temper was, and began by sounding him before he ventured to deliver the paper. 'My lord,' was the reply, 'ye know what is fit for you to represent, and I know what is fit to me to hear and consider; and therefore do or do not upon your peril.' After another attempt Rothes put the document in his pocket and made no further effort to obtain a hearing.

Balmerino could not rest satisfied with this conclusion. He showed the paper in the strictest secrecy to his notary, and the notary took a copy which he showed, also in the strictest secrecy, to a friend, who carried it to Spottiswoode. Spottiswoode forwarded it to the King.

The supplication, humble enough in outward form,

must have been most irritating to Charles. The sting of the paper is to be found rather in its general tone than in any particular charge brought in it. On the one hand, it tacitly treated the whole existing Church system, and still more the changes which were known to be impending, as illegal. Nothing lawfully rejected at the Reformation could be reintroduced without consent of the 'clergy lawfully assembled,' that is to say, in plain words, without the consent of a Presbyterian Assembly. The recent ecclesiastical legislation was rejected as 'importing a servitude upon this Church unpractised before.'

King and the Estates of the Realm.

The framers of the supplication must have been aware that Charles might answer, as it had been again and again answered in England, that it was for the King and the nation expressing their will in an Act of Parliament to impose these resolutions upon the clergy. They therefore proceeded to point out the obstacles which had been thrown in the way of that previous discussion without which Parliamentary proceedings are valueless. The Lords of the Articles had been chosen so as to make them merely the representatives of a party. The dissentient nobles had been hindered from representing their views to them in conference, and when the final vote was taken the King had forbidden that any one should state the reasons of the vote which he was about to give, and finally, by marking down the votes given, had shown that those who persisted in opposition were regarded by him as out of favour.[1]

The supplication, in short, discursively, and under forms of the highest respect, touched boldly on the sore point in Charles's government. His own will was predominant. The general opinion of the clergy had long

---

[1] These ideas are expressed in different parts of the supplication, but they are all there.

been neglected. The general opinion of the laity had not yet completely turned against him. But it required tender handling, and it might at any day become adverse in the process. Those who pointed out this to Charles were doing him a real service.

Charles did not perceive the service, but he did perceive that his whole system of government was threatened. Haig had prudently escaped to Holland, and Balmerino was selected as the victim. By giving the paper to his notary he had published a seditious libel, and was liable to the penalty of death under the Scottish law of 'leasing-making,' for stirring up enmity between the King and his subjects by false and malicious statements. It was not till March 1635 that the trial actually came on.[1] The jury acquitted Balmerino of every charge brought against him but one. They found that he was not the author of the libel, and had not divulged or dispersed it. But by a bare majority of eight to seven they found that he was guilty of concealing his knowledge of its existence.[2]

Already, before the day of trial, a remonstrance had been addressed to the King by a man of whom Scotland was deservedly proud. William Drummond of Hawthornden did not rise above the second rank of literary greatness. But he was a man of varied culture, and his writings in poetry and prose were widely read. He was the foremost of that band of men which broke the tradition that Scottish literature ought to be written in the Scottish national tongue, and which strove to express their thoughts in the language which had served the purposes of Shakspere and Jonson, and was one day to

---

[1] Mr. Burton, *Hist. of Scot.* vi. 384, suggests that this delay was caused by the hesitation of those entrusted with the conduct of the prosecution.

[2] *State Trials*, iii. 591. *Row*, 386.

VOL. I.   B B

serve the purposes of Scott and Campbell. He was withal an upright and honest man, craving for philosophic and literary culture rather than for Calvinistic orthodoxy, and fearing the inquisitive meddling of the Presbyterian clergy who would be sure to bear hard upon one of his tastes and opinions. He was one who, like Patrick Forbes, had formed part of that wave of liberal reaction, which, through the blunders of James and Charles, had already spent its force. As Forbes had warned James against his ecclesiastical mistakes, Drummond now warned Charles against his political mistakes. In a letter, evidently intended to be shewn to the King, he pointed out that it was impossible to secure popularity by muzzling men's tongues and pens. In so doing the King was shutting his eyes to that which it most imported him to know. "Sometimes it is great wisdom in a Prince not to reject and disdain those who freely tell him his duty, and open to him his misdemeanors to the commonwealth, and the surmises and umbrages of his people and council for the amending disorders and bettering the form of his government." The best way to treat political libels was to scorn them or answer them. "Wise Princes have never troubled themselves much about talkers; weak spirits cannot suffer the liberty of judgments nor the indiscretion of tongues."[1]

Drummond's letter was even a more impressive condemnation of Charles's system of government than the supplication had been. The tone is different, but

---

[1] Drummond's Apologetical Letter [to the Earl of Ancram], *Works*, 132. I need not refer the reader to Professor Masson's *Drummond of Hawthornden*, which should be in every one's hands who wishes to understand these times in Scotland. Unluckily he has passed over the affair of the tithes, without which no completely fair judgment can be formed. Mr. Napier, on the other hand, in his various works on the life of Montrose, is totally unable to see anything except the commutation of tithes and Presbyterian intolerance.

the fault complained of is the same. One man, however highly placed, cannot govern a nation from which he stands apart. It was because Charles could never learn this lesson that he fell at last. It was indeed morally impossible for him to send Balmerino to the scaffold. Even Laud told him that a man must be pardoned who had been acquitted by seven jurymen out of fifteen.[1] But the impression of the trial and the events which had preceded it could not be so easily wiped away. Charles had gone far to blot out the memory of the services which he had rendered to Scotland in enforcing the commutation of tithes.

When great national errors have been committed, smaller personal mistakes are certain to follow in their wake, and to obtain an importance which they would not otherwise have had. There can be no doubt that the absence of the King was an enormous difficulty in the way of governing Scotland. Not only was the King himself liable to be filled with ideas which were not Scottish ideas, but the Privy Council which ruled in his name was sure to deteriorate into the worst possible form of government. It was a Committee in which there was no master mind. Personal objects swayed its members, and those men who should have stood as the leaders of the nation became known as men jostling against one another for power or pelf. One great blow had been wisely struck at their supremacy by Charles at the beginning of his reign. He had ordained that, with the exception of the Chancellor, men who sat in the Privy Council as administrators of the Government, should not also sit in the Court of Session as Judges.[2] From time to time he had done his best to moderate the quarrels of his representatives at Edinburgh. But he had not sufficient knowledge of men to choose

[1] *Row*, 389. [2] *Balfour*, ii. 129.

Hamilton in favour.

The Bishops promoted in Scotland.

counsellors who were really worthy to govern, and his gradual alienation from the national feeling on the subject of religion made those who were really worthy shrink from his side.

Gradually Charles saw fit to take for his counsellor in England the Marquis of Hamilton. He chose him as he had chosen Buckingham and Weston, and resolved to support him against all complaints. It was not a wise choice. Hamilton was a weak and inefficient man, with just enough remembrance of his relationship to the Royal dynasty to keep him perpetually on the watch for occasions which might increase his credit in Scotland, whilst his double-dealing, springing from an anxiety to stand well with every party, deprived him of all value as an adviser.

Charles's choice of representatives at Edinburgh was even worse than his choice of a confidant in England. When nobles were grasping and lawyers intriguing, there was one body of men who had never crossed his path, and who had given him every reason to assure himself of their devotion. If the Bishops had given him full satisfaction when employed in Church affairs, why should they not give him full satisfaction when employed in political affairs? Man for man, there was in all probability more chance that a Bishop would be honest and self-denying than an Earl or a Baron would be. Charles at least thought so. Step by step he had pushed forward the Bishops into temporal rank and office. At his coronation he had been vexed by the refusal of Lord Chancellor Hay, whom he had just created Earl of Kinnoul, to allow Spottiswoode to take precedence of him. Kinnoul declared his readiness to lay the Chancellorship at his Majesty's feet. But whilst he kept it, 'never a priest in Scotland should set a foot before him as long as his blood was hot.'[1] In December 1634 the 'old cankered goutish man,' as Charles called him, died. In January 1635 the Archbishop of St. Andrews was appointed Chancellor in his place. Seven other Bishops had been gradually admitted to the Privy Council.

1635. Jan. Spottiswoode Chancellor.

It was all natural enough. But it was none the less a fatal step. It was a distinct challenge to all orders and classes of men. Those who were thus promoted were obnoxious to the Presbyterians because they were Bishops, and to the mass of religious Scotchmen who were not distinctly Presbyterians, because they supported the ceremonies, and were incorrectly believed to have been the authors of all the innovations which had had their real origin in England. The nobles hated them as intruders upon the dignities which they claimed by birth. The lawyers were jealous of them as intruders upon the dignities which they claimed by virtue of professional knowledge. They stood alone in Scotland as Charles stood almost alone in England.

In the summer of 1635 every element of a great conflagration was present in Scotland. Only the spark was wanting to set the country ablaze.

Dangers in the future.

[1] *Balfour*, ii. 141.

END OF THE FIRST VOLUME.

www.ingramcontent.com/pod-product-compliance
Lightning Source LLC
Chambersburg PA
CBHW032015220426
43664CB00006B/257